D1765113

University of Edinburgh

30150   027130225

Themes from G. E. Moore

Themes from G. E. Moore:

New Essays in Epistemology and Ethics

EDITED BY

Susana Nuccetelli and Gary Seay

OXFORD
UNIVERSITY PRESS

EDINBURGH UNIVERSITY LIBRARY
WITHDRAWN

OXFORD
UNIVERSITY PRESS

Great Clarendon Street, Oxford ox2 6DP

Oxford University Press is a department of the University of Oxford.
It furthers the University's objective of excellence in research, scholarship,
and education by publishing worldwide in

Oxford New York

Auckland Cape Town Dar es Salaam Hong Kong Karachi
Kuala Lumpur Madrid Melbourne Mexico City Nairobi
New Delhi Shanghai Taipei Toronto

With offices in

Argentina Austria Brazil Chile Czech Republic France Greece
Guatemala Hungary Italy Japan Poland Portugal Singapore
South Korea Switzerland Thailand Turkey Ukraine Vietnam

Oxford is a registered trade mark of Oxford University Press
in the UK and in certain other countries

Published in the United States
by Oxford University Press Inc., New York

© The several contributors 2007

The moral rights of the author have been asserted
Database right Oxford University Press (maker)

First published 2007

All rights reserved. No part of this publication may be reproduced,
stored in a retrieval system, or transmitted, in any form or by any means,
without the prior permission in writing of Oxford University Press,
or as expressly permitted by law, or under terms agreed with the appropriate
reprographics rights organization. Enquiries concerning reproduction
outside the scope of the above should be sent to the Rights Department,
Oxford University Press, at the address above

You must not circulate this book in any other binding or cover
and you must impose this same condition on any acquirer

British Library Cataloguing in Publication Data

Data available

Library of Congress Cataloging in Publication Data

Themes from G.E. Moore : new essays in epistemology and ethics / edited
by Susana Nuccetelli and Gary Seay.
p. cm.
Includes bibliographical references and index.
ISBN 978-0-19-928172-5
1. Moore, G. E. (George Edward), 1873-1958. 2. Knowledge, Theory of.
3. Ethics. I. Nuccetelli, Susana. II. Seay, Gary.
B1647.M74T44 2007
192—dc22
2007025748

Typeset by Laserwords Private Limited, Chennai, India
Printed in Great Britain
on acid-free paper by
Biddles Ltd, King's Lynn, Norfolk

ISBN 978–0–19–928172–5

CONTENTS

ACKNOWLEDGMENTS

We wish to acknowledge here a number of people who have been helpful to us in putting this collection together. Above all, Brian McGuinness deserves our thanks for his encouragement and advice in the early stages of the project, without which the book would not have appeared at all. We are also indebted to Stephen Schiffer and Charles Landesman, who both offered insightful criticisms that have helped to make the volume much better than it would otherwise have been. Michael Kelly should also be mentioned for his early advice on strategies for publication, as should Myron Anderson for his generosity in sharing with us some important Moorean literature from his own library. We are also grateful for the help of our editors at Oxford University Press, Peter Momtchiloff, Victoria Patton, Rupert Cousens, and Jaqueline Baker, who provided judicious guidance and patient attention to detail throughout the editorial and production processes.

CONTRIBUTORS

C. A. J. (Tony) Coady is Professorial Fellow in Applied Philosophy in the Centre for Applied Philosophy and Public Ethics at the University of Melbourne, where he was formerly Boyce Gibson Professor of Philosophy. His book *Testimony: A Philosophical Study* (Oxford University Press, 1992) was widely and enthusiastically reviewed internationally. His book for Cambridge University Press, *Morality and Political Violence*, will be published in 2007. His edited collection, *What's Wrong with Moralism?* was published by Blackwell (2006). In 2005 he presented the Uehiro Lectures on Practical Ethics in the University of Oxford. The lectures will be published by Oxford University Press under the title 'Morality and Feasibility'.

Jonathan Dancy is Professor of Philosophy at the University of Reading, UK, and at the University of Texas at Austin. He previously taught at the University of Keele, UK, and also held visiting positions at All Souls College, Oxford, at the Australian National University, at Christchurch University, NZ, and at Pittsburgh, Georgetown, and Northwestern Universities in the USA. He has written many articles on moral philosophy and the philosophy of reasons and action more generally, and his books include *Moral Reasons* (Oxford: Blackwell, 1993), *Practical Reality* (Oxford: Clarendon Press, 2000), and *Ethics Without Principles* (Oxford: Clarendon Press, 2004).

Stephen Darwall is John Dewey Collegiate Professor at the University of Michigan. He has written widely on the foundations and history of ethics. His books include *Impartial Reason, The British Moralists and the Internal 'Ought', Philosophical Ethics,* and *Welfare and Rational Care.* His most recent book is *The Second-Person Standpoint: Morality, Respect, and Accountability.*

Richard Fumerton received his Ph.D. from Brown in 1974 and is currently the F. Wendell Miller Professor of Philosophy at the University of Iowa. His research has focused mainly in epistemology, but he has also published in metaphysics, philosophy of mind, philosophy of science, value theory, and philosophy of law. He is the author of *Metaphysical and Epistemological Problems of Perception* (1985), *Reason and Morality: A Defense of the Egocentric Perspective* (1990), *Metaepistemology and Skepticism* (1996), *Realism and the Correspondence Theory of Truth* (2002), and *Epistemology* (2006).

Joshua Gert is Associate Professor of Philosophy at Florida State University. He is the author of *Brute Rationality* (Cambridge, 2004) and has written articles on metaethics, reasons for action, color, and the color/value analogy.

Terry Horgan is Professor of Philosophy at the University of Arizona. He is author (with John Tienson) of *Connectionism and the Philosophy of Psychology* (MIT, 1996). He has published work (often collaboratively) in philosophy of mind, metaphysics, philosophy of language, epistemology, and (collaboratively with Mark Timmons) metaethics. He and Timmons co-edited *Metaethics after Moore* (Oxford: Clarendon, 2006), and are currently working together on issues concerning the phenomenology of moral experience.

Michael Huemer received his Ph.D. from Rutgers University in 1998 and is presently Associate Professor of Philosophy at the University of Colorado at Boulder. He is the author of *Skepticism and the Veil of Perception* (Rowman & Littlefield, 2001) and *Ethical Intuitionism* (Palgrave Macmillan, 2005), as well as numerous academic articles in ethics, epistemology, and other areas.

William G. Lycan is William Rand Kenan, Jr Professor of Philosophy at the University of North Carolina. He is author of *Logical Form in Natural Language* (1984), *Knowing Who* (with Steven Boër, 1986), *Consciousness* (1987), *Judgment and Justification* (1988), *Modality and Meaning* (1994), *Consciousness and Experience* (1996), *Philosophy of Language: A Contemporary Introduction* (1999), and *Real Conditionals* (2001). He has also edited an anthology, *Mind and Cognition* (1990, 1999).

Ram Neta is Assistant Professor of Philosophy at the University of North Carolina at Chapel Hill. He has previously taught at the University of Utah, and at Carnegie Mellon University. He has published widely in his area of specialization, epistemology. He is currently at work on a book on perception and knowledge.

Susana Nuccetelli is Associate Professor of Philosophy at St Cloud State University in Minnesota. She is editor of *New Essays on Semantic Externalism and Self-knowledge* (MIT Press, 2003) and author of articles in epistemology and philosophy of language that have appeared in *Analysis, Metaphilosophy, Inquiry Philosophical Forum*, and *The Southern Journal of Philosophy*, among other journals. A native of Argentina, she has also written on Latin American philosophy.

Charles Pigden is a graduate of King's College, Cambridge, and completed his PhD at La Trobe University, Melbourne. Since 1988 he has taught philosophy at the University of Otago, Dunedin. His annotated collection of Russell's ethical writings, *Russell on Ethics,* won the Bertrand Russell Society Book Award for 2000.

Gary Seay did graduate work in philosophy at Georgetown and Rice and is currently Associate Professor of Philosophy at Medgar Evers College of the City University of

New York. He is the author of journal articles on various topics in ethics. With Susana Nuccetelli, he is the editor of *Philosophy of Language: The Central Topics* (Rowman & Littlefield, forthcoming, 2007).

Robert Shaver is Professor of Philosophy at the University of Manitoba. Recent publications include papers on Adam Smith, Sidgwick, Hume, utilitarianism, and hypothetical imperatives.

Paul Snowdon has been Grote Professor of Mind and Logic at University College, London, since 2001. Before that he was a Fellow and Lecturer in philosophy at Exeter College, Oxford. He has published articles about personal identity, perception, and other topics in the philosophy of mind. His first book, *Persons, Animals and Ourselves*, is due out in 2007.

Roy Sorensen is Professor of Philosophy at Dartmouth College. He is the author of *Blindspots, Thought Experiments, Pseudo-Problems, Vagueness and Contradiction*, and *A Brief History of the Paradox*.

Ernest Sosa is Professor of Philosophy at Rutgers University. He is the author of *Knowledge in Perspective* (Cambridge, 1991) and of *Virtuous Circles: Apt Belief and Reflective Knowledge*, Vol. 2 (Oxford University Press, 2007). He is the editor of *Philosophy and Phenomenological Research*, co-editor (with E. Villanueva) of *Philosophical Issues*, and has published widely on many topics in epistemology.

Mark Timmons is Professor of Philosophy at the University of Arizona. He is author of *Morality without Foundations: A Defense of Ethical Contextualism* (1999) and *Moral Theory: An Introduction* (2002). Along with Terry Horgan, he is co-editor of *Metaethics after Moore* (2006), and they are currently working together on issues concerning the phenomenology of moral experience.

Crispin Wright, Fellow of the British Academy, is Wardlaw University Professor at the University of St Andrews and Director of the Research Centre, *Arché*. He has taught at Columbia, Princeton, and Michigan, and is Global Distinguished Professor at New York University. His books include *Wittgenstein on the Foundations of Mathematics* (Harvard University Press, 1980), *Frege's Conception of Numbers and Objects* (Humanities Press, 1983), *Truth and Objectivity* (Harvard University Press, 1992), and *Rails to Infinity* (Harvard University Press, 2001).

Part I

Introduction

I

Nearly fifty years after the death of G. E. Moore, a revisionist consensus has begun to emerge about Moore's place in the history of philosophy and the nature of his contribution to the subject. Although the breadth of Moore's influence, as one of the founders of analytic philosophy, has never been in doubt, an entire generation of philosophers spent their professional lives dissenting from Moore's views, so that, by the middle of the last century, many had come to regard him as only a philosopher whose best arguments had been superseded by those of more insightful successors. But Moore is now being reassessed in light of subsequent developments in both epistemology and ethics that make clear the durability of Moorean ideas in twenty-first-century philosophical disputes. Renewed interest in the normative and evaluative dimensions of epistemology and in the connections between some central issues of epistemology and value theory and metaethics have sparked new interest in Moore's work. This is evident in recent literature on ethical non-naturalism, realism, and intuitionism, and also in debates about skepticism and common sense in epistemology. Some themes developed by Moore in epistemology and ethics are revisited in this volume in the light of contemporary controversies in those areas.

As these new essays make clear, Moore's arguments uncovered significant conundrums whose true import we have only begun to understand. The notorious difficulties encountered by the various attempts at resolving them have only brought us back to a more acute appreciation of just how difficult the problems were to which Moore set his hand. If the early history of twentieth-century philosophy in Britain seems to have been largely a history of philosophers disagreeing with Moore, that is because Moore's role in that history was that of an innovator who could see old problems in new ways, and because those ways sometimes hit wrong notes that were perceived immediately by his critics. But Moore clearly had an acute sense of where the fault-lines lay in moral philosophy and theory of knowledge, and his meticulous methods of analysis enabled him to point out fundamental issues and say provocative things about them, in a way that led other philosophers to jump into the fray. Where others appeared to make progress on a problem, Moore was happy to acknowledge it; and whenever his own positions proved unsupportable, Moore would revise or abandon them without hesitation.

Moore's interests were wide ranging, but his legacy to philosophy lies chiefly in his contributions to three areas: epistemology, ethics, and philosophical method,—the first two of which are the focus of this volume. In ethics, Moore defended a boldly cognitivist moral realism that incorporated a non-naturalist theory of intrinsic value, and argued that such value was knowable only through intuition. As we shall see presently, all of this was in the service of a normative theory that embraced an ideal utilitarianism. In epistemology, Moore famously broached a number of issues, though his main concerns were with the epistemic status of common-sense beliefs, the problem of knowledge and skepticism, the relation between sense data and physical objects, and what has come to be known as 'Moore's Paradox' (that to say, sincerely and competently, 'I believe that p but p is false,' seems consistent but absurd). Often raising questions of his own about these issues, he struggled to resolve them with arguments and strategies so influential that we may justly consider them *Moorean themes* in epistemology—topics that, in Moore's day, attracted the attention of contemporaries of the caliber of Wittgenstein, Russell, and Ayer. As the essays in this collection make clear, however, they continue to generate philosophical interest in our own time.

II

What, then, were some of the questions in epistemology that puzzled Moore? The historical Moore took a 'common-sense' view of the world to be not only predominantly true but generally known to be true. Questions arise, however, as to whether common sense has such features and, if so, on which grounds. And what, exactly, are the elements that make it up? The *locus classicus* for Moore's own answers is of course his 1925 essay, 'Defence of Common Sense'. Yet, as widely read there, his position often receives little credit. It comes out as championing a Yes answer to the first question, while providing only a viciously circular one to the second, and no view at all that could constitute an adequate answer to the third. On the other hand, more charitable critics argue that, with supplemental reasons, common sense may be shown to have the properties ascribed to it by Moore.[1]

Either way, dissatisfaction appears to be the shared response to at least the letter of Moore's account of common sense. For both skeptical and sympathetic readers have noticed that it ascribes to the relevant beliefs properties they might not have at all, and that it does so without argument. Surely any attempt to back up Moore's account would need to address how the items that make up common sense are individuated. The closest Moore himself came to providing a criterion for membership of the relevant class was perhaps the *Commonplace Book* (1962b: 280), where each item making up common sense is said to consist in 'a thing which every or very nearly every sane adult, who has the use of all his senses (e.g. was not born blind or deaf) believes or knows (where "believes" & "knows" are used dispositionally).' The items at issue, then, appear to be common-sense beliefs, construed as ordinary assumptions shared alike by philosophers and non-philosophers in their everyday lives. Moore is not alone in thinking that a great number of such beliefs have the features of being almost immune to falsity and epistemic failure (see for instance Huemer 2001; Lemos 2004; and Somerville 1986).

Yet the claim is vulnerable to well-known objections. For one thing, there is a long history of outlandish beliefs that were at one time or another shared assumptions of philosophers and non-philosophers in their ordinary lives. Since, as we shall see, Moore intended common sense to have ambitious metaphysical and epistemological cash value, he appears committed to providing a principled way of ruling out unwelcome shared assumptions. After all, a closer look at common sense may very well reveal that the class of actually shared beliefs is either quite small, or of no philosophical interest at all, or both. Moreover, some of Moore's putative common-sense beliefs, such as that *there exists at present a human body which is one's own body* and that *ever since one's own body was born, it has been either in contact with or not far from the surface of the earth* (1925, 33) are quite sophisticated and may therefore fail altogether to qualify for the class. For to understand their contents seems to require a certain cultural, and maybe even philosophical, training that 'nearly every sane adult' may *not* in fact have—a weakness in Moore's account pointed out independently by J. L. Austin (1962) and C. D. Broad (1970), among others.

It should be noted, however, that although Moore provided no explicit criterion for identifying common-sense beliefs, he did offer at the outset of 'Defence' a list of *truisms*, and these can be put at the service of articulating the following working hypothesis: a belief type qualifies for common sense if and only if its propositional-content type

[1] See, for example, Moore (1925, 44). The list of skeptics about Moore's common sense include Ayer (1984), Broad (1970), Butchvarov (1998), Strawson (1985), Stroud (1984), and Unger (1974). For more sympathetic readers, see, e.g., Klemke (2000), Landesman (2002), Lemos (2004), and Somerville (1986).

belongs to the domains carved out by Moore's list of truisms. Now the question becomes, *what, exactly, are those truisms*? They are propositions Moore took to express meanings that, though resistant to philosophical analysis, are none the less understood and known to be true *mutatis mutandis* by most of us, intellectual and layman alike. But, as we have seen, this claim has problems of its own. In any case, such propositions cannot *express* meanings—for they *are* the meanings of some utterances, as they also are the contents of beliefs and other psychological attitudes.

Let's say that a belief, whether dispositional or occurrent, qualifies as common sense just in case its propositional content is of the kinds illustrated in Moore's list (1925, 33–5). This list divides the included sentences into two 'classes', with many belonging to a metaphysical domain, since they can be used to express propositions about the reality of certain entities and their various relationships. Some involve the existence of one's own body, states of consciousness, recent memories, and/or various relationships with external things. In Moore's own examples, sentences of this sort can be used to express propositions, such as *that one has and has had for a period of time a human body and certain states of consciousness, is and has been near the surface of the earth*, etc. But other sentences in the same metaphysical domain are about others having and having had for a period of time human bodies that have had certain relationships and experiences, and about the existence of biological kinds and non-living things such as celestial bodies and artifacts. Moore's example of a common-sense epistemological belief is expressed by a single sentence asserting that the previously listed truisms are common knowledge: not only does he himself know them, but he knows that *most of us* also know *mutatis mutandis* a great number of them too (1925, 34).

Thus construed, common sense was intended to have ambitious metaphysical and epistemological consequences. For, given Moorean common sense, many of the beliefs instantiating the listed truisms would be true, and therefore entail the truth of some generalizations about the *reality* of the self, other minds, the past, and the external world. But if true, since they would also be justified by whatever reasons can be adduced to include them in that list, such beliefs would amount to *knowledge* in some sense, and therefore entail the truth of some generalizations about knowledge of propositions in those domains. In fact, Moore's argument often appears to aim at substantiating two conclusions at once: one metaphysical, the other epistemological.

Compare Moore's 'Defence' with his 'Proof of an External World'. In both cases it would be too naïve to read the paper as offering only one strand of reasoning—that against metaphysical anti-realist positions such as those held by idealists, solipsists, and the like—while ignoring the fact that it also targets skeptical positions about knowledge, of the kinds illustrated by the listed truisms. In the case of 'Defence', merely by holding that he was justified in believing certain metaphysical propositions because they belong to common sense (since these entail generalizations about the existence of the self, other minds, the past, and the external world), Moore was, in fact, thereby making a claim with anti-skeptical import. On the other hand, in his 1939 'Proof' if he could come to have a justified belief in the existence of an external world by deducing it from the assertion that *here is a hand* while holding up one of his hands (in good light, clear-minded, with eyes open, etc.), then his argument would *ipso facto* have an anti-skeptical import. And it would, of course, have it independently of whether Moore himself was willing to acknowledge it explicitly (cf. Moore 1942; Baldwin 1990). Let's now consider these two strands of reasoning separately. First, the metaphysical one, which may be reconstructed as follows:

HAND I

1 Here is a hand.

2 If here is a hand, then there is an external world.

> (For hands are objects in a world external to the mind.)

Therefore,

3 There is an external world.

HAND I is valid and may even be sound. Its premise (1) amounts to an empirical belief likely to be true, for example, when 'I' refers to Moore. To many, premise (2) is a priori true, given the concepts involved. By simple *modus ponens*, then, the general conclusion (3) follows. Yet, in light of well-known anti-realist arguments and thought experiments, **HAND I** strikes us as unpersuasive. It is difficult to see how any appeal to common sense to support premise (1) could be of any help in avoiding begging the question against anti-realists when it comes to premise (2). Something more is needed to get **HAND I** off the ground—and it may very well be one of the alternative strategies attempted by Moore himself elsewhere.

Let's now consider whether a Moorean argument against skepticism about the external world (hereafter, simply 'skepticism') could do any better. It may be taken to run,

HAND II

1 I am justified in believing that *here is a hand*.

2 If I am justified in believing *that here is a hand*, then I'm justified in believing *that there is an external world*.

> (For a hand is an object in a world external to the mind)

Therefore,

3 I am justified in believing *that there is an external world*.

Assuming the plausibility of a closure principle to the effect that, if one is justified in believing that p, and that p entails q, then one is also justified in believing that q, **HAND II** is valid. Yet questions arise as to whether its premise (1) is well supported. In light of well-known skeptical scenarios, it wouldn't do in this case to first invoke common sense to support that premise, and then argue that premise (2) is supported by reflection alone. Such a maneuver would clearly fall short of meeting the skeptical challenge.

Yet perhaps other grounds are available to the historical Moore to support **HAND II**'s premise (1). Is there logical space for him to hold, for example, that such beliefs are justified directly or non-inferentially? It seems not, given his views in theory of perception, which allow only for immediate introspective knowledge of one's own sense data (cf. Pryor 2004). Like other sense-datum theorists, Moore faced the obstacle that no inference from direct awareness of one's own sensedata, be it deductive, abductive, or analogical, could produce the kind of justification needed to counter the skeptic about beliefs such as *that here is a hand*. At the same time, Moore's own rejection of skepticism of the Humean sort (1909, 1910) commits him to avoiding the naturalist contention that such beliefs are justified on the grounds that we humans cannot help but have them (e.g., Strawson 1985). Let's suppose, then, that common-sense beliefs don't qualify for being direct or irresistible. Couldn't they still come to be justified if either epistemic externalism or semantic externalism turns out to be true? The first option is unavailable to the historical Moore, who enlisted himself in the epistemic internalist camp, often claiming not only to *know* many such beliefs but to *know them with certainty* (1941, 236–7), and at the same time conceding to the skeptic that if he did not know *that he was not dreaming*, then he did not know propositions such as *that here is a hand* (1941, 247). On the other hand, semantic externalism might not be an option worth fighting for, since it appears to face a reductio: when held, together with a plausible thesis of privileged self-knowledge, semantic externalism seems to have the consequence that one could deduce *that one has hands* from one's own belief that one has them. As shown by recent literature, the controversial character of any such deduction would speak against Moore's appeal to semantic externalism.

Relevant to the anti-skeptical reasoning of the historical Moore is his own reaction to the Cartesian-dream scenario, which he judged incompatible with knowledge of propositions such as that *this is a pencil* or *here is a hand*. In fact, he would have granted that many other well-known skeptical scenarios are also incompatible with knowledge of that sort. Although we need not rehearse here the details of any such scenario, let's briefly consider a possible Moorean response to the brain-in-a-vat (BIV) case. Imagine the skeptic invites Moore to entertain the possibility of his being a handless brain, electronically stimulated to have sensory experiences indistinguishable from those of a non-*BIV*. Contra Moore, the skeptic argues

BIV

1 Moore is not justified in believing *that he is not a BIV*.

2 If Moore is not justified in believing *that he is not a BIV*, then he is not justified in believing *that here is a hand*.

Therefore,

3 Moore is not justified in believing *that here is a hand*.

Since to Moore (1941, 247), however, skeptical arguments 'cut both ways', he might take *BIV*'s conclusion to be less plausible than the belief *that here is a hand* when he is holding up his hand in the appropriate circumstances. Accordingly, his rejoinder could consist in an equally valid argument such as

HAND III

1 I am justified in believing *that here is a hand*.

2 If I am justified in believing *that here is a hand*, then I am justified in believing *that I'm not a BIV*.

Therefore,

3 I am justified in believing *that I'm not a BIV*.

Could this defeat the skeptic's argument? Once again, it is difficult to see what resources are available to Moore in order to provide non-question-begging support for premise (1). Only by producing some reasons independent of his own perceptual experience can he prevail in this debate with the skeptic. This is, of course, a common objection to his 'proof' of an external world, when construed as an argument against skepticism. Whether or not the charge can be substantiated, it is clear—as noted by some of the papers in this volume—that any successful attempt to vindicate a Moorean anti-skeptical stance must give a compelling account of why it has been so widely thought to fail.[2]

---

[2] As is well known, Moore took his 1939 argument, cast here as **HAND II**, to be a rigorous proof, with a conclusion that differs, but follows validly, from premises known to be true. Although the premise that we have cast as 'Here is a hand' is controversial, Moore (1939, 147) believed himself to have 'evidence' for it, even if neither he nor anyone else could provide it. He rightly pointed out that it would be unreasonable to demand a proof for each step in a proof. But, since first proposed by Moore, the 'proof' has struck philosophers as both provocative and deeply unsatisfactory. It is often charged that, here again, Moore simply begged the question against the skeptic. Some objections to that effect are, for example, in Jackson (1987) and Wright (2002). See also Davies (2004) and Pryor (2004) for neo-Moorean rejoinders.

III

The straightforward realist and anti-skeptical convictions that mark Moore's meta-physics and epistemology appear also in his ethics. As noted above, Moore's normative ethical theory was an ideal utilitarianism. Influenced in some central ways by Sidgwick, Moore's theory held actions to be right only in so far as they produce in their results more overall good than other possible alternative actions (1903, 77). It is therefore not surprising that Moore's position reveals a consequentialist's concern with the objective, intrinsic value of the end in terms of which the rightness of the means is determined. On his view, the goodness that right actions bring about is not merely something subjective (1912, 50–105), but a mind- and language-independent property that good things have.

It is not, however, a natural property. Although the goodness of good things may be said to supervene[3] on their ordinary, observable, physical properties (so that it is in virtue of their having the latter that they are good), goodness itself is not reducible to, or analyzable into, any other quality, whether natural or metaphysical. This is because, according to Moore, 'good' denotes a simple, non-natural property. Given its non-naturalness, such a property is not a part of the physical world investigated by the sciences. Given its simplicity, it cannot be analyzed into parts, for it has no parts. In connection with this, it is a central claim of *Principia Ethica* that the term 'good' cannot be defined at all, since the sort of intrinsic value that it denotes is not equivalent to any other property, or to any combination of other properties (1903, 58–69).

In particular, goodness is not equivalent to any natural property, and the attempt to define 'good' in purely descriptive terms allegedly commits a 'naturalistic fallacy' (1903, 62).[4] Furthermore, to equate goodness with any natural property or properties, such as *what maximizes pleasure* or *what we desire to desire*, only makes the proponent of such an equation vulnerable to the Open Question Argument (*OQA*). Moore's *OQA* rests on some intuitions about the cognitive value of propositions relevant to analyses of value predicates into purely descriptive predicates. In light of those intuitions, although it is trivial, and so perhaps even unintelligible, to say 'Granted, *a* is what maximizes pleasure, but is it what maximizes pleasure', or 'Granted, *a* is what we desire to desire, but is it what we desire to desire?', it is informative and clearly intelligible to say 'Granted, *a* is what maximizes pleasure, but is it good?' or 'Granted, *a* is what we desire to desire, but is it good?' If 'good' were *semantically equivalent* to 'what maximizes

---

[3] Moore does not himself use the word 'supervene'.

[4] Strictly, the 'naturalistic fallacy' is the mistake of trying to define 'good' in terms of *any* other property, or combination of properties at all, whether natural or non-natural. But it is clear that Moore's chief concern in *Principia Ethica* was to deny that 'good' could be defined in terms of either natural or metaphysical properties.

pleasure' or to 'what we desire to desire', Moore reasoned, then questions such as the latter would have exactly the same cognitive value as the former. Yet they don't. He concluded that 'good' is not semantically equivalent to these purely descriptive predicates. And, given that similar arguments could be run for any other attempted naturalistic analysis of 'good', with always the same result, Moore inferred that value predicates such as 'good' are not analyzable at all into purely descriptive predicates.

What this suggests, he thought, is that goodness—or 'intrinsic value', as he often referred to it in *Principia*—is something *sui generis*: what we ordinarily denote by 'good' is never reducible to any natural property or combination of natural properties—or, indeed, to *any other* properties at all. Thus the *OQA*, arguably Moore's most important contribution, fueled Moore's conviction that goodness itself can only be a simple, unanalyzable, non-natural property. But a number of objections were early adduced against the *OQA*, ranging from its begging the question and leading to the so-called paradox of analysis (Frankena 1939) to its being invalid (Putnam 1981; Harman 1977). Ultimately there came to be a consensus that Moore had, in fact, discovered no naturalistic fallacy and that his *OQA* against naturalism in ethics could not be made to work (Darwall, Gibbard, and Railton 1992).

To sum up, Moore's metaethical stance in moral ontology may be said to rest on certain crucial doctrines, to which all other claims are corollaries. One is moral realism, the doctrine that moral properties exist and are mind- and language-independent. Related to this is cognitivism, the doctrine that whether something has an evaluative or normative property is something *objective* so that any judgment to that effect qualifies for a truth value. Another is non-naturalism, the doctrine that moral properties are something over and above natural properties. A corollary of non-naturalism is the so-called *autonomy-of-ethics* thesis, according to which ethics cannot be naturalized, since it is a philosophical discipline with its own subject-matter and methods completely independent of the natural and social sciences.

Another important question raised by Moore's moral ontology concerns its epistemology: how do we know that something has intrinsic value? Moore's answer is that, although the presence of goodness in good things is signaled by the observable, natural properties on which (we would say) it supervenes, goodness itself is knowable only *by intuition*: it is simply apprehended directly in reflecting on the intrinsic nature of the things that have it. Moore thought that the goodness of certain things—in the final chapter of *Principia* he names the states of consciousness associated with friendships and aesthetic enjoyments—was self-evident.

Now clearly, this moral ontology and epistemology amount to a combination of doctrines that could hardly fail to draw fire, and it has done so from the very outset. Moore's realist non-naturalist account of goodness,[5] together with his appeal to intuition to account for how goodness could be identified in the things that have it, were so thoroughly alien to the empiricist sensibilities of the younger generation of philosophers in the1930s and 1940s that some reacted by rejecting cognitivism and moral realism altogether and adopting non-cognitivist theories in various forms. Chief among these were the emotivism of Stevenson (1944) and Ayer (1936), which held that moral judgments were non-descriptive utterances without propositional content that express directly one's attitudes of approval and disapproval; and the prescriptivism of Hare (1952), which held that moral judgments were prescriptive utterances—like imperatives but typically requiring reasons in support—that were ordinarily framed as action-guides and, if assented to sincerely, would be action-guiding.

But many philosophers found these forms of non-cognitivism unpersuasive. Some objected that non-cognitivism could not give an adequate account of the distinctive content of moral judgments (Foot 1958) and required us to ignore what is in many cases a plainly propositional form (Geach 1960). Moreover, non-cognitivism, as an anti-realist view, was widely thought to be unable to account for the objectivity of moral judgments. Partly in response to these objections, descriptivist theories have now returned to favor. Developments in metaethics over the past half-century have seen a proliferation of new variations of cognitivism, usually embracing some form of moral realism,[6] to compete with innovative non-cognitivist positions presented under the banner of what is now called 'expressivism'. Furthermore, some cognitivist theories currently on offer present non-naturalist accounts of moral value.

All of these developments, clearly, are reasons to think that Moorean themes in ethics are well worth revisiting now. Among persistent concerns driving contemporary work in metaethics are two fundamental conceptions about ethical theory and the nature of morality that may justly be seen as among the principal products of the past hundred years' debate over Moore's views. First is the view that moral value is something objective, in the sense of being an agent-neutral consideration somehow built into the fabric of our common human experience, and, hence, that moral obligation comes to each of us *from without*, a view held both by some contemporary moral realists and by many philosophers who endorse what may be called 'practical reasoning' theories. Second is the notion that there is an irreducibly normative function of ethical judgments that any metaethical theory must be able to account for, a view that, though plainly not Moore's, is arguably the distillation of what was

---

[5] According to Baldwin (1990), Moore's moral realism is a remnant of the Bradleyan idealism that informed his earliest writing.

[6] But not always. Some cognitivists are error-theorists, holding that moral judgments are descriptive, but that there's nothing *real* that they describe (Mackie 1977).

most salient in Moore's non-naturalism, the idea that goodness was not reducible to, or definable in terms of, physical or psychical facts. In addition to these, there is also a conviction about the proper methodology of ethics that a growing number of contemporary moral philosophers share with Moore: namely, that appeal to intuition at some level is after all unavoidable in moral reasoning, and is to that extent a legitimate move in ethics.

IV

In this volume, a wide variety of Moorean themes in both ethics and epistemology are explored at length in relation to ongoing disputes in those areas. The opening contributions are devoted to Moore's anti-skeptical arguments. The first selection, by Crispin Wright, takes issue with a liberal conception of epistemic warrant recently articulated by the so-called dogmatists or neo-Mooreans (e.g., Pryor 2004; Davies 2004) and put at the service of vindicating Moore's 'proof'. To dogmatists, some *basic* perceptual beliefs, when entertained in the appropriate circumstances, are warranted by the believer's own sensory and bodily experiences alone, provided she has no reason to doubt them. Thus, if Moore believes *that here is a hand* while holding up his hand in the appropriate circumstances, his belief is warranted. Since, *pace* idealism, the other premise of the 'proof' is warranted by reasoning about the relevant concepts, it follows that, given dogmatism, Moore's 'proof' succeeds in deductively transmitting epistemic warrant from premises to conclusion. Although the proof may fail to persuade anyone in the skeptic's camp, its failure there involves dialectical, and not epistemic, space.

But to Wright, dogmatism faces unresolvable problems, and he ultimately rejects it as unable to be of any help within what he calls 'The Traditional Epistemological Project'. Wright's own sympathies are with a conservative conception of epistemic warrant. Accordingly, in Moore's 'proof', the warrant for 'Here is a hand' depends on some collateral information that includes that contained in the argument's conclusion. If this is correct, then it seems that such a conclusion must already be in place before Moore could reasonably take his bodily experience to warrant the controversial premise. Thus, the 'proof' turns out to be non-cogent, in the sense that having a warrant for its premises and recognizing its validity is not sufficient for having a warrant to accept its conclusion. As a result, the 'proof' fails to meet a challenge that points to a fundamental limitation in our knowledge. But, on Wright's account, the challenge can be met by appealing to non-evidential entitlements or presuppositions of the sort needed for getting our inquiries off the ground, provided there is no reason to doubt them.

Ernest Sosa's contribution also examines Moore's anti-skepticism. He reconstructs the original 'proof' in light of Moore's own understanding of what a proof is and who its primary intended target was—which Sosa identifies as idealism (and not skepticism about perceptual knowledge, as is usually assumed). On Sosa's view, although the reconstructed proof is more interesting and helpful than some *pseudo*-proofs, this result is compatible with its ultimately failing as a response to skepticism. Sosa looks closely at other anti-skeptical arguments offered by Moore in 'Certainty' and 'Four Forms of Scepticism', but finds them insufficient to support the crucial premise of his proof. Although Moore explicitly agreed with Descartes in that knowing that one is not dreaming is needed to refute skepticism, at the same time he held that he knew with certainty many ordinary perceptual propositions, such as *that here is a hand*. In addition, he granted that no such proposition is entailed by what he would consider foundational beliefs, which include only beliefs based on the data of immediate experience and short-term memory. Now, on Sosa's view, since Moore construes a proof as some kind of public demonstration, this may allow for having conclusive reasons for a claim, and even knowing it with *certainty*, without being able to produce a proof for it. In fact, depending on how 'certainty' is construed, a Moorean stance on skepticism may be defensible, provided it avoids some questionable epistemological assumptions made by the historical Moore. If we drop the assumption that knowing that one is awake is required to know *that here is a hand*, then knowledge of a sort Sosa terms 'animal knowledge' is possible. But knowledge of another sort, 'reflective knowledge', does require knowing that one is awake. Yet on Sosa's 'non-linear' conception of reflective knowledge, that condition need not be understood as amounting to *prior* knowledge.

Ram Neta's essay in this volume argues that although Moore's 'proof' cannot succeed in transmitting the epistemic warrant of its premises to its conclusion, it is none the less capable of rationally overcoming doubts about it. In this way, Neta attempts to accommodate the sense of inadequacy widely felt about the 'proof', while avoiding some dilemmas facing two current interpretations of that argument: Crispin Wright's (2002), and that of neo-Moorean rivals such as Martin Davies (2004) and James Prior (2004). Neta argues that, by denying that warrant transmits from premises to conclusion in Moore's argument, Wright's interpretation is at odds with common intuitions about how we acquire knowledge through deductive reasoning. And by holding that warrant does transmit in that argument, the neo-Mooreans run into the problem of easy knowledge (Cohen 2005). If Neta is right, then the neo-Mooreans have it exactly backwards. Moreover, both parties face equally troublesome dilemmas. Neta regards his own position as offering an alternative construal of the 'proof', one that is more congenial with the historical Moore and avoids both objections. According to this construal, the argument can rationally overcome skeptical doubts about its conclusion. Evidence from Moore's writings suggests that he took the 'proof' to *display* the knowledge we already have of its conclusion (cf. Sosa, this volume), rather than to transmit it from premises to conclusion.

William Lycan's essay also looks closely at Moore's strategies against skepticism, which he tracks from Moore's early writings on Hume to his classic essays on the topic. After reconstructing the arguments and considering possible objections, Lycan contends that it was not until 'Four Forms of Scepticism', where Moore proposed what we may call 'method of comparative certainties', that he managed to articulate an effective response to the skeptic. In fact, as recast by Lycan, what Moore is really up to in his response to skepticism is a plausibility comparison between the conclusion of the skeptical argument and any Moorean propositions based on sound experience, such as *that here is a hand* or *that one is standing up*. Since the skeptic's conclusion comes out as being less plausible than Moorean propositions, at least one of the skeptical argument's premises should be rejected. While skeptical claims are always seen to rest on some highly controversial philosophical assumptions, Moorean ones aren't. In light of this, Moore's anti-skeptical argument may be reconstructed in a way that resists the objections that it is question-begging against the idealist and that it dogmatically privileges propositions of a certain kind. It may be thought that Moore has provided a superfluous argument, or that he is committed to ignoring the requirement that the premises of the anti-skeptical argument be known. The latter would, of course, be consistent with epistemic externalism. But, on Lycan's view, given the plausibility-comparison strategy and epistemic externalism, no epistemological theory is needed to back up the choice of a Moorean proposition over its skeptical rival.

C. A. J. Coady's paper assesses the significance of Moore's defense of common sense. Coady argues that, as in the case of Reid, Moore's conception of common sense presupposes that the philosopher's role is not that of a radical always ready to reveal truths incompatible with what ordinary people believe to be true. At the same time, according to Coady, Moore is committed to neither the acceptance of all such beliefs nor to a conservative attitude about the philosopher's role (of the sort Wittgenstein seems to have adopted). On the other hand, far from being either the product of dogmatism or a non-serious response to skepticism, Moore's appeal to common sense has what Coady sees as a 'strategic' significance. For one thing, it suggests that there is a puzzle facing the absurdity of skeptical claims about ordinary beliefs. To some, however, any objection to skepticism along these lines can be met by a Humean maneuver invoking a distinction between what can be justified ordinarily and what can be justified 'in the study'.

But Coady holds that such a maneuver cannot succeed, since it presupposes a divide between the outcomes in the study and in reality, which has unwelcome implications for skepticism. Furthermore, he sees no good reason for thinking that Moore's strategy is vulnerable to the charges of dogmatism and question-begging. In arguing for this, Coady offers a charitable reconstruction of Moore's 'greater certainty argument', according to which it really rests on a comparative judgment of what is more *rational* to believe when one is faced with the choice of believing either that one is more certain about skeptical claims or that one is more certain about some common-sense propositions. After pointing out some widespread misunderstandings of Moore's appeal to common sense (including that underwriting Wittgenstein's dissatisfaction with Moore's list of the common-sense propositions allegedly known to be true), Coady concludes by suggesting a way to accommodate error in popular belief within a Moorean common-sensist framework.

For the historical Moore, there is a need to make his stance on skepticism about ordinary beliefs consistent with his views in theory of perception. As a sense-datum theorist, Moore granted that one can have direct knowledge of *only* the data of one's own current conscious sense experience. But, given this commitment, problems then arise for his claim to know *that he has a hand* while holding up his hand in the appropriate circumstances. Given his sense-datum theory, he seems committed to saying that the object of immediate awareness could not be the hand itself or its properties, but some mental entity directly given in perception which is related (in a way to be determined) to a physical object external to the perceiver's mind. To support the controversial premise of his anti-skepticism, it seems, Moore needs a suitable account of the epistemic relation between sense data and physical objects. A suitable account of that relation was a problem on which he struggled throughout his philosophical career.

In his contribution to this volume, Paul Snowdon examines Moore's writings on theory of perception, showing that the question of whether sense data are identical to external objects is the one on which Moore labored exclusively, thereby neglecting other issues raised by the phenomenon of perception. Moreover, Snowdon finds Moore's treatment of that question to presuppose further assumptions that are themselves in need of support. He argues that the views of the historical Moore cannot, in the end, really contribute to current discussions of perception, since some of the parties to those discussions reject the act-object analysis of experience to which Moore was committed, while others would require an act-object analysis of perceptual experience of a sort that Moore failed to provide.

Another focus of some contributions to this volume is the so-called Moore's Paradox, a problem originating in Moore's intuitions about what appear to be odd, yet logically consistent, statements of the form '*P* but I don't believe that *P*' and '*P* but I believe that not-*P*'. Michael Huemer proposes a number of such paradoxical sentences and contends that the exercise of trying to resolve the puzzle raised by them can itself bring needed illumination to a vexing epistemological problem: viz., the analysis of knowledge. For the attempt to resolve what's puzzling about them leads to a plausible norm bearing on the nature of belief and knowledge. Huemer disagrees with both Moore and Wittgenstein, who took the puzzle to be a purely linguistic phenomenon requiring a linguistic solution. To Huemer, any attempt to resolve it in that way would be 'incomplete', since one could generate a number of similarly puzzling phenomena for belief and other psychological attitudes. On his account, Moore-paradoxical sentences and attitudes are *akin* to contradictions. He is especially interested in epistemic versions of the paradox that arise with sincere utterances of sentences such as 'It is raining, but I do not *know* that it is'. Huemer contends that the puzzle thus generated supports the general conclusion that fully believing that *P* commits one to the view that one knows that *P*. He takes this to be a rule that governs and constrains rational belief.

On the other hand, Roy Sorensen argues that Moore detected a real anomaly of assertion: that paradoxical sentences, such as 'It is raining but I do not believe it' are unassertible (despite being consistent). Thus, Sorensen takes Moore's puzzling sentences to be illuminating for theories of assertion. He is especially interested in exploring what he sees as *the Moorean absurdity* of post-mortem statements, such as 'I am dead'. In connection with these, Sorensen rejects Alan Sidelle's contention that such statements are deferred utterances, which presupposes the existence of conditional assertions. To Sorensen, both deferred utterances and conditional assertions are Moorean absurdities. Given this view, it follows that the dead cannot make assertions. In arguing for the view, Sorensen appeals to David Kaplan's theory of indexicals, holding that a sentence intended to be read after death is similar to the answering-machine greeting 'I am not here now', in that both amount only to *displays*. This enables Sorensen to accommodate John Searle's Chinese-room argument against attributing mental states to computers: rather than asserting a sentence, what a computer offers is merely a display of it.

Contributions to this collection focusing on Moorean themes in ethics likewise reflect a variety of different issues bearing on contemporary disputes in philosophy. Stephen Darwall's essay argues that it was Sidgwick rather than Moore who better understood the essential normativity of ethics. For, although both agreed that there was a fundamental concept underlying all ethical judgments that made them irreducible to any claims of the natural or social sciences, they did not agree on what that concept was. Moore held that it was the idea of goodness or intrinsic value that was basic to ethics, so that all of ethics was based on goodness at the *conceptual* level. But Sidgwick rightly saw that a genuine ethical judgment is necessarily one that asserts of some attitude or action that it is supported by normative reasons, so that it's an attitude or action some person ought to have or take. Thus, on Sidgwick's view, judgments about intrinsic goodness are judgments about the normative reasons, or justification, for some attitude. But Moore could not accommodate this view, since he held that goodness was 'unanalyzable' and so could not be cashed out in other terms, such as what we have reasons to esteem, desire, or do; thus it was not, for him, a normative notion in this way. For this reason, Sidgwick's account is to be preferred to

Moore's, Darwall thinks, though both ultimately fail to appreciate a crucial dimension of ethical reasoning, for they miss what is most distinctive about normative judgments regarding the attitudes in which we hold one another responsible and direct moral demands to each other.

In the essay by Terry Horgan and Mark Timmons, they attempt to show how certain aspects of Moore's ethics that lend themselves to moral-phenomenological analysis can be adapted in a more general phenomenological account of the experience of moral obligation, and then discuss the ways in which facts about moral phenomenology bear on the metaethical problem of moral realism. In particular, they ask if it is a fundamental part of the phenomenology of direct, judgment-involving moral experiences that there be a sense of some action's appropriateness or inappropriateness in the circumstances. And if the related felt demand is experienced as coming to the agent *from without,* then isn't the intentional content of such experiences just a sense of their objective appropriateness or inappropriateness as an *in-the-world relational property?* And don't such experiences in this way purport to represent *objective moral facts?* Their answer is that a moral phenomenology of this sort would *not* carry descriptive purport—and, thus, neither does the Moorean moral phenomenology they present. The facts that moral phenomenology can provide, they conclude, do not support realist over irrealist views in ethics. Such an exercise does not, by itself, have the power to justify metaphysical judgments about what sorts of properties there are in the world.

In Richard Fumerton's contribution to this volume, he argues that although the philosophical legacy of the Open Question Argument (*OQA*) has persisted, it has done so in unexpected ways. Although no version of the argument is successful, he thinks, it raises fundamental metaphilosophical issues that have to do with the nature of analysis, and these recur in contemporary discussions of naturalistic analyses of ethical judgments and of naturalistic analyses of reasons for acting, chiefly in the denial that such analyses can take account of normativity. The real value of Moore's fundamental insight in the *OQA*, Fumerton believes, is mostly in the influence it has had on anti-naturalist arguments familiar in present-day moral theory, with their insistence on the irreducible normativity of ethical terms. These arguments are really little more than contemporary variations of the *OQA*, Fumerton thinks, and may in the end be vulnerable to the same criticisms.

Charles Pigden's paper contends that Moore has *two* arguments to the effect that 'good' denotes a non-natural property: the Barren Tautology Argument (*BTA*); and the open question argument (*OQA*). The *OQA*, he suggests, was probably proposed to deal with naturalistic theories, such as Russell's desire-to-desire theory, which are immune to the *BTA*. The *OQA* is valid and would, if sound, have disposed of the desire-to-desire theory. But, according to Pigden, two key premises were successively questioned: one because philosophers came to believe in synthetic identities between properties; and the other because it led to the so-called paradox of analysis. By 1989 David Lewis could put forward precisely the kind of theory that Moore professed to have refuted. But all is not lost for the *OQA*, says Pigden. He first presses an objection to the desire-to-desire theory derived from what he considers Kripke's epistemic argument, which he sees as a variant of the *OQA*. But Moore's argument does not lead to the Paradox of Analysis, Pigden believes, and this suggests three conclusions: (1) that the desire-to-desire theory is false; (2) that the *OQA* can be revived, albeit in a modified form; and (3) that the revived *OQA* poses a serious threat to *semantic naturalism*.

In the next contribution, Susana Nuccetelli and Gary Seay offer a qualified defense of the open question argument that recasts *OQA* in two different versions, depending on the variety of reductive naturalism each attempts to undermine. One is a non-question-begging extended argument that can transmit by entailment the apriority of its premises to the conclusion that no thesis of semantic reductive naturalists is true. According to Nuccetelli and Seay, this argument rests on the contention that Moorean questions have the privileges of cogito-like thoughts. The other, a non-deductive argument against metaphysical reductive naturalism, takes the failure of semantic naturalism as suggesting that some good reason is needed for the reductive naturalists' view that value predicates and purely descriptive predicates are co-extensional. Nuccetelli and Seay conclude that, in the absence of such a reason, the burden of proof is on the metaphysical reductive naturalists.

Recent interest in ethical naturalism, and in the viability of non-naturalist responses to it, is also evident in Robert Shaver's essay, 'Non-naturalism'. Shaver looks closely at two main objections facing non-naturalism: that it is epistemically and metaphyscially extravagant and that it solves no problems. He defends non-naturalism from both objections. The non-naturalism of Moore, Ross, Broad, and Ewing, he argues, was primarily a rejection of 'analytic' naturalism and, later, non-cognitivism.

Joshua Gert, in his essay included here, contends that most of the central doctrines of Moore's ethics, when subjected to more careful analysis using distinctions drawn with today's methods, actually undermine utilitarianism rather than support it. A number of core doctrines in Moore's theory can, in fact, be defended, he thinks, if reconstrued in updated terms; thus, for instance, the contextual invariance of goodness and the narrow dependence of goodness on the intrinsic nature of that which has it can be given revised interpretations that make them highly plausible. Likewise, the notion of 'intrinsic value' can be reconceived as 'what it is rational to choose for its own sake'—so that the primary normative notion is not 'good' or 'right' but 'rational.' Gert also defends a version of Moore's isolation test for intrinsic value that appeals to the notion of rationality instead of duty, and makes use of this test to defend both the universality and the supervenient nature of non-moral goods and harms. In the end, however, this same move from duty to rationality provides a diagnosis of Moore's attraction to a maximizing utilitarian view, and provides a way of avoiding it while retaining much of what is distinctive in his position.

Recent scholarship on Moore's metaethical theory has also included attention to the much-neglected Chapter 6 of *Principia Ethica*, in which Moore considers, among other things, the notion of 'organic unities', complex states of affairs wherein the value of the whole may not be equivalent to the sum of the values of its parts. In this volume's final essay, Jonathan Dancy considers two ways of thinking about organic unities: Moore's way, sometimes called the 'intrinsicalist' way; and the 'variabilist' way preferred by Dancy himself. The difference between these lies in the fact that Moore claims that value-bearers cannot change their non-instrumental value as they move from whole to whole, even though the value they contribute to a whole may depend on the nature of the other parts of that whole. Dancy claims, by contrast, that a feature cannot contribute value that it has not got, and so that intrinsicalism is incoherent. A test case for this debate is that of what Moore calls 'vindictive punishment'. Although some have raised doubts that this case can be treated in a variabilist way, Dancy contends that it can. He considers Moore's intrinsicalist treatment of punishment in the final chapter of *Principia Ethica* and tries to show that the variabilist can, in fact, describe the situation equally well. In the end, Dancy concludes that there is no counter-example to variabilism there.

Works Cited

Austin, J. L., *Sense and Sensibilia* (Oxford: Clarendon Press, 1962).

Ayer, A. J., *Language, Truth and Logic* (London: Gollancz, 1936).

_____ *Philosophy in the Twentieth Century* (New York: Vintage Books, 1984).

Baldwin, T., *G. E. Moore* (New York: Routledge, 1990).

Broad, C. D., 'Philosophy and "Common Sense"', in A. Ambrose and M. Lazerowitz (eds.), *G. E. Moore: Essays in Retrospect* (London: George Allen & Unwin, 1970), 193–203.

Butchvarov, P., *Skepticism about the External World* (New York: Oxford University Press, 1998).

Cohen, S., 'Why Basic Knowledge Is Easy Knowledge', *Philosophy and Phenomenological Research*, 70/2 (2005), 417–30.

Darwall, S., Gibbard, A., and Railton, P., 'Toward a *Fin de Siècle* Ethics: Some Trends', *Philosophical Review*, 101 (1992),115–89.

Davies, M., 'Epistemic Entitlement, Warrant Transmission, and Easy Knowledge', *Proceedings of the Aristotelian Society*, supp. vol. 78 (2004), 213–45.

Foot, P., 'Moral Beliefs', *Proceedings of the Aristotelian Society*, 59 (1958), 83–104.

Frankena, W. K., 'The Naturalistic Fallacy', *Mind*, 48/192 (1939), 464–77.

Geach, P., 'Ascriptivism', *Philosophical Review*, 69 (1960), 221–5.

Hare, R. M., *The Language of Morals* (Oxford: Clarendon Press, 1952).

Harman, G., *The Nature of Morality* (New York: Oxford University Press, 1977).

Huemer, M., *Skepticism and the Veil of Perception* (Lanham, Md. Rowman & Littlefield, 2001).

Jackson, F., *Conditionals* (Oxford: Blackwell, 1987).

Klemke, E. D., *A Defense of Realism: Reflections on the Metaphysics of G. E. Moore* (Amherst, NY: Humanity Books, 2000).

Landesman, C., *Skepticism: The Central Issues* (Oxford: Blackwell, 2002).

Lemos, N., *The Common Sense Tradition: A Contemporary Perspective* (Cambridge: Cambridge University Press, 2004).

Mackie, J. L., *Ethics: Inventing Right and Wrong* (London: Pelican Books, 1977).

Moore, G. E., *Principia Ethica* (1903), rev. edn., (Cambridge: Cambridge University Press, 2002).

_____ 'Hume's Philosophy', *The New Quarterly* (1909), repr. in Moore (1922), 147–67.

_____ 'Hume's Theory Examined' (1910), repr. in Moore (1962a), 108–26.

_____ *Ethics* (Oxford: Oxford University Press, 1912).

_____ 'Some Judgements of Perception', *Proceedings of the Aristotelian Society* (1918–19), repr. in Moore (1922), 220–52.

_____ *Philosophical Studies* (London: Routledge, 1922).

_____ 'Reply to My Critics', in P. A. Schilpp (ed.), *The Philosophy of G. E. Moore* (Lasalle, Ill.: Open Court, 1941), 533–677.

_____ 'A Defence of Common Sense', in J. H. Muirhead (ed.), *Contemporary British Philosophy*, 2nd ser. (1925), repr. in Moore (1959), 32–59.

_____ 'Proof of an External World', *Proceedings of the British Academy*, 25 (1939), repr. in Moore (1959), 127–50.

_____ 'Four Forms of Scepticism', in Moore (1959), 196–225.

_____ 'Certainty', Howison Lecture (University of California, Berkeley, 1941), in Moore (1959), 226–51.

_____ *Philosophical Papers* (London: George Allen & Unwin, 1959).

_____ *Some Main Problems of Philosophy* (London: George Allen & Unwin, 1953, and New York: Collier Books, 1962a).

_____ *The Commonplace Book of G. E. Moore, 1919–1953*, ed. C. Lewy (London: Allen & Unwin, 1962b).

Pryor, J., 'What's Wrong with Moore's Argument?', *Philosophical Issues*, 14 (2004), 349–78.

Putnam, H., *Reason, Truth and History* (Cambridge: Cambridge University Press, 1981).

Somerville, J., 'Moore's Conception of Common Sense', *Philosophy and Phenomenological Research*, 47/2 (1986), 233–53.

Stevenson, C. L., *Ethics and Language* (New Haven: Yale University Press, 1944).

Strawson, P. F., *Skepticism and Naturalism: Some Varieties* (New York: Columbia University Press, 1985).

Wright, C., '(Anti-)Skeptics Simple and Subtle: G. E. Moore and John McDowell', *Philosophy and Phenomenological Research*, 45/2 (2002), 330–48.

_____ 'Wittgensteinian Certainties' D. McManus (ed.), *Wittgenstein and Scepticism* (London: Routledge, forthcoming).

Part II

Moorean Themes
in Epistemology

1

The Perils of Dogmatism

In Memory of Paul Tomassi

Crispin Wright

'Dogmatism' is a term renovated by James Pryor (2000) to stand for a certain kind of neo-Moorean response to scepticism and an associated conception of the architecture of basic perceptual warrant. Pryor runs the response only for (some kinds of) perceptual knowledge but here I will be concerned with its general structure and potential as a possible global anti-sceptical strategy. Something like it is arguably also present in recent writings of Burge[1] and Peacocke.[2] If the global strategy could succeed, it would pre-empt any role in the diagnosis and treatment of sceptical paradoxes for the kind of notion of *entitlement* (rational, non-evidential warrant) I have proposed elsewhere (Wright 2004). But my overarching contention will be that dogmatism is, generally and locally, too problematic a stance to be helpful in that project.

I Neo-Mooreanism, dogmatism, liberalism, and conservatism

In recent literature Moore's 'Proof' of the existence of an external world is customarily represented as the transition from a single premise:

Here is a hand,

---

[1] Burge (1993) 458–9; and (2003), 264. [2] Peacocke (2003), chs. 3 and 4.

endorsed as a thinker (takes herself to) hold(s) up her hand in clear view in front of her face in a state of cognitive lucidity, etc., to the conclusion

There is an external material world,

the transition being mediated by the conceptual necessity that any hand is a material object existing in space. Familiarly, there has been general agreement both that the Proof is unsuccessful—though less clarity about how to describe the respects in which it is unsuccessful, or why it is so[3]—and that one who offers it as a response to material world scepticism[4] is somehow naïvely missing the point, or underestimating the severity of the challenge that the sceptical arguments present. We can regard as neo-Moorean any view of the Proof which rejects, or at least importantly qualifies, these normal negative assessments. So a neo-Moorean will hold, for example, that the proof is unsuccessful only for certain relatively specialized purposes, or when addressed to a particularly, perhaps unreasonably, demanding audience; and that, while it may be ineffective as directed against a sceptical adversary, it does at least demand a response from the sceptic,—a response which may betray an (in the best case, unmotivated) assumption that is somehow pivotal in the generation of sceptical doubt, and that one who advances the Proof may be seen as (tacitly) repudiating.

By these criteria, the *dogmatism* canvassed by James Pryor is prototypically neo-Moorean. The best way of bringing out the essence of the view is to contrast it with a diagnosis—following Pryor, we can call it the *conservative* diagnosis—of the failure of Moore's Proof which I have myself advanced in previous work. According to that diagnosis, the 'Proof' fails because the unarticulated ground for its premise—the thinker's sensory and bodily experience as she holds up her hand—is fitted to support the premise

Here is a hand

only in a certain kind of conducive informational context. It is a familiar Quinean thought that empirical evidence generally varies in its supportive potential as a function of the 'theory'—collateral background beliefs—within whose stage-setting it is enlisted. Suppose I am awakened from slumber by a brightness outside my bedroom window. It may depend on my knowledge of the lunar cycle and the positioning of my bedroom whether that is best taken as evidence for a setting full moon, or a stationary car headlight. Likewise, according to the conservative diagnosis, it is only in the context of the (presumed) collateral information that there is, indeed,

---

[3] Coliva (forthcoming a) provides a useful overview of the various analyses of the proof's failure offered in the literature, as well as an original diagnosis of the apparent *obviousness* of its failure.

[4] As it is by no means clear that Moore himself intended to do—cf. Coliva (forthcoming b), n. 1.

an external material world at all (and more, that ordinary sense experience is a more or les reliable guide to how things are with it) that the Moorean hand-waver's experience is fitted to support the Proof's premise. Replace that information with reason to believe that he is instead a handless brain in a vat, whose every experience is controlled by a computer-program designed by an evil scientist, and the experience supports instead the claim that

> The computer is right now implementing a phase of its program which requires me to suffer the illusion of having a hand and holding it up in front of my face.

According to the conservative diagnosis, then, the Proof fails because its premise is without evidence unless its conclusion is *already* part of the subject's information. It is only in an informational context in which the conclusion is already warranted (or known) that the relevant evidence can provide for warrant (or knowledge) of the premise. So the proof suffers from a kind of epistemic circularity: to take it that one knows its premise (on occurrent perpetual grounds) is to presuppose that one already knows the conclusion. Nor, assuming one does indeed know the premise, is any additional warrant conferred on the conclusion by Moore's simple reasoning. In that sense, the Proof fails to transmit to its conclusion any warrant one may have for its premise. To invoke Pryor's own useful summary way of looking at the matter: in Moore's Proof the logical order of premise and conclusion inverts their epistemic order. In a proof which is to generate a reason to believe its conclusion, by contrast, the orders must coincide.

The conservative diagnosis is not yet *per se* sceptical. Generalized to any proposition about the local perceptible environment, it says merely that apparent perceptual evidence for the proposition in question has that status only in an informational context which includes the existence of an external material world, broadly manifest to our perceptual faculties. We get a sceptical paradox when we further accept that the only justification for accrediting our informational context with that component would have to depend upon first getting warrant for particular propositions about the local perceptual environment—(compare the contention that the only justification we could have for accepting the brain-in-a-vat hypothesis would be by first getting experience-based justification for particular claims about the operation of the computer and the nature of its program). If that is accepted, then the basic architecture of perceptual warrant involves a hopeless circularity, comparable to that alleged in simple Humean scepticism about enumerative induction.[5]

Still, the conservative diagnosis can be maintained without sceptical cost provided there is a way of making out that we may indeed rationally avail ourselves of the

---

[5] I think it is felicitous to call this broad genre of sceptical argument *Humean*. I have characterized the argument in detail—terming it the I-II-III argument—in various writings. See Wright (2004).

collateral informational presuppositions which it calls for. One strategy for doing so—the path of *entitlement*—is to pursue the possibility that we possess a rational but non-evidential warrant for acceptance of those presuppositions. According to dogmatism, by contrast, the conservative diagnosis is already fundamentally mistaken. For the warrant provided by sense experience for propositions of the kind typified by 'Here is a hand' when entertained in the Moorean setting is not, in the dogmatist view, just one more 'theory-conditioned' kind of empirical warrant—albeit one drawing on a minimally controversial, maximally general 'theory'—but is rather unconditional and immediate. To have one's experience represent it to one as if P is true just is, absent other relevant information, to be presented with a defeasible warrant to take it that P is true. One does not need to presuppose any particular 'theory' or body of information—though the possession of certain kinds of unconducive information (for instance, that one is a brain-in-a-vat) will undermine the warrant-conferring power of the experience.

One way of articulating the dispute is thus to centre it on two construals of the sense in which the proposition that there is an external material world, broadly manifest in normal sense experience, is a presupposition of the evidential support of sense-experience for claims of the kind typified by 'Here is a hand' in the Moorean setting. According to the conservative, it is a presupposition in the sense that it something which a thinker requires some kind of prior reason to accept before he may rationally regard his experience as carrying such evidential force.[6] According to the dogmatist—or, as Pryor sometimes says, the *liberal*[7]—it needs to be presupposed only in the sense that a thinker who has reason to regard it as untrue may not rationally regard his experience as carrying such evidential force. No collateral epistemic achievement is required. The thinker need not even consider the issue. Not even a collateral entitlement, without epistemic work, is required. All that is required is that he lack reason to disbelieve it. The ordinary view of our situation in a material

---

[6] This is not to say that the required 'prior reason' must be deliberately thought through or entertained by the beneficiary. The best versions of the notion of rational entitlement will belong with a kind of 'welfare-state' epistemology: entitlements will be benefits by which one may live well, doxastically speaking, without having to do any epistemic work by way of qualification for them.

[7] I ought not to give an impression that Pryor's use of the terms is interchangeable. Roughly, "dogmatism", for Pryor, is restricted to perception: it is the view that the acquisition of knowledge, or warrant, by perception requires no additonal, enabling information, though it of course has potential informational defeaters. Thus both reliabilism and McDowellian direct realism, as well as Pryor's own internalist view, count as kinds of dogmatism. "Liberalism" denotes a view about a specific type of defeater (below, an "authenticity condition") in relation to a specific genre of evidence: to wit, that no reason to discount the obtaining of the defeater is required before one can capitalise on evidence of that genre—it is enough that one has no reason to suppose that such a defeater obtains.

world, impinging in various helpful ways upon our sense-organs, is presupposed only in the sense that it is required to be something which there is no reason to disbelieve.

It merits emphasis before we go any further that Pryor's own invocation of dogmatism is extremely sparing and selective, restricted to certain kinds of perceptual content. There could, in contrast, be a kind of *global* dogmatism. This would be something like the view that for every kind of broad region of our thought which can be called into (Humean) sceptical doubt—matter, other minds, the laws of nature, the future, and the substantial past—there is a kind of basic evidential warrant whose architecture is properly conceived along liberal lines: a type of evidence to possess which is, absent all other relevant information, *eo ipso* to be warranted in accepting a specific proposition of the kind proper to the region in question. One might attempt so to conceive the evidence of others' sayings and doings for their mental states, the evidence of one's own apparent memories for one's past, the evidence of observed regularities for hypotheses of natural law and specific predictions about the future, and the evidence of testimony for—well, for claims about whatever subject-matters a theorist thinks that testimony provides a kind of default warrant. And all these tendencies would stand opposed to corresponding forms of conservatism, with the attendant, overshadowing threat of Humean scepticism. Pryor himself, to stress again, has explicitly proposed dogmatism only for a small sub-species of the propositions which we normally take ordinary sense-experience as fitted to confirm. One question we shall come to later is whether he manages to give a principled demarcation of just which propositions these are. But our initial and principal interest will be in the structure of the proposal: in the very idea, at the heart of liberalism, of evidential relationships which are both defeasible but, in the sense noted, basic and unconditional.

II General Observations and Possible Constraints: (i) The Simple Elevation Hypothesis

Whenever the belief that *P* is formed for reasons, we will characteristically be able to find a number of justificational triads, each of the following form

1 A kind of evidence *that P* that constitutes the reasons for believing it

2 The proposition *that P* itself

3 An *authenticity-condition*

Examples are legion. Here are five:

Moore	Zebras	Red Wall	Stranger	Deduction
1 Experience as of a hand in front of my face	1 Observation of zebra-like animals	1 Observation of a red-looking wall	1 S tells you *that P*	1 Certain data given as premises
2 Here is a hand	2 Those animals are zebras	2 That wall is red	2 P	2 A conclusion
3 There is a material world	3 Those animals are not cleverly disguised mules	3 That wall is not a white wall bathed in red light	3 S is not likely to be untruthful	3 The inference from premises to conclusion is valid

In each case the third element of the triad—the authenticity-condition—is related to the first two like this: a thinker who doubted 3 could not rationally believe 2 just on the basis of evidence 1. Notice that the pattern runs both in defeasible cases—the first four—and in the case of deduction. And, of course, in each of the cases there will be many, many more authenticity-conditions besides those listed.[8]

Let a *warrant* for a belief be, roughly, an all-things-considered mandate for it: to possess a warrant for P is to be in a state wherein it is, all things considered, epistemically appropriate to believe P. Here I shall require no more specific an understanding of the notion of warrant than that. So the reader is free to construe it further as she thinks fit, whether *externally* (so that, for example, warrant may be constituted by a belief's formation by means of a *de facto* normally reliable cognitive mechanism) or *internally* (so that, for example, warrant may be constituted by a state of information which may be ascertained by a priori reflection and self-knowledge alone), or in more complicated (perhaps admixed) ways. However, I want to contrast the idea of possessing a warrant for P with another idea, namely, that of a thinker's *being in position to claim* possession of a warrant for P. And by this, I *do* intend something with internalist resonances. I want to understand the claimability of a warrant to be what is at issue when, for example, a philosopher feels that one has not been given everything one needs to address scepticism about the external world, say, merely by impressive arguments—if any such there be—that knowledge can be constituted by reliably generated true belief. To be sure, if the sceptical argument is taken to be to the effect that knowledge of the material world is *impossible*, then it must founder if a reliabilist conception of

---

[8] Note that authenticity-conditions are *presuppositions of cognitive project* in the sense of Wright (2004); see 191.

knowledge is sound; for even the most skilful monger of paradoxes cannot show that we are not *as a matter of fact* so situated in a material world that our cognitive faculties reliably generate mostly true beliefs about it. But the residual dissatisfaction with the externalist suggestion as a response to scepticism is that it merely points to a congenial *possibility*: nothing has been offered to put us in position to claim that it, rather than one of the many contrasting uncongenial sceptical scenarios, actually obtains.

It is important to realize that there is no room to articulate this dissatisfaction—whose mitigation I shall take to be a cardinal objective of the traditional epistemological project, properly conceived—merely by setting it as an assertion of second order ignorance: as the claim that, even if we, as it were, externally know all kinds of things about the material world, we do not know that we do. For the latter claim is, when knowledge is externally construed, no less presumptuous than the original first-order sceptical claim. The belief that we know all kinds of things about the material world may itself be a reliably generated true belief. The dissatisfaction—if felt at all—needs to be articulated in terms of the absence of a kind of assurance which cannot be remedied merely by external cognitive achievement. Since any epistemic operator, including—to be sure—the proposed '. . . *is in position to claim*', may always be subjected to externalist construal by an awkward customer, that may seem to leave us in difficulty when it comes to providing a cogent articulation of the dissatisfaction in question. A resolute externalist may simply refuse to hear anything as an expression of it—the suggestion that mere reliabilism provides us with no resources to challenge a scepticism focused not on the possibility of knowledge in a targeted region but on our right to claim it, may be dismissed as just as unsupported as regular first-order scepticism.

Fortunately (or unfortunately), this is not a dialectically stable stance. For consider how externalism promises to address simple first-order closure scepticism about knowledge. A sceptical scenario, SH, is selected whose obtaining is incompatible with the truth of any of a wide class of ordinary beliefs that we customarily regard as knowledgeable. It is alleged that we have no knowledge enabling us to discount SH. So, by closure, none of the beliefs in question is knowledgeable. Assuming that no issue is to be raised about closure, the only room for manœuvre is to challenge the allegation that we cannot know that SH does not obtain. The externalist counter will be precisely that this has not been shown: that for all that the sceptical argument has established, we *may* know that SH does not obtain—if, for example, the belief that it does not obtain is 'safe': is true in all relevantly close worlds. But consider what happens if we try to express this counter using an externally construed outer operator—it may as well be the very same operator—so that what it comes to is the contention that

We cannot know that: we cannot know that SH does not obtain.

Since the obtaining of SH would ensure that we cannot know that SH does not obtain, the externalist's counter commits him, by closure, to affirming that

We cannot know that SH does obtain.

But the externalist is committed to regarding that contention, externally construed, as just as inappropriate, and for the very same reasons, as the sceptical premise that we cannot know that SH does not obtain. On the contrary, we *may*, she should allow, know that SH does obtain—if, for example, the belief that it does obtain is safe: is true in all relevantly close worlds. To be sure, that is not a belief we actually—most of us—have. But the issue here is the *possibility* of knowledge.[9]

Moral: without recourse to some internalist notion of epistemic warrant, there is no prospect of utilizing external notions of warrant to address even the simplest of sceptical paradoxes. Naturally, merely to make that observation is not yet to explain how the requisite internal notion, or notions, are best to be construed. But when even externalist-minded theorists must, seemingly, have tacit recourse to them in bringing their characteristic proposals to bear on the challenge of scepticism, we are, I think, entitled to proceed on the assumption that some such notions are in good-standing and, more, are deeply rooted in our understanding of the issues and challenges in the vicinity.

Very well. Suppose now that a thinker T is presented with evidence 1 for a proposition 2, for whose relevance 3 is an authenticity-condition. Then here are two types of question we can ask about the situation:

Q^{level1}: What independent epistemic relation must T bear to 3 if having 1 (or warrantedly believing an associated proposition recording the possession of that evidence) is to give her warrant for 2?

Q^{level2}: What independent epistemic relation must T bear to 3 if, when 1 does give her warrant for 2, she is *to be in position to claim* a warrant for 2?

Q^{level1} and Q^{level2} will get the same answer if it is supposed that the very having of warrant puts one in position to claim it. The latter may be true on certain internalist conceptions of warrant. (It will be for Pryor to say whether it is true when warrant is understood in the kind of internalist way in which, unless I misread him, *he* wants to understand it.) However, it will not be true—at least not a priori true—on externalist

---

[9] This way of making the point exploits the factivity of knowledge. But that is inessential. Suppose merely that whatever the external conditions are that are conceived as making for warrant, they cannot be met simultaneously for both the belief that P and the belief that not-P, and that warrant is closed under (obvious) entailment. Then if W(SH), it follows that $\sim$W($\sim$SH). So if the latter—the sceptical premise—is to be deemed unwarranted, so must be W(SH). Hence the externalist's complaint, that the sceptical premise is unwarranted, requires an endorsement of $\sim$WW(SH). But how, when W is construed externally, is that endorsement to be philosophically justified? Whatever it externally takes to make a belief warranted, it cannot be ruled out just by philosophical reflection that the condition is met by my (perhaps perverse) belief that SH. If it is, W(SH) will be true. And now, what if I believe that too, and what if this belief likewise meets the requisite external conditions? Who is to say it doesn't?

conceptions of warrant possession in general and when being in position to claim warrant is understood as I have proposed.

What is dogmatism saying about the two questions? We take a dogmatist view of any particular such triad when we affirm that Q^{level1} gets this answer:

> A thinker's having the evidence 1 suffices to give her warrant for 2 provided she *has no reason to doubt 3*,

where having no reason to doubt is ensured in particular by having no relevant independent information of any kind that bears on 3.[10] But what about Q^{level2}? Does dogmatism intend to answer Q^{level2} at all? If not, it says nothing whatever to respond to (Humean) scepticism about claims of warrant. So its interest for the traditional epistemological project is immediately severely limited. But if so, what is its intended answer?

There is a simple proposal which, if correct, leaves dogmatism with no option but to answer Q^{level2} in one particular way. The proposal is that of the *Simple Elevation Hypothesis*:

> In general, whatever conditions C (a priori necessarily) confer warrant upon a thinker T for acceptance of 2, it will suffice to put T in position to claim warrant for 2 that she be in position to claim that C are met

Someone might demur from this on account of the following gap: conditions C may obtain, so that T has a warrant for 2, and T may be in position to claim that C are met, and yet in no position to claim warrant for 2 because she doesn't know that C *are* warrant-conferring for 2. However, I do not think this is a plausible reservation for a *dogmatist* to have. It is an intuitive strength of dogmatism that it seems to account for our intuitions about what it takes to have warrant for simple, perceptual beliefs on the part of thinkers who for the most part lack the conceptual resources even to formulate, still less to take attitudes to propositions articulating authenticity-conditions. Consider a 6-years-old

---

[10] Notice that the dogmatist stance can perfectly sensibly be authenticity-condition relative: one may hold that the answer above is appropriate only for certain choices of relevant authenticity-conditions for 3, while for others a conservative view is appropriate. I already emphasised that Pryor's dogmatism is local to the relation between perceptual experience and certain kinds of proposition concerning the external world—those involving 'perceptually basic' concepts. However, the observation just made involves a further potential locality. It is open to a dogmatist to insist that, even where perceptually basic judgments are concerned, experience may warrant them in the liberal manner only where certain authenticity-conditions are concerned, and that others *do* need to be part of a thinker's presumed information before she may warrantedly take the experience at face value. This is not, as far as I am aware, Pryor's view. But it is a possible view. Both the very existence of a material world and the thinker's occurrent perceptual receptiveness are authenticity-conditions for the transition from 1 to 2 in *Moore*. There would be no incoherence in combining a liberal view of the role of the first with a conservative view of the second.

child, Sophie. Sophie will form simple beliefs about her local environment—that her bedroom is untidy, that Tabitha is sleeping in her basket, and so on—purely on the basis of her experiences, and we are inclined, just as dogmatism would seem to predict, to say that these are beliefs for which she is fully warranted. Conservatism, by contrast, represents these warrants as hostage to the possession of collateral information about authenticity-conditions—hostages which, in the absence of any ability of Sophie's even to entertain such information, are presumably not redeemed. But notice that our inclination to grant Sophie's warrants is not in any way qualified if, possessed of at least a rudimentary mastery of the verb 'to know' and asked what she knows about her bedroom at the moment, or the cat's whereabouts, she replies that *she knows* that it is untidy, and that *she knows* that Tabitha is in her basket. These are effectively claims of warrant but they seem just as justified and rational, in the circumstances, as the claims they embed. It would be quite out of keeping with the general tenor of dogmatism to insist that they are not so—that warrant for them requires in addition a sophisticated piece of epistemological knowledge.

The Simple Elevation Hypothesis forces dogmatism to extend its distinctive thesis about the possession of certain kinds of warrant to the corresponding claims of warrant. More generally, it allows us test answers to Q^{level1} by appeal to our intuitions about *claimable* warrants. The dogmatist answer to Q^{level1} has it that it suffices for possession of warrant for 2 that T has the evidence 1 and no reason to doubt 3. So, by the Simple Elevation Hypothesis, it should suffice for T to be in position to claim warrant for 2 that she is in position to claim both that she has evidence 1 and that she has no reason to doubt 3. That is the answer that dogmatism must give to Q^{level2} unless the Simple Elevation Hypothesis is rejected. But is that answer acceptable in general?

To fix ideas, consider the case of *Stranger*. Suppose the dogmatist answer is here correct: it suffices to get warrant for *P* by testimony that one be told that *P* in a context where one has no reason to doubt the truthfulness of one's informant. Then by the Simple Elevation Hypothesis, it should suffice to be in position to claim a testimonial warrant that one be in position to claim that one was told that *P* and that one has no reason to regard one's opponent as untruthful. But that answer seems manifestly insufficient. Imagine the natural dialogue:

'Why do you believe that *P*?'

'Because S told me and I have no reason to regard him as untruthful or likely to be mistaken'

'So: you take it as reasonable to believe a stranger on a matter like whether *P* unless there is evidence that they are untruthful or likely to be mistaken'

'I *do not need to have a view about that*. Let that issue be open. I repeat: S told me and I have no reason to regard him as untruthful or likely to be mistaken. That suffices for warrant. I therefore claim my warrant for *P*.'

There is a strong intuition that the last response is irrational, or epistemically irresponsible. After his first answer, and once the issue is raised, the speaker *does* need to take the stance that it is reasonable to believe the testimony of strangers unless there is reason to regard them as untruthful or likely to be mistaken—or back off his claim to testimonial warrant for *P*. If so, then the testimony-dogmatist answer to Q^{level1} is faulty unless the Simple Elevation Hypothesis is wrong.

Can the Simple Elevation Hypothesis be wrong? We noted one way in which it might be questioned: the thought was the simple one that being in position to claim that conditions obtain which in fact constitute a warrant for a particular belief may none the less fail to put a thinker in position to claim warrant for that belief if she does not know that fact—is not enough of an epistemologist, as it were. We also noted that this does not seem a good tack for dogmatism to try. But there is another point. Irresponsibility in general is relative to the ability to understand relevant possibilities and take relevant corresponding precautions. So a child may be open to no charge of irresponsibility in acting on information which an adult who shared her objectives could not responsibly act on unless assured that a number of precautions were in place. Might it be that the single most impressive piece of evidence in favour of dogmatism—our apparent intuitions about what it takes to confer warrant on the perceptual beliefs of the young and unsophisticated—is actually drawing credibility from a version of this point? In that case, it would be true that an innocent might achieve warrant for 'Here is a hand' purely on the basis of her experience and, while lacking any relevant information about authenticity-conditions, only and purely because incapable of entertaining, or appraising, statements about such conditions. As soon as she acquired the conceptual and intellectual wherewithal to understand how their failure would invalidate the warranting power of sensory impressions, she would exile herself from a position of innocence in which there was no obligation even to take a view about the obtaining of authenticity-conditions, still less to assure oneself that they did obtain, or that it was justifiable to suppose so.

If this were the situation, the Simple Elevation Hypothesis would remain unchallenged. The mismatch between the dogmatist's answer to Q^{level1} and the answer it enforces, in accordance with the Simple Elevation Hypothesis, to Q^{level2}, would be explained by the consideration that the very conceptual sophistication required by the practice of *self-ascription* of warrant of the kind illustrated by the dialogue somehow 'ups the ante': that it raises the standards for *having* warrant in the first place. So the liberal answer to Q^{level1} would be correct only for relatively unsophisticated subjects; and no answer, liberal or conservative, would be generally correct.

Much more should be said about this, but I have no space to pursue the matter here. What is clear is that there is a dilemma for dogmatism in any area where a dialogue like that above for *Stranger* seems to accord with our intuitions (prejudices?)

about what it takes to be in position to claim warrant. If the dogmatist agrees with the Simple Elevation Hypothesis, these intuitions strongly suggest that his answer at Q^{level1} is wrong. He might save that answer by rejecting the Simple Elevation Hypothesis, or by pursuing the train of thought just canvassed. But, either way, he concedes that the answer to Q^{level2} that one might expect dogmatism to offer—the answer enforced by the Simple Elevation Hypothesis together with the dogmatist answer to Q^{level1}—is incorrect. And in that case dogmatism has nothing to offer when the sceptical challenge concerns our being in position to claim the wide sweeps of (perceptual) knowledge which we ordinarily take ourselves to have—and only little to offer, accordingly, to one pursuing the traditional epistemological project.

III General Observations and Possible Constraints: (ii) Warrant Transmission

A second kind of potential control on answers to Q^{level1} is provided by considerations of warrant transmission. In the typical run of cases, there will be no entailment in a justificational triad, {1, 2, 3}, from proposition 2 to the satisfaction of the authenticity-condition, 3. The redness of the demonstrated wall does not entail, for example, that the subject is not colour-blind; and the truth of S's testimony does not entail—the actual example—that S is characteristically truthful. But the first three examples in the table—*Moore, Zebras* and *Red Wall*—were precisely selected to illustrate how the satisfaction of certain authenticity-conditions may indeed sometimes be a consequence of the very proposition, 2, that is up for warrant. In any case of this kind—let's say: in any case where a justificational triad has the *entailment feature*—the correctness of the conservative answer to Q^{level1} will entail that the warrant given by 1 for 2 will fail to transmit to 3. A conservative answer to Q^{level1} will be (something like) this:

> A thinker's having the evidence 1 suffices to give her warrant for 2 only provided she *has independent warrant for* 3

Whenever that answer is correct, it would be absurd to regard 3 as confirmed, across the entailment of it by 2, by the evidence 1. You could not acquire a *first* warrant to think that 3 was satisfied in that way, since you would have to have warrant for 3 already in order to conjure a warrant for 2; nor is it intelligible how such reasoning could *strengthen* a warrant for 3 which you already possessed—for the warrant for 3 cannot, in the circumstances be stronger than the warrant for 2, and the latter, presumably, is bounded by the strength of the demanded anterior warrant for 3. Conservatism, then, predicts failure of warrant transmission in any such case.

Now, while *Moore* may be controversial, the prediction seems right for *Zebras* and *Red Wall*. That is why it was not implausible for Dretske, the author of those examples,[11] to offer them as examples of failure of *Closure*. If in *Zebras*, for instance, the warrant for 2 provided by 1 transmitted to 3, then the observations required by 1 would, in principle, suffice, by the inference from 2, to allow the subject to *learn* that 3 obtained, even though its failure to obtain is a possibility beyond the power of observation, of the envisaged level of refinement, to detect directly. That would be magic indeed! *Mutatis mutandis* for *Red Wall*.

However, on a liberal view of the justificational architecture involved in these examples, it remains unclear why there should be any issue about the transmissibility of the warrants involved. What could stand in the way of transmission of a warrant from a premise to an obvious, valid conclusion when no information about, or epistemic attitude to, the latter is prerequisite for appreciating the force of the evidence for the former? How is it ever going to be possible to learn anything by inference if there can be a good issue about transmission of warrant even in such a case? Dogmatism, it would appear, should predict that there will be no transmission worries in any justificational triad with the entailment feature for which the liberal view is correct. So our intuitions (defeasible as they may be) about warrant transmission can be used to test liberal and conservative views in such cases. If warrant seems to transmit to an authenticity-condition, that is strong evidence that its role in the support provided by the relevant kind of evidence for the relevant kind of belief is not as conceived by conservatism; but if it seems to fail to transmit, that is evidence that things are not as conceived by the liberal.

The application of this proposed control would obviously be compromised, however, if there are other kinds of pathology of argument which, though in some respects presenting like transmission-failure, are different and are consistent, moreover, with liberalism. Pryor (2004) has attempted to argue just this, for the case of *Moore* at least, by suggesting a distinction between transmission-failure properly so regarded, and a certain kind of *dialectical ineffectiveness*. Clearly, even a warrant-transmissive inference may be dialectically ineffective for a thinker who is already convinced of the falsity of the conclusion. In any such case, that antecedent conviction may overpower the evidence for the premises. More subtly—this is Pryor's actual thought—in the case of justificational triads with the entailment feature, doubt about the authenticity-condition stated by the conclusion is mandated by dogmatism itself as defeating the warranting power of the evidence for the premise. So *Moore* will quite properly be regarded as ineffective by a sceptic who doubts the existence of the external world, even if warrant-transmissive for an ordinary common-sense thinker like Moore himself. Furthermore, it is to be expected that *we* non-sceptics, tacitly recognizing that

---

[11] Dretske (1970).

the argument is no good when directed against such a sceptic, will likewise be inclined to dismiss it in the dialectical setting in which it was offered—when, that is, it is directed against scepticism—even though free of doubt about the conclusion ourselves.

I think there is no doubt that dogmatism does indeed predict that *Moore* should involve no failure of transmission. Still it is, to be sure, a further question whether the typical reaction of frustration with it is correctly diagnosed as an intuition of transmission-failure.[12] According to the proposal just canvassed, it is not. Rather, the frustration betrays—so it is open to Pryor to suggest—merely a less specific sense that the Proof is no good for its purpose. There are other ways that proofs may be no good for their purposes besides by being invalid, by containing false or unwarranted premises, or by virtue of failures of transmission.

The distinction between transmission-failure and dialectical ineffectiveness of the kind diagnosed by Pryor is clearly a good one in general. There is, however, an evident problem in the attempt to invoke the latter notion in a diagnosis of *Moore*. Liberalism and conservatism precisely divide over the question whether *agnosticism* about an authenticity-condition defeats the relevant kind of evidence: the conservative holds that it does; the liberal that it does not. So Pryor's diagnosis cannot kick in if the intended audience of a proof merely (considers that it) has *no* relevant information bearing on whether an entailed authenticity-condition obtains or not. To doubt that there is an external world in the manner needed to trigger Pryor's diagnosis has to be: to (incline to) believe that *there is no material world*. It cannot be merely a matter of lack of conviction, or disinclination to the contrary belief. Yet the doubt that is the stock-in-trade of scepticism is exactly that. Scepticism argues that we have no adequate reason to believe that there is a material world. It is no part of scepticism to take the further step to the *denial* of matter—to *idealism*.[13] If Moore's Proof is indeed transmissive, it should be able—at least for all the liberal account of its justificational architecture has to say about the point—to produce a warrant to believe in the external material world for such an agnostic. The sheer occurrence of suitable experiences ought to be enough to trigger a flow of warrant down to the common-sense world-view in exactly the manner articulated by the Proof. It is therefore bad for Pryor's view if—as I suggest it does—the sense remains strong that *Moore* produces *no* reason to believe its conclusion, not merely for one antecedently doubtful of it but even for one merely antecedently unconvinced of it.[14]

---

[12] See Coliva (forthcoming) for exploration of other possibilities.

[13] As stressed also in Coliva (forthcoming).

[14] As Annalisa Coliva has pointed out to me, a *principled* agnosticism about the existence of the external world—one not merely involving open-mindedness, or disinclination to a view, but resting on an argued stance that there can be no adequate evidence for or against the disputed matter—will have a motive for rejecting Moore's Proof which is not encompassed by the kind of Pryorian dialectical ineffectiveness characterized above. Such an agnostic thinker will discount the evidence of experience for

The proposed constraint on answers to Q^{level1} emerges from this discussion in the following form. For justificational triads with the entailment feature: (i) conservatism predicts failures of transmission of warrant; (ii) liberalism predicts that there should be no such failure: (iii) the distinction between mere dialectical ineffectiveness and transmission- failure proper turns on whether cogency is jeopardized by mere agnosticism—perhaps better: open-mindedness—about the satisfaction of the relevant authenticity-condition.

IV Four Perils for dogmatism in general

With these preparations, our catalogue of the forewarned Perils can be brisk. In this section, I shall outline four potential trouble-spots for dogmatism wherever it is proposed. In the next, concluding section, I'll sketch one more vexation for Pryor's specific proposals about perceptually warranted belief.

1 The pervasive threat of the insufficiency of the liberal account at second level

The pattern of dialogue outlined above for the case of Stranger and warrant by testimony may be replicated for any justificational triad, with the impression of irresponsibility that it provokes persisting—I conjecture—more or less exceptionlessly. Try it for the case of any belief P about one's local environment formed on the basis of visual experience

'Why do you believe that *P*?'

'Because it looks to me to be the case that *P* and I have no reason to regard my visual system as defective.

'So: you take it that it is reasonable to believe that your visual system is likely to be trustworthy unless there is evidence that it may not be functioning properly?'

'*I do not need to have a view about that.* I repeat: it looks to me that *P* and I have no reason to doubt that my visual system is working properly. I therefore claim warrant for *P*.'

---

the Proof's premise, 'Here is a hand', not because he disbelieves the relevant authenticity-condition—he can be open-minded about the existence of the external world—but because he regards the evidence as inadequate in principle in any case. It is an interesting question whether the ineffectiveness of the Proof for such an agnostic thinker demands a diagnosis distinct from transmission failure. However, nothing will turn on it in the sequel, so I defer discussion to another occasion. Pryor is of course aware of the issue—see his (2004) at pp. 367–8.

As before, all the dialogue does is to export the liberal view of the architecture of a justificational triad—here:

Eyes

1 Visual experience as of P

being the case

2 P

3 My visual system is working

properly

up to level 2, in accordance with the Simple Elevation Hypothesis, so that it is presented as sufficient for a thinker to be in position to *claim* warrant for P that she be in position to claim that exactly those conditions are met which dogmatism views as sufficient for *having* warrant. And, as before, there is a very strong sense that the last response is irrational, or epistemically irresponsible.[15] After his first answer, and once the issue is raised, the speaker *does* need to take the stance that it is reasonable to believe that his visual system is working properly unless there is evidence to the contrary—or back off his claim to visual warrant for P. If so, then the perceptual-dogmatist answer to Q^{level1} is faulty unless the Simple Elevation Hypothesis is wrong. But even if the Simple Elevation Hypothesis is wrong, that is of no very great avail to dogmatism since the point remains that there is a mismatch between the conditions which dogmatism regards as sufficient for warrant-possession and the conditions which our intuitions—at least as elicited by the dialogues—regard as necessary for warrant-claiming. Some of the latter have no counterparts among the former. So even in the best case, when the Simple Elevation Hypothesis is rejected, dogmatism has nothing to contribute to those of the challenges and problems of the traditional epistemological project that concern the level of claims.

As suggested, this difficulty threatens to be pervasive.

2 The problem of stand-off defeaters

The dogmatist view of any particular justificational triad returns this answer to Q^{level1}:

A thinker's having the evidence 1 suffices to give her warrant for 2 provided she has no reason to doubt 3

'Doubt' in English equivocates between uncertainty and disbelief (belief that not). However, for liberalism, crucially, 'having no reason to doubt' must pertain to the latter. For liberalism requires the status of having no reason to doubt to be consistent

---

[15] Here is a possible explanation why. In claiming visual warrant for P while disclaiming any view about the likelihood of proper visual function, the subject is steering dangerously close to claiming warrant for P while disclaiming any view about the likelihood of being right.

with having no relevant information either way—that is the whole point. So it appears the proviso, as it must be intended, is met by any thinker whose evidence—other than that given by 1—provides no sufficient reason for a view on 3, and thereby mandates open-mindedness on the matter.

But this cannot possibly be correct. What if one's evidence balances the scales? Consider an amalgam of *Eyes* and *Red Wall*:

Red-wall (II)

1 Observation of a red-looking

wall

2 That wall is red

3 My visual system is working

properly

Suppose you are knowledgeably participating in a double-blind trial of a new hallucinogen, affecting just colour vision. Half the trialists have the pill and half a placebo. The trialists are advised that the former group will suffer a temporary systematic inversion of their colour experience, but have no other relevant information, in particular none providing any reason for a view about which group they are in. Clearly this information defeats 1 as a warrant for 2. Its effect is that your evidence 1 now provides no reason whatever for believing 2. But it does not give sufficient reason to *doubt* 3 if that is required to mean: to believe not-3. You should be open-minded about 3.

It seems, then, that it is only when 'having no reason to doubt 3' in liberalism's answer to Q^{level1} is understood as compromised by a situation of balanced evidence for and against 3 that the answer has any plausibility. But balanced evidence for and against is what you have, trivially, in a position of *innocence*, when you have no relevant evidence either way. And there dogmatism precisely wants the warrant for 2 to stand. So, *what's the relevant difference*? Why does mandated neutrality conferred by balanced evidence defeat the warrant provided by 1 for 2, while mandated neutrality conferred by lack of all relevant evidence does no harm?

The conservative has no difficulty with the issue: if a thinker's having evidence 1 suffices to give her warrant for 2 only provided she has *independent warrant for 3*, it is readily intelligible—indeed it is predicted—that mandated open-mindedness about 3 will defeat that warrant. Specifically: once her information requires her to be open-minded about 3, she will fail to meet the condition on 3 demanded by the conservative answer to Q^{level1}. However, if, as dogmatism has it, no independent warrant to accept 3 is needed in any case, what of relevance has been lost when one's information mandates open-mindedness?

3 What are Pryor's 'priors'?

This is a concern first articulated by Stephen Schiffer.[16] Let us reconsider

Red-wall

1 Observation of a red-looking wall

2 That wall is red

3 That wall is not a white wall

bathed in red light

so that now we once again have a triad with the entailment feature. And suppose 1 is the only relevant evidence you have for 2 and that you have no other relevant evidence bearing on 3. What were your prior conditional probabilities of 2 given 1, and of not-3 given 1, respectively? Suppose your actual reaction to getting evidence 1 is a high degree of confidence—say, no doubt artificially, 90 per cent—in 2. Then, if you are rational, so subject to the laws of classical probability, your prior conditional probability of not-3 on 1 cannot have been higher than 10 per cent. Classical probability requires that a rational thinker acquires confidence that P on the basis of evidence e only if antecedently disposed to assign a correspondingly low conditional probability on e to any claim incompatible with P.

According to dogmatism, however, a rational thinker who acquires the evidence 1 and who has no other information bearing on 3—in particular none that should incline him to believe the negation of 3—is fully warranted in accepting 2, and so in discounting the negation of 3, without further ado. If this claim is intended to hold irrespective of the thinker's prior probability for the negation of 3 given 1, then it is in tension with the conception of rationality encoded in the laws of classical probability. If it is intended rather to import the idea that, absent any other relevant information, a rational thinker should assign a higher conditional probability to 2 given 1 than to not-3 given 1, then that seems to demand elucidation by reference to some thesis of the prior rational acceptability of at least some important class of authenticity-conditions—a thesis that would fit naturally with a conservatism that made use of the idea of non-evidential entitlement, but seems quite foreign to dogmatism.[17]

---

[16] Schiffer (2004), at 175–6.

[17] Christopher Peacocke repudiates this objection at 113–15 of Peacocke (2003). After glossing the concern, summarising its upshot as being that: 'It seems from the description of the case that my confidence [that I am not subject to a perceptual illusion] cannot be rationally enhanced simply from the enjoyment of the experience itself . . .', he then replies that: 'the default entitlement to take . . . perceptual experience at face value in the absence of good reasons for doubt should be located in a theory of outright, all-or-nothing, propositional attitudes. These are more fundamental than degree-theoretic attitudes, and I doubt that the outright attitudes can be elucidated in terms of degree-theoretic attitudes. A thinker may simply have no attitudes in advance about the likelihood of

4 'Easy-warrant' issues

Here is a difficulty first pointed out by Stewart Cohen.[18] In all cases where it appears visually to me that P, dogmatism allows that I can chalk up a warrant that P provided I have no reason to doubt that my visual system is working properly (and have no other defeating information). So in all such cases I am warranted in affirming each member of the pair

<It appears visually to me that P; P >

Chalk up enough such pairs and I shall have a large body of information recording nothing but matching correlations between my visual appearances and how matters stand in the real world—and indeed a body of information which I can grow as large as I like provided merely that I am fortunate enough to acquire no information at any stage suggestive that my visual system is *not* working properly. Innocence on the matter is bound, it seems, if dogmatism is correct, to inflate into an overwhelmingly inductively supported, rational confidence in the effectiveness of my visual system, just provided I encounter no independently countervailing information. Obviously, the point is independent of the choice of the example of vision and visually apprehensible subject-matter. It will engage whatever the subject matter of P, for whatever we conceive of as the relevant cognitive faculties.

This would clearly be an absurd consequence. But dogmatism has an effective response to it.[19] A pool of evidence should be regarded as providing inductive confirmation of a hypothesis only if it is reasonable to consider it as drawing upon a representative sample. And that, in turn, requires that a significant prior probability for the thesis that counter-examples would have shown up in the sample if there are any. But the body of 'confirming' data compiled by chalking up pairs of the form, <It

his being subject to perceptual illusions in his present circumstances. For such a thinker his enjoyment of an experience of a flat surface in front of him will not only entitle him to think that there is a flat surface in front of him. It will, by inference, give him an entitlement to think that he is not subject to an illusion, an entitlement that he did not have antecedently to his having the experience.' It is hard to see how this addresses the issue. Let it be—as Peacocke (merely) asserts—that the warrants that experience supplies for perceptual beliefs are warrants for irreducibly outright attitudes. It is an entirely different thing whether the rational formation of such attitudes should be somehow exempt from the broad constraints to which the degree-theoretic attitudes are subject. Of course, that is exactly what dogmatism must claim. But here is the basic dilemma: if taking myself to have a Peacocke-style entitlement to the outright belief that there is a flat surface in front of me has no bearing on what opinion I should rationally have about the likelihood of being right, then it is nothing I can use to address the sceptical misgiving that, for all I am entitled to think, I am as likely to be right as wrong about any particular perceptual claim. On the other hand, if Peacocke-entitlement *is* to warrant an opinion about likelihoods, it remains utterly unexplained why it is not subject to the broad pattern of constraint, in terms of conditional 'priors', that Schiffer's objection appeals to.

[18] Cohen (2002).   [19] Cf. Pryor (2001), 26–8.

appears visually to me that P; $P >$, in the way described, has no chance of containing any counter-examples to the contention of the reliability of my visual appearances. So it provides no inductive support for that contention in any case, for purely general methodological reasons quite independent of dogmatism.

However, there does remain a real 'easy-warrant' problem—the problem of unstoppable transmission in seemingly inappropriate cases. If the dogmatist view of the original *Red Wall* example is right, the visual warrant for 2 transmits to 3: so I get a *visual-cum-inferential* warrant for a claim—viz. that the wall in question is not a white wall bathed in red light—whose falsity would be visually undetectable. Indeed, if one thinks of the original visual warrant for 2 as conferring *knowledge*, then dogmatism has no resources to prevent the conclusion that I can acquire knowledge by vision plus elementary inference of a proposition whose being false would predict my enjoyment of exactly the same visual experience. That is absurd. Its being absurd is just the intuition that prompted Dretske (1970) to regard such cases as failures of Closure. Dretske's interpretation is, I think, mistaken. Nevertheless, there is no denying the datum.

The problem is once again pervasive, affecting a huge range of cases of justificational triads with the entailment feature. For instance, it afflicts each of

Pain	Seaweed	Lizard	Geiger counter
1 Jones leaps out of the dentist's chair with a howl	1 Observation of the sea-weed line on the West Sands	1 A bright light is shone on a nocturnal lizard revealing a stripy pattern of brown and black scales	1 A crescendo of rapid clicks is emitted by my Geiger counter
2. The dentist's drilling just caused Jones a dart of intense pain	2 Here is this morning's high-water mark	2 That kind of lizard is striped	2 The Geiger counter has detected a strong radiation source nearby
3 Jones is not faking a pain	3 The seaweed was not re-positioned by pranksters to make a point about warrant-transmission	3 That kind of lizard does not very rapidly become striped when irradiated in bright light	3 The Geiger counter is not malfunc-tioning

The adoption of a dogmatic stance with respect to triads such as these—the normal run of cases—is surely out of the question. But then: which are the cases where it is supposedly correct, and why?[20]

V An Additional Peril for Perceptual dogmatism

5 —Providing a principled restriction of the scope of the dogmatist thesis

In Pryor's view, the answer to the question with which the preceding section concluded is: when the judgement supported by one's experience is in a certain sense *perceptually basic*. A perceptually basic judgement is one whose content an experience may carry as *its* own proper content. The dogmatic cases are those where the experience's consisting in the reception of an appearance that P is a fact independent of any issue about *interpretation*, or the background beliefs of the subject.

Two points are salient if Pryor's suggestion is on the right strategic lines. One is that dogmatism will rest squarely on the presupposition that there is a core intrinsic content carried by an experience: a message, as it were, which is just what the experience strictly

---

[20] It is worth quickly reviewing one line of thought about these cases which, while denying—as I have suggested that dogmatism about them must deny—that they manifest any failure of transmission of warrant, can accommodate the datum to this extent, that in each case it would be acknowledged as absurd to think of the evidence 1 as *improving one's epistemic position* with respect to 3. There are cases where evidence for P, which entails Q, simultaneously raises the antecedent probability of P but lowers that of Q. In such cases, Q becomes less likely once we have to view it as true, if at all, because P is. Example: five snooker balls, two reds, two 'colours', and the cue ball, are placed in a bag. One will be drawn out at random. P is the proposition that the selected ball will be a red. Q is the proposition that the selected ball will not be the cue ball. The prior probabilities are respectively 40% and 80%. Then we learn that no colour will be selected. On this evidence, the probability of P rises to 66% but that of Q drops to 66%. Is this what is happening in our catalogue of alleged transmission-failures?

This model might explain a kind of illusion of transmission failure in certain examples, but it cannot plausibly be presented as suggesting an alternative, dogmatism-friendly account of the difficult cases. While it is true that, for example, the prior probability of

3 Jones is not faking a pain

drops once I acquire the evidence that he is at least behaving as if in pain—after all, there are innumerably many ways he might have acted so as to make 3 true which are now ruled out—the disanalogy remains that, in the snooker-ball case, it is intuitively perfectly reasonable to present one's knowledge of the original set-up, plus the new information that no colour will be selected, as direct warrant for, say, betting that the cue ball will not be selected. But absent any other relevant information—about, for example Jones's character and motivation—it would seem manifestly irrational to bet that Jones is not faking purely on the grounds that he is acting as he would if either faking or genuinely suffering a shoot of intense dental pain. Certainly, the matter needs more detailed discussion.

and literally conveys, more basic than anything which, in the context of her collateral information, it may be able additionally to convey to its subject.[21] Second, it would seem that dogmatism will be appropriate as a view about the epistemic relationship between any given kind of evidence and the propositions for which it is evidence only in cases where the former consists in the presentation of appearances that P that are intrinsically just that—appearances which carry a certain proper, invariant content. Memory might inherit that feature when based on perceptual experiences that had it in the first place. But it would be a stretch so to conceive of the relation between behaviour and mental states (indeed, at odds with the holism of the intentional)—and yet more of a stretch so to conceive of inductive confirmation. So if Pryor's own account of the province of dogmatism is correct, we shall need to seek elsewhere for materials to address scepticisms about other minds and inductive inference.

Let us scrutinize the proposal more carefully. If there are perceptually basic contents as characterized, then it follows that should such a content be false, the experience that carried it must somehow have misfired—a misperception must be involved. Pryor himself affirms this point, though he does not remark that it is a corollary of the very idea of a perceptually basic judgement as glossed above.[22] Moreover, it seems to indicate a usefully clear operational account: an experience dogmatically warrants the belief that P just in case, should the belief be false, the explanation must include misperception or some other form of illusion. This leaves Pryor free to accept the conservative diagnosis of the evidential relations in, for example, *Zebras*. No misperception need be involved in coming falsely to believe that the zebra-like animals are zebras—not if the zoo-keeper's fraud is skilful enough. However, it would also seem to put *Red Wall* beyond the scope of a dogmatist account. For it does not follow from my being mistaken about there being a red wall before me that my receiving the appearance of a red wall involved misperception—there need be no misperception precisely in the case when what I am seeing is a white wall cunningly illuminated by red light. Finally, the masthead case of Moore's Proof itself also seems to fall on the wrong side of the line: I may be mistaken about the presence of a hand in front of my face, notwithstanding the convincing visual appearances to the contrary, precisely because I am competently perceiving something that merely looks like a hand.

The point seems utterly general: external things may be mimicked (fake hands), and any property of them may be mimicked, too (mere seeming redness.) It would appear that it is only by restricting perceptually basic contents—at least when characterized

---

[21] In correspondence, Pryor has suggested that he would not wish to assign subject-invariant basic contents to perceptual experience—the kinds of basic contents that experiences can carry may vary as a function of, e.g., the conceptual resources of the thinker. This complication will not affect the discussion to follow.

[22] See Pryor (2001), n. 13.

as Pryor proposes—to the sphere of *appearances* that the difficulty can be avoided. Only then will error implicate misperception. More specifically, the needed retrenchment would seem to be that a dogmatist account of the relation between visual appearance and material world claims will be appropriate only when the latter are confined to the kind typified by:

Here is something that *looks like* a red wall,

Here is something that *looks like* a hand,

and so on.

How much of a loss is that? It would, to be sure, still be a point of epistemological significance if dogmatism did, indeed, give the correct account of the epistemological architecture even of claims of this restricted kind. For one thing, a version of Moore's Proof would still avoid transmission-failure since, for instance, something that merely looks like a hand will presumably be no less of an external material object than a real hand.

However, for the purposes of the traditional epistemological project, even restricted to the context of warrant for perceptual beliefs, the significance of the correctness of dogmatism, so limited, would be very marginal. For we have, of course, to get beyond claims about how external things appear. Yet with the legitimate scope of dogmatism so restricted, no resources will be to hand to resist an account of the epistemic architecture of the further transition from

Here is something that *looks like* a red wall,

to

Here is something that *is* a red wall,

which represented it as requiring independent warrant for an authenticity condition somewhat along the lines of

External objects are, by and large, as they appear to be.

And the problem of preventing the resulting conservative account of such triads from spawning Humean scepticism about the kind of proposition typified by the second component will then remain to be addressed by other, non-dogmatic, resources.[23]

---

[23] The ideas of this paper were first presented at my Topics in Epistemology seminar at NYU in Spring 2004. They have subsequently had some circulation via the handouts for that seminar and talks at other institutions, including the University of Texas and the Arché Epistemology Seminar. Part of the material was presented as the first Paul Tomassi Memorial Lecture at the University of Aberdeen in November 2006. I am grateful to the discussants on all these occasions. Special thanks to Annalisa Coliva, David Enoch, Hartry Field, James Pryor, Joshua Schechter and Stephen Schiffer.

References

Burge, Tyler, 'Content Preservation', *Philosophical Review*, 102 (1993) 457–88.

―――― 'Reply to Martin Davies', in M. J. Frapolli and E. Romero (eds.), *Meaning, Basic Self-Knowledge and Mind: Essays on Tyler Burge* (Stanford: CSLI Publications, 2003), 250–7.

Cohen, Stewart, 'Basic Knowledge and the Problem of Easy Knowledge', *Philosophy and Phenomenological Research*, 65/2 (2002), 309–29.

Coliva, Annalisa, 'The Paradox of Moore's *Proof of an external world*', *The Philosophical Quarterly*, (2006a).

―――― 'Moore's *Proof*, Liberals and Conservatives―is there a third way?' in A. Coliva, ed. *Mind, Meaning and Knowledge: Essays for Crispin Wright Volume I* (Oxford: Oxford University Press, forthcoming b).

Dretske, Fred, 'Epistemic Operators', *The Journal of Philosophy*, 67 (1970), 1007–23.

Goodman, Nelson, *Fact, Fiction, and Forecast*, 4th edn. (Cambridge, Mass.: Harvard University Press, 1983).

Peacocke, Christopher, *The Realm of Reason* (Oxford: Oxford University Press, 2003), see esp. chs. 3 and 4.

Pryor, James, 'The Skeptic and the Dogmatist', *Noûs*, 34/4 (December 2000), 517–49.

―――― 'Is Moore's Argument an Example of Transmission-failure?' (2001), prototype of Pryor (2004), available on his website at: *http://www.jimpryor.net/research/papers/Moore2001.pdf*

―――― 'What is Wrong with Moore's Argument?', *Philosophical Issues*, 14 (2004), 349–78.

Schiffer, Stephen, 'The Vagaries of Skepticism', *Philosophical Studies*, 119 (2004), 161–84.

Wright, Crispin, 'Warrant for Nothing', *Supplement to the Proceedings of the Aristotelian Society*, 78/1 (July 2004), 167–212.

I am grateful to the discussants on all these occasions. Special thanks to Annalisa Coliva, David Enoch, Hartry Field, James Pryor, Joshua Schechter and Stephen Schiffer.

2

Moore's Proof

Ernest Sosa

Kant thought it a scandal that the external world had never been proved to exist.[1] Moore raised a hand, saying 'Here is a hand', and raised his other hand, saying 'Here is another.' These being external objects, Moore concluded, there is indeed a world of external things (two at least). Written out as an argument, with a redundant hand dropped, the proof is as follows:

H-external   Here is a hand.

              Hands are external objects.

              Therefore, there is at least one external object.

His argument, Moore adds, satisfies three conditions for being a proof. First, the premises are all different from the conclusion. Second, the conclusion follows logically from the premises. Third, the argument's purveyor knows his premises to be true. While granting that perhaps something else may be required for a legitimate proof, Moore is confident that his Proof would satisfy such requirements as well. After all, how is his Proof inferior to the following?

M1   Here on this page is the expression: recieve

      The expression recieve is a misspelling.

      Therefore, there is at least one misspelling on this page.

Surely this *would* be a way of 'settling' whether there is a misspelling on this page, a way of proving to someone in doubt that there is one indeed.

---

[1] As he says in the preface to the second edition of his *Critique of Pure Reason* (1787).

His 'Proof' would be generally rejected, Moore grants, but such rejection is traced to a requirement that the premise must itself be proved. And this requirement Moore finds unacceptable. One knows plenty that one has not proved, and maybe could not prove. That is fortunate, he adds, as *he cannot prove that before him there is indeed a hand.* But on this point he is not obviously right.

Consider the following argument.

> Here is a left hand.
>
> Therefore, here is a hand.

This does satisfy Moore's three conditions for being a proof. What is more, the premise here might itself be 'proved' as follows.

> Here is an open left hand.
>
> Therefore, here is a left hand.

As for *this* premise, it too is easily 'proved' in keeping with Moore's three conditions. Here is a *modus ponens* proof:

> $1 + 1 = 2$
>
> $(1 + 1 = 2) \supset$ (here is an open left hand)
>
> Therefore, here is an open left hand.

And if this counts as a proof, then any known truth is easy to prove.

Our reasoning shows, not that it is easy to produce a proof, but that Moore makes it seem too easy. Moore's requirements for being a proof must be jointly *in*sufficient, even supposing they are severally necessary. Compare the case of someone in doubt as to whether there is a misprint on a certain page, and suppose he were offered the following 'proof':

> M2 The first misprint from the top of this page is a misprint on this page.
>
> Therefore, there is a misprint on this page.

Anyone who questions whether there is any misprint on this page thereby questions whether there is a *first* misprint from the top. If the conclusion of M2 is antecedently in doubt, the premise is equally in doubt, and it begs the question to just assert it.

Analogously, it may be thought, anyone who puts in doubt whether *any* external things exist puts in doubt whether this thing here, 'this hand', exists. Moore's Proof H-external seems relevantly different, however, from the supposedly analogous M2. Although the premise of M2 is equally in doubt once its conclusion is in doubt, neither premise of H-external suffers that fate. Take Bishop Berkeley. In Moore's shoes, with the hand before his nose, Berkeley would still reject the conclusion of H-external without doubting the premise.[2] Moore and Berkeley might even find it obvious that they are right in saying 'Here is a hand', while leaving it open whether hands are internally or externally constituted. Moore and Berkeley do, of course, part ways on the second premise. Moore argues for the truth of that premise, which Berkeley firmly rejects. So, Moore takes himself to have proved that there are indeed *external* objects, and to have offered his proof quite properly to his idealist opponents. Crucial to his anti-idealism is his painstaking inquiry into the very meaning of *externality*, which turns out to be a kind of mind-independence, so that the question whether there is an *external* world is that of whether there is a relevantly *mind-independent* objective reality.[3]

An analogy may help to show how Moore sees the matter. Suppose we wonder whether on a certain surface there is any figure with internal angles adding up to 180 degrees. And someone then provides the following argument:

> T Here on the surface (pointing) is a triangle.
>
> Triangles have internal angles that add up to 180 degrees.
>
> So, on this surface is a figure with internal angles adding up to 180 degrees.

We can, of course, buttress our second premise with a proof of its own drawn from plane geometry. As for the first premise, we know it by visual perception. But how we know the conclusion is by combining the two premises in just the way brought out by our argument T.

That, it seems to me is how Moore thinks his argument, H-external, works against the idealist, and how it works to give us justified belief and knowledge that there is an *external* world. How he knows (*one* way we know) that there is an *external* world (the conclusion of his Proof) is by combining the thing he knows by perception, that there before him is his hand, with something else that he knows by philosophical means (the reflection that takes up most of the article, for the thesis that hands, if there are any, are *external*, mind-independent entities). So his Proof displays reasons based on which he can properly believe that there is an external world (which is not to say that he might not have plenty of other reasons).

There are indeed at least two different ways in which a proof can work:

> A *persuasive* proof is a valid argument that can be used to rationally persuade one to believe its conclusion, if one has put the conclusion in doubt.

---

[2] Here and in what follows I will for simplicity imagine that the mind-independence that defines externality is not just independence from 'the minds of living human beings living on the earth', as Moore assumes ('Proof of an External World', *Proceedings of the British Academy*, 25 (1939), 273–300, repr. in Moore's *Philosophical Papers* (London: George Allen & Unwin, 1959), 143) but independence from intelligent minds, in line with Berkeley. This abstracts from a distracting complication.

[3] Do we really implicate *independence from the mind* in believing in hands and fires? Nor does it seem right that we must presuppose such a thing *with priority* to our ordinary singular thoughts. Recall Berkeley's claim that he, not the realist, is the champion of common sense.

EDINBURGH UNIVERSITY LIBRARY
WITHDRAWN

A *display* proof is a valid argument that displays premises on which one can rationally base belief in the conclusion, without vicious circularity.

Note how these notions are both relative (to the 'one' who is to be persuaded, or for whom the premises might function as proper reasons). Every persuasive proof would seem a display proof, but the converse is questionable. Consider, for example, an immediate inference from two propositions to their conjunction. This constitutes a display proof, but it is not clearly a persuasive proof. If one has put the conjunction in doubt, one is unlikely to be rationally persuaded by a simple conjoining of the premises. One is unlikely to grant both premises at the time when one doubts their conjunction. Despite this, however, the proof might be a perfectly proper display proof. That is to say, one might quite properly believe the conjunction on the rational basis provided by the two premises severally.

Moore can, and I think does, regard his Proof as a good display proof, and may well even regard it as a good persuasive proof against his idealist opponents. He is certainly right that it is a display proof, and probably right if he thinks it to be a persuasive proof as well. Take someone who has not seen clearly enough what is involved in externality, who is unaware of Moore's detailed analysis of that notion in his article.[4] Anyone so benighted would seem ripe for a persuasive proof of the sort provided by Moore in that same article.

In any case, what might distinguish Moore's Proof from our pseudo-proofs that clearly satisfy the three conditions offered by Moore? Can we buttress Moore's position by finding some further condition for being a cogent proof? There must surely be one, beyond the three he made explicit. Take our useless pseudo-proofs that satisfy Moore's three explicit requirements. Why are they not acceptable? Perhaps because they are so thin, so unhelpful. But how is Moore's Proof any better? Well, Moore's Proof may perhaps help to counter the idealist threat that he faced as a realist (along with Russell and a few others). Moore's Proof may help that way, at least when combined with his inquiry into what it is to be external, and on how and why hands qualify as external, an inquiry that takes up most of his article.

In order to understand Moore's Proof, it is important to consider its intended target. It is normally thought to be aimed at the skeptic, but Moore's target was not so much the skeptic as the idealist. He was opposing those who think that there is no external world, that empirical reality is internal (to our minds). Against these he aimed to show that there is an *external* world, one that contains hands and other such ordinary objects.[5]

---

[4] "Proof of an External World", *Proceedings of the British Academy*, 25 (1939); repr. in *Philosophical Papers* (Collier Books, 1962), 126–48.

[5] True, he also opposed the view that anything we cannot prove must be accepted on faith. Of course, *this* view he did not oppose by means of his proof. He opposed it rather by remarks such as the

If Moore's target is mainly the idealist, not the skeptic, this puts in question a recent interpretation of his proof as just ironic:

[On Moore's] . . . view, both the skeptic and the philosopher who tries to provide the proof demanded by the skeptic accept an unjustified theory of what knowledge consists in. This diagnosis brings out the ironic nature of Moore's presentation. Would anyone who believed that a proof of the external world was needed be satisfied by Moore's proof? No. Anyone who demanded such a proof would already have accepted the skeptic's restrictive conception of what knowledge is, and so would deny that Moore knew that he has holding up his hand. What then was Moore's purpose in presenting his proof? It was to show that there is no need for such a proof in the first place. What he wants us to see is that if there is scandal to philosophy in all of this, it is not the inability of philosophers to satisfy the demands of the skeptic; rather it is their uncritical acceptance of the legitimacy and presuppositions of their demands.[6]

Maybe Moore did want to call into question such uncritical acceptance. In fact, I am confident that he did, though we shall find below how unusual and surprising was his way of doing so. Nevertheless, he was also utterly serious in offering his Proof. Given how much of his article is devoted to establishing the nature of externality and the fact that hands count as external, there can be little doubt that he was serious in his attempt to *establish* a certain conclusion: namely, that, *contra* the idealist, there is indeed an *external* world, one populated by hands among many other items.

In line with that distinction between contra-skeptic and contra-idealist proofs, consider the following:

H-general There are hands (at least one)

          Hands are external objects

          Therefore, there is an external world

This, I believe, would have functioned about as well as Moore's actual proof, H-external, against his target idealists. And it functions about as well even if one's knowledge of the first premise is at the time not at all perceptual but only a piece of standing common-sense knowledge. Even so, this *is* a proof of the external world about as good as Moore's own Proof. True, the premise here *can* be proved, or so Moore

following, addressed to those who try to cast doubt on his knowledge of the premise that there before him was his hand: 'How absurd it would be to suggest that I did not know it, but only believed it, and that perhaps it was not the case! You might as well suggest that I do not know that I am now standing up and talking—that perhaps after all I'm not, and that it's not quite certain that I am!' ('Proof of an External World', ibid., 145).

  [6] This is from the chapter on Moore in Scott Soames, *Philosophical Analysis in the Twentieth Century*, Vol. I (Princeton University Press, 2003), 23.

would have insisted. But the fact that its first premise is provable certainly would not disqualify H-general from being a proper proof.

So, H-general can still function as a proof in the way Moore took his own Proof H-external to function, in opposition to the idealist. By contrast, H-general is obviously useless against the traditional external-world skeptic. What this skeptic wants, after all, is evidence for the proposition that there are indeed such things as hands, *whether external or not*, evidence that will establish that proposition just through our use of reason and of what is given to us in experience (or in experience and immediate memory).

Moore is at pains to prove not so much that hands exist but that they are external, and thereby that there is an external world. And this he can prove against the idealist by relying not on perception but just on his background knowledge that there are hands. Thus, he can use H-general in place of H-external. By contrast, no proof that engages the traditional external-world skeptic can start from the premise of H-general or any such general claim. One could hardly argue against the traditional skeptic about the world around us by taking for granted as a premise that hands just do exist in the world (whatever their ontological nature). Whatever may be the right ontology of hands—whether hands are independently real, or on the contrary socially constituted—our skeptic will in any case want their existence demonstrated through reasoning from the given. What the traditional external-world skeptic puts in doubt is precisely the existence of such objects *beyond the mind of the subject*. Therefore, one cannot just assume as a premise that there are such objects. Such objects beyond the mind of the subject remain in doubt for our skeptic, moreover, regardless of whether they are external or socially mind-constituted.

Against a familiar traditional external-world skeptic, then, Moore does not, and would not, argue just by way of H-general, nor even by way of H-external. A direct response to that traditional skeptic requires that we reason just from our given states of consciousness enjoyed at the time or remembered from the very recent past. But wait: does Moore perhaps reject any such requirement as that imposed by our skeptic: namely, the requirement that any real knowledge of the external world around us must be founded on the given through reason? No, actually, Moore quite clearly agrees with our skeptic on that much.[7]

How and why Moore agrees with the sort of foundationalism presupposed by our external-world skeptic emerges in three closely related papers from a short span in the early years of the Second World War. One, 'Proof of an External World',[8] was his British Academy lecture in 1939. The other two—'Certainty'[9] and 'Four Forms of

---

[7] So, Moore's Proof cannot have been just an ironic way of rejecting the foundationalist demands of our traditional skeptic.

[8] Ibid.   [9] *Philosophical Papers*, 223–46.

Scepticism'[10] —developed as he taught and lectured in the States for the next few years.

As emerges in these papers, to give a proof is, for Moore, a performance, perhaps a public performance: one must rehearse an argument, perhaps in words. Only reasons one might proffer can possibly constitute a proof. But in his view you cannot possibly *cite* the full set of reasons that support your belief that you are awake. Here is how he puts it:

How am I to prove now that 'Here's one hand and here's another'? I do not believe I can do it. In order to do it, I should need to prove for one thing, as Descartes pointed out, that I am not now dreaming. But how can I prove that I am not? I have, no doubt, conclusive reasons for asserting that I am not now dreaming; I have conclusive evidence that I am awake; but that is a very different thing from being able to prove it. I could not tell you what all my evidence is; and I should require to do this at least, in order to give you a proof.[11]

So, Moore distinguishes having reasons, *even conclusive reasons*, from having a proof. One crucial respect of difference is that a set of reasons need not be publicly articulable, whereas a proof that can be given to others must be. Moore, in fact, leaves it open that a set of reasons need not even be *privately* articulable, *in foro interno*. This is why, in his view, one cannot prove that one is now awake: Although one's belief that one is awake is based on evidence, on conclusive reasons, *these are reasons one could not fully cite, perhaps not even to oneself.*

Moore claims that, despite his inability to prove his claim that he is holding up a hand, he still knows the truth of what he claims (since one can know things that one cannot prove). But he is *not* thereby endorsing epistemic foundationalism. He is not endorsing the doctrine that some knowledge depends not at all on evidence or reasons. Take the fact that he is then awake. According to Moore, he is unable to prove that fact, but he *does* have reasons for believing it, indeed *conclusive* reasons. To know without proof, then, is not to know without reasons. One can know based on conclusive reasons without knowing based on any proof.

Although, as it turns out, Moore is not endorsing epistemic foundationalism in 'Proof of an External World', he does endorse it in another paper of the period, 'Four Forms of Scepticism'. There, in agreement with Russell, he has this to say:

I think I do know *immediately* things about myself. . . . But I cannot help agreeing with Russell that I never know immediately such a thing as 'That person is conscious' or 'This is a pencil', and that also the truth of such propositions never follows logically from anything which I do know immediately, and yet I think that I do know such things for certain.[12]

---

[10] *Philosophical Papers*, 193–222.

[11] 'Proof of an External World', penultimate paragraph.

[12] 'Four Forms of Scepticism', penultimate paragraph.

Moore agrees with Russell that

> (a) to know is to know for certain;[13] and, further, that
>
> (b) our knowledge of the world around us, including neighboring minds, is derived from what we know immediately, is derived through reasoning that is not deductive but inductive or analogical.

From these premises Russell concludes that we lack knowledge of our surroundings, and must settle for probable opinion. By contrast, Moore concludes that we can enjoy knowledge for certain of our surroundings, and that such knowledge does not require deductive *proof*; it can derive rather from reasoning that is inductive or analogical.

The assumption that Moore and Russell share is not obviously true. I mean the assumption that knowledge must be knowledge for certain. At a minimum, we must distinguish *absolute* certainty from a certainty that allows one to be more certain of one thing than of another. This distinction opens up a possibility: one might now cater to what is plausible in Russell's claim that non-deductive inference cannot yield certainty (absolute certainty), while agreeing with Moore that it can still deliver the level of certainty (a high enough degree of certainty) requisite for knowledge.[14]

Since our focus here is on Moore, let us adopt the sense of the word certainty compatible with his view, agreeing thus with him that one can know, and know for certain, things that one must base non-deductively (through inductive or analogical reasoning) on what one knows immediately. Having taken Moore's side on this much, we may now be baffled by the third of his three papers from those early years of the Second Would War entitled 'Certainty', where we find the following passage:

I agree . . . that if I don't know now that I'm not dreaming, it follows that I don't *know* that I am standing up, even if I both actually am and think that I am. But this first part of the argument is a consideration which cuts both ways. For, if it is true, it follows that it is also true that if I *do* know that I am standing up, then I do know that I am not dreaming. I can therefore just as well argue: since I do know that I'm standing up, it follows that I do know that I'm not dreaming; as my opponent can argue: since you don't know that you're not dreaming, it follows that you don't know that you're standing up. The one argument is just as good as the other, unless my opponent can give better reasons for asserting that I don't know that I'm not dreaming, than I can give for asserting that I do know that I am standing up. [15]

But *how*, exactly, *do* we know that we are awake and not dreaming? Recall the assumption that knowledge is knowledge for certain, which we have granted, if only

---

[13] In the concluding pages of 'Four Forms of Scepticism', for example, he repeatedly uses the two expressions as if they were interchangeable.

[14] A full discussion would go into the subtle and complex ways in which knowledge, certainty, and doubt, are related. I go further into the matter in 'Relevant Alternatives, Contextualism Included', *Philosophical Studies* (2003), 35–65.

[15] 'Certainty', twelfth paragraph from the end.

by allowing a threshold-dependent level of certainty requisite for knowledge.[16] And consider in this light what Moore has to say:

Now I cannot see my way to deny that it is logically possible that all the sensory experiences I am having now should be mere dream-images. And if this is logically possible, and if further the sensory experiences I am having now were the only experiences I am having, I do not see how I could possibly know for certain that I am not dreaming.[17]

Here Moore is facing the following question: how can he, as a committed foundationalist, account for his claimed knowledge that he is not dreaming if this does not follow from his having his sensory experiences when he makes his claim to know?

This problem Moore tries to resolve by relying not only on his present sensory experiences but also on his memories of the immediate past. Such memories can also in his view constitute immediate knowledge. And the *combination* of his present experiences and memories is now said to be sufficient.

But what if our skeptical philosopher says: It is *not* sufficient; and offers as an argument to prove that it is not, this: It is logically possible *both* that you should be having all the sensory experiences you are having, and also that you should be remembering what you do remember, and *yet* should be dreaming. If this *is* logically possible, then I don't see how to deny that I cannot possibly know for certain that I am not dreaming.[18]

Consider now the dialectical situation. Moore agrees with the skeptic that we must be able to reason from what is given to us in experience and short-term memory to any other contingent fact that we could hope to know. Yet he thinks we cannot prove the facts that we take ourselves to know perceptually. And why is this so? Because in order to prove any such fact we would need to be able to prove that we are not dreaming at the time. And this, he claims, he cannot prove. Yet he goes on to claim about the fact that he is not dreaming that it does follow by logic from what is given to him in experience and short-term memory! Moreover, these things thus given to him constitute conclusive evidence for believing that he is awake and not dreaming. But how then could he have thought that we *could not* prove that we are awake? How could Moore have thought that it was beyond him to prove that he was awake, when, amazingly, he himself seems to provide for such a proof?! The answer to our puzzle lies in Moore's distinction between, first, a 'proof', whose possession always requires the ability to cite its premises, so that it could be *given*, at least to oneself *in foro interno*; and, second, conclusive reasons, which one can still have despite being unable to cite them fully. Without the ability to cite the premises one can have no proof, regardless of how high a level

---

[16] Note, incidentally, how, in a paper ostensibly about certainty, Moore focuses on 'knowledge' (sans qualification).

[17] Ibid., third paragraph from the end.   [18] Ibid., penultimate paragraph.

of certainty one might attain for believing as one does based on such conclusive evidence.

Casimir Lewy, who helped prepare for publication the collection, *Philosophical Papers*, in which Moore's paper appears, adds the following footnote about the concluding paragraphs of Moore's paper, including the one just cited here. Lewy writes: 'It should, I think, be mentioned that Moore was particularly dissatisfied with the last four paragraphs of this paper, and I believe that he was thinking primarily of these paragraphs when he wrote, in the Preface, that the paper contains bad mistakes.' What might these mistakes be, and what might be said in favor of the position adopted by Moore in those passages, however mistakenly?

We have found an apparent incoherence in the position laid out by Moore in those three closely related papers. But we have seen how to defend Moore by appeal to his plausible requirement that in order to possess a proof one must be able to cite its premises, at least to oneself. Accordingly, that apparent incoherence is unlikely to be what bothered Moore about his paper.

However, something else is quite puzzling when we put those papers together. Moore rejects Russell's skepticism, despite agreeing that we know the external world *neither* immediately *nor* by deductive reasoning from what we *do* know immediately. In 'Four Forms of Skepticism' Moore argues against Russell that even if his beliefs about pencils, and about the minds of others, would require an 'inductive or analogical' basis, it could still amount to knowledge 'for certain'. If we can know facts without proving them deductively, however, why not include the fact that one is awake among those facts? Why do we need a *logical implication* from our experiences and immediate memories to the conclusion that we are awake and not dreaming? Why can't it be through some sort of inductive or analogical reasoning that we acquire our knowledge of that fact? Why can't we have *non-deductive* knowledge of that fact?

This much Moore can rebut as follows. Since no analogical argument is likely to take us from what we know immediately to knowledge of a hand we see, the argument would presumably be inductive. Now, inductive arguments come in two main varieties: enumerative, and hypothetical or explanatory. Clearly, there is no valid enumerative induction from our experience (exclusively) to the character of the world around us: any such argument would require correlational information as a basis for the induction. Moreover, one side of the correlation would involve knowledge of our surroundings, but how do we get such knowledge *in the first place*? We seek an account of how we get it without relying on a basis of other knowledge of the same sort.

Neither through analogical reasoning nor through enumerative induction could we know that we are awake and not dreaming. So, we are down to some hypothetical or explanatory induction. But note the content of the desired conclusion: namely, that one is *not* dreaming, that one's relevant experiences are *not* detached from externalia in the ways characteristic of dreams. On the face of it, this lacks the sort of content required for an explanatory induction. An explanatory hypothesis could not be just negative as this one is.

It might be thought that the inference could be an explanatory inference to the *presence* of a hand whose relation to our eyes helps explain the character of our experiences. The fact that we are not dreaming would then come along as a by-product of the inductive inference. And this is the tack that Moore apparently takes in his reply to Russell. Why does he diverge from it in this other passage of that period? Is this perhaps why he takes himself to have blundered in those concluding paragraphs of 'Certainty'?

Perhaps; but consider how problematic his stance would then be. He seeks to understand how he could possibly know that he is not just dreaming, which he needs to know in order to know about his hand. And now we are entertaining the following way out: he knows about the hand through an explanatory inference based on knowledge of his visual and other experiences as of a hand before him. Once in the know about such data, he can use them as a basis for the belief that he is not just dreaming. Thus, he can reason against the skeptic's challenge as follows: 'Here before me is a hand, one that is causing my experiences as of a hand before me. But this could not be so, if I were only dreaming. Therefore, I am not just dreaming.' How plausible can it be that one could *discover* that one is not dreaming as a by-product of any such inference?

Compare a case where one knows about one's current speed only by reading one's speedometer. And suppose this knowledge to depend entirely on an explanatory inference from the speedometer reading to the actual speed. Could one thereby *discover*, and come to know, that one's speedometer is properly connected so as to be sensitive to one's speed? If one asked oneself whether the speedometer was properly installed and operative, one could hardly settle that matter *exclusively* by inferring one's actual speed from the speedometer reading, as an explanatory inference, so as to draw the further inference that the instrument must indeed be properly installed and operative.

Here's another way to put the point: one could hardly discover that the speed/speedometer connection is good through the following reasoning: 'My speed is 40 mph, which is why my speedometer reads 40 mph. But this could not be so if the speedometer were disconnected from my actual speed. Therefore, my speedometer must not be disconnected from my actual speed.'

That is why Moore does have good reason to seek some other way in which he might know that he is not dreaming. And here's how he might have reasoned: 'That I am not dreaming is not something I could know by direct explanatory induction (it does not have the right content for such an inference)', he might have reasoned, 'nor could I know it as a by-product of such an inference. I must be able to presuppose *independently* that I am not dreaming, just as the speedometer reader must be able to presuppose independently that his instrument is properly connected and operative.' That is how he might have been led to require some other way to know that he was not dreaming, which might explain why he stretched towards some *deductive* knowledge of that fact.[19] So, this might explain why he thought we could not know ourselves to be awake and not dreaming unless this was implied logically by what we know immediately, by our present experiences and immediate memories. But this is really a desperate move, especially for the champion of a strong realist refutation of idealism.

None of the options considered by Moore holds much attraction to us now. What wrong turn leads to that blind alley? One mistake is to suppose that you can know about the hand only if you *know* you are not dreaming. You must *not* be dreaming, of course, but you needn't know it, not for animal knowledge. Animal knowledge of the hand requires no knowledge that it is not just a dream. So, we could just respond to the skeptic by denying what Moore is so willing to grant, as is Descartes if we believe Moore. 'What is required by our perceptual knowledge of a fire we see, or a hand,' we could respond, 'is just that we be awake, and not that we *know* we are awake'.

However, that would take us only part of the way out. For, we want a knowledge that is not just animal but also reflective. We want a knowledge that is defensible in the arena of reflection. And so we still have our problem: although animal knowledge that we see a fire requires only that we be awake, and not that we know we are awake, *reflective* knowledge still does require knowledge that we are awake, not just dreaming.

Although reflective knowledge requires knowledge that we are awake, fortunately this required knowledge need not be *prior* knowledge. Here's why.

The right model for understanding reflective justification is *not* the linear model whereby justification is a sort of liquid that flows through some pipe or channel of reasoning, from premises to conclusion. A good human system of beliefs is rather a web properly attached to the environment, whose nodes may gain status through mutual support. Any given node is in place through its connections with other nodes, but *each of these* is itself in place through *its* connections with the other nodes, including that original given node. By basing beliefs on other beliefs the rational weaver creates a web each member of which is held in place *in part* (perhaps in minuscule part) through its being based on each of many others, directly or indirectly. There is no apparent reason why such basing should be regarded as either causally or normatively

[19] The problems just under the surface of Moore's proof are subtle and difficult enough that we are still struggling with them in the latest journal issues and epistemology collections: they have figured large in the epistemology and philosophy of mind of the most recent years. So I do not suppose what I say in this brief account of the Proof to provide more than a preliminary sketch of the problematic. In recent discussion of these issues there are at least two particularly relevant threads. One derives from much discussed issues of content externalism and self knowledge, and the other from the closely related 'Problem of Easy Knowledge'.

asymmetrical; no reason why many beliefs could not constitute webs in which *each* node is in place by being based *partly* on *others*. What is more, each might thus gain its epistemic status partly through such relations with the others, where the whole web is also attached to the world through the causal mechanisms of perception or memory.

Consider now the proposition that there is an external world. And let's allow less restrictive conceptions of externality than Moore's mind-independence conception. For example, we might just think of the external as 'that which is to be *met with in space*', to take another Moorean notion from his 'Proof' article. It would then be quite plausible that in order rationally to believe that here is a hand, based on one's relevant perceptual experience, one would have to presuppose with *independent* justification that there is such an external world. But it would not follow, nor is it plausible, that one must presuppose such a thing with *prior* justification.

Reflective endorsement may now take its place in the web without any special problems. This seems to me the key to the Pyrrhonian problematic faced when we reflect on Moore's Proof. That it is the key is easier said than shown, however, and the showing is hard enough to require more time than is now at our disposal. [20]

[20] My own take on the problem of easy knowledge, and other problems of circularity in epistemology, is part of *Virtuous Circles: Apt Belief and Reflective Knowledge, Volume Two* (Oxford University Press, 2007). Here I have offered the barest sketch of my diagnosis and prescription.

3

Fixing the Transmission: The New Mooreans

Ram Neta

Some of the things that now exist have both of the following two features: first, they exist in space; and second, they can exist even if no one is conscious of them. For instance, the planet Earth exists in space, and it can exist even if no one is conscious of it. The Atlantic Ocean exists in space, and it can exist even if no one is conscious of it. Following G. E. Moore, let's use the term 'external things' to denote all such things—things that exist in space, and that can exist even if no one is conscious of them. Using this terminology, we may say, then, that there now exist some external things. The planet Earth, the Atlantic Ocean, and human hands are among the many external things that now exist.

Not only do some external things exist, but moreover, we *know* that some external things exist. For instance, we know that the planet Earth exists, that the Atlantic Ocean exists, and that human hands exist. And we know that all of these things are external things, and so some external things exist.

We know it, but can we prove it? Can we prove that there exist some external things? Kant thought it was a scandal to philosophy that we could not prove it. G. E. Moore attempted to remedy this scandal by proving that there are external things. His Proof goes as follows:

Here is one hand (he said, raising one of his hands).

Here is another hand (he said, raising the other hand).

If there are hands, then they are external things.

Therefore, there exist some external things.

Is this a successful proof of its conclusion? It is commonly thought that Moore's Proof is unsuccessful because it, in some sense, 'begs the question'. More specifically, it is thought, one cannot acquire knowledge of the conclusion of the Proof *by deducing it from the premises*. Even if one knows all of the premises to be true, and knows the conclusion to be true, still, one cannot acquire the latter bit of knowledge by means of deduction from the former bits of knowledge. One's knowledge of the premises does not 'transmit' across the Proof to the conclusion; the Proof thus suffers from what is called 'transmission-failure'. Crispin Wright has been the most prominent contemporary proponent of this line of objection against Moore's Proof. In section I, I will elaborate Wright's objection to Moore's Proof below. (I will also then give a substantially more precise and accurate rendering of Wright's objection than the one I just gave.)

But Wright's objection to Moore's Proof has not gone unanswered. Recently, some philosophers have defended Moore's Proof against Wright's objection, and more generally against the common objection that one cannot come to know the conclusion of the Proof by deducing it from the premises. Moore's Proof does not, according to these philosophers, suffer from the kind of 'transmission-failure' that Wright takes it to suffer from.[1] I will call these philosophers 'the New Mooreans', and in this paper I will focus on the work of the two most prominent New Mooreans: Martin Davies and James Pryor. These philosophers defend Moore's Proof as a successful, knowledge-transmitting proof of its conclusion. Its only epistemological shortcoming, according to them, is that the Proof cannot rationally overcome doubts about the truth of its conclusion—it cannot provide someone who doubts its conclusion with a reason to stop doubting. In section II below, I will examine their defense of Moore's Proof in some detail. (And, again, I will also then give a substantially more precise and accurate rendering of their response to Wright than the one I just gave.)

Finally, after presenting the dispute between Wright and the New Mooreans, I will argue for the following two claims:

(1) The only objection that the New Mooreans offer to Wright's epistemological views is no more or less powerful than an analogous objection that can be offered against the epistemological views of the New Mooreans themselves. If the objection works against Wright, the analogous objection works just as well against the New Mooreans. And if it doesn't work against Wright, then we have been given no good reason to prefer the New Moorean view. (I will argue for this in section III below.)

---

[1] Pryor says that Moore's Proof does not suffer from transmission-failure. Davies says that it suffers from transmission-failure, but from a different kind of transmission-failure from the kind that Wright takes it to suffer from. It is not clear to me that the difference between Pryor and Davies is anything more than terminological.

(2) As an interpretation of Moore, the New Mooreans have it exactly backwards. As Moore himself sees it, his Proof *does not* transmit knowledge from premises to conclusion, but *does* rationally overcome doubts. Its epistemological usefulness consists in the latter. (I will argue for this in section IV below.)

In short, I will argue that G. E. Moore would, and should, reject the gifts that the New Mooreans have offered him.

I Wright: We cannot know the conclusion of Moore's Proof by deducing it from the premises

It is widely believed that Moore's Proof 'begs the question'. But in precisely what sense does Moore's Proof 'beg the question'? Barry Stroud attempts to show how difficult it is to answer this question,[2] by appealing to the following analogous example suggested by Moore.[3] Suppose you ask a proof-reader to read over a page of printed material in order to see whether or not there are any typographical errors on that page. The proof-reader reads over the page and says 'yes, there are typos on this page'. You might ask her to prove that there are typos on the page, and she proves it as follows:

Here is one typo (she says, pointing to a typo on the page).

And here is another typo (she says, pointing to another typo on the page).

Therefore, there are some typos on the page.

Now, there doesn't seem to be anything wrong with this 'proof' that there are typos on the page. If the premises are known to be true, then, it seems, the proof provides knowledge of the truth of its conclusion. Why, then, isn't Moore's Proof of the existence of external things just as good as the proof-reader's proof of the existence of typos on the page? Despite his sense that there is something seriously wrong with Moore's Proof, Stroud admits that it is not easy to answer this last question: it is not easy to specify exactly how Moore's Proof 'begs the question' in a way that the proof-reader's proof does not.

But one way of understanding Crispin Wright's recent work on Moore's Proof is that it does just this: it attempts to specify exactly how Moore's Proof 'begs the question'. That's not quite the way Wright puts it: Wright describes himself as attempting to explain why Moore's Proof is not 'cogent'. But what does Wright mean when he speaks of a proof or inference, as being 'cogent'? Let's first consider some examples of

---

[2] Barry Stroud, *The Significance of Philosophical Scepticism* (Oxford: Oxford University Press, 1984), 84–5.

[3] *G. E. Moore: Selected Writings*, ed. by Thomas Baldwin (London and New York: Routledge, 1993), 167.

inferences that are cogent, then some examples of inferences that are not cogent, and then examine Wright's definition of cogency.

Note that throughout the following discussion, we will be using the term 'inference' to describe a type of act: an act of inferring a conclusion with a specified content from premises with specified contents. This is a *type* of act, and the type has many possible tokens. To say that an inference is cogent (or not) is to say that an act of that type is cogent (or not), but whether a token act of that type is cogent (or not) depends upon the situation in which that token act is performed. So, when we speak of a type of inference being cogent (or not), we will mean that, *in at least many easily imaginable situations*, acts of that type are cogent (or not). Thus, one and the same type of inference will be cogent relative to some situations, and not cogent relative to others.

So first, some examples of inferences that Wright regards as cogent:

Toadstool
    I Three hours ago, Jones inadvertently consumed a large risotto of *Boletus Satana*.
   II Jones has absorbed a lethal quantity of the toxins that toadstools contain.

  III Jones will shortly die.

Betrothal
    I Jones has just proposed marriage to a girl who would love to be his wife.
   II Jones's proposal of marriage will be accepted.

  III Jones will become engaged at some time in his life.

In each of the two inferences above, Toadstool and Betrothal, if one knows II to be true on the basis of the evidence stated in I, then one can—at least in many easily imaginable situations—acquire knowledge that III is true by deducing III from II. Of course, there are situations in which having the evidence stated in I will not give someone knowledge that II is true. (For instance, suppose that one has the evidence stated in I, but also has strong reasons to distrust the source of that very evidence. In such a situation, having the evidence stated in I would generally not suffice to give one knowledge that II is true.) But in many easily imaginable situations, one will be able to know that II is true by virtue of no more evidence than what is stated in I. Relative to those latter situations, then, Wright says, Toadstool and Betrothal are both cogent inferences.

Now here are some examples of inferences that Wright regards as not cogent:

Soccer
    I Jones has just kicked the ball between the white posts.
   II Jones has just scored a goal.

  III A game of soccer is taking place.

Election

    I Jones has just placed an X on a ballot paper.

    II Jones has just voted.

    III An election is taking place.

In each of these last two inferences, Soccer and Election, if one knows II to be true on the basis of the evidence stated in I, then one cannot—at least in many easily imaginable situations—acquire knowledge that III is true by deducing III from II. In those situations, the evidence stated in I can furnish one with knowledge that II is true only if one has knowledge—*independently of I*—that III is true. Relative to those same situations, Wright says, Soccer and Election are not cogent inferences.

Now, what does any of this have to do with Moore's Proof? According to Wright, Moore's Proof has an epistemological structure that is not fully explicit in the way the Proof is written above. If we follow Wright in making explicit this epistemological feature of Moore's Proof explicit, and we suppress the premise that hands are external things, then here's how Moore's Proof ends up looking:

Moore

    I It perceptually appears to me as if here are two hands.

    II Here are two hands

    III There are external things.

The two premises 'here is one hand' and 'here is another' that Moore gives when explicitly stating his Proof are conjoined to form II of this last inference. And I states the evidence on the basis of which Moore knows II to be true. So Wright's question is this: if Moore knows II to be true on the basis of the evidence stated in I, then can Moore, in the situation in which he finds himself in presenting his Proof, acquire knowledge that III is true by deducing III from II? Relative to that situation, is Moore's Proof cogent, like Toadstool and Betrothal typically are? Or is it rather not cogent, like Soccer and Election typically are? According to Wright, Moore's Proof is not cogent, at least not in the situation in which Moore finds himself. It falls into the same category that Soccer and Election would fall into in most situations, in that the evidence stated in I can furnish one with knowledge that II is true only if one has knowledge—independently of the evidence stated in I—that III is true. Therefore, Wright concludes, Moore cannot acquire knowledge that III is true by deducing III from II. Since one must have independent knowledge that III is true in order to know that II is true on the basis of I, one cannot acquire the knowledge that III is true by deducing it from II, if one knows that II is true only on the basis of I. For Wright, then, Moore's Proof—unlike Toadstool and Betrothal—is not cogent. But the proof-reader's proof is typically cogent: one can typically come to know that there are typos on the page by inferring it from the premises that here is one typo and here is another. This is how Wright can distinguish Moore's Proof that there are external things from the proof-reader's proof that there are typos on the page.

So far, I have characterized Wright's account of cogency in terms of knowledge-transmission. But it is not quite accurate to attribute this characterization of cogency to Wright, for although this characterization is similar to the characterization that Wright himself explicitly offers, it is not identical to the latter. Wright's own explicit characterization of cogency is in terms of epistemic properties other than knowledge, e.g., warrant, or rational conviction. For instance, Wright (2002, 332) explicitly defines a 'cogent' argument, or inference, as follows: '[A] cogent argument is one whereby someone could be moved to rational conviction of—or the rational overcoming of some doubt about—the truth of its conclusion.'

Given that Wright characterizes cogency in terms of the generation of *rational conviction*, why have I been describing cogency in terms of the transmission of knowledge? My decision was dictated by the fact that Moore himself is concerned with knowledge. Moore claims to know the premises of his Proof, and to know the conclusion of his Proof; Moore never explicitly talks about rational conviction. This is why I have been focusing, so far, on the issue of whether or not Moore's Proof transmits knowledge.

But, while this issue of knowledge transmission is not identical to the issue that Wright and the New Mooreans are explicitly arguing about, it is related to it. That's because the transmission of knowledge is related to the transmission of some other epistemic properties, such as rational conviction. When we speak of knowledge being transmitted from premises to conclusion, what we mean is that one knows the conclusion *by deducing it from the premises* (which one knows to be true). But knowing that T1 is true *by* deducing it from T2 involves at least this much: one's knowledge that T2 is true provides one with what is, in fact, a good reason to believe T1—and this reason is good enough that (at least under the circumstances) it renders one's conviction in T1 rational. Wright and Davies say that a belief or conviction is 'warranted' when it is held rationally, i.e., on the basis of reasons that are good enough to render it rational. Pryor says that such a belief or conviction is 'doxastically justified'. To know that *p* requires that one have a rational conviction that *p*. In Wright's and Davies's terminology, it requires that one have the warranted conviction that *p*. (According to Wright 2004, this conviction need not be a belief—it may be some other species of acceptance of a proposition.) In Pryor's terminology, it requires that one have the doxastically justified belief that *p*. Henceforth, I shall stick with Pryor's terminology, only because it is closer to being standard. Thus, I shall say that the transmission of knowledge always involves a transmission of doxastically justified belief from premises to conclusion. A necessary condition of having knowledge is having doxastically justified belief, and a necessary condition of an inference's transmitting knowledge is its transmitting doxastically justified belief. The transmission of doxastically justified belief is, however, not a sufficient condition for transmitting knowledge, since, for example, doxastically justified belief could be transmitted from premises to conclusion even when the conclusion is false, and so even when knowledge is not transmitted.

But a necessary condition of having doxastically justified belief is having what's often called 'propositional justification' to believe something—whether or not one believes it. And a necessary condition of an inference's transmitting doxastically justified belief is its transmitting propositional justification from premises to conclusion. Now what is it to have 'propositional justification' to believe something? To illustrate, suppose that you justifiably believe all of the premises of Toadstool to be true, and you do not believe, or have the slightest reason to believe, anything that makes those premises unlikely to be true. In that case, you have a very strong justification for believing that Jones will shortly die. But you might not actually form the belief that Jones will shortly die. You might simply stop short of drawing that conclusion. In that case, while you have a good justification for believing that Jones will shortly die, you do not have a rational belief that Jones will shortly die, because you do not have any belief that Jones will shortly die. In such a case, although you lack the belief that Jones will shortly die, you none the less have 'propositional justification' for believing that Jones will shortly die: you have very good reason, all things considered, to believe it. This is a case in which an inference transmits propositional justification from the premises to the conclusion, even though one doesn't have a doxastically justified belief that the conclusion is true, because one happens not to believe the conclusion. Transmitting propositional justification is a necessary condition for transmitting doxastically justified belief, which is, in turn, a necessary, but not sufficient, condition for transmitting knowledge. This distinction between propositional justification to believe and doxastically justified belief will become important below, when we articulate the New Moorean critique of Wright.

Wright himself does not explicitly talk about propositional justification, but he is not committed to anything that conflicts with the claims I have just made concerning the relations between knowledge, doxastic justification, and propositional justification. Wright would want to distinguish propositional and doxastic justification that are provided by evidence from propositional and doxastic justification that are provided by something other than evidence, and the latter are what he would call 'entitlement'. Some philosophers would reject Wright's claim that there are entitlements, i.e., forms of justification provided by something non-evidential. But we needn't enter into this dispute now.

According to Wright, cogency is what Toadstool, Betrothal, and the proof-reader's proof all supposedly possess, and what Soccer, Election, and Moore's Proof all supposedly lack. But notice that as Wright defines a 'cogent' argument, or inference, it is one that satisfies either of two conditions: first, it is one whereby someone could be moved to rational conviction of—or, as we've said, doxastically justified belief in—the truth of its conclusion. To be moved to rational conviction of the truth of its conclusion requires being given a reason to accept the truth of its conclusion, where this reason is a reason that one didn't already have, before going through the proof. And second, a 'cogent' argument is one whereby someone could be moved to rational overcoming of some doubt about the truth of its conclusion. That is, in going through the proof, one acquires a reason, perhaps a compelling reason, to suspend whatever actual doubt (rational or irrational) one might initially have had about the truth of the conclusion. Now, it might naïvely seem as though any argument, or inference, that satisfies either of these conditions will satisfy the other condition as well. But the New Mooreans disagree. According to them, an argument can satisfy the former condition (i.e., being one whereby someone could be moved to doxastically justified belief in the truth of its conclusion) without satisfying the second condition (i.e., being one whereby someone could be moved to rational overcoming of some doubt about the truth of its conclusion). Indeed, they will say that this is precisely what's going on in the case of Moore's Proof: it passes one of Wright's cogency tests, but not the other. According to the New Mooreans, this renders Moore's Proof a good argument in one way, but not in another. It's important to distinguish these two ways in which an argument can be good, so that we can understand precisely what Moore's Proof does and does not accomplish. The next section will elaborate these claims.

II The New Mooreans: We can know the conclusion of Moore's Proof by deducing it from the premises

The main thesis of the New Mooreans is that Moore's Proof does not suffer from the defect that Wright calls 'transmission-failure', although it suffers from another defect that Davies, though not Pryor, regards as a distinct kind of 'transmission-failure'. According to the New Mooreans, one can know (and have a doxastic and propositional justification to believe) the conclusion by deducing it from the premises. Unlike Soccer or Election, Moore's Proof transmits knowledge, doxastically justified belief, and propositional justification to believe, just as well as Toadstool or Betrothal or the proof-reader's proof does. But it does this by satisfying only one of Wright's two criteria for cogency: it is one whereby someone could be moved to rational belief or conviction that the conclusion is true, but it is not one whereby someone could be rationally moved to overcome doubts about the truth of the conclusion. Pryor elaborates on this point by distinguishing several types of epistemic dependence that premises of an argument can have on the conclusion of that argument. Among the various types that Pryor distinguishes, two are particularly important for our purposes. First, there is what Pryor calls 'Type 4' epistemic dependence. The premises of an inference have 'Type 4' dependence on the conclusion of that inference just in case evidence against that conclusion does, to at least some degree, *undermine* the kind of justification that the maker of the inference purports to have for the premises. What matters for Type 4 dependence is not simply that evidence against the conclusion can *defeat* one's justification for believing the premises—that is true of any deductive inference. Rather, what matters for Type 4 dependence is that evidence against the conclusion can defeat one's justification for believing the premises *by undermining that justification.*

Now, according to Pryor:

> Moore's argument clearly *does* exhibit this type of dependence. So long as we maintain the assumption that hands are external objects, any evidence that *there is no external world* will (to some degree) undermine Moore's perceptual justification for believing he has hands ... (Pryor 2004, 359)

So Moore's Proof exhibits Type 4 epistemic dependence. But is this a shortcoming of the Proof?

In order to explain why we should not answer this question in the affirmative, Pryor distinguishes Type 4 epistemic dependence from what he calls 'Type 5' dependence. Cases of Type 5 dependence are cases in which having justification for believing the conclusion of an inference is among the conditions that gives one justification for believing one or more of the premises of that inference. In such a case, one cannot have a justification for believing the premises of an inference unless one already has a justification for believing the conclusion, and so the inference itself cannot be the source of one's first justification for believing the conclusion: before making the inference, either one does have justification for believing the conclusion, or one does not. If one does, then, of course, the inference cannot itself be the source of one's first justification for believing the conclusion. But if one does not have justification for believing the conclusion, then one also does not have justification for believing one or more of the premises, in which case, again, the inference cannot give one justification for believing the conclusion. It is for this reason that Pryor says 'Type 5 dependence does clearly seem to be an epistemic vice' (Pryor 2004, 359.)

After distinguishing Type 5 dependence from Type 4 dependence, Pryor goes on to argue that it's possible for an argument to exhibit Type 4 dependence without exhibiting Type 5 dependence, and that such arguments (those that exhibit Type 4 dependence but not Type 5 dependence) may transmit propositional justification—and even rational belief or conviction—from their premises to their conclusion. If Pryor can establish this conclusion, then he can shift a burden of argument onto Wright: in order to make his case that Moore's Proof does not transmit rational belief or conviction,

Wright must argue that Moore's Proof is not a case in which there is Type 4 but not Type 5 dependence. And this is not something that Wright argues. So Pryor would then have shown at least that Wright has not shown that Moore's Proof suffers from transmission-failure.

Pryor would have shown this, if he had shown that some arguments exhibit Type 4 but not Type 5 dependence. But has he shown that some arguments exhibit Type 4 but not Type 5 dependence? His only explicit argument for this conclusion proceeds by considering the following example, and a couple of others very similar to it: suppose that you are now having a cold sensation, and you believe, on the basis of introspection, that you are now having a cold sensation. This introspective belief is not infallible: it could result from a priming mistake—for instance, you could come to believe that you are now having a cold sensation even if you are not having a cold sensation but are instead having a hot sensation, provided you have been led to expect in advance that you will have a cold senation. Now, according to Pryor, if you have evidence that you are making a priming mistake, then this undermines your introspective justification for believing that you are now having a cold senation. But, Pryor writes, 'it's not plausible that your justification to believing you're having a given sensation requires you to have antecedent justification to believe you're not making any priming mistakes' (Pryor 2004: 360). For instance, according to Pryor, you can have justification for believing that you're having a cold sensation, even if you do not also have justification for believing that you're not making a priming mistake. If this is true, then what sort of dependence is exhibited when you make the following inference?

(a) I am introspectively aware that I'm having a cold sensation now.

(b) I am having a cold sensation now.

(c) Therefore, I'm not making a priming mistake right now.

According to Pryor, the conclusion (c) is such that evidence against it would undermine (to at least some degree) the kind of propositional justification that I have for believing the premises. So clearly, this argument does exhibit Type 4 dependence. Why doesn't it exhibit Type 5 dependence? Because—according to Pryor—whatever it is that makes me have propositional justification for believing (c) is not among the conditions that make me have propositional justification for believing (a) and (b).

Now, why should we accept this last claim? Consider the following hypothesis about what it is that makes me have propositional justification for believing (c): what makes me have such justification is simply my introspective awareness of my cold sensation. (We can add that this introspective awareness suffices to make me have such justification only if there are no defeaters for the justification. Also, my having this justification for believing (c) does not require that I actually believe (c), or that I even have all of the concepts necessary to believe (c), e.g., the concept *priming mistake*. One can have a justification to believe a proposition even if one doesn't, or can't, actually believe that proposition.) If my introspective awareness of my cold sensation is what makes me have propositional justification for believing (c), then what makes me have such justification is—on at least some plausible views of the matter—precisely that very condition that makes me have propositional justification for believing the premises. *A fortiori*, my having justification for believing (c) is, in that case, among the conditions that makes me have propositional justification for believing the premises. In that case, the argument above would exhibit precisely what Pryor defines as Type 5 dependence.

So, for the example above to do the argumentative work that Pryor wants it to do, we need to know why we should believe that what makes me propositionally justified in believing the conclusion is not precisely the same thing that makes me propositionally justified in believing the premises. But Pryor never tells us why we should believe this. Pryor's case for the possibility of an argument that exhibits Type 4 but not Type 5 dependence is therefore crucially incomplete. Perhaps it is possible for an argument to exhibit Type 4 but not Type 5 dependence, but perhaps it is not possible: we're not yet in a position to say which, at least not on the basis of anything Pryor shows us about this example, or the other examples like it that he cites.

Consideration of the introspection argument has not yet given us any good reason either to accept or to reject the possibility that an argument can suffer from Type 4 but not Type 5 dependence. But might there be another reason to accept that this is possible? And, indeed, might there be another reason to accept that this possibility is realized in the case of Moore's Proof? Pryor would say that there is another reason to accept that this possibility is realized in the case of Moore's Proof: namely, it is a consequence of Pryor's own view of perceptual justification (a view that Pryor calls 'dogmatism') that Moore's Proof exhibits Type 4 but not Type 5 dependence, and so whatever reason there is to accept Pryor's dogmatist view of perceptual justification also provides us with a reason to accept that Moore's Proof exhibits Type 4 but not Type 5 dependence. According to Pryor's dogmatist view of perceptual justification, having a perceptual experience that has the propositional content p constitutes a prima-facie defeasible propositional justification for the experiencer to believe that p, and, by closure, constitutes a prima-facie defeasible propositional justification for the experiencer to believe anything that she knows to follow from p. Thus, having a perceptual experience that has the propositional content I have two hands constitutes a prima-facie defeasible propositional justification for me to believe that I have two hands, and, by closure, constitutes a prima-facie defeasible propositional justification for me to believe that there are external things. In order to have all-things-considered propositional justification to believe that I have two hands, I do not need to have any distinct justification to believe that there are external things, though it is necessary that there be nothing to defeat the prima-facie justification provided by my experience. It is a consequence of dogmatism, then, that Moore's Proof exhibits Type 4 but not Type 5 dependence.

But what reason is there to accept Pryor's dogmatist view of perceptual justification, rather than Wright's non-dogmatist view of perceptual justification? Pryor (2000) tells us that the dogmatist view is intuitively plausible, but—even granting both that this is true and that it is a reason to accept the dogmatist view[4]—why isn't Wright's non-dogmatist view of perceptual justification equally intuitively plausible?

Davies (2004) suggests an answer to this question.[5] According to Davies, Wright's own view of perceptual justification conflicts with some of our ordinary thinking concerning the generation and transmission of evidentially based doxastic justification, and this conflict with ordinary epistemic thinking is avoided by a dogmatist view of perceptual justification.[6] If we hold a dogmatist view, we can then account for the apparently questionable character of the Proof by claiming that—even though it does transmit evidentially based doxastic justification—it cannot rationally overcome doubts about the truth of its conclusion. That is the New Moorean account of Moore's Proof.

So at what point does Wright's own view supposedly conflict with our ordinary thinking concerning the transmission of doxastic justification? Consider Moore's Proof again. According to Wright's own view, we have a non-evidential entitlement to accept the conclusion of the Proof, and it is, *inter alia*, our possession of this entitlement that enables us to have evidentially based doxastically justified beliefs in the premises. Our beliefs in the premises (what Wright calls 'II' in his reconstruction of Moore's Proof) are doxastically justified by the evidence of our senses—but this sensory evidence succeeds in justifying our beliefs in the premises of the Proof only if, and only because, we have a non-evidential entitlement to accept the conclusion of the Proof. It's only because he is non-evidentially entitled to accept the existence of external things that Moore's sensory evidence can provide him with evidentially based

---

[4] In my paper 'Perceptual Evidence and the New dogmatism', *Philosophical Studies*, 119 (2004), 199–214, I call into question the intuitive plausibility of Pryor's case for dogmatism.

[5] In his paper 'Epistemic Entitlement, Warrant Transmission, and Easy Knowledge', *Proceedings of the Aristotelian Society*, Supp. Vol., 78 (2004), 213–45, Davies does not explicitly endorse the dogmatist view of perceptual justification that I am describing in this section, though he strongly suggests endorsement of that position. Davies does, however, explicitly endorse dogmatism about perceptual justification in his 'Armchair Knowledge, Begging the Question, and Epistemic Warrant', Carl G. Hempel Lectures, Princeton University, (2003).

[6] Although Davies claims that this objection is not devastating to Wright's non-dogmatist view, it is the only objection that Davies offers against Wright. And so I treat it as the strongest point that Davies has to make against Wright. If there are other theoretical arguments that a dogmatist would wish to offer against Wright's position, I do not know what they might be.

doxastically justified beliefs that here are hands. Now, suppose that Wright is correct about all of this. In that case, Moore might start with a non-evidential entitlement to accept that there are external things, then subsequently gain some sensory evidence for the existence of his two hands, and thereby acquire doxastically justified beliefs that here are hands. But suppose he has these doxastically justified beliefs, and then he notices that it follows from them that there are external things. Can he not then deduce the latter from the former, and thereby acquire *evidentially based* doxastically justified belief, that there are external things? It seems that Moore ought to be able to do so: after all, he just deduced the conclusion from premises, and he has an evidentially based doxastically justified belief in each of those premises. Shouldn't such evidentially based doxastic justification be transmitted to the conclusion across this deductive inference?

Wright faces a choice here: he can either deny that such evidentially based doxastic justification is transmitted to the conclusion across this deductive inference; or he can allow that, by means of nothing more than deductive inference, we can convert a non-evidential entitlement to accept that there are external things into an evidentially based doxastically justified belief that there are external things. Wright takes the former option; but Davies regards both of these two options as in conflict with our ordinary thinking concerning the generation and transmission of evidentially based doxastic justification. Thus, he thinks, Wright's view of perceptual justification faces a dilemma, both horns of which are unappealing.

Davies thinks we can give a better account of Moore's Proof, an account that avoids this dilemma. The account that Davies has in mind is a dogmatist account according to which Moore's Proof suffers from Type 4 but not Type 5 dependence. When, on the basis of his sensory evidence, Moore acquires evidentially based doxastically justified beliefs about his hands, and then he deduces that there are external things, he thereby acquires an evidentially based doxastically justified belief that there are external things. No non-evidential entitlement to accept the existence of external things need have been involved in Moore's gaining evidentially based doxastically justified beliefs about his hands, so there is no problem of converting non-evidential entitlement into evidentially based doxastic justification by the mere act of deductive inference. So, on this view, Moore's Proof does not suffer from Type 5 dependence. It may still suffer from Type 4 dependence, of course—indeed, if dogmatism is true then it will suffer from Type 4 dependence—but it can do so without suffering from Type 5 dependence.

According to this New Moorean view, although Moore's Proof transmits knowledge, evidentially based doxastic justification, and propositional justification, it cannot rationally overcome doubts about its conclusion. Why can't it rationally overcome doubts about the truth of its conclusion? Because, according to Pryor and Davies, such doubts—whether rational or irrational—would render the doubter doxastically unjustified in accepting the premises. And so the doubter cannot employ the arguments to transmit doxastically justified belief from the premises to the conclusion, because the doubter has no doxastically justified belief (in the premises) to transmit. Of course, the doubter might actually believe the premises, and she might even have propositional justification to believe the premises. Indeed, she might also perform the inference and, as a result, believe the conclusion, and have propositional justification to believe the conclusion. But so long as she has—or even entertains—doubts concerning the conclusion of the argument, she cannot rationally believe the premises, and so she cannot have a doxastically justified belief in the premises. And so the argument cannot transmit doxastically justified belief to the conclusion, since in such a case there's no doxastically justified belief in the premises to begin with.

Both Davies and Pryor take this inability rationally to overcome doubts to be the source of the apparent problem with Moore's Proof.[7] In section III, I will argue that the dogmatist epistemology that leads them to this view of Moore's Proof faces a dilemma very similar to the dilemma faced by Wright's epistemology. Then in section IV, I will show that Moore's own epistemological view was inconsistent with dogmatism, and with the New Moorean reading of Moore's Proof. The New Mooreans have it exactly backwards, in fact, since Moore thought that his Proof *could not* transmit knowledge or justification, but *could* rationally overcome doubts about its conclusion.

III Is There Reason to Prefer the dogmatist View of Perceptual Justification to Wright's Non-dogmatist View of Perceptual Justification?

According to Davies, Wright's view faces the following dilemma: either deny that evidentially based doxastic justification is closed under known entailment (which he does); or allow that by means of nothing more than a deductive inference from a Type II proposition one is evidentially justified in believing, one can convert a non-evidential entitlement to accept a Type III proposition into an *evidentially based* doxastic justification for believing a Type III proposition. Each option, Davies

---

[7] William Alston (1986) and Michael Bergmann (2004) are also committed to claiming that some apparently 'question-begging' arguments have precisely this characteristic: they can transmit justification (both propositional and doxastic) but they cannot rationally overcome doubts. I do not include Alston and Bergmann as New Mooreans only because, so far as I am aware, they have not explicitly discussed the issue of whether Moore's Proof has this characteristic.

claims, conflicts without our ordinary thinking about doxastic justification, but a dogmatist does not have to grant either of these two options, and so this is a point in favor of dogmatism over Wright's own non-dogmatist view of perceptual justification.

Of course, there may be non-dogmatist views of perceptual justification that allow that Moore's Proof suffers from Type 4 but not Type 5 dependence, but the New Mooreans do not explicitly advocate such views. The question before us now is whether there is a reason to claim that Moore's Proof suffers from Type 4 but not Type 5 dependence, and the answer that we're presently considering on behalf of the New Mooreans is as follows: there is a reason to claim that Moore's Proof suffers from Type 4 but not Type 5 dependence, which is that this claim follows from dogmatism, and we should accept dogmatism because, unlike Wright's view, it avoids having to choose between the horns of an uncomfortable dilemma.

One problem with this dilemma argument against Wright's view is that dogmatism itself faces a dilemma that is analogous to—and no less serious than—the dilemma faced by Wright's own non-dogmatist account of perceptual justification.[8] So either Davies's argument does not present a serious problem for Wright's view, or an analogous argument presents an equally serious problem for dogmatism.

Here's the dilemma for dogmatism. According to the dogmatist, Moore's epistemic situation is the following. He has some fallible perceptual evidence for the proposition that he has two hands—let's say that it *perceptually appears* to him that he has two hands. And, on the basis of this perceptual appearance, he believes that he has two hands. Since (we may suppose) there are no defeaters, he has propositional justification to believe that he has two hands, and his belief enjoys evidentially based doxastic justification, and he knows that he has two hands. But Moore also has propositional justification to believe *that it perceptually appears to him as if he has two hands*: the perceptual appearance itself provides him with such propositional justification. Now suppose, plausibly enough, that Moore believes that it perceptually appears to him as if he has two hands, and he believes this on the basis of the appearance, and there are no defeaters. In that case, Moore once again has an evidentially based doxastically justified belief that it perceptually appears to him as if he has two hands, and he knows that it perceptually appears to him as if he has two hands. So Moore, we may suppose, has the following two evidentially based doxastically justified beliefs: he has two hands, and it perceptually appears to him as if he has two hands. But from these two premises, he can deduce, and therefore (assuming closure of evidentially based doxastic justification) have an evidentially based doxastically justified belief, that his perceptual appearance is, in this case, not misleading.

---

[8] The dilemma faced by dogmatism is a special case of a dilemma faced by an internalist fallibilist epistemological theory, as I argue in my unpublished manuscript 'A Refutation of Internalist Fallibilism'.

But how could Moore have an evidentially based doxastically justified belief *that his perceptual appearance is, in this case, not misleading*, if the only evidence that he has in favor of that proposition is the fallible perceptual appearance itself? It seems that the dogmatist faces a dilemma here: either he has to deny that evidentially based doxastic justification is closed under known entailment, or he has to allow that by means of nothing more than deductive inference from beliefs that one holds on the basis of a bit of perceptual evidence, one can acquire an evidentially based doxastically justified belief that that very bit of perceptual evidence is, in this case, not misleading. dogmatists would opt for the latter of the two horns of this dilemma, but why is this dilemma any easier for the dogmatist to handle than the analogous dilemma is for Wright to handle?

In order to review, let's compare the two dilemmas side by side. Here's the dilemma that Wright faces: either Wright has to deny that evidentially based doxastic justification is closed under known entailment, or he has to allow that by means of nothing more than a deductive inference from a Type II proposition that one is evidentially justified in believing, one can convert a non-evidential entitlement to accept a Type III proposition into an *evidentially based* doxastic justification for believing a Type III proposition.

Now, here's the dilemma that dogmatists face: either they have to deny that evidentially based doxastic justification is closed under known entailment; or they have to allow that by means of nothing more than deductive inference from a Type II proposition that one is evidentially justified in believing and another proposition that one is introspectively justified in believing, one can convert one's trust in a bit of fallible perceptual evidence into an evidentially based doxastically justified belief that that very bit of fallible perceptual evidence is, in this case, not misleading.

Each dilemma involves one horn that denies closure, and another horn that seemingly generates evidentially based doxastic justification miraculously, by means of some 'epistemic alchemy'.[9] Wright accepts the former horn of his dilemma, and the dogmatist accepts the latter horn of her dilemma. But if the very fact that Wright faces the first dilemma is (as Davies suggests) a reason to resist Wright's account of perceptual justification, then why isn't the very fact that dogmatists face the second dilemma a reason to resist their dogmatist account of perceptual justification? And if neither dilemma operates as an objection to the view that faces it, then we still have seen no reason to prefer the dogmatist view of perceptual justification to Wright's non-dogmatist view. And, in that case, we still have seen no reason to accept the view that Moore's Proof does not suffer from Type 5 dependence. It's still possible, of course, that Moore's Proof does not suffer from Type 5 dependence, but we haven't yet been given any more reason to accept this claim than to reject it.

---

[9] The phrase is from Davies (2004).

Of course, if we *must* choose either Wright's view of perceptual justification or the dogmatist view of perceptual justification, then perhaps we have no choice but to settle for facing one or the other of the two dilemmas stated above, and we will have to settle for whichever dilemma we find less discomfiting. But, as I will argue in the next section, this is not a choice that we must make. Moore himself would have rejected this choice, for he would have rejected both Wright's view and the dogmatist view of perceptual justification.

IV The Views of the New Mooreans are Inconsistent with Moore's own Views

According to the New Mooreans, the reason that Moore's Proof appears to be epistemically defective is not that it suffers from the kind of defect that Wright calls 'transmission-failure'. Moore's Proof transmits knowledge, doxastically justified belief, and propositional justification to believe—at least it does so for anyone who does not have, and is not entertaining, skeptical doubts. The reason that the Proof may *appear* to suffer from what Wright calls 'transmission-failure' is that it cannot be used rationally to overcome actual, or even hypothetical, doubts as to whether or not the conclusion is true. It cannot be used to overcome such actual or hypothetical doubts, because the very existence of such doubts would rob the doubter of doxastically justified belief in the premises, and so the doubter could not employ the Proof to achieve doxastically justified belief in the conclusion.

Now, is this how Moore viewed his Proof? No. For one thing, it is reasonably clear that Moore thought that his Proof *did* rationally overcome actual and hypothetical doubts about its conclusion. Although he does not say this explicitly, he does say the following shortly after offering his Proof:

My proof, then, of the existence of things outside of us did satisfy three of the conditions necessary for a rigorous proof. . . . all of us do constantly take proofs of this sort as absolutely conclusive proofs of certain conclusions—*as finally settling questions, as to which we were previously in doubt.* (Moore 1993b, 167, emphasis added.)

While Moore does not explicitly say here that his Proof rationally overcomes doubts about its conclusion, the text above strongly suggests that he takes his Proof rationally to overcome doubts. Indeed, immediately after the quoted passage Moore compares the cogency of his own proof to that of the proof-reader's proof of the existence of typos on a particular page. If Moore did not take his Proof rationally to overcome doubts about its conclusion, then it is not clear what point there would be to his writing the paragraph quoted above. (Nothing that comes further on in Moore's text helps to make it clear what point there would then be.) Indeed, if he did not take his Proof rationally to overcome doubts about its conclusion, then it is not clear what he could have taken his Proof to accomplish.

If Moore takes his Proof rationally to overcome doubt about its conclusion, then mustn't he also think that his Proof provides us with knowledge of the truth of its conclusion, and so does not suffer from transmission-failure? No. As I will argue in the remainder of this section, there are strong textual grounds for understanding Moore as thinking of his Proof not as *providing* us with knowledge of the truth of its conclusion, but rather as *displaying* our knowledge of the truth of the conclusion—knowledge that we already had prior to the Proof. The Proof itself does not in any way enhance our epistemic status *concerning the existence of external things*, even though the conclusion of the Proof is about external things. Rather, Moore's act of giving the Proof enhances our epistemic status concerning *our knowledge* of the existence of external things, even though the conclusion of the Proof is not about our knowledge.

On Moore's own view, his Proof does suffer from transmission-failure: we could not so much as have propositional justification to believe the premises—let alone knowledge of the truth of the premises—unless we had knowledge of the truth of the conclusion. But that doesn't make it pointless for Moore to give the Proof: Moore's goal in giving the Proof is not to give us knowledge of the existence of external things, but rather to display our knowledge of the existence of external things, and thereby to give us knowledge that we already have knowledge of the existence of external things. Just as I might ride a bicycle in order to display the knowledge that I already possess of how to ride a bicycle, or point to Jones in order to display the knowledge that I already possess of who Jones is, or tell someone the time in order to display the knowledge that I already have of what time it is, Moore gives his Proof in order to display the knowledge that he already has of the existence of external things.

It is not entirely straightforward to defend these attributions to Moore, since Moore's terminology is so different from the terminology that we, following Pryor and other contemporaries, have been using. But I will mount some defense of these attributions below.

Yet before arguing for this interpretation of Moore, we must first deal with the following worry: if we were in any doubt as to the truth of the conclusion of Moore's Proof, then could we have already possessed knowledge of the truth of the conclusion? Not according to the New Mooreans. Such doubts are, according to them, precisely what render us incapable of knowledge, or of having doxastically justified belief in, the premises or the conclusion of the Proof.

On this point, however, the New Moorean view is simply wrong. In fact, I can know that p even while I doubt that p, so long as my doubt is unreasonable. For instance, if a philosopher talks me into doubting whether or not the universe has existed for more than 5 minutes, it doesn't follow that I no longer know that the universe has existed for more than 5 minutes. I still know that I ate breakfast 3 hours ago, even if I harbor silly philosophically induced doubts concerning the reality of the past. And if I know that I ate breakfast 3 hours ago, then I can also know that the universe has existed for more than 5 minutes. My doubt is unreasonable, of course. But it need not be what Pryor calls a 'pathological' doubt: a doubt that I recognize to be unreasonable. It could be a doubt that I don't recognize to be unreasonable. But still it does not destroy my belief, or my knowledge, that I ate breakfast 3 hours ago. I can know that I ate breakfast, even when I also (unreasonably) doubt that the universe if more than 5 minutes old. There is no problem for Moore, then, in admitting that his Proof rationally overcomes doubts about its conclusion by displaying our antecedent knowledge of the truth of that conclusion: such doubts are perfectly compatible with our believing, and even knowing, the truth of that conclusion.

So the question that remains for us to answer is this: did Moore think that his Proof could transmit justification from premises to conclusion? Although Moore does not address the question in these terms, an examination of his general account of perceptual knowledge strongly suggests a negative answer to this question. On Moore's view, knowing that there are external things—or at least having learned that there are external things—is a necessary condition of knowing that here are two hands, so whatever epistemic properties the Proof might transmit, it cannot transmit knowledge. In a 1941–2 entry in his notebooks, Moore says the following about what he takes to be a representative case of our empirical knowledge of perceptible objects:

> [My knowledge that this is a dog is] not immediate, because I only know it because I have learned from past experience that things like this always have a substantial thickness and an inside. If I only saw, felt, and remembered what I do at this moment, I shouldn't know that it was a dog: this knowledge is due to my having learned by experience how things generally behave . . . My grounds are *generalizations* which I've learned by past experience. . . . Having learned these things is having grounds . . .   (Moore 1993a, 176)

For Moore, our empirical knowledge of such particular truths as that *this is a dog* or *here is a hand* requires our having learned various empirical generalizations to be true, including empirical generalizations to the effect that particular perceptible objects have 'a substantial thickness and an inside'. But only external things can have a thickness and an inside, for to have a thickness and an inside requires that something exist in space and have some portion that can exist without our being aware of it.[10]

---

[10] Also, in discussing a list of particular truisms given at the beginning of his 1925 'A Defence of Common Sense', Moore writes: 'I do not know them directly; that is to say, I only know because, in the past, I have known to be true other propositions which were evidence for them' (*G. E. Moore: Selected Writings*, ed. by Thomas Baldwin (London and New York: Routledge: 1993), 118).

Moore's analysis of such particular truths as that *this is a dog* or *here is a hand* puts some pressure on him to hold the view that our knowledge of such particular truths requires us to know some generalizations. In his 1925 'A Defence of Common Sense', Moore writes: 'the analysis of the proposition "This is a human hand" is, roughly at least, of the form "There is a thing, and only thing, of which it is true both that it is a human hand and that *this surface* is a part of its surface" '.[11] If the latter existential claim is the *analysis* of 'There is a human hand', then our knowledge that this is a human hand requires us to know the truth of the existential claim. On Moore's view, you cannot know that this is a human hand unless you know that there are human hands. Your knowledge that there are human hands is, for Moore, based on sensory evidence, just as is the knowledge that this is a human hand. But no particular bit of sensory evidence, all by itself, gives us any particular bit of knowledge. Rather, on Moore's view, a whole lot of sensory evidence in tandem gives us a whole lot of empirical knowledge (of both particulars and of generalizations) at once.[12] In this respect, Moore's account of empirical knowledge is like the views defended in Rosenberg (2002) and Sosa (1997).

It seems clear, then, that Moore does not think that his Proof transmits knowledge: one must know the conclusion in order to know the premises. But knowledge-transmission is not what is most directly at issue between Wright and the New Mooreans. They are chiefly concerned about whether the proof transmits doxastic justification. Since Moore never uses any term that is clearly equivalent to 'doxastic justification', his view on this issue is not obvious. But we get a hint from the following passages, taken from his 1905–6 article 'The Nature and Reality of Objects of Perception': '[A] good reason for a belief is a proposition which would not be true unless the belief were also true . . . (1968, 35), and '[I]t is plain that if anyone ever believes what is false, he is believing something for which there is no good reason, in the sense in which I have explained, and for which, therefore, he cannot possibly have a good reason' (1968, 37).

For Moore, then, believing something for a good reason involves believing it for a reason that could not be true unless one's belief is true. Here's a similarly infallibilist passage, though of narrower scope, from his 1941 lecture 'Certainty': '[I]f a man at a given time is only dreaming that he is standing up, then it follows that he has not at that time the evidence of his senses in favor of that proposition . . . ' (1993b, 191).

[11] See also this passage from Moore's 1918–19 article 'Some Judgments of Perception': '[I]f there is anything which is this inkstand, then, in perceiving that thing, I am knowing it only as *the* thing which stands in a certain relation to this sense-datum' (G. E. Moore, *Philosophical Studies* (Totowa, NJ: Littlefield, Adams & Co., 1968), 234).

[12] Moore (1993b, 129). This is the view that Moore held in the 1920s and later, throughout the period in which he composed his Proof. He entertained—but did not clearly endorse—a different view in his 1910–11 lectures entitled *Some Main Problems of Philosophy*. See Moore (1953, 142).

These passages strongly suggest that Moore would have been an infallibilist about doxastic justification: one cannot hold a belief on the basis of good reasons—i.e., what we would call a 'doxastically justified' belief—unless one's reason for the belief is such that it could not be true unless the belief itself is true.[13] But it's not clear how such doxastically justified belief falls short of knowledge. It involves a true belief held on the basis of infallible reasons. Moore never says precisely what suffices for knowledge, so it is not clear that he would have regarded such a belief as sufficing for knowledge. But it is also not clear what more he could have required for knowledge. Perhaps Moore never used a phrase equivalent to 'doxastically justification' simply because he would not have taken there to be any difference between doxastic justification and knowledge. In that case, then, Moore would also have taken it to be a necessary condition of having a doxastically justified belief that here are two hands, that one have a doxastically justified belief that there are external things.

On Moore's view, then, its merely seeming to you as if there are two hands before you does not suffice for you to have a good reason to believe that there are two hands before you. To have a good reason to believe that there are two hands before you, you would need to have a lot of sensory evidence, and to have learned various generalizations. (Of course, one cannot have learned these generalizations by inference from merely our knowledge of instances, since knowing the generalizations is required to know the instances in the first place. One must get all this knowledge—of generalizations and of instances—as a package deal.) No single bit of sensory evidence is an infallible indicator of there being two hands before you, but the totality of your evidence taken together must be such an infallible indicator, or else it cannot give you knowledge—or even good reason to believe—that there are two hands before you.

So, while Moore's text is not explicit on this last point, I think we can reasonably draw the following conclusions: First, Moore pretty clearly would have thought that his Proof did *not* transmit knowledge from premises to conclusion: one could not achieve knowledge of the conclusion solely on the basis of inferring the conclusion from antecedent knowledge of the premises. And second, although it's not clear whether Moore had any views about the property that we call 'doxastic justification',

---

[13] Yet in a different passage in 'On the Nature and Reality of Objects of Perception', Moore explicitly claims to use the expression 'reason for a belief' as follows: 'If, for instance, the *Times* stated that the King was dead, we should think that was a good reason for believing that the King was dead ... We should not, indeed, think that the statement in the *Times* rendered it absolutely certain that the King was dead. But it is extremely unlikely that the *Times* would make a statement of this kind unless it were true; and, in that sense, the fact of the statement appearing in the *Times* would render it highly probable—much more likely than not—that the King was dead. And I wish it to be understood that I am using the words "reason for a belief" in this extremely wide sense' (Moore 1968, 41.)

there are some textual grounds for thinking that he would not have thought that his Proof transmits that property from premises to conclusion either. By Moore's lights, his Proof is not intended to give us knowledge that we might not already have, but rather to display to us the knowledge that we already have, and thereby rationally to overcome our doubts, i.e., to give those of us who happen to doubt the existence of the external world a reason to stop doubting.[14]

Works Cited

William Alston 'Epistemic Circularity', *Philosophy and Phenomenological Research*, 47 (1986), 1–30.

Bergmann, Michael, 'Epistemic Circularity: Malignant and Benign', *Philosophy and Phenomenological Research*, 69 (2004), 709–27.

Davies, Martin, 'Armchair Knowledge, Begging the Question, and Epistemic Warrant', Carl G. Hempel Lectures, Princeton University (2003).

_____ 'Epistemic Entitlement, Warrant Transmission, and Easy Knowledge', *Proceedings of the Aristotelian Society*, supp. vol., 78 (2004), 213–45.

Moore, G. E. *Some Main Problems of Philosophy* (New York: Collier Books, 1953).

_____ *Philosophical Studies* (Totowa, NJ: Littlefield, Adams and Company, 1968).

_____ *Commonplace Book 1919–1953*, ed. by Casimir Lewy (Bristol: Thoemmes Press, 1993a).

_____ *G. E. Moore: Selected Writings* ed. by Thomas Baldwin (London and New York: Routledge, 1993b).

Neta, Ram, 'Perceptual Evidence and the New dogmatism', *Philosophical Studies*, 119 (2004), 199–214.

_____ 'A Refutation of Internalist Fallibilism', ms.

Pryor, James, 'The Skeptic and the dogmatist', *Noûs*, 34 (2000), 517–49.

_____ 'Is Moore's Argument an Example of Transmission Failure?', *Philosophical Issues*, 14 (2004), 349–78.

Rosenberg, Jay, *Thinking about Knowing* (Oxford: Oxford University Press, 2002).

Sosa, Ernest, 'Reflective Knowledge in the Best Circles', *Journal of Philosophy*, 94 (1997), 410–30.

Stroud, Barry, *The Significance of Philosophical Scepticism* (Oxford: Oxford University Press, 1984).

Wright, Crispin, 'Facts and Certainty', *Proceedings of the British Academy*, 71 (1985), 429–72.

_____ '(Anti-)Sceptics Simple and Subtle: G. E. Moore and John McDowell', *Philosophy and Phenomenological Research*, 65 (2002), 331– 49.

_____ 'Warrant for Nothing (and Foundations for Free)', *Proceedings of the Aristotelian Society*, supp. vol., 78 (2004), 167–212.

[14] I am grateful to Mark Greenberg, Marc Lange, and Bill Lycan for their comments on an earlier draft of this paper, and to Dylan Sabo for his enormous assistance in finding passages from Moore's corpus. I am also grateful to an audience at the University of Melbourne (especially Graham Priest, Francois Schroeter, and Laura Schroeter) and at the Australian National University (especially David Chalmers, Martin Davies, and Frank Jackson).

4

Moore's Anti-skeptical Strategies

William G. Lycan

> And this state of things is an excellent illustration of a principle, which many
> philosophers are, I think, apt to forget: namely, that the mere fact that one
> proposition coheres with or follows from another does not by itself give us the
> slightest presumption in favour of its truth.[1]

Moore is best known for his distinctive critiques of idealism and of skepticism. Few
philosophers have defended idealism against him, because since his day few have
defended idealism at all. But skeptics and their sympathizers have spoken out. For
the most part, their responses have been shallow dismissals—that Moore has begged
the question, that his privileging of 'common sense' is arbitrary and dogmatic,
etc.—though there have been more extensive rebuttals as well.

I think the main problem has been that Moore made several different anti-skeptical
moves, without distinguishing them, and they differ in their failings. My purpose in
this paper is to note the differences and to identify the reasoning that I believe has the
most force. I shall proceed in chronological order of his writings.

I 'Hume's Theory Examined'

Moore's first foray, in a lecture given in 1910,[2] was against a skeptical argument based
on two epistemological principles he ascribed to Hume:

---

[1] G. E. Moore, *Some Main Problems of Philosophy* (New York: Collier Books, 1962), 137. Originally published
in London by George Allen & Unwin (1953).

[2] But not published until decades later, as ch. 6 of *Some Main Problems*.

You see, the position we have got to is this. If Hume's principles are true, then, I have admitted, I do *not* know *now* that this pencil—the material object—exists. If, therefore, I am to prove that I *do* know *that* this pencil exists, I must prove, somehow, that Hume's principles, one or both of them, are *not* true. In what sort of way, by what sort of argument, can I prove this? (136)

That argument is so straightforward as not to need reconstructing. But, Moore continues:

It seems to me that, in fact, there really is no stronger and better argument than the following. I *do* know that this pencil exists; but I could not know this, if Hume's principles are true; *therefore*, Hume's principles, one or both of them, are false. I think that this argument is really as strong and good a one as any that could be used: and I think it really is conclusive. In other words, I think that the fact that, if Hume's principles were true, I could not know of the existence of this pencil, is a *reductio ad absurdum* of those principles. But, of course, this is an argument which will not seem convincing to those who believe that the principles are true, nor yet to those who believe that I really do not know that this pencil exists. It seems like begging the question. And therefore I will try to shew that it really is a good and conclusive argument. (ibid.)

It is noteworthy that, even in this earliest effort, Moore anticipated the charge of question-begging and tried to block it. He 'consider[s] what is necessary in order that an argument may be a good and conclusive one', which he equates with an argument 'which enables us to *know* that its conclusion is true' (136–7).[3] First, of course, the argument must be formally valid; his is, but as he says in the passage that serves as epigraph to this paper, that shows nothing either way. (And in any case, every question-begging argument is valid.)

A second requirement is that if the argument is to yield knowledge, we must know its premises to be true. On pain of regress, we cannot suppose that *every* piece of knowledge is deduced from something already known, so we must suppose that there is 'immediate knowledge' (140), by which Moore means just knowledge that is not inferred from something known. Now:

It is certain, then, that if any proposition whatever is ever known by us mediately, or because some other proposition is known from which it follows, some one proposition at least, must also be known by us *immediately*, or *not merely* because some other proposition is known from which it follows. And hence it follows that the conditions necessary to make an argument good and conclusive may just as well be satisfied, when the premiss is only known *immediately*, as when there are other arguments in its favour. It follows, therefore, that my argument: 'I know this pencil to exist; therefore Hume's principles are false'; may be just as good an argument as

I do not count 'The Refutation of Idealism' (1903). It is not about skepticism at all, though its last two pages contain some remarks on the nature of awareness that could easily be made into an unusual argument against skepticism

[3] Here and throughout, italics are original. Moore liked italics.

any other, even though its premiss—the premiss that I do know this pencil to exist—is only known immediately.   (141–2)

But does Moore know (immediately or not) the premise that he knows the pencil to exist? He is 'inclined to think' that he does (142). He surveys and rebuts two obviously bad objections.

But there are good objections. First, he has not, after all, directly addressed the question-begging charge.[4] His 'immediate' premise is that he does know that the pencil exists. But the skeptic's already defended position is that no one knows any such thing. Moore wants to say that his argument is no less clearly unsound than the skeptic's, and that is true; but the skeptic was there first, and Moore has raised no independent objection to either of Hume's principles. (I am assuming a rule of dialectic to the effect that if A has tenably defended the claim that no F are G, then B cannot refute A *simply* by alleging that here is an F that is G, without finding a flaw in A's argument. B may refuse to accept the argument and propose to turn it on its head, and not unreasonably so, but A is not thereby refuted.)

Also, Moore's reasoning in support of immediate knowledge assumes the falsity of skepticism: the skeptic, by assuming that what is known must have been conclusively proved, could equally use the regress to show that nothing empirical is known; and, much more to the point, Moore infers the actual existence of immediate knowledge directly from the impossibility of all knowledge's being mediate.

Second, Moore's tentative claim that he knows the pencil to exist is too highly disputable to be advanced as itself known. Skepticism is a viable philosophical position, and its denial is a substantive philosophical claim. I for one do not think that any philosophical claim is known to be true.[5] Indeed, Moore himself had a low regard for philosophical claims in general, and I believe he was right in that. If he does not know skepticism to be false, then it is hard to grant the supposition that his premise is itself known to be true.[6] (Nor can I guess why he was inclined to think it was.)

But at the tail end of the lecture, Moore says casually,

---

[4] Indeed, he seems to have conceded the charge a year previously, in 'Hume's Philosophy', in *Philosophical Studies* (Totowa, NJ: Littlefield, Adams & Co., 1968), 159–60. Originally published in *The New Quarterly* (1909).

[5] D. M. Armstrong argues this convincingly in 'The Scope and Limits of Human Knowledge', *Australasian Journal of Philosophy*, 84 (2006), 159–66. Throwing in impromptu advice to undergraduates when he used to present the paper as a talk, he would add that 'if you go into philosophy as your life's work, you will die never having known whether anything you said was true.' I say it is worse than that: though the skeptical meta-induction does not work against science, it certainly does against philosophy. If we know anything, it is that we are always wrong.

[6] I am temperamentally hostile to closure principles, but what I have just said still seems true.

But whether the exact proposition which formed my premiss, namely: I do know that this pencil exists; or only the proposition: This pencil exists; or only the proposition: the sense-data which I directly apprehend are a sign that it exists; is known by me immediately, one or the other of them, I think, certainly is so. And all three of them are much more certain than any premiss which could be used to prove that they are false; and also much more certain than any other premiss which could be used to prove that they are true. That is why I say that the strongest argument to prove that Hume's principles are false is the argument from a particular case, like this in which we do know of the existence of some material object. And similarly, if the object is to prove *in general* that we do know of the existence of material objects, no argument which is really stronger can, I think, be brought forward to prove this than particular instances in which we do in fact know of the existence of such an object. (142–3)[7]

That remark is slightly amplified eight years later, in another oddly isolated passage from 'Some Judgments of Perception'[8]:

But it seems to me a sufficient refutation of such [skeptical] views as these, simply to point to cases in which we do know things. This, after all, you know, really is a finger: there is no doubt about it. And I think we can safely challenge any philosopher to bring forward any argument in favour either of the proposition that we do not know it, or of the proposition that it is not true, which does not at some point, rest upon some premise which is, beyond comparison, less certain than is the proposition which it is designed to attack. The question whether we do ever know such things as these, and whether there are any material things, seem to me, therefore, to be questions which there is no need to take seriously: they are questions which it is quite easy to answer, with certainty, in the affirmative. (228)

---

[7] Similarly, from 'Material Things', the following chapter of *Some Main Problems*: '[T]he attempt to prove by means of such a principle as Hume's, that we cannot know of the existence of any material object, seems to me to be a characteristic instance of a sort of argument which is very common in philosophy: namely, an attempt to prove that a given proposition is false, by means of a principle which is, in fact, much less certain than the proposition which is supposed to be proved false by its means' (160–1).

Just prior to that, Moore has asserted that 'any general principle to the effect that we can never know a particular kind of proposition, except under certain conditions, is and must be based upon an empirical induction: upon observation of the cases in which we obviously do know propositions of the kind in question, and of those in which we obviously do not, and of the circumstances which distinguish the one class from the other.' His point is that there are empirical propositions of which the skeptic cannot say that we *obviously* do not know them. But why should anyone grant that a skeptical argument must be based on an induction of the sort Moore has in mind? (For further discussion of this byway, see Thomas Baldwin, *G. E. Moore* (London: Routledge, 1990), 272–3.)

[8] In *Philosophical Studies*. Originally published in *Proceedings of the Aristotelian Society* (1918–19).

II 'A Defence of Common Sense'

Moore begins 'A Defence of Common Sense'[9] by 'enunciating . . . a whole long list of propositions, which may seem, at first sight, such obvious truisms as not to be worth stating: they are, in fact, a set of propositions, every one of which (in my own opinion) I *know*, with certainty, to be true' (32). The list begins: 'There exists at present a living human body, which is *my* body. This body was born at a certain time in the past, and has existed continuously ever since . . .'. The body has been in physical contact with other things 'having shape and size in three dimensions', such as the pen he is holding; and so on at considerable length (33). (Perhaps the least obviously *known* of those propositions is that 'the earth had existed also for many years before my body was born; and for many of these years, also, large numbers of human bodies had, at every moment, been alive upon it; and many of these bodies had died and ceased to exist before it was born.')

Further, Moore contends, nearly every human being 'has frequently, during the life of his body, known, with regard to *him*self or *his* body . . . a proposition corresponding to each of' those on his list. Moreover, again, the latter knowledge claim itself 'seems an obvious enough truism' (34).

But this essay, though classic, adds nothing good to Moore's earlier case against skepticism. He contends in (a bit ironically) Humean fashion that even the philosophical skeptics in practice believe not only the relevant common-sensical propositions but that they are certain of them, and he maintains that they thereby contradict themselves.[10] Dialectically speaking, that is a rubber arrow. Though it is true and important that we are unable in practice to doubt the things we are theoretically obliged to doubt, that shows no contradiction in the skeptic's theory itself.[11] Also,

---

[9] In *Philosophical Papers* (New York: Collier Books, 1962). The book was originally published in London by George Allen & Unwin (1959), the article in J. H. Muirhead (ed.), *Contemporary British Philosophy*, second ser. (Allen & Unwin, 1925).

[10] '[S]uch philosophers . . . seem to me constantly to betray the fact that they regard the proposition that those beliefs *are* beliefs of Common Sense, or the proposition that they themselves are not the only members of the human race, as not merely true but *certainly* true; and *certainly* true it cannot be unless one member, at least, of the human race, namely themselves, has *known* the very things which that member is declaring that no human being has ever known' (43).

There is a later passage that is very puzzling unless we understand it along the same lines. Moore says: '[I]f we know that they are features of the "Common Sense view of the world," it follows that they are true: it is self-contradictory to maintain that we know them to be features in the Common Sense view, and that yet they are not true; since to say that we know this, is to say that they are true' (44).

[11] Possibly all Moore meant was that there was a contradiction within *the skeptic*, i.e., as between the skeptic's theory and her/his private, personal beliefs. But that, too, would show nothing wrong with the theory.

it is questionable whether, even in real life, skeptics believe *that they are certain* of the common-sensical propositions, even if to the observer they usually act as if they do.

Then Moore says merely, 'I think I have nothing better to say than that it seems to me that I do know them, with certainty' (43; he adds the disclaimer that he does not know them directly or immediately). Here he has wisely backed off the claim that he knows that he knows them; but its seeming to him that he does by itself contributes nothing to his case as it stands.

III 'Proof of an External World'

This immortal work[12] rises to Kant's famous 'scandal to philosophy' challenge, and offers to prove the existence of material things ('things which are to be met with in space'). Moore argues by holding up his hands. 'Here is one hand, and here is another', he says, making 'a certain gesture' with each. He adds the premise that hands are material things external to our minds. He calls the result a 'Proof' of the existence of material things, indeed a 'perfectly rigorous' proof. He repeats that phrase, and adds that it is probably impossible to give a better or more rigorous proof of anything (146).

How, exactly, does that argument bear on skepticism? The skeptic contends that Moore does not know he has hands. But if Moore can produce a perfectly rigorous proof that he does, such a proof would be an adequate basis for knowledge. Else it is hard to see what the skeptic could be demanding.

An idealist would charge Moore with question-begging once again, since the idealist has already argued that there are no material things in the sense Moore means; either there are not really any hands at all, or hands are not material things. Moore heads off that objection by pointing out that neither of his premises is equivalent to his conclusion.

Moore concedes that his argument would not count as a proof unless he knew each of its premises to be correct. But he maintains that

I certainly did at the moment *know* that which I expressed by the combination of certain gestures with saying the words 'There is one hand and here is another.' ... How absurd it would be to suggest that I did not know it, but only believed it, and perhaps it was not the case! You might as well suggest that I do not know that I am now standing up and talking. ...   (145)

Well, yes, you might. Indeed, the skeptic has more than suggested it; skeptics have provided a battery of arguments for just such a claim. But an externalist move is available to Moore here: for an argument to count as a proof, its premises must *be*

---

[12] In *Philosophical Papers*. 273–300. Originally published in the *Proceedings of the British Academy*, 25 (1939).

known, but (on pain of regress) they need not be shown to be known (cf. his remarks on this in *Some Main Problems*). Nor is Moore question-beggingly *assuming that* they are known; though he believes they are, that claim is not part of the proof itself.[13]

Yet I think the argument as it stands here is dialectically improper all the same. Though it does not formally beg the question, it comes close. For, as noted above, we know in advance that no idealist will grant both of the proof's premises. Moore is wasting the idealist's time. The idealist has taken a position and given an argument in its support. Taking that position and not being an idiot, the idealist obviously rejects either 'There really are hands' or 'Hands are material things', so Moore's own argument contributes nothing to the conversation, even if Moore is right.[14]

Moore goes on to point out that existential generalization is a common and generally unexceptionable form of inference, as when I convince you that there are misprints on a certain page by showing you three of them. But my merely showing you the misprints would (rightly) not convince you if you had already and independently defended the claim that all the apparent misprints in the book are really just variant spellings.

IV 'Certainty'

'Certainty'[15] does not attack skepticism directly. Moore spends a long time scouting some very simple and accordingly very bad arguments for skepticism. Then he turns to the more formidable Dream argument. He makes some surprising concessions to it, at least for the sake of discussion:

(i) that if I do not know that I am not merely dreaming that *P*, I do not know that *P* (242), which would be disputed by present-day opponents of closure of knowledge under known entailment;[16]

---

[13] For doughty further defense of Moore on this point, see Michael Watkins, 'I Know That You Know What You Don't Know That You Know' (Auburn University, MS).

[14] Subtler dialectical issues here have been raised by Crispin Wright in '(Anti-)Sceptics Simple and Subtle: G. E. Moore and John McDowell', *Philosophy and Phenomenological Research*, 65 (2002), 331–49, and pursued by Martin Davies ('Epistemic Entitlement, Warrant Transmission, and Easy Knowledge', *Proceedings of the Aristotelian Society*, suppl. vol. 78 (2004), 213–45) and James Pryor ('Is Moore's Argument an Example of Transmission Failure?', *Philosophical Issues*, 14 (2004), 349–78). See Ram Neta's article in this volume.

[15] Howison Lecture delivered at the University of California, Berkeley, 1941. First published in *Philosophical Papers*.

[16] Most notably Fred Dretske, 'Epistemic Operators', *Journal of Philosophy*, 67 (1970), 1007–23; Robert Nozick, *Philosophical Explanations* (Harvard University Press, 1981); Colin McGinn, 'The Concept of Knowledge', in P. French, T. E. Uehling, and H. Wettstein (eds.), *Midwest Studies in Philosophy IX:*

(ii) that it is possible for me to experience 'dream-images' that are exactly like the presumably veridical sensory data I am now experiencing (244–5), which was disputed by J. L. Austin and would be opposed, though on quite different grounds, by present-day 'disjunctivists.'[17]

(iii) that '[i]f it is logically possible for some dream-images to be exactly like sensory experiences which are not dream-images, surely it must be logically possible for *all* the dream-images occurring in a dream at a given time to be exactly like sensory experiences which are not dream-images, and logically possible also for all the sensory experiences which a man has at a given time when he is awake to be exactly like all the dream-images which he himself or another man had in dream at another time' (245), which was vehemently scorned as a scope fallacy by Wittgenstein and by Austin.; And even

(iv) that if it is logically possible that 'all the sensory experiences I am having now should be mere dream-images . . . and if further the sensory experiences I am having now were the only experiences I am having, I do not see how I could possibly know for certain that I am not dreaming' (245) (!).[18]

Moore goes on to suggest that current sensory experiences *plus recent memories* might logically rule out the experiences being dream-images, but rightly admits having no reason to think that is so.

And now he makes the further concession that

(v) if experiences-plus-memories do not logically rule out dreaming, 'then I don't see how to deny that I cannot possibly know for certain that I am not dreaming; I do not see that I possibly could' (245) (!!). This sounds just about like bawling 'Kamerad' and throwing himself at the skeptic's feet.[19] How could he possibly still stand firm? This is what he then says:

But can any reason be given for saying that it *is* logically possible? So far as I know nobody ever has, and I don't know how anybody ever could. And so long as this is not done my argument,

---

Causation and Causal Theories (1984); and especially Mark Heller, 'Relevant Alternatives and Closure', *Australasian Journal of Philosophy*, 77 (1999), 196–208.

[17] E.g., J. M. Hinton, *Experiences* (Oxford: Clarendon Press, 1973); P. Snowdon, 'Perception, Vision, and Causation', *Proceedings of the Aristotelian Society*, 81 (1980/1), 175–92; John McDowell, 'The Content of Perceptual Experience', *Philosophical Quarterly*, 44 (1994), 190–205; M. G. F. Martin, 'The Transparency of Experience', *Mind and Language*, 17 (2002), 376–425.

[18] Myles Burnyeat and Barry Stroud have considered (iv) disastrous. Burnyeat, 'Examples in Epistemology: Socrates, Theaetetus and G. E. Moore', *Philosophy*, 52 (1977), 381–98, 396–7; Stroud, *The Significance of Philosophical Scepticism* (Oxford: Oxford University Press, 1984), 122 ff.

[19] It should be pointed out that in his 1958 Preface to *Philosophical Papers*, Moore says of 'Certainty' that '[t]here are bad mistakes in it which I cannot yet see how to put right' (9), and the editor, Casimir Lewy, indicates (246) that this passage occurs within the span of four paragraphs that Moore meant to repudiate.

'I know that I am standing up, and therefore I know that I am not dreaming,' remains at least as good as his, 'You don't know that you are not dreaming, and therefore don't know that you are standing up.' And I don't think I've ever seen an argument expressly directed to show that it is not.   (245)

Notice that there are here two quite different points. There is the question of whether the skeptic can defend the compossibility of experiences-plus-memories and dreaming, and there is that of whether the Dream argument can be turned on its head. I myself do not think the compossibility claim needs defending,[20] but the second question should be considered in its own right, independently of the memory issue. Why should the skeptic get to start with 'You do not know that you are not dreaming' and infer that I do not know that I am standing up, any more than I get to start with 'I know that I am standing up' and infer that I know I am not merely dreaming that I am? Given the concessions, those arguments are both valid. So the skeptic's case is not proved.

That is true and (I shall contend) important. And one might think that it affords a positive argument against skepticism: 'I know that I am standing up; therefore I know that I am not dreaming.' But in the latter cause Moore's point does not help. He himself has made what he grants is a good case for the skeptic's premise. To *start* with 'I know that I am standing up' would certainly beg the question.[21]

Moore's arguments seem to be getting worse. At this point, if my earlier criticisms are sound, he has accomplished nothing whatever against the skeptic. But things are about to look up.

V 'Four Forms of Scepticism'

Here[22] Moore is primarily concerned to bash some unconvincing skeptical arguments of Russell's. His exegesis and criticism go on for pages and pages, until the paper's very last paragraph. Suddenly:

What I want, however, to emphasize is this: Russell's view that I do not know for certain that this is a pencil or that you are conscious rests, if I am right, on no less than four distinct assumptions: (1) That I don't know these things immediately; (2) That they don't follow logically from any

---

[20] I think hardly any compossibility claim, on any topic, needs defending; see my 'Free Will and the Burden of Proof', in Anthony O'Hear (ed.), *Minds and Persons*, Royal Institute of Philosophy Supplement, 53 (Cambridge: Cambridge University Press, 2003).

[21] In 'How to Defeat Opposition to Moore', *Philosophical Perspectives*, 13 (1999): 141–53), Ernest Sosa suggests an externalist move for Moore at this point, based on the counterfactual notion of 'safety'. Baldwin, *G. E. Moore*, ch. 9, also considers an externalist line.

[22] In *Philosophical Papers*.

thing or things that I do know immediately; (3) That, *if* (1) and (2) are true, my belief in or knowledge of them must be 'based on an analogical or inductive argument'; and (4) That what is so based cannot be *certain knowledge*. And what I can't help asking myself is this: Is it, in fact, as certain that all these four assumptions are true, as that I *do* know that this is a pencil and that you are conscious? I cannot help answering: It seems to me *more* certain that I *do* know that this is a pencil and that you are conscious, than that any single one of these four assumptions is true, let alone all four . . . I agree with Russell that (1), (2) and (3) *are* true; yet of no one even of these three do I feel *as* certain as that I do know for certain that this is a pencil. Nay more: I do not think it is *rational* to be as certain of any one of these four propositions, as of the proposition that I do know that this is a pencil. . . . (222)

Bingo. Finally, he has got it. What he has got is that his point against the skeptic is *comparative*.[23] The odd thing is that less fully developed versions of the point had been popping up here and there from the start; recall the isolated passages I quoted from 'Hume's Theory Examined' and 'Some Judgments of Perception':

And all three of them are much more certain than any premiss which could be used to prove that they are false; and also much more certain than any other premiss which could be used to prove that they are true. That is why I say that the strongest argument to prove that Hume's principles are false is the argument from a particular case, like this in which we do know the existence of some material object.

I think we can safely challenge any philosopher to bring forward any argument in favour either of the proposition that we do not know it, or of the proposition that it is not true, which does not at some point, rest upon some premise which is, beyond comparison, less certain than is the proposition which it is designed to attack.

But he had made nothing more of those until now.

The point needs still further development. Notice that it is a perfect instance of what in 'The Conception of Reality'[24] Moore had called 'translat[ion] . . . into the concrete' (209). (I admit I cannot think why Moore does not mention that.) In that paper he was attacking Bradley's idealist claim that time is unreal. First, he argued that that claim should be taken to entail that there are no temporal facts, such as the fact that he, Moore, had had his breakfast before he had his lunch; if it did not mean that, then what was it supposed to mean?

---

[23] Notice carefully that the 'nay more' comparison is about *rationality*, the normative notion. That disposes of the dilemma posed by Thomas Baldwin (270) as between merely a subjective feeling of certainty and the relevant proposition's objectively being 'established as' certain. The latter distinction is Moore's own, from 'Certainty', but Baldwin's dichotomy is false: For it to be normatively rational to prefer the knowledge claim to one of the skeptic's purely philosophical assumptions, we need not drag in any further material that 'establishes' the knowledge claim; see below. (However, to his credit, Baldwin discerns the more basic point about comparativity; see section 2 of ch. 9. Michael Williams gets it also, in *Unnatural Doubts* (Princeton University Press, 1996).)

[24] In *Philosophical Studies*.

Now of course Bradley had defended his thesis, by a deductively valid argument. But, obviously, his argument had premises which were not themselves defended. So we are confronted by those premises and a valid derivation of the conclusion that time is unreal, from which Moore further derives the corollary that he did not have his breakfast before he had his lunch.[25]

But, as we have seen in the case of the Dream argument, Moore was well aware that any deductive argument can be turned on its head. So far, we have no more reason to accept the conclusion on the strength of the premises than to reject one or more of the premises because the conclusion's denial is more credible. We must make a comparative judgment: is it more rational to accept each of the premises and also the conclusion, or is the conclusion implausible enough that we should reconsider and reject one or more of the premises?[26]

We apply that (n.b.) inevitable question to Bradley's argument: since the reality of time is directly entailed by something Moore finds tediously obvious, that he did have his breakfast before he had lunch, he must look at the premises of Bradley's argument and see whether each and every one of them is more credible than that he had breakfast before he had lunch. But when he does that, he finds that at least one premise is, if not gobbledegook, distinctively abstract and philosophical. For example, one of Bradley's assumptions was that *even if time is infinitely divisible* it must involve a relation of 'immediately before' and the converse 'immediately after'.[27] But why would anyone accept that? And, much more to the point, how could it possibly be more reasonable to believe it, than to believe that we had breakfast before we had lunch?

As we know, all philosophy is contentious; that is why it is (counter-etymologically) called 'philosophy'. Not counting mathematical logic, its track-record in establishing results is not as good as poor or even dismal; it is zero.[28] Every philosophical proposition is perpetually open to challenge; and, in fact, no matter how secure is an orthodoxy reigning at a given time, it will later be overturned.[29] A purely

---

[25] I owe this way of understanding the 'translation' procedure to lectures many years ago by Vere C. Chappell.

[26] I am deliberately being loose in my use of terms like 'rational', 'credible', and 'plausible'. This is because, as I shall argue in Section VI, one need not do any philosophical epistemology to make or appreciate a Moorean plausibility comparison.

[27] *Appearance and Reality*, 2nd edn. (London: Swan Sonnenschein, 1893; with an appendix, London: Swan Sonnenschein (1897); 9th impression, corrected, Oxford: Clarendon Press, (1930), 39–40.

[28] Here I depart from Moore, who I doubt would have agreed. Also, I would never deny that philosophy sometimes gets one of its areas into good enough methodological shape that the area turns into a science: physics, biology, psychology, and most recently (1957) theoretical linguistics. As Rob Cummins says, science is philosophy that worked. But that is of no help to the idealist or to the skeptic.

[29] I am disgusted, but not surprised, to see the strong resurgence of mind–body dualism among the younger generation of philosophers of mind. And I do not doubt that idealism will be back before long.

philosophical assumption—n.b., a *bare* assumption, because we are talking about an undefended premise—could not possibly be as rationally credible as an everyday fact supererogatorily well supported by perception and short-term memory.

Returning to Russell: if his (1)–(4) are true, then I do not know that this is a pencil, or that I have hands or that my name is 'William Lycan' or that I just typed the word 'that'. But which is more rational to believe: that I do not ever know any such things, or that all of (1)–(4) are true? Considered as a comparison, as Moore is saying it must be considered, the question hardly leaves room for discussion. Russell loses. (1)–(4) are contentious and eminently disputable philosophical assumptions. I strongly doubt they will ever be settled one way or the other. Meanwhile, Moore has excellent grounds for his competing proposition: he is looking right at the pencil and can feel it in his hand.

Moore's proof of the external world can be reconstructed in this same way, though at a cost. The reality of material objects is entailed by something Moore altogether reasonably believes, that he has hands. So, presented with any philosophical argument designed to show that there is no external world, we must look at the argument's premises and compare their plausibility to that of our belief that we have hands. It is a sure bet that the philosophical argument will have some characteristically abstract and contentious premise, one that certainly pales in credibility beside 'Here is one hand, and here is another.'[30] Thus, dialectically speaking, it is hard to see how any purely philosophical argument could show that there is no external world, and Moore's proof stands.

As above, Moore maintained that an argument should be called a *proof* only if its premises are known. But nothing in the present comparative version guarantees that they are known. Moore believed that they are, and on the present interpretation of his rebuttal of skepticism, they are. From the externalist point of view, that is fine. But if we are to assure ourselves that those premises are known, we need the present anti-skeptical argument, and if we have that, the proof of the external world is superfluous. So (this is the cost aforementioned) either the proof is superfluous, or Moore must ignore the requirement that a proof's premises be known.

VI Virtues of this interpretation

This way of understanding Moore avoids both the two standard shallow objections and also each of my criticisms of his attempts prior to 'Four Forms of Scepticism'.[31]

---

[30] Duh!

[31] I have defended the view here attributed to Moore, in 'Moore Against the New Skeptics', *Philosophical Studies*, 103 (2001), 35–53—but only in its own right, not as correct interpretation.

First shallow objection: it is not surprising that Moore should have been accused of begging the question, because although he never did actually beg, he came very close at least twice. But on the present interpretation, there is no such issue. Moore is only inviting a plausibility comparison. As before, the comparison is between: (i) 'I had my breakfast before I had lunch'; and (ii) Bradley's purely philosophical assumption, that even if time is infinitely divisible it must involve relations of 'immediately before' and 'immediately after', or between Russell's four premises (especially (3)) and 'I know that I have hands'. It is conceivable that some person in the grip of a philosophical view might insist that a tenet of that view is more credible than 'I had breakfast before I had lunch' or 'I know that I have hands'. It is *conceivable* even that were we to go around and take a survey, a large number of people would rate 'If (1) and (2) are true, my belief that this is a pencil must be based on an analogical or inductive argument' as in itself more credible than 'I know that I have hands', and if so Moore's strategy would have failed; but I cannot see that outcome as even faintly likely, and certainly Moore would not. In any case, though, Moore has in no way begged the question.

Many philosophers have felt that even if he has not begged in the strict sense, Moore's response to the skeptic is shoddy and superficial, and that a more profound response is required. But could there be a deeper or more fundamental philosophical method than the plausibility comparison enforced by a deductive argument? What form could a more profound response possibly take?[32]

---

[32] I can think of two non-rhetorical answers to that rhetorical question. First, suppose our knowledge of our own sensory experiences is incorrigible and absolutely certain. And suppose that, as Russell once hoped, there is a construction of physical objects and indeed all of physics out of sensory data, such that statements about physical objects could actually be validly deduced from statements about the sensory data. That would be a more profound answer to the skeptic (and proof of the external world), because due to the supposed certainty and incorrigibility of the premises, the 'plausibility' comparison would be automatic and decisive. But, for familiar reasons, I do not think that our beliefs about our own experiences are certain or incorrigible; and I doubt anyone now living thinks that physics can be deduced from statements about sensory data. Also, notice that the Russellian strategy would still not satisfy the skeptic: as Keith Lehrer has pointed out ('Why Not Skepticism?', *Philosophical Forum*, 2 (1971), 283–98), deduction is as vulnerable to the Evil Demon as is any other method of belief formation.

The other non-rhetorical answer would be a transcendental argument, i.e., reasoning to show that skepticism necessarily presupposes the existence of an external world and so self-destructs. For the record, I do not see how any such reasoning could succeed; my reasons are similar to those of Barry Stroud ('Transcendental Arguments', *Journal of Philosophy*, 65 (1968), 241–56) and Tony Brueckner (e.g., 'Transcendental Arguments I', *Noûs* 17 (1983), 551–75.

Aside from the Russellian and transcendental strategies, the sort of deeper response that some anti-Mooreans long for would have to proceed from some kind of 'first philosophy'; it would have to be the deliverance of some distinctive faculty higher and more authoritative than our ordinary perceptual and cognitive faculties. It would have to have both the vantage point and the power to critique those lower faculties and to show that, whatever their everyday usefulness, they cannot show us the world of what is really and ultimately true as opposed to merely plausible or convenient to believe. But (news

Barry Stroud is a leading example of those who complain that Moore's strategy is a non-starter: 'In the [philosophical] . . . context [Moore's claims] are simply dogmatic and without probative force.'[33] As we have seen, some of Moore's claims are indeed without probative force. But Stroud's contention goes well wide of the present interpretation. It simply does not address Moore's plausibility comparison, once we realize that the ordinary knowledge-claim is one term of the comparison. To respond—at all, much less adequately—Stroud would have to produce the relevant skeptical argument, consider its premises, and ask in each case whether the premise is really more plausible than that he knows he has hands. He has not done that.[34]

The second shallow objection was the complaint about privileging common sense. But nowhere in the present argument has Moore used the expression 'common sense' (much less capitalized it, as in 'Hume's Theory Examined'). He does not call attention to any particular class of propositions under that heading, much less propose that 'common-sense' propositions have any particular good-making property, much less invest them with a 'right of ancient possession' or give them any other epistemic blessing. There is no privileging of a special type of proposition. Nor, a fortiori, is there any premise about either commonsensical propositions or philosophical propositions. There is only piecemeal credibility comparison. On this interpretation, it is not that 'I have hands', 'This is a pencil', etc. are known in virtue of their being common-sense propositions; it is only that the relevant knowledge-claims themselves are more plausible than are the premises of any philosophical argument intended to show that they are false.[35]

flash) there is no such faculty. The most powerful probative tool we have is the deductively valid argument, and even a deductively valid argument is at best a comparison of plausibility.

[33] *The Significance of Philosophical Scepticism*, 279.

[34] He does elaborate a skeptical argument, a version of the Dream argument. And his version has a *highly* contentious premise: that 'if somebody knows something, *p*, he must know the falsity of all those things incompatible with his knowing that *p* (or perhaps all those things he knows to be incompatible with his knowing that *p*)', (*The Significance of Philosophical Scepticism*, 29–30; notice that that condition requires second-order knowing). But he gives no hint as to why we should accept that abstract and arbitrarily demanding principle to the exclusion of 'I know that I have hands.'

Stroud demands a truly philosophical rather than merely practical or comparative reply to the skeptic. But see the concluding paragraph of n. 32 above, and for an extensive and detailed Moorean reply to Stroud, see my 'Moore Against the New Skeptics'.

[35] A related complaint, made by Peter Unger ('An Argument for Skepticism', *Philosophical Exchange*, 1 (1974), 131–55), is that Moore is being dogmatic, insisting on holding common-sense beliefs come what may. But Moore is doing no such thing. In particular, he does not contend that common sense is impervious to scientific discovery. (See, e.g., 'What Is Philosophy?', in *Some Main Problems*.) He certainly does not deny that everyday beliefs held with great confidence have sometimes proved to be mistaken. On my interpretation, his claim is only that at any given time, some of my knowledge claims will be more plausible, and rationally more credible, than are the purely philosophical premise(s) of any skeptical argument.

Actually there is only one further objection I made to the earlier arguments, that was not a version either of the question-begging charge or of the privileging charge: I complained against 'Hume's Theory Examined' that Moore could not fairly claim to know that he knows the pencil to exist. That is moot; the claim is not made here.

VI Moore's own reservations

Moore himself expressed two reservations about the argument as presently interpreted. One follows immediately after the crucial passage from 'Four Forms of Skepticism' (in fact, the ellipsis dots at the end of my quotation were not innocent). He adds a further sentence, the concluding sentence of the article: 'And how on earth is it to be decided which of the two things it is *rational* to be most certain of?'

I suppose he was thinking that, if pressed, he would not yet be able to defend his comparative claim. A defense might require some *criterion of* 'rationality', credibility, or comparative certainty. But it is important to note that no such particular criterion is, or need be, invoked; (i) beats Bradley's (ii) by any reasonable standard whatever. Although the epistemology of such judgments is both important and controversial, it is a meta-issue in the present context. Actual, real-life plausibility comparisons do not wait upon epistemology. That some people sometimes take long walks is more credible than that most people often walk 3 miles in a day, or that more people walk to work than take any other form of transportation, or that there is no life anywhere else in our galaxy, or that the cause of an idea must have at least as much formal reality as the idea itself has objective reality. No one has to have any particular *epistemological theory* in order to be entirely justified in preferring one claim to another,[36] any more than I have to have a particular philosophical theory of meaning in order to understand what someone has just said. To make his anti-skeptical point, Moore need not defend his comparative judgment.

The second reservation is expressed in Moore's reply to critics in his Schilpp volume:[37]

In the case of the proposition 'Nobody knows that there are any material things' it does seem to me more obvious that some further argument is called for, if one is to talk of having *proved* it to be false, than in the case of 'There are no material things;' and this difference is, I think, connected with the fact that an immensely greater number of philosophers have held that *nobody knows*, than have held that *there are none.*

[36] Of course, it would be a good thing if one does have such a theory. I have one: *Judgement and Justification* (Cambridge University Press, 1988), chs. 7 and 8.

[37] 'A Reply to My Critics', in P. A. Schilpp (ed.), *The Philosophy of G. E. Moore* (LaSalle, Ill.: Open Court Publishing, 1942), 669.

On the present interpretation, Moore has assimilated 'I know that I have hands' to 'I have hands'. It is hardly obvious that the plausibility of 'I know that I have hands' is nearly as great as that of the logically weaker 'I have hands', especially since the skeptic contests all empirical knowledge-claims. The logical point alone shows that, even among what Moore considers the most plausible propositions, some are decidedly more secure than others. But, as before, Moore is not isolating a particular class of propositions that are supposed to share a special sort of security. His credibility comparisons are always and everywhere piecemeal. It matters not whether 'I know that I have hands' is necessarily less plausible than 'I have hands'; all that matters is whether 'I know that I have hands' is more plausible than at least one premise of the argument put forward to refute it.

I believe that, as here interpreted, Moore's anti-skeptical move succeeds.[38] I wish that he had seen more clearly what he had had hold of from the first, and not given so many other distractingly bad arguments.[39]

[38] See again 'Moore Against the New Skeptics'.

[39] Thanks to Ram Neta for helpful discussion and comments on an earlier draft, and to each of two anonymous referees of the present volume.

5

Moore's Common Sense

C. A. J. Coady

G. E. Moore made many important contributions to philosophy, but it is fair to say that his views on common sense are what most come to mind when his name is mentioned today. Many philosophers reject the views out of hand; others admire them; and many, perhaps most, are puzzled by them. My aim is to evaluate them and their significance for the practice of philosophy.

Moore was not the first philosopher to appeal to common sense, so it is remarkable that there is no reference to his predecessors, such as Thomas Reid and Charles Sanders Peirce, in any of Moore's writings explicitly defending common sense. Moore knew of Reid, as is clear in the early paper 'The Nature and Reality of Objects of Perception' (1905), where Moore queries whether Reid's analysis of perception is compatible with his belief that we do, in some sense, observe the thoughts and feelings of others.[1] Moore suggests that this analysis conflicts with Reid's commitment to common sense. Yet he never explores differences and similarities between his and Reid's views on this matter.[2] I shall say something about this later, but for now I want to note one similarity, namely, that both Moore and Reid stand opposed to a certain picture of the philosopher's role.

That picture has appealed to many students beginning philosophy and inspired many philosophers in their work. It is the picture of the philosopher as a radical exposer of delusions and confusions in the plain thoughts of ordinary people and as

---

[1] G. E. Moore, 'The Nature and Reality of Objects of Perception', in G. E. Moore *Philosophical Studies* (London: Routledge & Kegan Paul, 1922), 57.

[2] I have no space to explore the possible roots of Moore's silence, though it is an interesting question of philosophical biography.

provider of radically different ways of thinking of the world. Subjectivists and cultural relativists about morality, epistemological sceptics, and revisionary metaphysicians all seem cheerfully to cut against the grain of what ordinary folk think and daily act upon. Moore and Reid believe that there is a kind of arrogance and, more importantly, a certain absurdity in the stance of the radical philosophers with respect to some of these views. There have, of course, been many widely held popular delusions and confusions, some dangerous, others harmless follies; critique and exposure of these must always be an intellectual duty, for philosophers and for others sometimes better placed. This is why the delineation of what Moore and Reid are defending is so important and often so elusive. Neither Moore nor Reid want to canonize all popular beliefs, nor to endorse the extraordinary conservatism that seems inherent in Wittgenstein's remarkable dictum: 'Philosophy leaves everything in its place'. Yet they stand opposed to anything like the view of philosophy as a 'project of pure inquiry' (to borrow a phrase from Bernard Williams) which could build up a world view from scratch in total defiance of, or at least lack of primary respect for, the most basic common convictions by which ordinary folk make their way around the world, and have done so for centuries. So Descartes planned to 'make a clean sweep, in all seriousness and with full freedom, of all my opinions.'[3] He hopes to restore many basic beliefs of common sense after the 'clean sweep', but he allows them no intellectual standing in the first place. Of course, in stressing Moore's and Reid's rejection of this approach, I am only so far sketching an attitude, not defending it, but it is important to emphasize this distinctive stance at the beginning.

I The strategic significance of common sense appeals

There is something strategic about Moore's appeal to common sense that needs elaboration. By 'strategic' I mean the importance of his defence for our understanding of the *point* of philosophical arguments and theories. Moore was clearly aware that his defence had such a point, and this emerges in what seems to be his earliest explicit resort to common sense in chapter 1 of his book *Some Main Problems of Philosophy* under the heading 'What is Philosophy?' In this chapter, Moore gives an ambitious account of the scope of philosophy, but mixes this with a prominent role for common-sense knowledge. One way of elucidating the strategic significance of this role is to confront the suggestion that some sceptical argument has shown that we do not know extremely salient facts, such as the fact that human beings have heads, or

[3] René Descartes, *Meditations on First Philosophy, (First Meditation)* in *Descartes:* Philosophical *Writings*, ed. and trans. Elizabeth Anscombe and Peter Thomas Geach (London: Thomas Nelson and Sons, 1954), 61.

that generations have preceded us. Anyone who seriously held that such facts are unknown would be holding something absurd; as Moore himself puts it: '... to speak with contempt of those "Common Sense beliefs" which I have mentioned is quite certainly the height of absurdity.'[4] Indeed, serious commitment to denying such beliefs would demonstrate insanity. But perhaps the sceptic is undeterred. How do we know that we are not insane? How does he know that he is not insane? People could, of course, be in the unfortunate situation of wondering whether they might be insane, but sceptical philosophers typically display none of the anxieties of such unfortunates.

Moore's strategy should be seen as insisting that we ought to be more puzzled by the ease with which philosophers court absurdity and insanity. These predicates are among those that most philosophers do not use readily except sometimes, with the term absurdity, in dismissing their opponents by way of reductio. Even there, the opponents often nullify the objection by embracing the absurdity, leaving their critic with nothing to say. No sceptical philosopher will profess or act upon her scepticism when she is dealing with normal folk. Is this just an appropriate caution in transactions with the unwashed? Is this what prevents a sceptical philosopher from saying to the surgeon who is to operate on her: 'You are about to operate on my brain, but remember that there is no good reason to believe that I have a brain, or even a head.' Perhaps, but more likely our sceptical philosopher knows that any such comment (intended seriously) would be literally mad.

At this point, it is likely that what might be called the Humean manœuvre will be invoked. The sceptical conclusion is legitimate and rational but is only possible in the study, or, as Hume has it, in the 'chamber or in a solitary walk by a river side';[5] for the outside world of commerce, love, friendship, work, and gardening such a belief is indeed preposterous, and nature forces us out of it. There are different standards in the solitary quiet of the philosopher's study. But how could there be different standards in the study or in a solitary walk by the riverside? Are these not part of reality? Not 'in the world'? Or are they havens for temporary lunacy? These reactions may seem rather crude and unsympathetic. Are there not subtle and intriguing arguments in the study that may seem out of place elsewhere but have a force and fascination for the solitary philosopher? There are indeed complex and fascinating arguments, but the question concerns not their complexity, subtlety, and fascination, but the real force, conviction, and meaning to be attached to their conclusions. It is surely bad faith to profess knowledge and belief (or the lack of them) that cannot be exhibited

---

[4] G. E. Moore, 'A Defence of Common Sense', in G. E. Moore, *Philosophical Papers* (London: George Allen and Unwin Ltd., 1959), 45.

[5] David Hume, *A Treatise of Human Nature*, Vol. I, Part IV, Section VII, intro. (London: A. D. Lindsay, J. M. Dent & Sons, 1911), 257.

and acted upon in our daily lives—and what other lives do we have? There is a sort of dishonesty in the harbouring of 'beliefs' that apparently concern everyday matters but that you cannot relate to those matters. Of course, there may be difficulties in relating complex theoretical conclusions to the everyday language and convictions of lay people. Some of the findings of contemporary theoretical physics are bizarre enough to challenge our capacities to translate them into the vocabulary of everyday. None the less, there is a cottage industry hoping to explain such curiosities and their relevance to the world at large. How can normal people appreciate similarly the claim that they do not know, or are not entitled to believe, that they have heads or a past?

The attempted bifurcation of study and reality has unrealized implications for the products of the study. As Moore points out, the sceptical philosophers' claim to be agnostic about the existence of the very audience that they address and strive so rigorously to divest of the deepest convictions is just one of the bizarre oddities of their position. Moore thinks it makes their position self-contradictory. As he says of the sceptical philosophers who deny that propositions about other minds and physical objects can be known for certain: 'They seem to me constantly to betray the fact that they regard the proposition that those beliefs *are* beliefs of Common Sense, or the proposition that they themselves are not the only members of the human race, as not merely true, but *certainly* true; and *certainly* true it cannot be, unless one member, at least, of the human race, namely themselves, has *known* the very things which that member is declaring that no human being has ever known.'[6] Perhaps the theorists in question can ingeniously respond that they do not really mean to be committed in any way to knowing that they seek to persuade an existing audience having definite beliefs, but only that if there *were* an audience with the common-sense beliefs, the members of it should consider that they could not know that any other members of it existed (including those who present them with the arguments). But could this really be seriously propounded, as opposed to being contrived to avoid incoherence? A similar response to a related problem could be envisaged. It is, for example, palpably problematic that the sceptical philosopher expresses his doubts and critical arguments in a language that requires visible or audible signs that have quite specific, stable meanings. It seems obvious enough—indeed part of common sense, though not remarked by Moore—that these are shared public meanings in the relevant language. If the sceptical doubt is supposed to reach to these facts, it is very hard to see what the sceptical claim can amount to, for a quite definite meaning much be attached to the sceptical philosopher's utterances if they are to bother us at all. The sceptic might reply that he doesn't know whether his thoughts are expressed in a public language or private language or whatever, he only knows that he has these thoughts and they contain the problematic he possibly expresses for possible others

---

[6] Moore, 'A Defence of Common Sense', 43.

in a possible public language. He might say that he is certain of the meaning of his sentences to him but that their being embodied in a public 'external' world of sounds and marks is quite uncertain. Can any philosophy which is so unserious be taken seriously?

At the very least, this strategic significance, as I have called it, of Moore's stance calls upon the sceptic to elucidate the real import of her scepticism. Moore's challenge should make it clear that the sceptic cannot be asserting a plain truth about our knowledge or belief. There are, of course, plenty of plain truths or falsehoods that philosophers do speak, or aim to speak. Political philosophers who defend or explore democracy or human rights or pacifism do so in the hope of showing something important for real life about democracy or human rights or war. As do logicians who devise logics that may be useful for better expressing some of the puzzling claims of theoretical physics. But the sceptic's claims, and the claims of many revisionist metaphysicians who are not outright sceptics, do not have this character. Just what character they do have and what Moore thinks of it, is an important question that I shall explore later.

II Two common reactions

Moore's dogged commitment to the validity of the plain facts he adduces commonly produces a sort of bafflement in many other philosophers, not all of whom are sceptics. This is exhibited in two common reactions. One is to charge Moore with engaging in mere dogmatism, and the other is to allege that he is 'begging the question'. Let us consider these in turn. The two allegations are clearly related, but they have a different emphasis. The former is concerned with Moore's attitude rather than his argument, indeed it accuses him of rejecting argument in favour of mere confident assertion; the latter objects that Moore provides an argument but that it has a fatal flaw—the fallacy of begging the question. The accusation of dogmatism is often mere abuse: someone who is resistant to my persuasive arguments is stubbornly dogmatic in her unrelenting opinions where my firm attachment to arguments and conclusions is calm and rational. None the less, the allegation can sometimes express a real concern. Dogmatists, it is held, have an unyielding attitude that shows an unwarranted confidence in their own views and a disregard for arguments or reasons that count against them. In Moore's case, the philosophical sceptic produces arguments that purport to show that we have no knowledge of independent material things or of other minds, and Moore responds by giving examples of what he takes to be evidently instances of such knowledge. The sceptic argues that we can know nothing of the material world (even that there is a material world) and Moore holds up his two hands and says: 'Here is one hand and here is another'. Shocked by this dogmatism, the sceptic demands to know *how* Moore can know whether he has a hand, but Moore treats that as a further matter that cannot be allowed to intrude upon the palpable fact *that* he knows it. As he says: 'We are all, I think, in this strange position that we do *know* many things, with regard to which we *know* further that we must have had some evidence for them and yet we do not know *how* we know them, i.e., we do not know what the evidence was.'[7] This emphatic determination is partly what evokes the charge of mere dogmatism. Those who make this criticism think that one should approach philosophical inquiry with a completely open mind, an approach that is captured by Descartes' comments at the start of his Discourse, where he says in beginning his method of doubt: '. . . as to the opinions I had so far admitted to belief, I could not do better than to set about rejecting them bodily, so that later on I might admit to belief other, better opinions, or even the same ones, when once I had made them square with the norm of reason.'[8] Those who are not quite so pure as Descartes' imaginary inquirer, perhaps allow that one has some minimum baggage for the journey in the form of some a priori logical procedures, but Moore is convinced that one must start with more substantial convictions.

Moore's supposed dogmatism is also connected with the objection that his approach denies, or at least ignores, exciting speculative dimensions of philosophy and simply disregards the powerful arguments philosophers use to upset the dull world view of the common people. But the charge that Moore is not interested in his opponents' arguments does not, I think, survive close examination, though it is often made. Thomas Nagel, for instance, objects to Moore's appeal to common sense by saying: 'he has done nothing to dispute the sceptic's argument either for the possibility that there are no material objects or for the impossibility of any evidence against its truth'.[9] On the contrary, Moore spends a good deal of time analysing such arguments, as in his essay 'Four Forms of Scepticism' and in 'Certainty', where the structure of a sceptical argument from dreaming is painstakingly examined, and a careful and perceptive discussion of different types of possibility and their relations to contingency occurs. This issue of possibility and contingency is central to many sceptical arguments. So, the complaint that Moore's appeal to common sense is mere dogmatic counter-assertion cannot be quite right, and indeed Moore backs up his assertions with some supportive arguments, in particular the argument from greater certainty.

---

[7] Ibid., 44.

[8] René Descartes, *Discourse on the Method of Rightly Conducting one's Reason and of Seeking Truth in the Sciences*. in *Descartes: Philosophical Writings*, ed. and trans. Elizabeth Anscombe and Peter Thomas Geach (London: Thomas Nelson and Sons, 1954), 17.

[9] Thomas Nagel, *The Last Word* (Oxford: Oxford University Press,1997), 85.

III The greater certainty argument and the remaining scope of philosophy

This is really an amplification of the primary appeal to common sense rather than a quite different strategy, but it is none the less worth separate discussion. Moore's basic move is to challenge the idea that we could have anywhere near as much certainty about the philosophical arguments for scepticism and reductive metaphysics as we have about the common-sense beliefs they are meant to topple. One place where Moore appeals to the greater certainty argument is at the end of his paper 'Four Forms of Scepticism'. He has been discussing Russell's arguments for the conclusion that we do not know for certain all sorts of propositions that Moore would call propositions of common sense. After closely scrutinizing Russell's arguments and arguing that there are various defects in them, Moore concludes his discussion by pointing out 'no less than' four distinct assumptions that Russell makes in presenting the sceptical case: '(1) that I don't know any of these things immediately; (2) that they don't follow logically from any thing or any of the things that I do know immediately; (3) that, if (1) and (2) are true, my belief in and knowledge of them must be 'based on an analogical or inductive argument'; and (4) that what is so based cannot be *certain knowledge*.'[10] Moore then expounds what I am calling the argument from greater certainty as follows:

Is it in fact, as certain that all these four assumptions are true, as that I *do* know that this is a pencil and that you are conscious? I cannot help answering: It seems to me *more* certain that I *do* know that this is a pencil and that you are conscious, than that any single one of these four assumptions is true, let alone all four.[11]

Moore goes on to say that, in fact, he does regard (1)–(3) as true, but even so his certainty in knowing the common-sense propositions (here, 'this is a pencil' and 'you are conscious') is greater than his certainty in any one of the philosophical propositions. And he adds that he believes it is not as rational to be as certain of any one of the four propositions as of the proposition that he knows that there is pencil in front of him. He then ends with the question: 'And how on earth is it to be decided which of the two things it is *rational* to be most certain of?'[12] This final comment seems to weaken the greater certainty argument by allowing that it *may* not be rational to prefer the greater certainty to the lesser, but I think it is more consistent with Moore's outlook to treat this exasperated cry as expressing his dissatisfaction with the prospects for finding a decision procedure or criterion for determining rationality in such a situation. Here, as elsewhere, Moore stands by his conviction about what is more rational, while candidly admitting that he does not see how to provide some proof that it is the more rational course.

[10] G. E. Moore, 'Four Forms of Scepticism', in *Philosophical Papers*, 226.   [11] Ibid.   [12] Ibid.

As for the complaint that Moore merely dismisses the exciting and imaginative dimensions of philosophy, of which scepticism is supposedly one, the matter is more complex. The first thing to be said is that Moore's critique of scepticism as contrary to common sense is not *ipso facto* a critique of all speculative metaphysics. At one stage, at least, he believed that the 'most important and interesting thing that philosophers have tried to do' is 'to give a general description of the *whole* of the Universe'.[13] More fully, he describes the task as:

To give a general description of the whole of the universe, mentioning all the most important kinds of things which we know to be in it, considering how far it is likely that there are in it important kinds of things which we do not absolutely know to be in it, and also considering the most important ways in which these various kinds of things are related to one another.[14]

This seems to leave considerable room for discussion of metaphysics, since Moore does not rule out the possibility that philosophers may have many surprising truths to convey about our common world. His discussion of the reality of time, for instance, makes it clear that some powerful and surprising metaphysical conclusions need not fully conflict with common sense. He distinguishes at one point between two types of metaphysical claim about time: (1) the view that time is unreal in the sense that 'nothing whatever really exists or happens *in* Time';[15] and (2) that there is such a thing as Time and 'ever so many different things do exist in it' but that things existing in Time and 'even, perhaps, Time itself, are, in some sense, mere Appearances . . . of something else, which does not exist in Time at all . . . '.[16] The former view, he thinks, 'plainly and flatly' contradicts common sense and 'an enormous proportion of our ordinary beliefs'.[17] The latter view does not contradict these beliefs and we might therefore allow that it is not in conflict with common sense. It does not deny (at least according to Moore) that many things exist in time, but it asserts that there are other things that exist timelessly and that these other things (or Thing) stand in a special relationship, that of reality to appearance, with those that do exist in time. Moore, however, is uncertain whether the second view contradicts common sense or not; he seems to vacillate between saying that it contradicts common sense to a mild degree, and that it is uncertain whether it contradicts common sense at all. The problem seems to be that 'the notion of timeless existence is certainly a very difficult one to grasp'.[18] Eventually, he says that it is only the first view that he is going to treat as contradicting common sense, but the question raised by the second view is an interesting one with respect to the ambitions and scope of the appeal to common

---

[13] G. E. Moore, 'What is Philosophy', ch. 1 in his *Some Main Problems of Philosophy* (London: George Allen & Unwin, 1953), 1.

[14] Moore, 'What is Philosophy', 1.

[15] G. E. Moore, 'Is Time Real', Ch. XI in *Some Main Problems of Philosophy*, 201.   [16] Ibid.

[17] Ibid., 202.   [18] Ibid., 201.

sense. I shall turn to this question later, but it is surely clear from the above that Moore did not think that the appeal to common sense exhausted all that could be done in philosophy, indeed, a good deal of his own work, in ethics, for instance, and in perception, goes much further than this, though a respect for common sense is usually involved at some point.[19] He denied being committed to any one method in philosophy, saying: 'I started discussing certain kinds of question because they happened to be what interested me the most; and I only adopted certain particular methods (so far as I have adopted them) because they seemed to me suitable for those kinds of question. I had no preference for any method.'[20]

IV Begging the question?

This returns us to the issue raised earlier about the special character of philosophical questions and problems. But before turning to direct discussion of that, I want to examine the charge of question-begging. Earlier, I quoted an objection of Thomas Nagel's and it is worth giving Nagel's criticism in more detail since, in part, he seems to be articulating this sort of worry. Nagel says: 'When G. E. Moore rebuts scepticism about the external world on the ground that he has two hands, he *is* begging the question; because if there are no material objects, then he doesn't have two hands, and he has done nothing to dispute the sceptic's argument either for the possibility that there are no material objects or for the impossibility of any evidence against its truth. A non-question-begging refutation would have to resist the sceptic en route to his conclusion.'[21] There are two parts to Nagel's objection that he does not himself distinguish. I have already discussed the part alleging that Moore 'does nothing' to dispute the sceptic's arguments. The other part insists that Moore's argument is question-begging because Moore's premise that he has two hands would be false if the sceptic's conclusion that there are no material objects is true. But, of course, it is equally the case that the sceptic's conclusion must be false if Moore's premise is true. If we can be independently assured of the truth of Moore's premise, then Moore's procedure is no more question-begging than the sceptic's. There is room for debate about just what the term 'question-begging' means, but if it means that you will be

---

[19] A good deal of Moore's theorizing in ethics requires some effort to harmonize with common sense. His view that goodness is a simple non-natural property is one example, as is his support for consequentialism. In perception theory, his support for sense-data, and, at one stage, his sympathy for phenomenalism provide further examples.

[20] 'A Reply to My Critics', in *The Philosophy of G.E. Moore*, ed. Paul Arthur Schilpp (Evanston and Chicago: Northwestern University Press, 1942), 676.

[21] Nagel, *The Last Word*, 85.

begging the question if you use a premise that is inconsistent with your opponent's conclusion, then this poses a threat to the very strategy of counter-argument. If, however, it means that you cannot use a premise that relies upon or is derived from the mere denial of the opponent's conclusion, then Moore can plead that he does no such thing. He does not derive the proposition that he has two hands from some prior proposition that material objects exist, even if the former proposition entails or even presupposes the latter. Consider a debate between two people, Tom and Muriel, about a mutual friend, Lucy. Tom maintains that Lucy is in the university cafeteria because he saw her go in at 2 p.m. and he has been standing outside for 10 minutes and she hasn't come out the only door for entry or exit. Muriel denies that Lucy is in the cafeteria and gives as her argument the fact that she (Muriel) has just come from the library next door where she saw Lucy immersed in a book at 2 p.m. until Muriel left at 2:09 p.m. Granted that people cannot be in two places at once, Muriel's key premise that she saw Lucy in the library from 2 p.m. to 2:09 p.m. is clearly inconsistent with Tom's conclusion, but it is not derived from the falsity of that conclusion, and is in no way question-begging. She might indeed be interested in how Tom got things so wrong but, if she is convinced of her observations of Lucy (her eyesight is fine, she knows Lucy well, she spoke to her, the light was good, etc.), then she can be equally confident he is wrong whether she works out why he has gone wrong or not.[22] Of course, if Tom is right and Lucy has been in the cafeteria all along, then Muriel's conclusion and her premise are false. So, there is a sense in which her premise depends upon the falsity of Tom's conclusion, but it doesn't depend on it viciously since she doesn't use that falsity in her reasoning. Similarly, with Moore.

V Is Moore missing something?

We have seen that Moore allows that philosophical claims, even rather strange ones, need not conflict outright with common sense, but there may remain doubts about whether the blunt dismissal of those claims that do so conflict is missing something important. Where a philosophical position conflicts with plain facts known to all, should this not move us to see whether the philosopher is really up to something else? And here the problem with Moore's approach could be said to be that he ignores possible answers to this further question. This complaint, expressed that bluntly, would, however, be unfair. Moore does not ignore this further question: he addresses it through what he says about the *analysis* of the claims that the sceptical

---

[22] Noah Lemos argues for a similar refutation of the question-begging objection in his *Common Sense: A Contemporary Defense* (Cambridge: Cambridge University Press, 2004), 85–91.

or metaphysical philosophers seem to reject. Moore allows that, in addition to the plain meaning and truth of the common-sense claims, there is a further question as to their philosophical analysis. So, he says when discussing what he calls 'a point of a very different order', that he is himself 'very sceptical as to what, in certain respects, the correct *analysis* of such propositions is.'[23] He then refers to problems with the analysis of the proposition 'Material things have existed' (or 'Material things exist'), which he takes to require analysis of simpler propositions such as 'I am perceiving a human hand' and '*This* is a human hand'. Moore's distinction between meaning and truth, on the one hand, and analysis, on the other, has several important implications, many of them contentious. A primary one, however, is that it leaves room for an explanation of what is otherwise puzzling, namely, how highly intelligent and not conspicuously insane intellectuals could have come to assert so many thoroughly absurd propositions as those that Moore rejects in the name of common sense.

Moore's comments about 'analysis' seem at least to gesture in these directions, as do certain remarks he makes elsewhere about different meanings of expressions that are significant in the debate, most notably the word 'know'.[24] A philosopher who argues that time is unreal (in the fashion of McTaggart) can be refuted in a way by showing that taken 'plainly' the claim is in direct conflict with such palpable truths as that it has taken me longer than 5 minutes to write this paper, and that before I had lunch today I had breakfast. But such a refutation requires the metaphysician (and his interpreters) to clarify how his argument and conclusion are compatible with such truths, and many would think that this is where the real interest should lie. For McTaggart, much depends on what the word 'real' is to mean in his conclusion, and this is partly determined by his insistence that nothing can be real if asserting it leads to contradiction and the assertion of temporal propositions does precisely that, and also by the metaphysics that he develops as an account of what is real. There seem to be two opposed errors lurking here: one is to believe that your metaphysical or critical arguments could show the plain falsity of the Moorean propositions; the other is to believe that there is nothing further to be said and explored about the arguments and the appropriate conclusions, once their incompatibility with Moorean truths is revealed. Acknowledging the first error should lead philosophers to tailor their theoretical cloths to the realities they hope to explain. A theory of meaning that results in the conclusion that no natural language sentences mean anything is a defective theory of meaning. Similarly, a theory of knowledge that concludes that plain and palpable knowledge claims are all false seems to be equally defective. Even

---

[23] Moore, 'A Defence of Common Sense', 53.

[24] See, e.g., his paper 'Certainty', in G. E. Moore, *Philosophical Papers*, esp. his remarks on 'know' and 'possible', 236–7.

so, the second error should alert us to the possibility that such theories (either of meaning or knowledge) are telling us something different from plain falsehoods, for example, that certain commonly held thoughts about knowledge or meaning are more problematic than they seem at first blush, or even that they are false. Such thoughts might be that meanings are private mental items or that whatever is known must be believed on the basis of a proof or at least inferred from another proposition that is known.

I have already discussed what is involved in the first error, but, with regard to the second error, it is worth noting that Moore himself thinks that his appeal to common sense leaves untouched various philosophical positions apparently in conflict with common sense. In reply to a criticism by John Wisdom, for instance, Moore concedes that some advocates of phenomenalism do not intend to affirm that there are no human hands when they conclude: 'There are no material things'. He insists that some really do, but, of others, he allows that they are not refuted by the existence of human hands because their assertion 'there are no material things' is 'merely an assertion that a certain kind of analysis of such a proposition as "This is a human hand" is true; and it is obvious that from the truth of the assertion "This is a human hand" it cannot follow that this analysis is false.'[25] Elsewhere, Moore makes it clear that he does not think that common sense includes any beliefs at all about sense-data, so that phenomenalism as such is not necessarily in conflict with common sense.[26] As well as talking of different analyses, Moore here also talks of different meanings, usages, and uses. In his earlier crucial papers invoking common sense, he tended to distinguish analysis from meaning, though he is not always consistent in doing so. There is clearly room for further debate about the best way to put the point, and I do not want to suggest that such debate is unimportant, but the thrust of Moore's idea is clear enough, at least at one level. He wants sceptics and metaphysicians to see that their theories must be concerned with something other than denying the plain truths of common sense. This 'something other' refers to the special character of philosophical discourse; it may be the giving of 'a general description of the whole of the universe', or it may be something else again to do with the special character of analysis or whatever. We cannot settle that here, but it is clear enough that Moore's appeal to common sense leaves the question open to exploration.

One thing that analysis might involve in the case of sceptical propositions is the idea of knowledge itself. Wittgenstein, for instance, who was clearly impressed by Moore's appeal to common sense at one level (he is reported to have told Moore that his 'A

---

[25] Moore, 'A Reply to My Critics', 669–70.
[26] G. E. Moore, 'The Nature of Sensible Appearances', *Proceedings of the Aristotelian Society*, Supp. Vol. 6, (1926), 186–7.

Defence of Common Sense' was his best article),[27] but dissatisfied at another, spends some of his book *On Certainty* objecting to Moore's use of the word 'know'. The basic idea is that it would be a misuse of ordinary language to say that we knew the Moorean propositions. As Wittgenstein puts it: 'Now, can one enumerate what one knows (like Moore)? straight off like that, I believe not.—For otherwise the expression "I know" gets misused. And through this misuse a queer and extremely important mental state seems to be revealed.'[28] There is an echo here of Wittgenstein's comments on first-person knowledge claims about sensation in the *Philosophical Investigations*, where he says: 'It can't be said of me at all (except perhaps as a joke) that I *know* I am in pain.'[29] In the case of the Moorean common-sense claims, Wittgenstein does little to show in what the misuse consists. In the quoted passage the inappropriateness seems to be related to the revealing of 'a queer and extremely important mental state', and Wittgenstein stands opposed to the idea that knowledge involves a certain sort of inner illumination. Elsewhere, there is the suggestion that knowing requires the having of grounds that can be stated. So, in paragraph 18, Wittgenstein says: ' "I know" often means: I have the proper grounds for my statement. So if the other person is acquainted with the language-game, he would admit that I know. The other, if he is acquainted with the language-game, must be able to imagine *how* one may know something of the kind.'[30] Now it is true that it is hard to find ordinary conversational contexts where such utterances would be naturally made, but it is a big step from that to claim that they somehow cannot be understood. For reasons that have been presented forcefully by Grice and Searle, merely noting that 'we do not say' or 'it would be queer to say' certain things is insufficient to establish interesting philosophical objections to the meaning and, indeed, truth of utterances not normally made. Moore's sample utterances are all too obviously true in normal contexts to bear remarking. Hence, their oddity arises from the violation of conversational maxims (in Grice's terms) that flow from a Co-operative Principle and prohibit pointless remarks and not from violating the meanings of words such as 'know'.[31] It is, however, easy enough to eliminate the oddity by providing suitable

[27] This remark is cited by Anscombe and von Wright in their preface to Ludwig Wittgenstein, *On Certainty* (New York: Harper Torchbacks, Harper & Row, 1969), p. vi.

[28] Wittgenstein, *On Certainty*, para. 6.

[29] Wittgenstein, *Philosophical Investigations*, trans. G. E. M. Anscombe, 3rd edn. (Oxford: Basil Blackwell, 1976), para. 246.

[30] Norman Malcolm also claims that Moore's propositions are not the sort that could be known. He insists that 'know' is misused unless there is some doubt to remove or the possibility of a proof. His argument for this turns on what is supposed to follow from our finding Moore's utterances 'strange and outlandish'. See Norman Malcolm, 'Defending Common Sense', *The Philosophical Review*, 58/3 (1949), 201–20.

[31] See Paul Grice, *Studies in the Way of Words* (Cambridge, Mass.: Harvard University Press, 1989), esp. 3–40 for the relevance of conversational maxims; and J. R. Searle, *Speech Acts: An Essay in the Philosophy of*

contexts. Take the case of 'I know that I'm in pain'. When my wife was in labour with our first child, an officious nurse insisted that she couldn't be in pain, to which the remark Wittgenstein rejects was a perfect reply. This strongly suggests that any oddity in Moore's propositions is conversational rather than semantic. Surely, the better move for Wittgenstein is to grant the truth of the knowledge claim but then object to what further philosophical beliefs or 'pictures' the truth of the claims might, as asserted by Moore, suggest.

VI Some remarks on philosophical method

A further strategic significance of the Moorean appeal to common sense is that it helps to provide some anchorage for the sensible conduct and possible resolution, or at least advance, of philosophical debate. It has often been remarked as a notable virtue of analytic philosophy that it puts a refreshing premium upon clarity of presentation and the process of rigorous argument. It is also, however, a virtue of its procedures that they provide some prospect of restraining extravagant, untethered philosophical speculations and theories, and, hence, more opportunities for at least limited agreement in a discipline famous for the irresolvability of its problems. This virtue is partly related to the demand for clarity and respect for logical probity, but partly to the requirement that philosophical theories pay more heed to their relation to everyday fact and common understanding. In contemporary analytic philosophy, this latter requirement is signalled by the constant appeal to what is intuitive and, more emphatically, what is counter-intuitive, and the consequent proposed defeat by counter-example. No one takes this appeal to be decisive on every occasion, but it has a certain presumptive and restraining effect. It is still possible to argue, and argue ably, for theses that are surprising and even shocking, such as David Lewis's realist ontology of possible worlds, or Derek Parfit's account of the self and his critique of common-sense morality, but there is a debt to be discharged to concrete realities and common understanding. If this burden cannot be met, then the theory is to that degree unsatisfactory, and explanation of the failure is required. It is this aspect of analytic philosophy that other traditions often find surprising. To speak anecdotally, I have often encountered this surprise in the past from philosophers raised in 'the Continental' tradition, or in relatively enclosed philosophies like Thomism or Marxism. They were used to stating and elaborating a position and defending it perhaps in terms of its internal coherence, but not to its being confronted with

Language (Cambridge: Cambridge University Press, 1969), 141–56 for an alternative approach based on conditions for specific speech acts.

'counter-examples' drawn from what 'we' accept in ordinary life and experience.[32] This illustrates a difference in style of doing philosophy for which Moore's appeal to common sense can lay some claim of ancestry. Of course, the ancestry is more complex and ancient than the single example of Moore would allow; it takes in at least Reid, Mill, Sidgwick, and elements in the empiricist tradition, as well as Aristotle's insistence on the value of common opinion. None the less, Moore's example in this matter has been profound, even among philosophers who are not sympathetic to Moore's own idea of common sense.

This aspect of the methodology of analytical philosophy has, I believe, been on the whole beneficial, but it is not beyond criticism. For one thing, the testing of theories and theses by counter-example sometimes appears to have developed a life of its own, in which it can move far from reality and common sense. The construction of very complex and often fantastic examples and counter-examples has become a striking feature of some strands in analytic philosophy to the point where its power to illuminate and check theoretical extravagance is much diminished, even dissipated altogether. We can learn something about the structure of our concepts by testing their range against imaginary circumstances, but too much stretching into the fantastic can create a fog of incomprehension rather like that the analytic movement originally reacted against in its critique of idealism. It is often difficult to know of some exotic examples *what* description of them would be appropriate in terms of testing the relevant philosophical definition or theory. This trend seems itself an abuse of common sense.

It remains to say something all too briefly of Moore's relation to C. S. Peirce and to Thomas Reid. Reid clearly had some influence on Peirce, who was similarly critical of Descartes and Hume. Peirce is both an imaginative theorist and an emphatic champion of common sense which he links to instinct. So he dismisses Humes's sceptical arguments as 'exhibiting the intensely ridiculous way in which a man winds himself up in silly paper doubts if he undertakes to throw common sense, i.e., instinct, overboard and be perfectly rational.'[33] None the less, Peirce, respectful as he is of 'the old Scotch school', opts for a 'critical common-sensism' that aims at a blend of Reid, Kant, and his own insights, but gives a certain primacy to the potential for a critical attitude to all beliefs. By contrast, Moore's emphasis on the absolute

---

[32] A wry example of this opposition at work is J. L. Austin's confrontation with the French existentialist Gabriel Marcel. Marcel had been invited to read a paper in Oxford to the Philosophy Society attended by Oxford philosophy teachers and researchers. Austin's relentless attempts to give an everyday cash value to Marcel's ideas reduced him to a refusal to answer further questions. A version of this exchange is given by George Pitcher in 'Austin: A Personal Memoir', in Isaiah Berlin (*et al.*), *Essays on J. L. Austin* (Oxford: Oxford University Press, 1973), 27. My version derives from others who were present.

[33] C. S. Peirce, *Collected Papers*, ed. Charles Hartshorne and Paul Weiss (Cambridge, Mass.: Harvard University Press, 1974), Vol. 6, para. 500, *p.* 344.

certainty of specific common-sense propositions leaves no room for the idea that such propositions are revisable in the light of future experience or theory. Here Peirce *seems* more an ancestor of Quine than of Moore. Moore's greater certainty argument counts against the revisability of the common-sense examples he gives. Neurath's famous analogy of the ship needing repair at sea which cannot be abandoned wholesale without disaster, but may have *any* plank removed and replaced, is inconsistent with Moore's position, though clearly consonant with Quine's holism, and possibly with Peirce's fallibilism. To continue the metaphor, Moore would have insisted that the planks directly and solidly in contact with the water were too indispensable to be abandoned on behalf of any future reconstruction with less solid planks from the upper part of the boat.[34]

As for Reid, the most striking contrast is that he is interested in first principles of common sense in a way that Moore does not address. Reid seems to think both that particular convictions of common sense are known with certainty since common sense is judgement concerned with what is evident, and that common sense also delivers abstract 'first principles' that are indubitable, and in some way ground the particular convictions. He is more interested in an architectonic of knowledge than was Moore, and his first principles vary in their degree of generality, ranging from ' . . . the natural faculties, by which we distinguish truth from error, are not fallacious' to ' . . . certain features of the countenance, sounds of the voice, and gestures of the body, indicate certain thoughts and dispositions of mind'. Reid faces problems to do with the relation between evident particular truths and evident first principles related to them that are reminiscent of Moore's occasional vacillation between holding that his common-sense propositions need no proof, and that they have a proof but he is not in a position to say what it is though their certainty is not affected by this.

VII Two final issues

Finally, there are two issues that need brief attention here, though they merit fuller exploration elsewhere. The first is that neither Moore nor I have provided anything approximating a definition of common sense. Moore is content to list beliefs or propositions that he regards as palpable candidates falling under the heading. His list

---

[34] Peirce's position is, however, complex and subtle. His endorsement of common sense is emphatic and in some tension with his commitment to critical revision. He says that the decisions of common sense do not attain infallibility, but then adds that if the 'substance' of common sense 'is in harmony with individual good judgement from general experience, then the authority of common sense as to the practical truth of the conclusion (subject to minute modification) is so weighty that special experience can hardly attain sufficient strength to overthrow it.' (see *Collected Papers*, Vol. 6, para. 574, *p.* 383).

at the beginning of 'A Defence of Common Sense' is both extensive and somewhat motley, and it is not clear that he regards all of them as equally certain. They contain statements maintaining the existence of certain things and states of affairs, and also statements claiming knowledge of such matters. Moore, it seems to me, treats both these types of proposition as equally certain, though he later says in a response to critics that they are differently related to the idea of proof, at least with respect to the idea of an external world. From the existence of his hands, he can, he believes, prove the existence of the external world, but he thinks that his knowledge that his hands exist only provides 'a good argument' and not a proof that he *knows* that the external world exists.[35]

The idea seems to be that the holding up of his two hands provides a proof of the following kind:

> Here is one hand, and here is another hand,
> Therefore, at least two human hands exist
> If a human hand exists, the external world exists
> Therefore, the external world exists.

In fact, in his 'Proof of an External World', Moore presents the Proof as only the first two lines above, but he has earlier analysed the concept of an external world in such a way that the third proposition is true, so he takes the move from line 3 to 4 to be already conceded. (It remains something of a puzzle why Moore thinks he needs to show the existence of two hands when surely one would do. Perhaps the thought lingers in the background that a world must have some plurality!) Yet if this is 'a Proof', and if, as Moore says, it will only be a Proof if he knows the premise in line 1, and he insists that he does, then it seems odd that he has not proved what he elsewhere claims to know, namely, that he *knows* that there is an external world. He is not worried about possible problems of opaque contexts, since he thinks this a good argument, and elsewhere relies upon such arguments, but gives as an objection to claiming a Proof that, with regard to material things, 'an immensely greater number of philosophers have held that *nobody knows,* than have held that *there are none*'.[36] But if Moore is right that hands and so on are just the sort of things that constitute an external world or must count as material things, it cannot matter what the numbers are in the philosophical headcount. That headcount might make one think that there is disagreement at the level of 'meaning in the sense of analysis' of the term 'know', but this is another matter.

A second point is that, absent a definition of common sense, any commitment to the power of common beliefs or natural instinct (in Peirce's phrase) faces the difficulty that,

---

[35] See Moore's 'A Reply to My Critics', 668–9. Moore somewhat recasts his 'Proof' in this Reply and talks of proving that 'there is at least one material thing' rather than 'an external world' but it seems clear that he means much the same manoeuvre to much the same conclusion.

[36] Ibid., 669.

over time, there have been remarkable shifts in common beliefs, and that much work in psychology has shown, or purported to show, that we are prone to quite fundamental mistakes of thinking in our ordinary lives.[37] In a somewhat similar spirit, Paul Grice objects to Moore's practice by saying that it is merely appealing to the obvious and 'the conception of the obvious is not in any appropriate sense an objective conception'.[38] Grice claims that something cannot be obvious unless all concerned agree that it is. But, apart from the fact that no claim can be guaranteed against merely obdurate rejection, Moore's examples challenge his audience precisely because the plain denial of their obviousness is beyond serious comprehension. Doubts about the definition and scope of common sense certainly indicate a need for some circumspection in appealing to common beliefs, and it is important to recognize that Moore's common sense is narrower than what is sometimes meant by the term. This is shown by Moore's comment 'for all I know there may be many propositions which may properly be called features in "the Common Sense view of the world" or "Common Sense belief" which are not true, and which deserve to be mentioned with the contempt with which some philosophers speak of "Common Sense beliefs." '[39] Even so, Moore insists that 'the Common Sense view of the world is, in certain fundamental features, *wholly* true'.[40] It is these fundamental features that are exhibited in Moore's examples. Widespread errors in popular belief do nothing to impugn the hard core of common sense that Moore, Peirce, and Reid are primarily concerned with. The absurdity of psychologists 'proving' that we are all of us mistaken in believing that we each have a head or that Germany was defeated in the Second World War is manifest. In the nature of the case, Moore's central appeals to common sense are safe from such rebuttals.

References

Descartes, Rene, *Discourse on the Method of rightly conducting one's Reason and of seeking Truth in the Sciences*, in *Descartes: Philosophical Writings*, ed. and trans. by Elizabeth Anscombe and Peter Thomas Geach (London: Thomas Nelson and Sons, 1954).
_____ *Meditations on First Philosophy (First Meditation)* in *Descartes: Philosophical Writings*, ed. and trans. by Elizabeth Anscombe and Peter Thomas Geach (London: Thomas Nelson and Sons, 1954).
Gilovich, Thomas, *How We Know What Isn't So: The Fallibility of Human Reason in Everyday Life* (New York: The Free Press, 1991).

[37] A good deal of this work is summarized in Thomas Gilovich, *How We Know What Isn't So: The Fallibility of Human Reason in Everyday Life* (New York: The Free Press, 1991).

[38] Grice, *Studies in the Way of Words*, 145.

[39] Moore, 'A Defence of Common Sense', 45. Likewise, in *Some Main Problems of Philosophy*, 3, Moore considers some cases in which 'the views of Common Sense have changed.'

[40] Moore, 'A Defence of Common Sense', 44.

Grice, Paul, *Studies in the Way of Words* (Cambridge, Mass.: Harvard University Press, 1989).

Hume, David, *A Treatise of Human Nature* (London: A. D. Lindsay J. M. Dent & Sons, 1911).

Lemos, Noah, *Common Sense: A Contemporary Defense* (Cambridge: Cambridge University Press, 2004).

Malcolm, Norman, 'Defending Common Sense', *The Philosophical Review*, 58/3 (1949), 201–20.

Moore, G. E., 'A Defence of Common Sense', in G. E. Moore, *Philosophical Papers* (London: George Allen and Unwin, 1959).

—— 'A Reply to My Critics', in Paul Arthur Schilpp (ed.), *The Philosophy of G.E. Moore* (Evanston and Chicago: Northwestern University Press, 1942).

—— 'Certainty', in *Philosophical Papers* (London: George Allen and Unwin, 1959).

—— 'Four Forms of Scepticism', in *Philosophical Papers* (London: George Allen and Unwin, 1959).

—— 'Is Time Real', in *Some Main Problems of Philosophy* (London: George Allen & Unwin, 1953).

—— *Some Main Problems of Philosophy* (London: George Allen & Unwin, 1953).

—— 'The Nature and Reality of Objects of Perception', in G. E. Moore *Philosophical Studies* (London: Routledge & Kegan Paul, 1922).

—— 'The Nature of Sensible Appearances', *Proceedings of the Aristotelian Society*, supp. vol. 6, (1926).

—— 'What is Philosophy', in *Some Main Problems of Philosophy* (London: George Allen & Unwin, 1953).

Nagel, Thomas, *The Last Word* (Oxford: Oxford University Press, 1997).

Peirce, C. S., *Collected Papers*, ed. by Charles Hartshorne and Paul Weiss (Cambridge, Mass.: Harvard University Press, 1974).

Pitcher, George, 'Austin: A Personal Memoir', in Isaiah Berlin *et al.* (eds.), *Essays on J. L. Austin* (Oxford: Oxford University Press, 1973).

Searle, J. R., *Speech Acts: An Essay in the Philosophy of Language* (Cambridge: Cambridge University Press, 1969).

Wittgenstein, Ludwig, *On Certainty* (New York: Harper Torchbacks, Harper and Row, 1969).

—— *Philosophical Investigations*, trans. by G. E. M. Anscombe, 3rd edn. (Oxford: Basil Blackwell, 1976).

6

G. E. Moore on Sense-data and Perception

Paul Snowdon

In 1958, the year of Moore's death, Professor A. R. White published his book *G. E. Moore: A Critical Exposition*.[1] White's study, though now, presumably, rarely read, is extremely acute and based on a close reading of Moore's work as he knew it. In it White says: 'There are three main topics dealt with in Moore's writings, namely, philosophical method, ethics, and perception.'[2] As a general description, the only reservation that can be felt about this remark is that it would be more accurate to add epistemology as a fourth main topic. Moore obviously grappled in a variety of ways with the problems raised by scepticism. Now, it might be that White included epistemology under the title of 'perception', and it is, indeed, not uncommon to think of the name 'philosophy of perception' as covering epistemology. But another, and I think more likely, possibility is that White underestimated Moore's epistemological concerns, perhaps because when White was writing a number of Moore's essays on the subject were not widely known (or, at least, not known to White).[3] However, what is undoubtedly correct in what White says is that perception is one of the topics about which Moore both thought, and wrote, a great deal. His last published work in 1958 was entitled 'Visual Sense-data', and it is obvious that Moore was, at that stage,

---

[1] A. R. White (1958) *G. E. Moore: A Critical Exposition* (Oxford: Blackwell). [2] Ibid., 1.

[3] White hardly mentions Moore's 'proof of the external world', and does not cite the group of articles on epistemology that were published in Moore's *Philosophical Papers*, itself published in 1959. Presumably, White was writing his book before they came to his attention. Significantly, White's list corresponds to the three categories into which Moore himself grouped his Replies in the Schilpp volume.

as fully engaged with problems raised by perception as he had been in such an early publication as 'The Nature and Reality of Objects of Perception', published fifty-three years earlier, and also as he was in the lectures he delivered in 1910 (published later under the title *Some Main Problems of Philosophy*.)

It would be misleading to describe Moore as simply interested throughout his life in the nature of perception. Rather, he repeatedly engages, with his characteristic intensity of focus and single-mindedness, with just a small cluster of problems. More or less every time he writes about perception Moore asks the same questions, scrutinizes the same arguments and examples, and embeds his discussion within the same set of assumptions. In fact, I think that it is no exaggeration to say that Moore's obsession with perception is really an obsession with two questions, the second of which has the rather special status of being a hard question only if the first one is answered a certain way. The first question, leaving out certain elements that Moore regards as crucial, is: what is the relation between sense-data present in our experience when we perceive our environment and the perceived physical objects? Moore's view is that in all perceptual experiences, e.g., seeing an ink-pot or hearing a piano, the subject directly perceives, or apprehends, a sense-datum. The question that concerns Moore is: how does the sense-datum involved in the experience relate to the physical object perceived? Moore, like many philosophers, thought most about visual experience, and in relation to the visual case Moore poses this question in the following distinctive way: what is the relation between the sense-datum and the *surface* of the object that is seen? The second general issue is: what is the correct analysis of what Moore calls 'judgements of perception'?[4] They are, roughly, judgements such as 'That is an ink-pot', in which a perceived object is described as being of a certain kind. Moore's view is that if the sense-datum involved in the (visual) experience can be counted as identical to the surface of physical objects then the analysis of such judgements is not difficult to give, but if it is not then the analysis is very difficult to give. In fact, Moore's main point about the analysis of such judgements, granting the assumption that makes the question difficult, is that it is so difficult that no satisfactory full analysis has been given! It is, therefore, really only the first question about perception that is the one Moore agonized about his entire philosophical life.

I have tried to capture the questions to which Moore repeatedly returns. From our perspective, two questions stand out as demanding a more extensive treatment than Moore provides in relation to the theory he develops. First, Moore says remarkably little as to the *nature* of that relation, which he calls 'apprehending', in which we

---

[4] I have chosen to formulate the second question along the lines that Moore adopted in 'Some Judgements of Perception', see 228. At other times, he puts what is, in effect, the same question in the words: what is the analysis of 'S sees (e.g.) an ink-pot'?

stand, according to him, to sense-data. What is it? How does it *work?*[5] Second, Moore does not explain how an occurrence which is the apprehending of a sense-datum (as conceived by him) can be the core element in something that ultimately amounts to the gaining of knowledge of our *environment.* How exactly does it fit into this broader occurrence? Moore does not explain how the apprehending of a sense-datum can yield an experience with the right character to generate the right epistemological consequences.

Whenever Moore discusses the central question that I have identified, he standardly expresses considerable uncertainty about the answer he is at that time inclined to give. Here are two typical passages by Moore, expressing his uncertainties about the matter. The first is from 'The Status of Sense-data', published in 1913–14: 'I now pass to the question how sensibles [i.e., sense-data] are related to physical objects. And here I want to say, to begin with, that I feel extremely puzzled about the whole subject. I find it extremely difficult to distinguish clearly from one another the different considerations which ought to be distinguished; and all I can do is to raise, more or less vaguely, certain questions as to how certain particular sensibles are related to certain particular physical objects, and to give the reasons which seem to me to have most weight for answering these questions in one way rather than another. I feel that all that I can say is tentative.'[6]

Here, again, is Moore, in 1925, expressing a similar uncertainty in 'A Defence of Common Sense': 'Am I, in this case, really knowing about the sense-datum in question that it itself is part of the surface of a human hand? Or, just as we found in the case of "This is a human hand", that what I was knowing about the sense-datum was certainly not that it *itself* was a human hand, so, is it perhaps the case, with this new proposition, that even here I am not knowing, with regard to the sense-datum, that it is *itself* part of the surface of a hand? And, if so, what is it that I am knowing about

---

[5] There is, it seems to me, a gap at this point in Moore's account, but perhaps a number of things need saying to soften somewhat the rather blunt nature of that complaint. (1) Moore does not fail to fill out what the relation of apprehending is more conspicuously than anyone else. In this failure, he simply resembles other philosophers. (2) It should also be pointed out that he does try to get clear about various aspects of nature of the relation. Thus, in section I of 'The Status of Sense-data', Moore distinguishes what he there calls 'direct apprehension' from that link a subject has to something when he or she remembers it, and he also agonizes about its relation to attention. (3) Further, in the 'Refutation of Idealism' (24), although his language there is different, he can be taken to be saying that apprehending is itself what he calls a transparent element, that is one not manifest to the subject (or at best manifest only with the greatest difficulty), and that it can be thought of as a form of awareness or knowing. In so far as he offers a cognitive analysis, Moore is endorsing what Sellars, in Part I of *Empiricism and the Philosophy of Mind,* called 'the mongrel classical concept of a sense datum'. This would open up Moore's account to the difficulties that Sellars brings out in that conception, as well as, of course, to others. It is not, though, clear whether Moore stuck by such a cognitive approach after that.

[6] G. E. Moore (1913–14), 'The Status of Sense-data', in *Philosophical Studies,* 185.

the sense-datum itself? This is the question to which it seems to me, no philosopher has hitherto suggested an answer which comes anywhere near to being certainly true. There seems to me to be three, and only three, alternative types of answer possible; and to any answer yet suggested, of any of these types, there seems to me to be very grave objections'.[7]

In his last article, 'Visual Sense-data' Moore finally, with a fair degree of confidence, declares that visual sense-data are *not* identical to the surfaces of objects. He says: 'But I have to own that I now think that I was mistaken in supposing that, in the case of 'seeing' an opaque object, where in seeing it you are seeing only one visual sense-datum, the sense datum can possibly be identical with that part of the opaque object's surface you are seeing. I now think that it cannot possibly be identical with that part of the object's surface . . . '.[8] This quotation reveals the final unequivocal re-emergence in Moore's thinking of some sort of confidence as to what to say about his main question, a confidence that he had lost officially towards the end of 'Some Judgements of Perception' (in 1918/19). Moore's confidence in how to answer the first and basic question means, of course, that he has no confidence in how to answer his second once. This passage also illustrates the point, already made, that Moore's discussions over a long period focused on precisely the same question.

I Moore's Framework

As I have said, Moore's reflections on perception (like those of most philosophers) mainly concerned vision. For that case Moore's main question can be put, perhaps with a degree of looseness that Moore would not have liked, in these words; when an object (of, perhaps the opaque kind) is seen by a subject, what is the relation between the sense-datum involved in the subject's visual experience and the seen surface of the seen object?

There are two features of this Moorean question that would attract immediate scrutiny nowadays. The first is that it is assumed in the question that there are sense-data involved in visual experience. The presence of this assumption in the question is likely to elicit the following complaint. 'Surely the (or a) fundamental question is *whether* there are sense-data. We should not assume in the very formulation of what is supposed to be the central question in the philosophy of perception that there are

---

[7] G. E. Moore (1925), 'A Defence of Common Sense', in *Philosophical Papers*, 55. I have eliminated some paragraph breaks in the quotation. For the sake of accuracy, it should be pointed out that in this passage Moore is expressing his uncertainty about the second of his two main questions. But the particular source of the uncertainty is the difficulty of answering the first.

[8] G. E. Moore (1958), 'Visual Sense-data', in R. J. Swartz (ed.), *Perceiving, Sensing and Knowing*, 136.

sense-data.' A reply to this complaint which is in the spirit of Moore's approach would run as follows: 'When I assume in posing the question that there are sense-data I am not assuming anything that is objectionable, or, indeed, that is disputable. My notion of sense-datum is a thoroughly neutral one. Given what I mean by "sense-data" no-one can deny that there are sense-data. You might perhaps, given the way the term has come to be used, quibble with my use of the word "sense-data" for these thoroughly unobjectionable items, but that is not a serious philosophical worry, and, moreover my usage is as long standing and as well known as any other.' How, though, are we to understand the *neutral* notion of sense-data that Moore supposedly employed? The way to think of Moore's conception is to contrast the *theory* that is built into Moore's use with the one that is built into a more committal and disputable use. Thus, when it is said that there are sense-data on such a committal use the claim amounts to saying that there are things which satisfy a certain complex theoretical condition. We can say, then, that on this conception to claim that:

Ex (Sense-datum (x))

is equivalent to:

Ex (in accordance with theory C (x)),

(where 'C' stands for committal). Being in accordance with theory C will be equivalent to and will be spelled out in terms of being P1 ... .PN, for certain values of those predicates specified by the committal theory as definitive of sense-data. The properties picked out might include being non-physical, being private to the experience of a single subject, and, possessing qualities such as those of colour, shape etc.[9] For Moore the assertion that:

Ex (Sense-datum (x))

will be equivalent to:

Ex (in accordance with Theory M (x)),

(where 'M' stands for Moorean). Theory M will define the conditions for being a sense-datum as being PM1, ...PMN, for values of those predicates which are supposedly such that no-one would deny that there are things of this sort involved in perceptual experiences. One central question, therefore, is whether the characterization which is built into Theory M is totally uncontroversial even *in the perceptual case*. A further important question, though, is whether the theory M applies uncontroversially in *all* the cases of experience to which Moore thinks it applies. At this stage, then, it is built into the framework which Moore endorses that there is a property (or properties)

---

[9] For one list of this sort, see H. Robinson, *Perception* (London: Routledge, 1994), 1–2.

which apply to certain objects in perceptual experiences, but also to certain objects involved in some other sorts of experiences as well, which no-one can really deny does (or do) apply to *something or other* in those cases. On Moore's conception the crucial question is what further *real nature* these objects have.

I shall later examine in more detail the theory that is built into Moore's employment of the term 'sense-data'. It is, however, easy enough to say what the central assumption is. Moore's root notion of the sense-datum present in an experience is that it is the item which the experience enables the subject demonstratively to pick out in what might be called an unmediated way. By talking of an unmediated way (which is not Moore's way of speaking) the point is to exclude a type of demonstrative designator which according to Moore exists. The excluded type of demonstrative is one where 'that F' (e.g., 'that cup') is equivalent to the definite description: the F which is R-related to that G. Moore evidently envisages that the R-relation slot in such a description can be occupied by a specification of considerable semantic complexity. Thus 'that F' might be equivalent to: 'the F which is G-related to the H which is I-related to that J'. An unmediated demonstrative is one not equivalent to a designator with this sort of structure. It is not clear, of course, that Moore is right to think that there are demonstratives with this mediated character, but that is not a question that needs considering at this point. Moore's concept of sense-data is that they are the items which experience enables subjects to demonstrate unmediatedly. He thinks that it is undeniable that experience enables us to do this and so there is nothing problematic in defining the category of sense-data in this way. Moore's question is: what sort of thing is that immediately demonstrable object?

There is, however, a second special feature of the way that Moore almost always formulates his central question which would strike most people nowadays as puzzling. Moore's question is whether the sense-datum present in the visual experience is identical with *part of the surface of the seen object* or not. Why does Moore suppose that the visual sense-datum is a candidate for being identical with, at best, parts of the *surface* of the seen object O rather than with the object O itself? That Moore did suppose this is the second ingredient in what I am calling his framework. Moore supposed this because he thought there are powerful considerations to show that even if we are seeing on object O, say an ink-pot, the relation in which we stand to O, the ink-pot, cannot be the same as the relation we are standing to the sense-datum. Hence, according to Moore, the only external candidate we might stand to in that relation (in the case of vision) is (part of) the surface of the seen object.

The two assumptions that I have tried to express are the two main ingredients in Moore's framework. There is, however, a third assumption that is very important to Moore and that influences his treatment of these issues. This is the assumption that it is obviously true, and so not a proposition for debate or possible revaluation in the course of philosophical discussion, that we do see external physical objects. Here is Moore expressing this attitude right at the beginning of 'Visual Sense-data'.[10] 'It seems to me quite plain that one of the commonest senses in which the word 'see' can be correctly used in English, perhaps the commonest of all, is that in which a particular person can be said, at a particular time, to be seeing such objects as, for example, a particular penny, a particular chair, a particular tree, a particular flower, or a particular horse, his own right hand, the moon, the planet Venus, etc.—objects which I shall call 'physical objects'. I have, indeed, once met a philosopher who told me that I was making a great mistake in thinking that such objects are ever seen. But I think that this philosopher was certainly wrong, and was thinking that the various correct uses of 'see' are limited in a way that they are not in fact limited. ... I, personally, have in fact often seen pennies and often seen the moon, and so have many other people. But, nevertheless, I think there is a puzzle as to how the word 'see' is being used in this common usage'.[11]

The two questions raised by this passage are: (1) what exactly is the attitude to which Moore is committing himself here?; and (2) is it an attitude that it is reasonable to endorse? Although I want to say something in response to these questions they are, it seems to me, very difficult in that they concern Moore's conception of philosophy and its tasks. This is both too large an issue to confront properly and also one about which I do not have a definite interpretation to offer. It is also not essential to do so in order to get Moore's account of perception in focus.

The most extreme view that might be ascribed to Moore is that it is not a matter for debate or question that, say, the sentence, 'S sees O' is true at t at p. An acceptable analysis of what 'S sees O' says must, therefore, fit what, on investigation, obtained at t and p. Beyond this constraint, however, mere reflection, unaided by an investigation of what did obtain, gets us no way to an analysis.

It would be natural to object to such a conception that we can in advance at least say that 'S sees O' entails that S exists and that O exists. The analysis of the sentence cannot remain neutral about its commitment to the existence of those two entities. There are, however, two replies to this comment that a proponent of the extreme attitude might make, the first of which, in fact, corresponds closely to something that Moore himself was at one time prepared to say. Consider first what Moore might say about the subject side of the sentence (the side of S). One might assume that if 'S sees O' entails the existence of S, then the sentence 'S directly apprehends the sensible X' would entail the existence of S, too. Moore's attitude to the latter entailment is, though, rather complicated. He says, in his early article 'The

---

[10] Moore expresses the same attitude to the claim that we see physical objects in 'Some Judgements of Perception', 233.

[11] Moore, 'Visual Sense-data', 130.

Status of Sense-data' the following; 'It is quite possible, I think, that there is no entity whatever which deserves to be called "I" or "me"...; and hence nothing whatever is ever directly apprehended by me.'[12] Moore himself is, therefore, extremely cautious about admitting what seem to be fairly obvious entailments. The second point is that even if it is conceded that 'S sees O' entails that 'S exists' and 'O exists' are true, this is insignificant if the analyses of the two entailed sentences are themselves completely open. All that is established is that the conditions built into the analysis of the second pair of sentences must be such that they come out true when the conditions built into the analysis of the first sentence is true, which is in effect no constraint at all.

Still, although there are elements in Moore's account which fit this extreme interpretation, it is, surely, not an attractive view, nor one that is forced on Moore by what he says. First, the position contains no satisfactory account of analysis. To offer such an account it is necessary to say both (i) what 'the analysis of P is Q' means; and (ii) how the analysis is to be determined. Now, the previous suggestion says nothing in relation to (i) and so gives no insight at all in to what an analysis is, and, in relation to (ii) the suggestion is purely negative, to the effect that it is not an a priori method. That, however, is both very extreme and incomplete. No indication is given as to how to distinguish those claims which figure in the analysis of 'P' and those claims which also happen to be true at the same time. Second, an explanation is needed, and it is by no means obvious how to provide it, of the epistemological status of the claim that S saw O at p at t. What provides the entitlement to regard it as settled, given the possibly massive ignorance as to what else obtains there and then? Third, there is, I think, nothing in what Moore says that means we have to think that he held such a view. Moore's remarks about the self illustrate how cautious, but also, to some extent, how bold, he is about analysis, but do not suggest that a priori analysis is impossible. The status that Moore ascribes to 'I have seen e.g. a coin' does not, I shall argue, require any such view, but can be interpreted differently.

An alternative interpretation of Moore's approach might be introduced by reflection on the following simple example. I can investigate the number of chairs in a room and determine that it is twelve. I am therefore entitled to affirm that is so, even though I do not know what my claim entails, (for example, I do not know that my claim entails that there is the square root of 144 chairs in the room). The fact that I myself have not yet achieved the a priori insight which is available into what is entailed by my claim does not undermine my entitlement to accept that it is. Of course, this example leaves unilluminated what the requirements of the entitlement are, but it reveals that they can exist in the absence of a complete, or

---

[12] Moore, 'The Status of Sense-data', 174.

even nearly complete, analysis of entailments. Further, Moore might hold that the determinate analysis is a priori but simply very hard. Or he might hold that what is a priori determinable are claims of the form 'If C then [the analysis of 'P' is 'Q']' and 'If B then [the analysis of 'P' is 'R'], where the choice between C and B is not a priori.

What I have been offering here is not intended to be a vindication of Moore's position, but rather a sketch of options for understanding it. It does need to be pointed out that there is something disingenuous in what Moore says in the quoted passage. Moore certainly insinuates, in the way he writes, that there is something very eccentric in the suggestion that maybe we do not actually see such objects as the moon or coins. In fact, this is simply the idea of what Mackie has famously called an 'error theory'. Philosophy is replete with error theories in general, and many have, of course, been tempted by the idea that our thought about perception is an error. It is quite unfair of Moore to represent this view as virtually unknown, and to support his own attitude on that basis. Second, Moore nowhere demonstrates, or even provides the beginning of a reason for believing, that we are entitled to hold, so firmly, that we do actually see such external objects.

Having worked through it somewhat, Moore's framework can be summarized in this way. Every experience puts the subject in relation to an entity in such a way that he or she can pick out the object by direct demonstration as 'that'. This is the supposedly uncontroversial sense-datum assumption. Moore's question is: what *is* that? Second, it can be shown that that is not identical to an object, say an ink-pot, but it remains open whether it is the surface of such an object. Whether it is or not is the central question. Finally, there are, definitely and without doubt, situations where we count as seeing external objects, and in those situations the sentence 'That is an external object' is true, but this 'that' cannot be a direct 'that' and is equivalent to 'The object which is R-related to that is an external object'. What 'R' is cannot be decided until we know the relation of that and the surface, and even then both in general direction and detail it might be beyond us to say. Moore's interest in perception is, really, an interest in determining the *truth* of certain identity judgements, and in determining the analysis of certain others.

It is what I have called the second element in Moore's framework that I want to investigate first.

II Moore on Surfaces and Seeing

We can attempt to understand and evaluate the line of thought which leads Moore to formulate the basic question in terms of surfaces of objects (rather than solely in terms of objects) by studying his last formulation of the argument in 'Visual Sense-data'.[13] I begin with a fairly extended quotation.

'There are two kinds of physical objects which we may at a particular moment be said to be 'seeing' in this common sense: namely (1) objects which are transparent, like a drop of clear water or any ordinary glass tumbler or wine glass; and (2) objects which are opaque, like a penny or the moon. In the former case it seems possible that you may, in certain cases, see the whole object at once, both every part of its surface and its inside; it is, at all events, not clear that, in certain cases, you don't do this. But in the case of opaque objects, it seems perfectly clear that you can be correctly said to be 'seeing' the object, in cases where (in another sense of 'see') you are *only seeing* one or several sides of the opaque object, i.e., *some* parts of its surface, but emphatically *not* all parts of its surface nor its inside. It seems, indeed, doubtful whether you can be correctly said to be seeing it unless you are seeing a sufficiently large part of its surface, and I am inclined to think that how large a part of its surface is 'sufficient' to entitle you to say you are seeing it is different in the case of different objects: e.g. it is quite plain that you can correctly be said to be seeing the moon when you only see the very thinnest crescent, whereas if you only saw such a small part of the surface of a penny it would be doubtful if it could be correctly said that you were seeing the penny; you would be inclined to say that you did not see it, but only a small part of its rim. But where, for instance, you see the whole 'tail' side of a penny, but don't see the 'head' side there is no doubt whatever that you can correctly be said to be seeing the penny. What is meant by 'seeing' the penny in such a case? There seems to me to be no doubt that, if you said to yourself, as you might, 'That is a penny', the demonstrative 'that' would be short for a phrase of the kind which Russell has called a 'definite description'; and if you only said this to *yourself*, there would, of course, be no need for you to point or touch anything, in order to show which object you were referring to, since you would be able to identify the object without any such gesture. The 'definite description' for which your 'that' would be short would be 'the object of which *this* is part of the surface' . . . '.[14]

This is a difficult passage to analyse. The chief problem is that what we are looking for is a reason for thinking that the sense-datum involved in a visual experience in which S sees O, if is it to be identical with something external, can, at best, be identical with the surface of O, but not with O itself. Moore, however, does not formulate this claim explicitly and so does not properly argue for it. Further, in the passage Moore starts by making assertions about what someone can see, relative, according to him, to various senses of 'see'. However, in the middle Moore shifts focus to discuss the analysis of certain types of demonstrative judgements (which, as I remarked, in an

---

[13] An earlier exposition of the same type of consideration is in 'The Status of Sense-data', 185–9.

[14] Moore, 'Visual Sense-data', 130–1.

earlier period he calls 'judgements of perception'). He does not properly explain the link between the claims about 'see' and the claims about demonstratives. Nor does Moore explain the link between the claims about demonstratives and the limitation on what the sense-datum involved could be identical with.[15]

These two, not properly explained, transitions—the first in the middle of the passage, the second moving on from its end—having been noted, I want to make a few critical or clarificatory remarks about what Moore says. (1) Moore attaches importance to the distinction between opaque objects and transparent objects (Moore 1958: 130), and, having drawn the distinction, he focuses on the case of seeing opaque objects. Why is that distinction of importance to him? The answer is that he is quite sure that in the case of an opaque object when S sees it, S does not see the whole of the object; whereas, in the case of transparent objects, it is not clear that this is so. Moore wants to develop his argument for cases where we do not see the whole of the object. Now, it seems fairly clear that when we see an opaque object we do not see the whole of the object. There are parts, for example, the bits inside it or on the far side of it, which are not then seen. It is wrong, though, to contrast this with the transparent case. On our current understanding of what parts there are to objects there will obviously also be parts of seen transparent objects that are not seen. They are the small microscopic parts, the molecules, atoms, and sub-atomic parts. These are surely parts of the object and they are not seen. There is, therefore, no contrast between the two cases, at least in respect of whether the whole of the object is seen. The distinction between the opaque and the transparent to which Moore attached importance throughout his writings on the philosophy of perception cannot rest on this point.

(2) It seems that Moore is interested in the opaque case because in cases of seeing an opaque object we do not see the whole of the object or, as he also puts it, the whole object. Now, the first claim seems correct, but we can ask why it is true. Compare seeing with the two following cases. If I say 'put the whole of that chocolate in your mouth', it seems easy enough to do what I say. If instead I say 'touch the whole of the cup' it would be very hard to carry out the command. Even if you touch the whole of the surface you would not have touched the whole of the cup. What about the inside bits? What makes sense of this is that the meaning of the expression 'the whole of

---

[15] In order to keep the quotation as short as possible consistent with discussing it properly, I have ended it before the end of the paragraph in question, hence at a point where Moore probably did not think of his line of argument as complete. It may be felt that this is unfair. However, immediately after the end of the quotation, but in the same paragraph, Moore shifts focus on to the different question of whether Russell is right to talk of *knowledge* by description in relation to ways of thinking or talking about objects which pick out the objects by descriptions. This does not engage with either question that I have claimed Moore does not clearly answer, and, I think, it is fair to say that Moore does not return to them.

X' is: every part of X. The noun phrase 'The whole of . . . ' is a universally quantified expression. The whole of the chocolate can be in your mouth because every part is, in fact, within your mouth, but the whole of the cup has not been touched because you have not touched every part of it (indeed you cannot do so). If this is right then we must deny the X is *identical* to the whole of X. X is not identical to every part of itself. What is confusing here is that there is a use of 'whole X' which means, roughly, an X which has not lost any of its parts. Now, if a particular X has not lost any of its parts it is a whole X, hence X is identical with the whole X. Thus if I see a cup which has not lost any parts, I see a whole cup but I shall not see the whole of the cup. Most importantly, the non-identity between X and the whole of X means that both the following inferences are invalid. First, S does not see the whole of X, so S does not see X. Second, that is not the whole of X, therefore, that is not X. If Moore relied on such inferences, then he is mistaken.

(3) Moore seems to think that from the claim that S does not see the whole of X it follows that the parts S is seeing are *parts of the surface*. He seems to make a contrast between the whole of X and its surface (and the surface's parts). In fact, what should be contrasted with seeing the whole of X (i.e., every part of X) is seeing at most some of the parts of X, which need not be surfaces. Thus, in looking at a two-handled cup I can see the handle towards me, that part, but not the handle away from me. There is, therefore, no obvious route from not seeing the whole of X to seeing at most parts of the *surface* of X. Moore's concentration on surfaces and their parts cannot be justified that way.

(4) In the third sentence of the passage, Moore thinks that he is entitled to say there is a sense of 'see' in which with opaque objects you only see some parts of the object's surface. Moore's reason for asserting that there is a sense of 'see' in this usage is presumably the following: (i) the sentence 'S sees O' is true (an assumption that Moore repeatedly endorses); (ii) there is a truth expressed in the words 'S sees only parts of the surface of O'; (iii) in the same sense of 'see' it cannot be that S sees O and also only sees parts of the surface of O; so, (iv) there are at least two senses of 'see'. This looks to be a cogent argument if the premises are true. However, the second premise is not obviously strictly true. Why cannot we say, more carefully than Moore, that strictly S saw O itself, as well as the part S also saw? Moore has no reason to affirm the ambiguity.

We can also ask what the relevance would have been if there had been a sense of 'see' in which we do not see opaque objects but merely parts of the surfaces of those objects. Whatever the answer in general, it does not seem to be something that in itself could imply that the demonstrative contact we have to objects has to be analysed in such a way that the contact reduces to homing in on the object via a description containing demonstrative reference to something else. The existence of a separate sense could not imply that. Although, therefore, we need not accept the ambiguity thesis, nothing of relevance would have followed from its existence.

(5) Moore, it will be remembered, begins the paper from which the passage being analysed comes, by affirming that we do see physical objects. Moore has to claim, therefore, that if we merely see (in his supposed second sense of 'see') a part of the surface of an opaque object O, we might also see O. Moore assumes that there will be conditionals linking seeing objects and seeing parts of their surfaces. In fact, Moore fairly obviously assumes that we should analyse seeing objects, where they are opaque, in terms of seeing parts of their surfaces. His suggestion is that we count as seeing O when we see a *sufficiently large part* of the surface of O, where what is sufficiently large varies from case to case. He claims that seeing only a small part of the surface of a coin would not amount to seeing the coin, whereas a proportionately small part of the surface of the moon does amount to seeing the moon. Moore does not pursue the questions that arise for this view, as to why there is such variation, and as to what determines what amount of a surface needs to be seen in each case for the object to be seen.

However, the claims that Moore makes which lead to these questions need not be accepted. Consider first that non-perceptual relation of touching. Even if S touches, ever so gently, a very small part of O, S can be said to have touched O. If someone is ordered to touch each college in Oxford, he carries out the order if he touches a part, however small, of each college. So there are some relations R such that if S stands in relation R to any part, however small, of O then S stands in relation R to O. There is, surely, evidence that 'seeing' is such a relation. Consider this example: I order you to bury O so that it cannot be seen. If you leave a small part visible, then you have failed to carry out the order. I can say; 'O is still visible'. Consider this second example: S, who is dying, wishes to see England for a last time. He is so seriously ill that we fly him to a field in England, open the door, and allow him to see a tiny patch of the ground. We have, it seems reasonable to me to say, enabled him to fulfil his last wish, however small the patch. These examples fit the suggestion that 'see' has the same logic as 'touch'.[16]

There are certain counter-examples which are often suggested when this proposal is made. It is sometimes said that you do not see a person if you see a small part of them, say the tip of the little finger on their left hand. Consider, though, this case: S is looking through a keyhole into a room where there is a meeting. If S can see the tip of

---

[16] Assuming that it is correct to say that 'see' has this logical property, then it is a property that provides a reason for saying about statements to the effect the S sees O that they contain little information about what one might call the character for the subject of the perceptual episode being reported by them. Thus if I say that S saw O, then it is consistent with what is said that S saw a tiny and unrecognizable part of O.

a moving little finger, then if he is asked whether he can see anyone he can, surely, say that he *can* see someone, even if he cannot make out who it is. There is also a tendency to suppose that other perceptual verbs do not have the logic specified, which, if true, would make one doubt that it could apply to 'see'. Thus, it is said that one does not hear a Beethoven symphony if one only hears just one chord from its performance. However, if a deaf person has his hearing restored for a second and during that second merely hears the first chord of the symphony, it can be said that for a second he was able to hear a Beethoven symphony. It seems to me that examples like this do not count against the proposal.

Two more general points can be added. (i) There is an incentive to avoid the type of approach that Moore suggests because, as I pointed out above, it raises difficult supplementary questions. (ii) We can explain why there is a reluctance to *say* in some of these cases simply that S perceived in some way or other O. It would be more helpful for a speaker who knows that S's perception was of such a small part of O to inform the hearer that that was so, since there will be some tendency for the hearer to make mistaken assumptions if told merely that there was perceptual contact between S and O.

(6) It seems to be an element in Moore's view that 'S sees O', where O is an opaque object, entails 'S sees (part of) the surface of O'. Moore indicates that he thinks we could analyse seeing opaque objects in terms of seeing the surfaces of opaque objects. Such a proposed analysis could not be correct if the entailment did not hold, but the entailment might hold even though the analytical proposal was mistaken. Does the entailment hold? It seems to me not to. Here are some counter-examples. (a) You can see a man in silhouette against the night sky without being able to see his surface. (b) You can see the bright glowing filament in a light bulb without being able to see its surface. (c) You can see a far distant object, say a ship, which is just visible, as a black dot, on the horizon, without being able to see its surface. (d) You can see a far distant star in the night sky without being able to see its surface. (e) Staring out of a window you can see a tiny branch on a tree in the near distance without seeing its surface. (f) You can see the dirty water you are swimming beneath without seeing its surface. (g) You can see a thick mist engulfing you without seeing its surface. (h) Consider a kind of object which can be found in gift shops. It consists of glass, the exterior parts of which are transparent, whereas the inner glass is opaque. Looking at it, in certain conditions, one does not see its surface but can see the object.[17]

The conclusion that emerges from these observations is that Moore has not, in 'Visual Sense-data' really assembled any evidence or provided an unconfused reason to

---

[17] The last example on the list raises questions about Moore's practice of dividing objects into two groups, the opaque and the transparent. Single objects can have both transparent and opaque parts. In which category do such objects belong? Another issue here, though, is what counts as the surface of an object. Consider a human body. Suppose that in an operation a hole is cut in its surface and S sees the heart inside it. Does S thereby see that body? Does he see its surface?

believe that we cannot make unmediated demonstrative reference to opaque objects as opposed to their surfaces. There is, as far as I can see, no reason to adopt the second part of Moore's standard framework.

A remark in one of his earlier papers provides a significant insight into the roots of Moore's thinking about objects and surfaces. In 'A Defence of Common Sense', Moore says: 'That what I know with regard to the sense-datum, when I know that "This is a human hand", is not that it is itself a human hand, seems to me to be certain because I know that my hand has many parts (e.g., its other side, and the bones inside it) which are quite certainly not parts of this sense-datum.'[18] The question this little argument raises is how Moore knows that the sense-datum in question does not have the other parts that he mentions. If Moore wishes to be as neutral as possible about sense-datum talk, then there is, I believe, no answer to that question. Thus, if the sense-datum is just that thing, whatever it is, that is unmediatedly demonstrable by, say, Moore then unless he has already proved that it is not his hand he has no grounds for saying the thing has no other parts. The basis for Moore's claim that the sense-datum lacks these other parts must be that he is *assuming or stipulating* certain further things about it. One possible stipulation might be that the sense-datum is the unmediatedly demonstrable item which has no other parts which are themselves not currently unmediatedly demonstrable. This stipulation, though, runs the risk of guaranteeing that nothing fits it. It would probably rule out an identity between the sense-datum and the actual surface. The reason is that looking at a surface in normal conditions from a normal distance means that there are parts of the surface that are not there and then perceived. This is why getting closer, etc. reveals more of the surface and its details. Alternatively, Moore might be stipulating that the sense-datum must be, as one might say, surface-like. The question is: why should such a stipulation be made? It seems to me that it must be that the insidious conception of sense-data as fundamentally two-dimensional is having an influence. It does not, of course, actually fit Moore's neutral conception of sense-data. The insight from this passage, then, is that Moore often slips into assumptions about sense-data with which his neutral conception is inconsistent.

The overall conclusion remains that the second element in Moore's framework is without support.

III The Status of Sense-data

I argued, so far, that Moore's conviction that visual sense-data could, at best, be identical to external surfaces is not properly justified. But I wish to ask now whether

---

[18] Moore, 'A Defence of Common Sense', in *Philosophical Papers*, 55.

Moore advances any arguments that determine whether this crucial identity does hold or not.

In the published work that I am concentrating on Moore advances, from time to time, a number of arguments aimed at establishing the non-identity. I want to look briefly at two such arguments, before analysing in a little more detail the argument that moved Moore at the end of his life in 'Visual Sense-data'.

In 'The Status of Sense-data', Moore says that it is certain that the 'visual sensible', which is the term he was there using for what elsewhere he calls the 'sense-datum', which he apprehends when he is seeing a coin, is not identical with the upper side of the coin.[19] The reason is that if two people, say Moore himself and S, see the same coin, it cannot be that the sensibles apprehended by both are identical to the upper surface, because there is one surface but two sensibles, Moore's and S's, which are not identical. As Moore points out, some extra work is needed to get from this to a definite conclusion about the status of Moore's own individual sensible. However, the major mistake in this argument is that Moore is not entitled to claim that his and S's sensibles are not identical. If the sensible is simply that thing, whatever it is, which the experience makes apprehensible by the subject, who is to say that the experiences of the two people do not make exactly the same thing apprehensible by both of them? Moore is, surely, under the influence again of a more committal notion of sensible (or sense-datum) according to which such an item is *private* to the apprehender.

In 'A Defence of Common Sense', Moore proposes what he calls a 'serious objection' to the identity (between sense-datum and the seen surface of the seen object) based on the occurrence of double vision.[20] This resembles the previous argument in its general structure, except that the two supposedly distinct sense-data are apprehended by a single subject, rather than by two. The assumption is that double vision involves two sense-data, at least one of which cannot, in consequence, be identical to the surface (since there is only one surface). Moore does not explain how a general conclusion about sense-data can be elicited from the occurrence of such a case (although it is true that such cases are very common.) However, the more serious problem is that Moore is not entitled to the claim that there are two sense-data in the double vision case. Maybe there are two apprehendings of a single entity. Maybe, that is, the total experience enables the subject to apprehend the same entity twice, so there is no need for two things to be one.

Moore's problem in these arguments is that they work by affirming a non-identity at the level of sense-data between two items as a basis for proving a non-identity of at least one (and ultimately both) of these items with a single external thing. But

---

[19] This is stated in 'The Status of Sense-data', in *Philosophical Studies*, 187.

[20] This is presented in 'A Defence of Common Sense', in *Philosophical Papers*, 56.

the non-identity affirmed in the premises is not something that Moore is entitled to affirm while being genuinely neutral as to the nature of the 'apprehensibles'.

In such debates about the identity with external items of certain 'presented' or 'apprehended' things, those who deny the identity suppose they can prove their position by locating property differences between the apprehended item and the external thing. Those who wish to affirm the identities cannot, usually, demonstrate them, but must rather render acceptance of the objections non-obligatory and make some other sort of case for their identity.[21] To render acceptance of the objections non-obligatory, it is necessary to explain how the property ascriptions to which the non-identity affirmer is appealing need not be accepted. Now, in 'Some Judgements of Perception', Moore made a suggestion which, it seems to me, must form a component in any view that claims to defend these identities. Moore made his suggestion in the course of weighing up a style of argument commonly known as 'Arguments from Illusion'. Within the Moorean framework one such argument might run thus. Suppose that at t S is seeing a coin, viewing it from above. S moves and at t + n views the same coin from an angle. The sense-datum apprehended by S at t is (perceptibly) different (in its shape) from the sense-datum apprehended by S at t + n. However, the coin itself, and its surface, has not changed (and is no different) between those two times. It follows that at least one of the sense-data is not identical with the coin's surface. Moore commented, though, that it maybe that the sense-datum at t and the sense-datum at t + n are not really different, but merely that they *seem* different. If there has actually been no change, but it merely seems as if there has, between the different times with the sense-data, then the fact that the surface itself has not changed would not show that there is a non-identity between the sense-data and the surface. Let us, because we shall need a name for it, call this suggestion the Seems Idea. Moore puts the point this way: 'The great objection to such a view [that is, the Seems Idea] seems to me to be the difficulty of believing that I don't actually perceive this sense-datum to *be* red, for instance, and that other to *be* elliptical; I only perceive, in many cases, that it *seems* so. I cannot, however, persuade myself that it is quite clear that I do perceive it to be so.'[22] Now, I am not claiming that the Seems Idea originates with Moore, but, rather, that it represents a resource on which any defender of the identity between sense-datum and surface must rely. Further, once this possible response was acknowledged by Moore, he became very (and properly) cautious about accepting arguments against the identities of visual sense-data and surfaces.

It is, of course, in 'Visual Sense-data' that Moore eventually decides that the Seems Idea can be rejected. Why does Moore (in 1958) think that it is inadmissible? Since this

---

[21] For example, it may be said that non-acceptance of the identity involves postulating an extra range of objects and, moreover, renders the explanation of perception more difficult.

[22] 'Some Judgements of Perception', in *Philosophical Studies*, 246.

is a major development in Moore's thinking, one would have expected the reason to be advanced clearly, but, in fact, it is not entirely obvious what Moore's reasoning is. There are, as far as I can see, possibly three routes that Moore took to the conclusion. In the first place, Moore says that 'it seems to me quite plain that the proposition that a physical surface looks bluish-white to me, entails that I am directly seeing an entity that *is* bluish-white.'[23] This claim is simply a straight affirmation of what the Seems Idea denies, and in itself it offers no reason why we should accept the 'plainness' of the entailment. In the second place, Moore raises the following question: 'If I am not directly seeing a bluish-white expanse which has some relation to the wall which is not bluish-white, how can I possibly know that the wall is looking bluish-white to me?'[24] The person who accepts the Seems Idea does, of course, accept that a subject can know that, for example, that thing looks bluish-white, without directly seeing a bluish-white thing. The weakness in Moore's response is that he merely asks the question as to how such knowledge is possible, and really provides no reason to think it is not possible.

What I read as Moore's third point is both richer and more interesting. Moore says this: 'Until very recently I had thought that, although some of the arguments that purported to show it [namely, the claim that the sense-datum is identical to the surface of the seen object] cannot [be true] were very strong, yet they were not conclusive, because I thought that e.g. in the case where you directly see an 'after-image' with closed eyes, it is just possible that the after-image only looked to have certain colours . . . and did not really have them. . . . I well remember that, at the Aristotelian meeting at which I read that paper, Russell said that the suggestion certainly was nonsensical. I now feel that he was right . . . '.[25] Although this reason is fuller than either of the other two, there is significant compression in its presentation. Moore does not explain why he now thinks, nor attempts to persuade us that, Russell's judgement is correct. We are expected to concur.

Moore's line of thought raises two fundamental questions. The first is whether Russell is right in claiming that it is nonsense to suggest that an after-image might, for example, look reddish but actually be bluish. The second question is this: if Russell's claim is correct, what does that imply about the Seems Idea?

In response to the first question, it seems to me that Russell's verdict is correct. The argument in favour of saying this is that where we can make a genuine distinction

---

[23] 'Visual Sense-data', 135. I have ignored part of Moore's discussion at this point. He distinguishes two sorts of looks-judgements, and restricts the thesis that he is suggesting is plain to one of them. Having the distinction provides no reason, though, for supposing that it is plain in relation to the one that Moore is talking about.

[24] 'Visual Sense-data', 134.

[25] 'Ibid., 136. There is something very charming in Moore's recollection of an Aristotelian meeting where Russell told him that he was speaking nonsense!

between an object's being F and its seeming F (say, its looking F), in such a way that it can seem F and not be F, and also can be F without seeming F, there needs to be *enough* involved in the relation or relations in which a subject stands to the object to account for these possibilities. Thus, a tree can be brown without seeming brown to a subject S because the tree might fall outside the subject's range of experience, by being, for example, on the other side of a mountain. Again, it might be perceived by S but conditions of viewing be sub-optimal, because the light is bad or itself coloured. Again, S's sense organs might be defective, and so distort the tree's appearance. Similar factors, of course, ground the possibility that the tree might look F and not be F. Ultimately these possibilities are grounded in the huge complexities built into the causal relation between the object and the experiencer. Now, these complexities are not present in the experience of after-images. Nothing can come between a subject and his or her after-images, there is no space for sub-optimal viewing conditions, nor can the subject's sense organs distort appearances. It would not be right to put this point by saying that a subject's view of his or her after-images is guaranteed perfect; rather it is the negative point that there is nothing in the experience of after-images which can ground this is-seems distinction.

If this is a good reason to agree with Russell, then the second question, in effect, answers itself. We can first ask why Moore thinks that if after-image experience does not contain enough to ground the is-seems distinction then the kind of experiences that Moore is interested in, namely seeing an external object, cannot ground such a distinction. The reply that Moore would make is that he *does* think that the overall experience in seeing an external object contains enough, because it grounds a contrast between how the external object is and how the sense-datum is. This response is not, however, adequate, and merely prompts us to ask why the experience of the directly apprehended thing, that is to say of the sense-datum, *in itself* does not actually contain enough to ground the possibilities. Moore's problem at this stage is that he is simply working with the notion of the sense-datum as the unmediatedly demonstrable thing. The item's nature, and equally importantly, the real nature of its relation to the subject, aside from its enabling unmediated demonstrative contact, has *not been determined*. Moore has, therefore, as yet no reason for thinking that the relation to that thing does not contain enough to ground the is-seems distinction. The answer, then, to the second question is that from the fact (if it is a fact) that the experience of after-images does not contain enough to ground that contrast, it does not follow that there is not enough in the experience of the directly demonstrable item in vision.

My conclusion, then, is that Moore's final renunciation of the Seems Idea is ungrounded, and that with the Seems Idea in play the types of arguments that at various times he advanced against the identity in vision of surfaces and sense-data totally fail. I do not mean to say that there are not other sorts of arguments here which cannot be defused simply on the basis of the Seems Idea. However, these are not arguments that particularly attracted Moore.[26]

IV Moore's Neutral Conception of Sense-data

We have arrived at a point where we need to put Moore's neutral conception of a sense-datum under the microscope. In effect, though, much has emerged about it in the previous discussion and so it is possible to be brief at this point.

Although there are variations over time in the way that Moore speaks and in what he stresses, Moore's idea is that it is right to talk of a sense-datum as involved in an experience so long as that experience relates the subject to an entity or thing in such a way that the subject can demonstratively think about that object in an unmediated way. Moore takes this, rightly I suspect, to be what Russell means by acquaintance. Moore himself talks about apprehending or directly seeing the item.

This conception of sense-datum is correctly called neutral, in that in supposing that an item qualifies as a sense-datum so explained nothing more is being supposed about it other than that it is available for unmediated thought in virtue of an experience of the subject. There is no commitment as to its nature or existence conditions. Indeed, it would not even be legitimate to assume in advance that all sense-data have the same nature, or existence conditions. Professor Baldwin in his discussion of Moore has, following Ayer, suggested that this possibility, that maybe some sense-data (in Moore's sense) have one nature and others another, is not really available, because 'as far as the content of experience goes, the two experiences, one hallucinatory, the other perceptual, can be as similar as one likes; so, whatever reasons there are for supposing that in the hallucinatory experience subjective sense-data are apprehended apply equally to the perceptual experience'.[27] This argument is, though, too quick to eliminate the possibility. It invites a two-sided reply. First, the similarity to the subject between one type of experience and another is quite consistent with their having a different nature. Second, the reason for introducing what Baldwin is calling subjective

---

[26] There is, I am inclined to think, a difference between the account offered here and that offered by Professor Baldwin. The question is why Moore abandoned what I have been calling the Seems Idea. Baldwin selects as crucial Ducasse's paper which made it clear to Moore that 'his sense-datum theory is inconsistent with direct realism' (Baldwin 1990: 250). But if by the 'sense-datum theory' Baldwin simply means Moore's idea that experience involves the presentation of an object of some kind or other (available, therefore, for demonstrative thought), it cannot be said that the emergence of what is now called adverbial theories of experience reveals any such inconsistency. That does reveal a new way of thinking of experience, not properly considered by Moore, but it does not demonstrate that there cannot be object-involving experiences which permit an is-appears contrast.

[27] Baldwin, G. E. Moore, 244.

sense-data might precisely be the unavailability in the relevant cases of the so-called objective sense-data.

There are three respects in which Moore's use of 'sense-datum' is not neutral. The first is that its explanation relies, ultimately, on what I am calling the idea of unmediated demonstrative thought. This is clearly a theoretical notion, which needs to be properly explained, and its employment may be disputed, say on grounds of obscurity, incoherence, or possible lack of application. Now, it has to be conceded that I have not here properly investigated whether some such notion is in good conceptual standing and does sometimes apply.[28] I wish myself not to object to Moore's employment of such a notion, and here shall restrict myself to two remarks in its favour. The first is that I know of no grounds for being sceptical of its coherence, or querying its application. The second is that there is a very strong intuition that some such notion does have application. Both Russell's and Moore's practice is evidence of this intuition. If this is granted to Moore, what further issues can be raised about his neutral notion?

Another respect in which Moore's approach is not neutral is the range of experiences which he thinks involve sense-data. At the beginning of 'the Status of Sense-data' Moore, in effect, says this about having ordinary images, having dreams, hallucinations, after-images, and also when having what he calls 'sensations proper'.[29] Moore is evidently counting, from the very beginning, perception as 'sensation proper'. There is, though, an issue or a question here: is it right to think of all these cases as involving the presentation to the subject of an item that the subject can directly demonstrate? The first point to make here is that the fact, if it is a fact, that these cases *seem* to involve (or to be) the presentation of an object does not mean that they do (or are). This is, in effect, the re-application of the Seems Idea to the description of the general structure of the experience. Maybe it seems to be the presentation of an object even though it is not. Appearance cannot settle this question, and there is nothing for it but to work out the requirements for, and the consequences of, thinking of an experience as object-involving, as opposed to thinking of it in some other way.[30] The point is that there are, or maybe there are, significant theoretical commitments in analysing an experience as the apprehending of an object. It is not, therefore, a neutral matter to think this way.

[28] This question is, in effect, one that I have tried to investigate elsewhere, without, however, there relating it, except in a very small way, to Moore. See P. Snowdon, 'How to Interpet "Direct Perception" ', in T. Crane (ed.), *The Contents of Experience* (Cambridge: Cambridge University Press, 1992), esp. sections 5–7.

[29] Moore, 'The Status of Sense-data', 168.

[30] A gigantic step in this debate was made by Ducasse in his engagement with Moore in his paper 'Moore's Refutation of Idealism', in A Schilpp (ed.), *The Philosophy of G. E. Moore* (La Salle, Ill.). Moore failed to appreciate this, but the emergence of adverbialism, as we call it, supplied an alternative way of thinking about experience.

The third non-neutral aspect of Moore's conception of sense-data is an extension of the previous point. According to some, it is wrong to think even of the experience in a perceptual occurrence as being, or involving, on its own the presentation of an object. On this view, which is the most extreme application of the conception begun by Ducasse, no experience consists in a relation to an object. According to such an account, it is not that there are no direct demonstratives, rather, they are not possible solely on the basis of experiences, but require experiences in the right object-involving context. Again, it has to be agreed that such a conception cannot be ruled out as a possibility. Since Moore's notion of sense-data in his application of it does rule this out, it is not properly neutral.

These remarks are in agreement with Professor Baldwin's judgement that 'Moore's conception of a sense-datum is grounded in the act/object philosophy of mind'. [31] Such a conception is not neutral. The most important thing to add, though, is that it is one thing to think of experiences as relations to objects (which thereby become available for demonstrative thought) and another to explain the character of the experience in terms of the actual features of the presented objects. Moore throughout his reflections seems to have subscribed to the former, but to the latter only in his early and then in his late accounts.

Finally, there is another sense in which Moore's own discussion is not neutral. In tracing the details of his arguments, we have seen a number of occasions on which he makes assumptions about sense-data, importing features into his premises which a properly neutral conception would require him to argue for.

My aim in these remarks about Moore's conception of sense-data has not been to settle how we should think about experience, but rather to display the assumptions built into Moore's conception.

V Conclusion

There are obvious limitations to Moore's writings about perception. First, he really only discusses one question: are sense-data identical to external objects? He totally neglects the myriad other questions which perception as a phenomenon raises. Second, his formulation and discussion of this central question incorporates a number of assumptions, both general and specific, which seem not to be properly grounded. An abiding distorting influence (as one might say, a snare and delusion), which I hope the analysis has made clear, is Moore's employment of the sense-datum vocabulary. Third, and as a result, Moore has really nothing to say in relation to

---

[31] Baldwin, *G. E. Moore*, 250.

certain research programmes about perception currently being pursued. One such programme involves commitment to the total renunciation of the act-object analysis of experience, an analysis Moore himself sustained at all times. The other involves providing an act-object analysis of perceptual experience (but not other types of experience), with, however, what I have been calling the Seems Idea built into the model. Moore cannot contribute to that approach. However, if it is right to think that some of the central philosophical questions about perception can be formulated as questions about the truth of certain identity judgements involving demonstratives, as Moore evidently thought, and as I also think, Moore's engagement with those questions displays such concentration, ingenuity, care, and intelligence that his writings are, and will continue to be, of major importance.[32]

Bibliography

Baldwin T., *G. E. Moore* (London: Routledge, 1990).

Bouwsma O. K., 'Moore's Theory of Sense-data', in P. A. Schilpp (ed.) (1942).

Crane T., (ed.), *The Contents of Experience* (Cambridge: Cambridge University Press, 1992).

Ducasse, C. J., 'Moore's Refutation of Idealism', in P. A. Schilpp (ed.) (1942).

Moore G. E. 'The Refutation of Idealism' (1903), in Moore (1922), 1–30.

——— 'The Nature and Reality of Objects of Perception' (1905–6), in Moore (1922), 31–96.

——— 'The Status of Sense-Data' (1913–14), in Moore (1922), 168–96.

——— 'Some Judgements of Perception' (1918–19), in Moore (1922) 220–52.

——— 'A Defence of Common Sense' (1925), in Moore (1959), 32–59.

——— 'A Reply to My Critics', (1942), in P. A. Schilpp (ed.) (1942).

——— *Some Main Problems of Philosophy* (London: Unwin and Allen, 1953).

——— 'Visual Sense-data' (1958), in R. J. Swartz (ed.) (1965).

——— *Philosophical Papers* (London: Allen and Unwin, 1959).

Robinson, H., *Perception* (London: Routledge, 1996).

Schilpp, A., (ed.), *The Philosophy of G. E. Moore* (La Salle: Open Court, 1942).

Sellars, W., *Empiricism and the Philosophy of Mind* (London: Harvard University Press, 1997).

Snowdon, P. F., 'How to Interpret "Direct Perception" ', in Crane (1992).

Swartz, R. J. (ed.), *Perceiving, Sensing and Knowing* (New York: Anchor Books, 1965).

White, A. R, *G.E. Moore: A Critical Exposition* (Oxford: Blackwell, 1958).

[32] I am very grateful to Professors Susana Nuccetelli and Gary Seay for their invitation to contribute to this volume and their patience and encouragement. A version of this paper was discussed in a class at UCL, and I wish to thank Lee Walters, Ian Phillips, and Hong-Yu Wong for their comments. Thanks also to Stephan Blatti for comments, and especially to Mark Kalderon, whose responses have contributed significantly to my thinking.

7

Moore's Paradox and the Norm of Belief

Michael Huemer

I Moore's Paradox

G. E. Moore discovered what at first seems a minor puzzle concerning such statements as 'It is raining, but I don't believe it'. This statement strikes us as something akin to a contradiction, but in fact the statement is consistent, since it is logically possible that it should be raining at a time when the speaker does not believe that it is. As Moore also observed, it is possible for another person to say of me, 'It is raining but *he* doesn't believe it', or for me to say, at a later time, 'It *was* raining, but I didn't believe it', and in either of these cases the speaker would apparently assert the same proposition as in the original 'It is raining but I don't believe it' (said by me), yet there is no air of inconsistency or absurdity about these statements.[1] I shall refer to sentences that are absurd in the same way (whatever that is) as 'It is raining but I don't believe it' and 'It is raining but I believe it isn't' as 'Moore-paradoxical sentences'.[2] Moore's Paradox is the puzzle of explaining why Moore-paradoxical sentences are absurd.[3]

In my view, the epistemological lessons of Moore's Paradox are rich. Reflection on the Paradox assists us in the analysis of the concept of knowledge, it leads us to an account of the deep philosophical significance of that concept, and it suggests an important general constraint on rational belief.

---

[1] Moore (1993).   [2] Here I follow Shoemaker's (1996, 74) terminology.
[3] The term 'Moore's Paradox' is from Wittgenstein (1968, 190), who appears to use it to refer to this puzzle, rather than to the Moore-paradoxical sentences themselves.

II Linguistic Accounts

Most who have weighed in on Moore's Paradox have offered purely linguistic solutions. These are solutions that seek to explain the absurdity of Moore-paradoxical sentences in terms, broadly speaking, of rules of language. This includes G. E. Moore's own solution, according to which, in asserting that *p*, one *implies*, even though one does not actually say, that one believes it. I take it that the sense of 'implies' here is something like the sense in which, in asking, 'Have you stopped beating your wife?' one implies that the addressee has beaten his wife. Moore observed that not only is it absurd to say, 'It is raining but I don't believe it', but it is also absurd to say, 'It is raining but I don't know that it is'. He went on, therefore, to propose that in asserting that *p*, one generally implies that one *knows* that *p*. This explains the air of contradiction: 'It is raining' implies that I know that it is raining, but 'I don't know that it is' denies that I know this; so when I say, 'It is raining but I don't know that it is', something that I *say* contradicts something that I *imply*.[4]

Wittgenstein offers another linguistic solution. He contends that although in most contexts '*x* believes that *y*' means that the person referred to by '*x*' believes the proposition expressed by '*y*', sentences of the form 'I believe that *p*' are a special case: rather than meaning that the speaker believes that *p*, they function as a kind of hesitant assertion of *p*. Thus, 'It is raining, but I believe that it isn't' is actually contradictory: the first part asserts that it is raining, while the second part denies, albeit hesitantly, that it is raining.[5] Perhaps the best way to see the futility of the Wittgensteinian approach is to introduce a new term, say, 'schmelieve', with the stipulation that 'I schmelieve that *p*' —perhaps unlike 'I believe that *p*' —is to mean only that the speaker believes that *p*. We could then ask why 'It is raining, but I schmelieve that it isn't' is an absurd thing to say, even though it is not contradictory. And since this question would be just as puzzling as our original question involving 'believe'—indeed, 'It is raining but I schmelieve that it isn't' seems to be absurd in exactly the way we originally thought that 'It is raining but I believe that it isn't' was absurd—nothing is accomplished by positing the sort of ambiguity in the word 'believe' that Wittgenstein posits.

A third linguistic solution is Timothy Williamson's, according to which the activity of assertion is governed by a *constitutive norm* (roughly, a norm whose general recognition is a precondition on there being such a thing as assertion). This constitutive norm is the rule that one ought to assert only what one knows to be the case. Thus, in saying, 'It is raining but I don't know it is', I necessarily violate a norm essential to the practice

---

[4] This account appears in Moore (1993).

[5] Wittgenstein (1968, 190–2; 1980, 472–8, 501). Malcolm (1995) defends Wittgenstein's view at greater length.

of assertion, since I cannot know that it is raining and that I do not know that it is raining.[6]

One or more linguistic solutions may well be correct, as far as they go. I suspect that Moore is right to say that an assertion of p implies that the speaker knows that p, and this fact may, in turn, be explained by Williamson's thesis that the norm governing assertion is 'assert only what you know'. But all purely linguistic solutions are incomplete. Moore's Paradox cannot be fully resolved by appeal to rules governing solely the use of language, because it is easy to construct non-linguistic versions of the Paradox. It would be absurd to think to oneself, even without giving any overt expression to the thought, that it is raining but that one does not believe this. And presumably if we can explain why this *thought* would be absurd, we would also thereby understand why the corresponding assertion expressing such a thought is absurd. So it seems that we should rather focus on the question of why what we may call 'Moore-paradoxical beliefs' are absurd.[7]

III The Self-intimation Account

Perhaps Moore-paradoxical beliefs are absurd because (typical) beliefs are *self-intimating*, in the sense that if one believes that p (or if one *explicitly* believes that p, or *consciously* believes that p), then, if one considers whether one believes that p, one must believe that one believes that p. The Moore-paradoxical thinker believes something like (1) or (2) below:

(1) It is raining, but I do not believe that it is.

(2) It is raining, but I believe that it is not.

This (plausibly) entails that he believes that it is raining.[8] This, given the self-intimation thesis (and suitable background conditions), implies that he believes that he believes that it is raining. If he also accepts the second half of (1), then the Moore-paradoxical thinker has contradictory beliefs: he believes both that he believes it is raining, and that he does not believe it is raining. And if he accepts the second half of (2), then the Moore-paradoxical thinker must *take himself* to have contradictory beliefs: he believes both that he believes that it is raining, and that he believes that it is not

---

[6] Williamson (1996, esp. 506–7).

[7] Shoemaker (1996, 75–6) and de Almeida (2001, 33) stress this point.

[8] I do not assume that belief is closed under entailment in general. But the idea that believing a conjunction implies believing the first conjunct seems an especially plausible instance of doxastic closure.

raining. In either case, it is plausible that the Moore-paradoxical thinker must be irrational.[9]

This sort of account seems plausible when applied to (1) and (2). But what about the epistemic version of the Paradox, in which a thinker accepts something of the form of (3)?

(3) It is raining, but I do not know that it is.

Can something along the lines of the self-intimation account explain the absurdity of believing (3)? Only if there is a plausible self-intimation thesis that involves *knowledge* in the appropriate way. Some epistemologists find it plausible that, if one knows that *p*, and one considers whether one knows that *p*, one can always know by reflection that one knows that *p*.[10] It is important to realize that *this* is not the self-intimation thesis required to explain the absurdity of (3). Rather, to explain the absurdity of believing (3), one would have to adopt the stronger assumption that if one *believes* that *p*, and one considers whether one *knows* that *p*, then one must believe that one knows that *p*. From there, we could infer that the thinker who accepts the first conjunct of (3) accepts (if he considers the question) that he knows that it is raining. If he also accepts the second conjunct of (3), this thinker must have contradictory beliefs.

But in fact it is not true that whenever one believes that *p* and considers whether one knows it, one believes that one knows that *p*. To take an extreme case, Peter Unger undoubtedly has many beliefs. But when he considers whether he knows the things he believes, he does not come to believe that he knows them; instead, he comes to believe that he does not know any of them.[11] Doubtless Unger is *misguided* to think this way; but, as long as he does, he is a counter-example to the thesis that if one believes a thing and one considers whether one knows it, one will take oneself to know it.

IV Metacoherence and the Knowledge Norm

While it is undoubtedly false that anyone who believes *p* will on reflection believe that he knows *p*, I think there is a principle in this vicinity that is very likely correct: if one believes that *p*, one is thereby *rationally committed* to taking one's belief to be knowledge.[12]

---

[9] Shoemaker (1996) defends essentially this account of Moore's Paradox, albeit with more qualifications and complications.

[10] Sosa (1997, 232–3).   [11] I refer here to the Unger of *Ignorance* (1975).

[12] This principle is advanced by David Owens (2000, 37–41) and criticized by Klein (2004). I use 'committed' here in the sense commonly used in philosophical discourse, as when one says, 'Utilitarians are committed to the view that one should kill the healthy patient and harvest his organs'. I discuss the concept further in the text below.

I shall call this principle the *Knowledge Norm (for Belief)*. If correct, the principle provides a satisfying resolution of Moore's Paradox. A person who believes (3), 'It is raining, but I do not know that it is', must thereby believe that it is raining. According to the Knowledge Norm, this commits the believer to the view that he knows that it is raining. In denying, in the second half of (3), that he knows that it is raining, the believer thus contradicts something to which he is rationally committed. This seems like a satisfying account of our sense that Moore-paradoxical beliefs are something akin to contradictions. The absurdity of Moore-paradoxical statements is also easily explained, in terms of the fact that such statements express Moore-paradoxical beliefs; a statement expressing something akin to a contradictory belief is itself something akin to a contradictory statement.

There is more to be said for this account of Moore's Paradox. The Knowledge Norm account predicts that we should find all statements of the form 'p but $\sim\Phi(p)$', where $\Phi(p)$ is a condition on the speaker's knowing that p, absurd in much the same way as the original examples of Moore-paradoxical statements. Thus, consider the following proposed examples of Moore-paradoxical statements:

(1) It is raining, but I do not believe that it is.

(2) It is raining, but I believe that it is not.

(3) It is raining, but I do not know that it is.

(4) It is raining, but that isn't true.

(5) It is raining, but I have no justification for thinking so.

(6) It is raining, but my reason for thinking so is false.

(7) It is raining, but there are (non-misleading) facts that neutralize my reasons for believing that.

(8) It is raining, but my belief that it is was formed in an unreliable way.

(9) It is raining, but I would believe that even if it were false.

(10) It is raining, but I am not sure that it is.

(11) It is raining, but it is not certain that it is.

Each of these is based on a different putative requirement on knowledge.[13] And it is worth noting that each of (2) through (11) seems an irrational thing to assert or believe, something akin to a contradiction, just as (1) does. With respect to each of (10) and (11), note that the statement is not to be read as one in which the speaker asserts that it is raining and then, a second later, thinks better of his assertion and adds

---

[13] (6) is based on Clark's (1963) fully groundedness condition. (7) is based on the defeasibility analysis (Klein 1971). (8) is based on reliabilism (Goldman 1992, 105–26). (9) is based on Nozick's (1981, 172–8) tracking condition.

a qualifier; rather, the speaker means to assert that it is raining, and to continue to stand by that assertion while also admitting that he himself is not sure it is raining or that it is not certain that it is raining.[14] A speaker might very well say, as one often does, something of the form of 'It is *probably* raining, but I am not sure (or, it is not certain) that it is' or 'I *think* it is raining, but I am not sure (or, it is not certain) that it is'. But, again, we are to imagine a speaker who asserts that it *is* raining, and not merely that it is probably raining or that he thinks it is. That said, it should be fairly clear that (10) and (11) are Moore-paradoxical. (Compare the similar 'It is raining, but it may not be', whose unassertability is perhaps more patent.) Furthermore, there do not seem to be any *other* kinds of Moore-paradoxical propositions, of the form '*p* but $\sim\Phi(p)$' where $\Phi(p)$ is *not* plausibly regarded as a condition on the speaker's knowing that *p*. So it seems that the Knowledge Norm for Belief can be used to explain the absurdity of all Moore-paradoxical statements and beliefs.

One might object that, while the second conjunct in each of (1)–(11) contradicts something that is a condition on one's knowing that *p* according to *some* proposed analysis of knowledge, there is no proposed analysis of knowledge on which *all* of these second conjuncts contradict a requirement on knowledge; no epistemologist has yet proposed, for example, that knowledge is justified, true, fully grounded, certain belief that tracks the truth, formed by a reliable method, with no non-misleading defeaters. I think, however, that it is plausible that knowledge really does have all, or nearly all, of these requirements. This does not mean that the best analysis of knowledge ought to be a very complicated one, containing all these miscellaneous conditions. Rather, it is plausible that some of these conditions entail the others, making the latter redundant. For instance, if a belief is formed in an unreliable way, that fact, plausibly, constitutes a defeater for the belief's justification; hence, the no-defeater condition entails the reliability condition. Be that as it may, I think that if one can really *know* that it is raining while the second conjunct in one or more of (1)–(11) holds, then it is not absurd to assert that conjunct while affirming that it is raining. In fact, I think this is true of proposition (9)—I think one may know that *p* even when one's belief does not track the truth—but I shall discuss this point further below.

The thesis that it is irrational to believe any of (1)–(11), if true, renders the Knowledge Norm for Belief very plausible. For if, in believing that it is raining, one were *not* rationally committed to the belief that one knows it is raining, then why could one not rationally go on to accept something that implies that one does *not* know this?

We have not yet satisfactorily resolved Moore's Paradox, because we have not yet explained *why* the Knowledge Norm should hold. And this is something that is initially

---

[14] The difference between (10) and (11) lies in the fact that while (10) refers merely to the speaker's actual attitude toward *p*, (11) refers to the state of the evidence supporting *p*.

puzzling. In believing that p, I am, obviously, rationally committed to accepting that p is true; and if belief is self-intimating in some sense, or under suitable conditions, then I shall (under suitable conditions) also be committed to accepting that I believe that p. But my *knowing* that p is a much stronger condition than my having a true belief that p. So the question is why I should be rationally committed to thinking that this very strong condition holds.

The Knowledge Norm, in my view, is best explained by two further principles: the Principle of Metacoherence, and the Endorsement Theory of Knowledge:

> *Metacoherence*: Consciously believing that p commits one, on reflection, to comprehensively, epistemically endorsing one's own belief that p;
>
> *Endorsement Theory of Knowledge*: Knowledge attribution is the most comprehensive epistemic endorsement.

To explain what these claims mean: first, what is it to *endorse* a belief? It is to hold a metabelief that positively evaluates the first belief—more specifically, it is to believe that one ought to hold the first belief, or at least that it is not the case that one ought not to hold it. An *epistemic* endorsement is, roughly, an endorsement according to one of the criteria or goals peculiarly applicable to belief, or according to the criteria of epistemic rationality, as opposed, say, to a moral or prudential endorsement. 'Belief B is true' is an epistemic endorsement; 'Jon's faith in God is very comforting to him' is a prudential endorsement.

Second, what is it to be rationally committed to Φing? 'Believing that p commits one to Φing' does not entail that, if one believes that p, one rationally ought to Φ; it entails only that, if one believes that p, then one rationally ought either to Φ or to withdraw one's belief that p. For example, suppose that, on reflection, it becomes clear to me that my belief in the afterlife is purely a product of wishful thinking. In that case, it is false that I ought rationally to endorse my own belief in the afterlife; rather, I ought (epistemically) to surrender the belief. Indeed, I ought to surrender it *because* I cannot rationally endorse it epistemically (this is, roughly, because I know that beliefs based on wishful thinking are unlikely to be true). This is in accord with the Principle of Metacoherence, which simply dictates in this case that I cannot rationally continue to believe in the afterlife while reflectively refusing to epistemically endorse that belief.

Third, why the qualifier 'on reflection'? A subject believing that p might simply fail to consider whether his belief that p is epistemically acceptable; this would not render the subject irrational. What the Metacoherence Principle requires is that, if the subject comes to reflect on whether his belief is epistemically acceptable in some respect, then the subject is committed to the view that his belief *is* acceptable in that respect; that is, the subject should believe that his belief that p is acceptable or, if he cannot rationally do that, withdraw the belief that p. This does not require a subject to endorse his belief that *p* with respect to every dimension of epistemic appraisal, but only with respect to those dimensions that the subject considers. Similarly, the qualifier 'consciously' is included because a subject who merely unconsciously believes that *p* might, on reflection, rationally believe that he ought not to believe that *p*; perhaps if he is unaware of his actual belief that *p*, its persistence under such conditions would not mark him as irrational. In any case, I wish only to consider the case of conscious beliefs.

Fourth, what is meant by the qualifier 'comprehensively'? The modifier 'comprehensively' indicates that a subject is committed to epistemically endorsing his belief across the board, that is, with respect to every dimension of epistemic evaluation that he considers, as opposed, say, to endorsing it on some epistemic criteria but not others. For instance, a subject who considers both whether his belief that *p* is true and whether it is formed by a reliable method is committed to taking the belief *both* to be true *and* to have been formed by a reliable method; if he doubts either of these things but continues to believe that *p*, then he is to some extent irrational.

Fifth, what does it mean for knowledge to be the most comprehensive epistemic endorsement? The idea here is that to say that a person knows that *p* is to endorse his belief that *p* on all criteria, or along all dimensions, of epistemic evaluation; it is to say that there is no sufficient (epistemic, as opposed to prudential, moral, etc.) reason why that person should not believe that *p*. This is not meant as an illuminating *analysis* of the concept of knowledge, partly because I have given at most a sketchy account of the concept of epistemic endorsement, and because it may be impossible satisfactorily to explain that concept without employing the concept of knowledge. Nevertheless, the Endorsement Theory of Knowledge is non-trivial and interesting—it is non-trivial and interesting to say that there exists a distinctive type of evaluation applicable to beliefs, such that '*S* knows that *p*' offers the most comprehensive positive evaluation, of that kind, of *S*'s belief that *p*.

The Principle of Metacoherence and the Endorsement Theory of Knowledge, I suggest, offer a satisfying account of why the Knowledge Norm for Belief should hold and, hence, in turn, of why Moore-paradoxical propositions are unfit for belief or assertion. It is not hard to see why Metacoherence should be true. It seems reasonable that if I cannot endorse my belief that *p*, even in the minimal sense of holding it to be epistemically *acceptable*, then I ought, epistemically, to withdraw that belief. Consider some practical analogies. If, on reflection, one cannot rationally hold a course of action to be morally permissible, then one ought, morally, to refrain from that course of action. If, on reflection, one cannot rationally hold a course of action to be an acceptable way of pursuing one's goals, then one ought, prudentially, to refrain from that course of action. There ought, in short, to be a sort of coherence between what one does (believes) and one's attitudes about what one ought to do (believe).

The Endorsement Theory of Knowledge is more controversial. In my view, one's failure to satisfy one of the conditions (other than the belief condition) on knowing *p* implies that, in some sense, one ought not to believe that *p*. For instance, that *p* is false implies that, in some sense, one ought not to believe that *p*. Consider one objection to this claim: suppose that *p* is adequately *justified* for me, even though *p* is false. It seems to follow from this that I *should* believe that *p*. A similar objection applies, arguably, to every condition on knowledge that goes beyond justified belief. Thus, suppose that *p* is adequately justified for me, although I lack a reliable belief-forming method whose output would be *p*. Still, given just the fact that *p* is justified, it seems to follow that I ought to believe that *p*. Some would question, of course, whether *p*'s being justified is compatible with my lacking any available reliable belief-forming method whose output would be *p*.[15] Nevertheless, it is generally agreed that knowledge requires more than justified belief. So whatever further conditions may be required for knowledge, suppose that one of these conditions does not hold, yet one is still justified in believing that *p*; in such a case, it seems, one should believe that *p*, even though one does not know that *p*. This suggests at least that knowledge-ascription is not *merely* epistemic endorsement of a belief in my sense.

But, in fact, while my having justification for believing that *p* may entail in some sense that I ought to believe that *p*, there is still a sense in which, if I do not satisfy the other conditions (apart from justified belief) on knowledge with respect to *p*, I ought not to believe that *p*. Consider a practical analogy. In driving to the airport, I must decide whether to take Interstate 25, or 104th Avenue. I-25 is normally about 10 minutes shorter, although the scenery is less attractive. I decide that, because I do not care much about the scenery, I shall take I-25. Assume that this is a rational decision. But suppose that, after getting on the freeway, I discover that an accident, which I could not have anticipated, has caused a traffic jam. As I sit there stuck in traffic on I-25, I say to myself: 'Damn, I should have taken 104th Avenue'. This is a reasonable thing to say. But I would not say that my choice was irrational or unjustified, given my information at the time. The 'should' here is one that takes account of the actual, external facts, whether they were available to me at the time of decision or not, that bear on the achievement of my goals. In *this* sense of 'should', that a decision was justified is compatible with the observation that one should have chosen differently. Similarly, there is a sense in which a person epistemically should not believe that *p*—even if *p* is, epistemically justified—if *p* is, in fact, false, or his grounds for believing that *p* are false, or his belief-forming method is, in fact, unreliable, etc.

But, whether or not you are convinced that this external sense of 'should' to which I refer is legitimate, it is clear in any case that if I *take* my belief that *p* to be false, my grounds for the belief to be false, my method of forming the belief to be unreliable,

[15] Goldman (1992, 122–3).

or the like, then I should not believe that p. Since, pursuant to the Metacoherence principle, I am committed by my belief that p to the view that it is not the case that I should not believe that p, I must *not* take my belief that p to have any of those undesirable, knowledge-canceling features. And more than this, it seems plausible that I am committed, positively, to taking my belief to have the desirable features of truth, reliability, and so on. If, on reflection, I find that I can at best remain neutral concerning whether my belief-forming method is reliable, then it seems that I am not justified in relying on that method, and thus that I should not believe that p.

V The Problem of Certainty

Perhaps the most puzzling aspect of Moore's Paradox is that it seems almost contradictory to think 'It is raining, but it may not be'. Why should this be? I take it that the 'may' here indicates epistemic possibility, so it would seem that 'it may not be raining' would be true as long as one's evidence that it is raining is less than conclusive. The statement that it *may* not be raining is, of course, compatible with the possibility that it is actually raining. Moreover, surely one might have adequate justification for believing that it is raining, while realizing that this justification is less than 100 per cent conclusive. In such a situation, would one not be both justified in believing that it is raining, and justified in believing that it *may* not be raining? If so, what is so odd about the belief that it is raining but it may not be? The fact that 'It is raining, but it may not be' strikes us as absurd suggests that the belief that it is raining commits one to its being *certain* that it is raining. The problem is that it seems that the standards for justified belief ought to be lower than the standards for certainty.

To add to the puzzle, consider that it does *not* strike us as odd to say or think, 'I *believe* it is raining, but it may not be'. This suggests that, while one cannot rationally believe both that it is raining and that it may not be, one *can* rationally believe both *that one believes* it is raining and that it may not be. But this would be very odd.

What I think is going on here is this. First, we need to draw a distinction between *high degree of belief*, and *outright belief* or *categorical belief*.[16] Degree of belief, or subjective probability, is the sort of thing that explains the betting odds one would be willing to accept. High degree of belief is necessary but not sufficient for outright belief. Two individuals may agree in regarding p as 99 per cent probable, and yet one may consider this good enough to accept p, while the other continues to withhold judgment.

---

[16] My conception of outright belief here is largely based on Owens's (2000, 142–5) conception of belief, though Owens and I differ over whether one can have reflective control over belief and over whether inconclusive reasons can motivate belief.

There would be a qualitative difference in these two individuals' attitudes: the first individual, for example, can be expected to cease to gather evidence or conduct inquiry about whether *p*. In his reasoning and practical deliberations, where the truth of *p* is relevant, he will proceed on the assumption that *p*, without taking account of *p*'s probability. He will not treat alternatives to *p* as relevant in his decision-making or theoretical reasonings about further facts. However, the second individual, the one who has a high degree of belief but not outright belief, will enter the *probability* of *p* (at least in some rough sense) into his practical and theoretical reasonings. He will consider it appropriate to gather evidence and conduct further inquiry into whether *p*, assuming the costs of doing so are manageable and the question of whether *p* is of some interest to him; he will not, at any rate, reject the idea of conducting further inquiry on the grounds that it has already been settled whether *p*. And while the first individual might agree to conduct inquiry into whether *p* for some ulterior purpose—for instance, to humor more skeptical colleagues—he cannot do so for the purpose of answering the question as to whether *p*, since, again, he regards that question as already settled in favor of *p*. This attitude of categorical belief need not be irrevocable—one's categorically believing *p now* is compatible with one's later losing that belief, perhaps as a result of evidence of the kind that one did not consider worth looking for, or perhaps even as a result of pragmatic considerations (if the costs of error should suddenly rise, one may rethink one's earlier view of the amount of evidence required to justify outright belief in a given proposition).

Next, we need to understand the concepts of certainty and epistemic possibility. Certainty, at least in one important sense of the word, is a matter of one's being justified in taking the attitude of categorical belief as I have just described it. In other words, it is certain that *p* when the available evidence makes it reasonable to close the inquiry into whether *p*, regarding the matter as having been settled in favor of *p*; to conduct future deliberation and reasoning on the assumption that *p*; and to dismiss alternative possibilities as irrelevant. Epistemic possibility I take to be the dual of certainty: it is epistemically possible that *p* (it may be that *p*) if and only if it is not certain that $\sim p$. In this sense, many propositions are certain for me now. For example, notwithstanding skeptical scenarios, it is certain that other people exist, and that they have conscious experiences. I do not need to conduct any further inquiry into that. When deciding whether to rob the local liquor store, I do not need to take into account the possibility that the store owner is a mindless automaton or the product of an elaborate hallucination.

Stronger conceptions of certainty exist. One could propose that it is certain that *p* only if one's justification for *p* (or one's having the justification one has) is logically incompatible with the falsity of *p*. Or one might propose that *p* is certain only if it is impossible that anything be more justified than *p* is. I reject these notions because they do not appear to match the ordinary usage of such words as 'certain' and 'possible'. Thus, imagine the following dialogue:

A: Do you know where your shoes are?

B: Yes, they're by the door. I remember leaving them there just 10 minutes ago.

A: Might they be on the moon instead?

In any normal context, B's only appropriate response is 'No' (or, perhaps, 'What on Earth are you talking about?'). But on either of the stronger conceptions of certainty just mentioned, a more apt response would be something like this: 'Well, *of course* they might be on the moon. Isn't that obvious?' For, after all, it is obvious that one's justification for believing that one's shoes are by the door, when one remembers leaving them there 10 minutes ago, is logically consistent with their now being on the moon.

We now have an explanation for how certainty can be a requirement on rational belief: certainty just *is* justification for outright belief in a proposition. When we think that it would be absurd to believe 'It is raining but it may not be', we are imagining the believer *categorically believing* that it is raining but that it may not be; on my view, this amounts to his categorically believing that it is raining and that he is not justified in categorically believing that. If we explicitly imagine a weaker doxastic attitude, Moore's Paradox does not arise. Thus, imagine someone regarding it as highly probable that it is raining, but also believing that it *may* not be. Or imagine (what is perhaps slightly different) one's having a high degree of belief that it is raining (being willing to offer strong odds on the proposition, and so on) while believing that it may not be. In these cases, I think it is clear that there is nothing self-defeating or contradiction-like in the subject's attitude. To find something contradiction-like, we must ascribe to the believer some quite robust sort of belief.

However, in those contexts where one says something of the form, 'I *think* that p, but I may be wrong' or 'I *believe* that p, but perhaps $\sim p$', 'think' and 'believe' refer merely to having a high degree of belief, not outright belief. This is why these statements escape Moore-paradoxicalness.

VI Lessons for the Analysis of Knowledge

Moore's Paradox can aid us in the analysis of knowledge. The fact that it is in some manner self-defeating to declare 'p, but I do not know that p' suggests a test for proposed conditions on knowledge: $\Phi(p)$ is a genuine requirement on knowing p only if believing (or asserting) that p rationally commits one to accepting that $\Phi(p)$.

Some alleged conditions on knowledge fail this test. Robert Nozick's proposed counter-factual tracking condition—if p were false, S would not believe that p—is a case in point. The same arguments that show tracking to be unnecessary for knowledge also show that one is not rationally committed to believing that one's beliefs track the truth. First, consider the failures of closure.[17] Though Nozick was happy to reject the closure principle, *some* failures of closure seem particularly counter-intuitive, such as cases in which one knows that $(p \& q)$ without knowing p. On Nozick's account, for example, one may know that one is not a brain in a vat *and* one has two hands, but one cannot know that one is not a brain in a vat.[18] This seems an unacceptable result.

The Knowledge Norm for Belief leads us to a similar conclusion; indeed, the Knowledge Norm generates a general argument for closure. Suppose that $\Phi(p)$ is a condition on knowledge that violates the closure principle: then it is possible that I know p and I know that p entails q, but because $\Phi(q)$ does not hold, I do not know q. Suppose in addition that, as presumably might also be the case, I know myself to be in such a situation. In this case, I am rational in believing p, but—given the Knowledge Norm for belief—I cannot rationally accept q since I know that I do not know q. This seems unacceptable, because it also seems that my acceptance of p, together with my knowledge that p entails q, rationally *commits* me to accepting q. So my only rational recourse would be to withhold both p and q. One problem with this is that it seems that my knowing p should give me license to (continue to) believe p. Another problem is that, at least on Nozick's view, failures of closure are so pervasive that, in the end, I would be forced to withhold judgment about nearly everything—for nearly every proposition p that I believe, there exists a proposition q such that q does not satisfy the tracking condition and I can see that p entails q. This can be seen from the fact that most things I believe entail that I am not in one sort of skeptical scenario or another, and, as Nozick notes, we do not satisfy the tracking condition with respect to the negations of skeptical scenarios.[19] The point is made even clearer by the example immediately below.

The second problem with the tracking condition is that it entails, falsely, that it is impossible ever to know that one is not mistaken about something that one

---

[17] Here, I shall take the closure principle as the principle that if one knows that p and that p entails q, then one knows that q.

[18] The nearest possible world in which it is false that (I am not a brain in a vat and I have two hands) is a world in which I do not have two hands, perhaps through some horrible accident a few years ago, but I am still not a brain in a vat. In this world, I do not believe (I am not a brain in a vat and I have two hands). So I track the truth with respect to the proposition (I am not a brain in a vat and I have two hands). But I do not track the truth with respect to the proposition (I am a brain in a vat), since in the nearest world in which I am a brain in a vat, I falsely think I am not one.

[19] Nozick (1981, 200–4).

believes. For, if one were mistaken about whether *p*, one would still believe that one were not mistaken.[20] This example also shows that one is not, in general, committed to believing that one's beliefs satisfy tracking. For although it is obvious that the belief that I am not mistaken about *p* fails to satisfy the tracking condition, surely it is false that I therefore ought to withdraw the belief. I can recognize that if I were mistaken, I would think I was not mistaken, but still reasonably go on to say that, in fact, I am not mistaken. (Compare this case: a murder suspect asserts, 'If I *had* committed the murder, I would probably lie to you and say that I did not do it; however, in fact I am not lying and I did not do it'. Though the hearer may well distrust the subject's word, the assertion makes perfect sense and is not Moore-paradoxical.)

The tracking condition, then, is one example of a spurious condition on knowledge. Doubtless there are others; the writings of philosophical skeptics are the most likely places to find them. Thus, suppose a skeptic maintains that one knows *p* only if one's justification for *p* is logically inconsistent with the negation of *p*. This putative condition on knowledge would make it mysterious why 'It is raining, but I do not know that it is' should be Moore-paradoxical. For it hardly seems that, in believing that it is raining, one is committed to believing that one's evidence for the claim that it is raining logically entails that it is raining—notice that 'It is raining, though my evidence for that claim does not logically entail that it is raining' does not seem Moore-paradoxical. Therefore, if the skeptic's condition were a genuine condition on knowledge, there should also be nothing paradoxical about saying 'It is raining, though I do not know that'.

VII The Significance of Knowledge

Finally, Moore's Paradox illuminates what is so philosophically important and interesting about the concept of knowledge. Initially, it may seem puzzling that this particular concept should give rise to an entire major branch of philosophy. Why is the concept of knowledge more philosophically significant than, say, the concept of belief, or of matter, or of happiness? Our puzzlement is likely, if anything, to increase once we see the sort of complex and seemingly gerrymandered accounts of knowledge that philosophers in this field have devised.

[20] Nozick (1981, 179–80) later adds a qualification to the tracking condition, resulting in roughly the following: *S* knows that *p* only if, if *p* were false and *S* used the same method to form a belief about whether *p* as *S* actually used, then *S* would not believe that *p*. My objection can be posed also to this principle: on Nozick's view, one could never know that one's actual belief-forming method did not deliver a false result.

The Knowledge Norm and the Endorsement Theory of Knowledge alleviate this puzzlement: they suggest that knowledge is *the strongest condition that one must take to hold when one believes a thing*. All areas of human inquiry, both inside and outside of philosophy, are centrally concerned with the attempt to form and transmit beliefs about their subject. Physicists form and transmit beliefs about the physical world; historians form and transmit beliefs about the past; and so on. The most comprehensive intellectual commitments of any inquirer are, therefore, of the form 'I know that *p*'. The nature and extent of knowledge are thus of central importance for all intellectual endeavor. In a sense, epistemologists study the conditions for the legitimacy of all claims.

Now, in spite of what I have said, some philosophers will doubt my claims. Some may feel that the Knowledge Norm is too strong, that there are conditions on knowledge that one need not take to obtain when one believes a thing. This is a particularly likely position for those who take knowledge to require certainty in some very strong sense. Nevertheless, the concept of *the most comprehensive rational commitment of belief*, or the strongest condition that one is committed to taking to obtain when one consciously believes that *p*, is an important and interesting one, whether or not that condition is knowledge. Furthermore, I should think it clear that this concept is at least strikingly close to that of knowledge. Clearly, if I consciously believe that *p*, I am rationally committed to taking my belief to be both true and justified; I am also committed to taking it to be fully grounded (not based directly or indirectly on any false beliefs). This is already quite close to knowledge. If 'knowledge' in ordinary English actually requires some further, very stringent, condition, such as a demanding form of certainty, such that one is not committed to taking this condition to hold when one believes a thing, then I should think the concept of *the most comprehensive rational commitment of belief* more interesting than that of *knowledge*. In any event, I consider the former concept worthy of the attention of epistemologists, and it is to that concept that Moore's Paradox directs our attention.[21]

References

Clark, Michael, 'Knowledge and Grounds: A Comment on Mr. Gettier's Paper', *Analysis*, 24 (1963), 46–8.

de Almeida, Claudio, 'What Moore's Paradox is About', *Philosophy and Phenomenological Research*, 62 (2001), 33–58.

Goldman, Alvin I., *Liaisons: Philosophy Meets the Cognitive and Social Sciences* (Cambridge, Mass.: MIT Press, 1992).

[21] I would like to thank Peter Klein and the numerous participants of the *Certain Doubts* weblog for very interesting and helpful discussion of the issues in this paper.

Klein, Peter, 'A Proposed Definition of Propositional Knowledge', *Journal of Philosophy*, 68 (1971), 471−82.

——— 'Skepticism: Ascent and Assent?', in J. Greco (ed.), *Ernest Sosa and His Critics* (Malden, Mass.: Blackwell, 2004), 112−25.

Malcolm, Norman, 'Disentangling Moore's Paradox', in G. H. von Wright (ed.), *Wittgensteinian Themes: Essays 1978−1989* (Ithaca: Cornell University Press, 1995), 195−206.

Moore, G. E., 'Moore's Paradox', in *G. E. Moore: Selected Writings*, ed. Thomas Baldwin (New York: Routledge, 1993), 207−12.

Nozick, Robert, *Philosophical Explanations* (Cambridge: Cambridge University Press, 1981).

Owens, David, *Reason without Freedom: The Problem of Epistemic Normativity* (London: Routledge, 2000).

Shoemaker, Sydney, 'Moore's Paradox and Self-Knowledge', in *The First-Person Perspective and Other Essays* (New York: Cambridge University Press, 1996), 74−93.

Sosa, Ernest, 'How to Resolve the Pyrrhonian Problematic: A Lesson from Descartes', *Philosophical Studies*, 85 (1997), 229−49.

Unger, Peter, *Ignorance: A Case for Scepticism* (Oxford: Clarendon Press, 1975).

Williamson, Timothy, 'Knowing and Asserting', *Philosophical Review*, 105 (1996), 489−523.

Wittgenstein, Ludwig, *Philosophical Investigations*, 3rd edn., trans. by G. E. M. Anscombe (New York: Macmillan, 1968).

——— *Remarks on the Philosophy of Psychology*, vol. 1, ed. by G. E. M. Anscombe and G. H. von Wright, trans. by G. E. M. Anscombe (Oxford: Basil Blackwell, 1980).

8

Can the Dead Speak?

Roy Sorensen

Do not pass by my epitaph,
Wayfarer, but when you have stopped,
hear and learn, then depart.
There is no boat, To carry you to Hades,
No ferryman Charon, No judge Aeacus, No Dog Cerberus.
All of us below have become bones and ashes.
Truly, I have nothing more to tell you.
So depart, wayfarer, Lest dead though I am
I seem to you to be a teller of vain tales.

Epitaph of 'a third century Roman cynic'

After G. E. Moore suffered a stroke, his physician advised against excitement or fatigue (Malcolm 1958, 67). Accordingly, Moore's wife limited his philosophical conversations to 90 minutes. Ludwig Wittgenstein disapproved. A conversation with Moore should continue until it reached a proper ending. Moore had spent his whole life in the pursuit of truth. If he collapsed in the course of philosophical discussion, that would be a fitting death.

Mrs Moore could have replied to Wittgenstein (and perhaps did!) that more truth would be obtained through a longer life. When G. E. Moore died, in 1958, his remarks were put at an end.

Death is generally assumed to be the end of all communication. Of course, people are quoted after their deaths. That has long been a solace to authors. Here is the epitaph of the first important Roman poet, Quintus Ennius (239–169 BC):

Behold, citizens, this portrait of Ennius as an old man,
He who told the story of the greatest deeds of your fathers.

> Let no one adorn my tomb with tears. Why?
> Because I lit about alive through
> the mouths of men.

(Shore 1997, 70)

Quintus Ennius is only speaking metaphorically about being alive. Is he only metaphorically speaking? When you read the epitaph of Quintus Ennius does he thereby make a fresh assertion?

Alan Sidelle answers 'yes'. He thinks people can defer assertions. People make fresh assertions each time their answering machine says 'I am not here now'. Wills are another example. The assertion takes effect after death.

If deferred assertions are possible, then G. E. Moore was mistaken in claiming that one cannot assert sentences such as 'I went to the pictures last Tuesday, but I don't believe that I did' (1942, 543). The trick is to put it in a suicide note.

I shall defend Moore (and David Kaplan's theory of demonstratives) by arguing that deferred assertions are as impossible. Since deferred assertions would be possible if there were conditional assertions, I argue also against these conditional speech acts. We can affirm conditionals but cannot conditionally affirm. Our extant categories of linguistic forms can accommodate the data marshaled in support of examples of conditional assertions. For instance, many 'conditional assertions' are just hedged assertions.

But Sidelle's case for deferred assertions forces conservatives to acknowledge a new category of speech act: displaying sentences. A display has a status intermediate between assertion and quotation. When you display an automated email message explaining why you cannot promptly reply to messages, you take responsibility for the accuracy of your automated message—but not as much responsibility as when you personally reply. As the channel for conveying information becomes increasingly indirect, the connection between utterances and the speaker's mental states becomes too weak to count as assertion. We may adopt the fiction that an assertion has transpired (say at the moment of death). Composers of wills prepare sentence displays that are designed to have postmortem effects. I can display 'I am the late the Roy Sorensen' but cannot assert it.

Some automated speech acts are fictive speech acts. When the automated teller says, 'It has been a pleasure to serve you. Have a nice day!', the machine has neither thanked you nor has it bid you to have a nice day. Instead, you have participated in make-believe reminiscent of the make-believe children enjoy with talking dolls and ventriloquists.

But displays are literal just as guesses are literal (as opposed to being make-believe assertions). Their intermediate status explains why the automated email response 'I cannot immediately reply to your message' is not self-refuting, even though it is sent immediately.

I apply the concept of a sentence display to the automated inscriptions and utterances of computers. This includes a parting treatment of Searle's Chinese Room thought experiment.

I The relevance of Moore's Paradox

At age 12, G. E. Moore became an evangelical Christian. Christians believe that some of the dead, at least Jesus, communicate after death. In John 20: 19–29, Jesus reappears after his crucifixion and speaks with his disciples.

Spiritualists attempt to document their contacts with photography and auditory recordings. The inventor Thomas Edison wished to improve on the poor reception that plagues *séances*:

> I am inclined to believe that our personality hereafter will be able to affect matter. If this reasoning be correct, then, if we can evolve an instrument so delicate as to be affected, or moved, or manipulated by our personality as it survives in the next life, such an instrument, when made available, ought to record something.   (quoted by Austin Lescarboura 1920, 47)

Members of the American Association of Electronic Voice Phenomena hunt for voices with the latest acoustic equipment. Their efforts became better known through Don DeLillo's supernatural thriller *White Noise* (which was turned into a movie in 2005 starring Michael Keaton).

G. E. Moore's religious phase was short lived. Moore was a shy boy, who experienced emotional difficulty discharging his obligation to convert others. He did not like to preach or distribute religious tracts. This made him receptive to intervention by his eldest brother, the poet Thomas Sturges Moore. The poet persuaded the philosopher that there was no evidence that God exists and almost as little evidence that God does not exist.

Moore stopped being an evangelical Christian. Did he also stop believing in God? Like other philosophers of his generation, Moore became an idealist. This belief, that reality is fundamentally mental (or, as Moore would say, 'spiritual'), was widely perceived as a substitute for religion. The leading British idealist, Francis Herbert Bradley, acknowledged this role: 'Metaphysics is the finding of bad reasons for what we believe upon instinct, but to find these reasons is no less an instinct' (1893, xiv).

G. E. Moore soon stepped back from his contemporary Bradley and became a follower of Immanuel Kant. In *The Critique of Pure Reason*, Kant presented his refutations of proofs of God's existence as a *service* to religion. Kant's idea was to make room for faith by showing that there was no hope of gaining evidence for God's existence.

At the start of the twentieth century, Moore's allegiance retreated even further backward, towards the Revd Thomas Reid's (1710–96) common-sense philosophy. Instead of becoming a follower of Reid, Moore developed his own distinctive philosophy (disagreeing with Reid on key issues such as the existence of sense-data). Moore gives almost as much weight to common sense as did Reid. (Reid is susceptible to grandiose thinking about this touchstone to reality.) Moore is more circumspect about what it implies. He thinks these entailments are most accessible through careful study of ordinary language. Moore pays unprecedented attention to locutions such as 'good', 'believe', and 'see'. The smaller the word, the more attention Moore lavishes on it. His (often exasperating) attention to detail makes Moore's writings technical, pedantic, and extraordinarily fruitful.

In 1946 Moore published a discovery that, in my opinion, undermines agnostic theism (and much else—for a survey read Mitchell Green's and John Williams's introduction to their anthology *Moore's Paradox*). Moore's immediate target was Charles Stevenson's (1942, 80) thesis that 'It was right of Brutus to stab Caesar' means 'I now approve of Brutus' stabbing of Caesar'. Moore objects that this ethical subjectivism confuses what a speaker implies with what he means. The speaker *implies* that he approves of Brutus stabbing Caesar, but Moore denies that this is what the assertion *means*. When a speaker says 'It is raining', he implies that he believes that it is raining. But the content of the assertion does not contain this claim about the speaker's mental state. Stevenson may have been misled by the inconsistency of 'The stabbing was right but I do not approve of it'. This sounds like a contradiction, but it is only odd in the way the following statement is odd: 'It is raining but I do not believe it'. The content of that sentence is consistent; it just reports a mistake. The inconsistency lies in the saying of the sentence rather than in what is said. If the speaker's approval were part of the meaning of 'The stabbing was right', then there would be a genuine contradiction in the content of 'The stabbing was right but I do not believe it'. But there is not, so Stevenson's analysis of ethical statements is mistaken.

According to Moore, we almost always believe what we assert. The prevalence of sincerity makes 'It is raining but I do not believe it' surprising. This statistical characterization of the anomaly is generally regarded as shallow—even as a naïve underestimate of the frequency of lying. Wittgenstein complains that Moore opened a wasp's nest but the wasps were too listless to get out.

Moore's detection of the anomaly, in contrast, was hailed as an important advance. Ludwig Wittgenstein praised it as Moore's greatest discovery (Malcolm 1958, 56). The historical record is bearing out Wittgenstein's assessment.

Moore shies away from the topic of religion. Consequently, I have no textual support for my application of Moore's Paradox to agnostic theism. But the basic idea is straightforward. Recall Kant's interest in making room for faith by removing the possibility of evidence for God's existence. Now consider the analogy between 'It is raining but I do not believe it' and

1 It is raining but I have no evidence that it is raining.

2 I believe it is raining for reasons that are independent of whether it is raining

Sentence 1 is odd because the speaker cannot sincerely assert what he thinks he does not know. When the speaker asserts a proposition, he implies that he has a reason for thinking it true. Sentence 2 helps us to see that not any reason will do. Practical reasons (such as there being a reward for believing that it is raining) do not produce belief. Only reasons for the truth of p generate belief that p.

This Moorean argument works only if 'evidence' includes meta-evidence. Sometimes the absence of familiar forms of evidence is evidence at a higher level (as when police discovered the total absence of fingerprints in the Hillside Strangler's apartment). Perhaps Tertullian had a higher level evidential principle when he said 'I believe because it is absurd'; perhaps his premise was that the correct creed was the one that put the greatest strain on our credulity.

Higher order principles (such as simplicity) are also needed charitably to interpret atheists who infer that God does not exist from the absence of evidence that God exists. In the absence of higher order principles, agnostic atheism will share the Moorean absurdity of agnostic theism.

Moore's theory of belief and his areligious lifestyle suggest that he did not believe in God. After he adopted a common-sense philosophy, he denied that the near universality of belief in the supernatural makes belief in God common sense.

II A Moorean Case Against Postmortem Assertions

If Moore had been asked whether postmortem assertions are possible, he would have answered 'no'. Moore would have granted that he spoke to us and would have granted that these remarks could be remembered or discovered and then repeated to others. But we are only repeating what the dead asserted, not what they are presently asserting or will assert. Moore might well have regarded 'People do not say anything after they die' as part of common sense.

As is often the case, common sense can be reinforced by the self-defeat incurred in attempts to deny it. 'I am dead' is a pragmatic contradiction. Although internally consistent, the statement is disconfirmed by the fact I am asserting it. Conversely, reports of being alive are pragmatic tautologies. The serious illness of James Ross Clemens led to a report that his cousin Samuel Clemens had died. In May 1897 Samuel

Clemens wrote to set the record straight: 'The report of my illness grew out of his illness, this report of my death was an exaggeration.'

According to Moore, a speaker can only assert what he intends others to take him to believe. This explains the self-defeating nature of 'It is raining but I do not believe it'. Although the sentence is consistent, one cannot consistently assert it. In general, you cannot assert a proposition that plainly implies that you lack the psychological state you aim to evince. A person who is dead plainly has no beliefs. That is why it is self-refuting for someone to say 'I am dead'. All subsequent accounts of assertion labor to accommodate Moore's result (Williamson 1996, 506).

III Recalcitrant postmortem assertions

But how are we to reconcile the Moorean verdict of unassertibility with the quotation that opens this essay? The cynic continues his epitaph:

> Do not favor this monument with sweet smelling oils
> or garlands, for it is but a stone.
> Do not feed the funeral flames, it is a waste of money.
> If you can give, give while I live.
> Pouring wine on the ashes will only turn them to mud,
> and besides the dead will not drink.
> For so I shall be. And you have heaped up earth on these remains,
> say that what this was, it will never be again.

> (Shore 1997, 72)

The cynic is not assuming that he somehow survives death. His point is that there is no afterlife. He is dead, dead, dead. The cynic is urging us to devote ourselves to those who are truly alive.

The practical import of the cynic's message militates against the hypothesis that he is *pretending* to assert. Generally, it is easier to pretend to do something than really to do it. But speaking is an exception. If the absence of an appropriate intentions and beliefs prevents the dead from speaking, then that absence also prevents the dead from pretending to speak.

One might reply that it is the *hearer* who is pretending that the dead speak. One can suppose of a corpse that it is alive and speaking. Children play with talking dolls this way. The scope of the pretence does not include the doll's lack of mental states. But, in the above passage, the dead's absence of mental states is the cynic's central theme. One would be pretending that a speaker correctly believes he is without beliefs.

While strolling through the Dartmouth College cemetery, I solemnly read inscriptions for the edification of my 6-year-old son, Zachary. This graveyard is full of dedicated professors, virtuous alumni, and altruistic benefactors of the college. Bored, my son enquired where the bad people were buried. The pretence hypothesis conflicts with the possibility of epitaphs being deceptions. If lapidary puffery were a game of make-believe, then the players would never be fooled.

Finally, some postmortem statements are not designed to be read by anyone. The spacecrafts Voyager 1 and 2 carry messages about humanity that have almost no chance of being received. But someone who believed that his epitaph about humanity would never be read might still wish to post the statement in the safety of empty space. This commemoration would not be a prop in a game of make-believe.

IV The Impact on Direct Reference Theories

I have focused on how postmortem assertions are an anomaly for G. E. Moore. But they are also anomalies for philosophers of language who came after Moore, especially those who work on direct reference.

In 1985 the famous actor Yul Brynner made an anti-smoking commercial in which he grimly says 'When you see this commercial, I'll be dead from lung cancer from years of smoking'. The enduring force of Brynner's warning is magnified by his use of the indexicals 'I' and 'you'. My oldest son, Maxwell, was born in 1995, ten years after Brynner died. But when Maxwell viewed a rerun of this commercial, he understood that the 'you' includes him.

Yul Brynner's referential success would be an anomaly for theories of direct reference. According to David Kaplan 'you' secures its reference by the addressee's causal connection with the speaker. So Brynner should not be able directly to refer to people who come into existence after he goes out of existence. He can indirectly refer to a future individual by means of a description such as 'the eldest son of Roy Sorensen'. Brynner cannot directly refer, as I do, by *pointing* to my eldest son, or by using the name 'Maxwell', or by using the demonstrative term 'that' as in 'That is my boy'. But if Brynner can make fresh assertions after death, then he can refer to postmortem people.

Indexical words are governed by rules that borrow properties from the utterance itself: 'I' means the speaker of the sentence, 'you' means the addressee of the utterance, 'now' means the time at which the utterance is made, 'here' means the place at which the utterance is made. However, 'I am not speaking' does not mean the semantic contradiction 'The speaker of this sentence is not speaking'. According to Kaplan, 'I' is a directly referential term. The individual rather than the description 'the speaker' is part of the proposition.

Kaplan thinks that some sentences are contingently analytic. 'I am not here now' should always result in a false utterance. If 'I' picks outs the speaker, and 'here' picks out the place of the utterance, and 'now' picks out the time of the utterance, then necessarily the proposition will be true. The proposition itself is not a necessary truth. The *character* of the sentence is analytic in the sense that its meaning guarantees a truth but the *content* of what is expressed will be contingent. Thus Kaplan (1989, 540) describes 'I am here now' as contingently analytic. Indeed, he says Descartes's cogito is analytic.

V Deferred Utterances

David Kaplan is vexed by the 'answering machine paradox'. When an answering machine says 'I am not here now', the utterance is normally an informative truth, not a self-defeating falsehood.

Alan Sidelle's ingenious solution is that the recorded message is a 'deferred utterance'. Instead of being uttered at the time of the recording, the message takes effect when a caller rings the telephone. 'Now' is therefore indexed to the time when the message is activated. Since the time of utterance is the time at which the call is made, 'now' is indexed to this later time.

On Sidelle's analysis, Kaplan was right about the rule being that 'now' means the time of utterance. He was wrong about when the utterance must occur. Since utterances may be deferred, 'I am here now' is not a contingent a priori truth.

Can Kaplan escape the answering-machine paradox by instead denying a truth-value to the recorded messages? No. Suppose that the owner of the answering machine is home but allows the machine to respond 'I am not home now'. Sidelle characterizes this as lying (1991, 533).

Thus, one tells the truth when one's answering machine plays 'I'm not here now,' and one is not at home, and to tell the truth is to make a true assertion. We can perform utterances at a distance . . .   (1991, 534)

We can perform many other acts at a distance. After loading his clothes in a washing machine, Sidelle can hurry over to the supermarket. When he meets a friend there, Sidelle can explain his haste by reporting that he is doing his laundry.

VI Conditional Assertion

Although Alan Sidelle does not mention conditional assertion, deferred utterances can be considered a species of this genus. W. V. Quine credits the idea of conditional assertion to Philip Rhinelander:

An affirmation of the form 'if *p* then q' is commonly felt less as an affirmation of a conditional than as a conditional affirmation of the consequent. If, after we have made such an affirmation, the antecedent turns out true, then we consider ourselves committed to the consequent, and are ready to acknowledge error if it proves false. If on the other hand the antecedent turns out to have been false, our conditional affirmation is as if it had never been made.   (Quine 1950, 12)

The standard analogy is with a conditional bet. If the condition is not satisfied, then the whole thing is off. Commentators on conditionals have suggested that conditional assertion may help to resolve the paradoxes of material implication, the raven paradox, and even provide a foundation for understanding all other types of conditionals (DeRose and Grandy 1999).

Deferred utterances can be reduced to conditional assertions. 'I am not here now' can be paraphrased as 'If you are receiving this sentence, then I am not here now'. One might object that in a deferred utterance it is a matter of *when* the message will be received rather than *if*. But a traveling salesman can record 'I am not here now' on his hotel answering machine just to cover the possibility of a call. Every deferred utterance S that lacks an explicit antecedent has an elliptical antecedent; it is elliptical for 'If you are receiving this sentence then S'.

A deferred utterance can itself be a conditional assertion. For instance, the answering machine could say 'If you are calling about the picnic, it is cancelled because of the weather forecast.' The reduction thesis says this is elliptical for a conditional assertion embedded in another conditional assertion. The reduction schema links the fate of conditional assertions to deferred utterances.

VII Postmortem Assertions

If the owner of the answering machine dies, does he continue to make assertions through the machine? Sidelle imposes limits on some deferred utterances. If he finds an old note from his wife saying 'I am at the store ', Sidelle (1991, 537) dismisses the deferred utterance as defunct. Does Sidelle think all deferred utterances expire with their speakers?

No. Sidelle points out that wills have sentences that are designed to be read after the speaker has died. Consider 'If my nephew is by now no longer an alcoholic and a gambler, he receives one-sixth of my estate':

It seems to me that the most natural, and perhaps necessary way of taking this is as an utterance by the writer of the will (to vouchsafe the reference of 'my'), an utterance that takes place at the time of the reading of the will (to vouchsafe the reference of 'now')—and thus, an utterance which he makes after he is dead. Put so baldly, this sounds peculiar—but not if we understand it as a deferred utterance. If one can defer utterances, there is no reason why one cannot defer them until after one has expired.   (1991, 526)

I agree with Sidelle's conditional that *if* we can make deferred utterances, then we can make them after we are dead. But where he infers by *modus ponens*, I infer by *modus tollens*.

If a deferred utterance does not say anything prior to the time it takes effect, then it might as well be in a sealed envelope. The envelope would describe when the envelope was to be opened but contain no more information than this. All of Sidelle's specimens, however, say something from their inception. This is especially vivid with wills. Octavian discredited Mark Anthony by divulging the contents of Mark Anthony's will. Octavian was merely revealing what Mark Anthony had *already* said (especially his concessions to Cleopatra—whom the Romans feared would become their queen).

The assertions contained in wills are deferred with respect to their institutional effects (principally the transfer of entitlements), not with respect to their status as assertions. President Richard Nixon announced his resignation on 8 August 1974. He remained president until the declaration went into effect the next day at 1 p.m. Nixon could have deferred his declaration or deferred the institutional effect of his declaration (by designating a later ending for his presidency). He could even have composed a draft of the declaration and then submitted it as a written resignation. The declaration would then be dated to the time of submission. In the case of a will, one submits the document to a legal representative for safe-keeping. Full disclosure of the document is generally scheduled after death. Since wills can be amended, death has the effect of finalizing what was last said.

When Nixon's spokesman made remarks, Nixon was responsible for what the speaker said. But no one can assert by proxy. Nixon could not concede his loss to John F. Kennedy in 1960 by having his spokesman concede. The spokesman can only report Nixon's concession. Nixon cannot confess to a crime by having his attorney confess to the crime. His attorney can only report Nixon's confession.

Even autographs must be done in person. If Nixon orders his press secretary to autograph fan photographs, then he issues an impossible command. The best the press secretary can do is to forge Nixon's signature. The problem is not that another *agent* has been inserted into the causal chain. Secretary of Defense Donald Rumsfeld was criticized in 2004 for using an automatic signing machine to imprint his signature on condolence letters to families of slain soldiers. Bereaved families complained that signing a letter means personally signing it.

Advisors to the president can often predict what he will say. But their prediction of what the president will say tomorrow does not advance the date of his assertion. Assertion is a causal concept. For an utterance to be the president's assertion, it must originate or be sustained by the president's mental states. Since the utterance must be an outward sign of the president's inner psychology, there cannot be a significant time delay.

For legal purposes, we need a decisive interpretation of what counts as been said. These rules for accepting a remark as an assertion are often so esoteric as to create a resemblance to fiction. For instance, a man can avoid the charge of perjury by pointing out that the lies contained in his letter were never mailed (because the police interrupted his plan to mail the letter). The written lies are assertions but not in the eyes of the law.

VIII Booby Traps and the Killing Paradox

Are all postmortem messages legal fictions? No, because some postmortem messages do not rely on any legal authority for their creation or sustenance. Herodotus (*History* IV, 2) reports that the tomb of the Babylonian queen Nitocris bore the inscription 'If any king of Babylon after me should be short of money, he may open this tomb and take as much as he wants, but only if he really is in need of it.' The king of Persia, Darius I (550–486 BC) had conquered the Babylonian empire. Although wealthy, Darius thought it a shame to let riches go to waste. He opened Nitocris's tomb. Instead of finding money, he found a second message beside the body of the queen: 'If you had not been greedy of gold and fond of base gain, you would not have thought of ransacking the graves of the departed.' King Darius could not undo the insult by royal fiat.

Queen Nitocris's insult was a literary extension of the booby trap. Tombs of the great are commonly portrayed as protected by covered pits, poison powders, and automatic crossbows.

There is a dilemma about dating the killing when the booby dies *after* the trapper. If the trapper killed the booby when the booby died, then the dead act. If the trapper killed the booby while the booby was still alive, then the booby was killed prior to the booby's death!

Action theorists have proposed solutions to the killing paradox. Donald Davidson (1969) reduces actions to bodily movements. His answer to the riddle is that the trapper killed the booby when he set the booby trap. The booby was 'dead on his feet'.

Sidelle must reject Davidson's reductive unification. He must join the 'action multipliers' who argue that agents perform new actions by virtue of the effects of their bodily movements. The action multiplier's answer to the riddle is that the dead trapper kills the booby when the booby dies.

The trapper may kill again. . . . and again . . . and again . . . . Given an endless sequence of boobies, the trapper can act endlessly, apparently drawing a vampire's immortality from his victims. Some philosophers argue that death is bad because the dead can no longer act (Hetherington 2005, 217). But action multipliers, such as Sidelle, allow for an open sequence of postmortem deeds.

Some object that since the dead no longer exist, there is no agent to be the killer. But Davidson's solution would face a parallel problem when the booby is born after the death of the trapper. Given that the booby does not exist before he is born, the trapper lacks a victim. *Both* unifier and multiplier must reject the principle that killing requires temporal overlap between killer and victim.

IX Scattered Events

In an earlier treatment of the killing paradox (Sorensen 1985), I characterized killing as a temporally scattered event. The first sub-event is the setting of the trap and the last sub-event is the death of the booby. The date for a scattered event must encompass all of its sub-events. There is a parallel requirement for scattered objects such as the United States. When asked 'Where is the United States?', you can answer 'In the Northern Hemisphere' because the Northern Hemisphere includes all of its parts. But you cannot answer 'In North America' because that leaves out the state of Hawaii (which is itself a scattered object). Unlike connected objects, scattered objects fail fully to occupy their places. Although the United States includes Hawaii, none of its parts lies in the Pacific Ocean between California and Hawaii.

Scattered events, such as the dripping of the faucet, are also incomplete occupiers. They resemble 'intermittent objects' because their stages are separated by temporal gaps.

My solution to the killing paradox is to reject the disjunction 'Either the trapper killed the booby when he set the trap or he killed the booby when the booby died'. Since the killing is a scattered event, the killing incompletely occupies its available intervals. The killing has no parts during the interlude between the trapper's bodily movements and the death of the booby. The serial trapper gains as much immortality from his killing of an endless sequence of boobies as he gets from any other postmortem effects. Which is to say, he gets no immortality at all.

The only peculiarity is that there is no complete date for the action. We can report when he set the trap but cannot report when he completed his killing spree (because he never does complete it). We can say that he killed after he decided to set up the booby trap. But we cannot find a time t to finish the sentence 'The trapper killed the booby at time t'. Thus there are some events in time that cannot be completely dated.

When Sidelle explains to his friend at the supermarket that he is doing his laundry now, his 'now' spans the time from his past bodily movements to the future completion of the wash cycle. When Sidelle leaves a note on the washing machine, 'I am now at the supermarket', his communication with the reader is a scattered event. The date of the communication must encompass both the composition of the note and its receipt. So we should not concede 'Either he communicated with the recipient when he wrote the note or when the recipient read the note'. We must date the communication diffusely with a period that encompasses both events. However, the charitable reader of Sidelle's note must choose a narrower period. Sidelle cannot be in two places at one time! Since indexing to the time the note was written yields a patent falsehood, the reader will index 'now' to the time he is reading the note.

The same broad intervals govern non-indexical bequests. Since the bequest is dated broadly, there is a living agent setting up the communication. It is false to date the bequest exclusively at the time that the will is read. That leaves out the act of composing the bequest.

IX Postmortem Interests

People wish to extend their influence into their postmortem future—well beyond the period in which they can actively participate. Thus they are drawn to projects that have postmortem effects.

As noted in recent literature on the Non-Identity Problem (Parfit 1984, 351—5), each of us mightily affects the course of history. Just saying 'Hello' to a man affects which of his millions of sperm will unite with the egg of his wife and thus affect the identity of his child. Our most casual effects ramify, ensuring that each us makes a bigger and bigger difference as time rolls on. We are far more powerful than is commonly assumed.

But mice have the same sort of ramifying influence over the future of mankind. Our interests in our postmortem futures go well beyond mere power. We want control. We are interested in the integrity of our effects.

Just as the graceful dance movements of a ballerina degenerate into disorganized heat, our effects dissolve into background noise. Special efforts are needed to keep our effects in a recognizable form. Ancient booby traps, for instance, wear out. They pose little danger to current archeologists (contrary to the Indiana Jones movies).

The word is more enduring than the sword. The poetry of Quintus Ennius persists, even though every sentence token he wrote has been destroyed. Those who hope to ease the sting of death by postmortem activity are well advised to try their hand at literature.

G. H. Hardy argued that mathematics provides a better opportunity for 'immortality'. Mathematicians often use as epitaphs 'eternal sentences'—so-called because their content does not vary with time and place. For instance, a diagram was etched onto Archimedes' tombstone to convey the principle that the sphere has a volume and area in the same ratio as that of a circumscribed straight cylinder.

Archimedes will be remembered when Aeschylus is forgotten, because languages die and mathematical ideas do not. 'Immortality' may be a silly word, but probably a mathematician has the best chance of whatever it may mean. (Hardy 1941, 21)

Hardy underestimates the portability of poetry. Latin is a dead language but the poetry of Quintus Ennius has been translated into living languages.

More importantly, eternal sentences lack the element of audience participation. A sentence that uses the indexical 'you' acquires new content with each new occasion of use. It is nice to be remembered for an abstract theorem. But it is also nice, and often nicer, to make a personal impression.

Human beings fear being left behind and forgotten. This fear is rooted in our hunter-gatherer past. Hunter-gatherers survive by teamwork. They have intense attachments starting from their mothers. The top priority of a separated hunter-gatherer is to reunite. There is an echo of this drive for reunion in the practice of co-burial. My friend Patrick Grim and his wife bought their tombstones early. They placed the monuments in their backyard to enjoy them while still alive. His tombstone says, 'I'm with her'. Her tombstone says, 'I'm with him'.

The second-best option for a separated hunter-gatherer is to join another group. There is an echo of this later drive in the extroversion of some epitaphs. From the grave, the outgoing dead hail strangers, offer advice, or a humorous remark. People want to be friendly and useful. Old habits die hard.

Death is an irreversible form of separation. The prospect of death triggers the drive for reunion without any realistic hope of fulfilling the desire.

We plan by editing fantasy. Since the desire for postmortem reunion is impossible to fulfil, we get stuck at level of fantasy. The only scope for editorial work lies in literary effects such as consolation and the promotion of solidarity. Authors sometimes magnify these emotional effects by presenting their fiction as fact. For instance, J. R. R. Tolkien presents *The Lord of the Rings* as a historical account of the origin of man's dominion over the earth (written by a hobbit). Myths of an afterlife develop as people seek intersubjective validation of their fantasies.

Separation anxiety can also be channeled, more realistically, into services for those who come after our deaths. An author can have a rational desire to entertain and inform people who are spatially distant from him. He can also have these desires about people who are temporally distant. For instance, G. E. Moore arranged to have his nine notebooks (written informally from 1919 to 1953) published posthumously as the *Commonplace Book*. This was done partly for contemporaries who survived him, but partly in the hope that his remarks would be of interest to future generations.

X Displays

In addition to defending Moore, I am defending David Kaplan. I say Kaplan's theory of indexicals only applies to *assertions*. The rules are more flexible for *displays* of sentences.

Displaying is compatible with asserting. We often assert by exhibiting a prefabricated sentence (as when the janitor posts the portable sign: WET FLOOR). But the user of the display has less control over the sentence and so he has less responsibility for what it says. When the janitor forgets to take down the sign, we do not regard him as lying.

People are responsible for the accuracy of their displays in the standoffish way clockmakers are responsible for the accuracy of clocks. Even a broken clock displays the correct time twice a day. The clockmaker must make his timepiece reliably display the correct time (when properly set and maintained). If the clock runs slow, then he is culpable for the inaccuracy but is not thereby a liar. The clockmaker is not *asserting* the incorrect time.

When the speaker asserts a proposition, he takes responsibility for it being true. This is how knowledge is transmitted by testimony. To stabilize the speaker's knowledge-claim, indexicals are indexed to his situation.

Speakers can abuse their authority. A deceptive asserter can cause his audience to mis-index his utterance (Weatherson 2002). Consider a wily phone caller who says 'I am having a good time here' while playing loud background music. The hearer is misled into believing 'here' refers to a lively bar. Actually 'here' refers to the caller's apartment (where he is surreptitiously having a good time reading about indexicals).

This kind of deception is more difficult for displays. When there is no asserter to serve as an accessible, salient index for the indexicals, the hearer's reasonable interpretation of the sentence becomes the correct interpretation. The displayed message can be false, even though the designer of the display intended an interpretation under which it would be true.

The speaker's responsibility for the accuracy of a sentence display need not be any more focused than the clockmaker's responsibility. Since the speaker leaves the scene, the hearer dominates displays.

Attempts to index a display in accordance with the speaker's time of utterance often yield absurdity. When the *Mission Impossible* message concludes, 'This tape will self-destruct in ten seconds' the hearer does not face any practical ambiguity about whether to relativize the future tense from the time of encoding or the time of decoding.

The displayer's psychological relationship with his display can be quite remote. A responsible displayer is not required to know the proposition that will be expressed by the display. He need not even know which proposition will be expressed by the display. All he needs to know is that the display will express a true proposition. For instance, suppose Mr French tells Mr English to tell Mrs French 'Il pleut'. Mr. English does not know any French, but he can memorize French sentences and does know that Mr French is telling the truth. When Mr English says 'Il pleut' to Mrs French, he is not asserting 'Il pleut'. He lacks the understanding needed for asserting 'Il pleut'. Mr English can assert the metalinguistic statement ' "Il pleut" is true'. But that is a different remark.

Mr English is not merely quoting the sentence. He is inviting Mrs French to take it as a truth. Mr English is displaying the sentence to Mrs French.

Yul Brynner did not understand all semantic features of the sentence in his television commercial. In Kaplan's terminology Brynner understands the character and part of the content. But he did not understand the content of 'you'. Brynner could be sure that the sentence tokens in broadcast were going to be true. But he did not understand whom 'you' would refer to. Sentence meaning transcends speaker meaning.

XI Delegated Assertions

The Roman politician Scipio Nasica Serapio called upon his old friend Quintus Ennius only to be told by a slave that Quintus was not home. Nasica glimpsed the poet slip into a back room of the house. But Nasica said nothing and left. A week later Quintus Ennius went to visit Nasica. From behind the door, Nasica said 'Not at home!' Quintus chided him: 'You can't expect me to believe that—I recognize your voice.' Nasica retorted 'Why, you are a nice fellow, I believed your slave, and you won't believe me' (Fadiman 1985, 493).

The slave's assertion was not self-defeating. When Quintus says 'I am not here now' to his slave, the slave understands that he is to report 'He is not here now' to the caller. Thanks to the grammatical change to the third person, the content is no longer in the format of a pragmatic paradox (even though it is still false). Similar transformations can remove the paradoxical air of 'I do not speak any English', 'I am a mute', 'I am dead', 'I am asleep', 'I do not exist', and G. E. Moore's 'It is raining but I do not believe it'.

When the slave asserts the master's falsehood, the slave lies. The master does not lie because he did not assert anything. After all, Quintus said nothing to Nasica. And Quintus did not *assert* anything to the slave (though he uttered a sentence that displayed the content of the lie he was ordering). Quintus shares responsibility for the slave's lie because he instigated the deception. A man who never lies can be guilty of soliciting perjury.

Sidelle's call screener is responsible when his answering machine falsely displays 'I am not here now'. The call screener is deceiving the caller by letting the false message play. But nothing is being asserted, so there is no lie.

Like Quintus' slave, the phone caller hears the unassertible sentence 'I am not here now'. But pragmatic paradoxes are relative to an illocutionary force. 'Never give advice' is paradoxical as advice but not as an order. The very fact that 'I am not here' is a pragmatic paradox relative to assertion flags the sentence as a non-assertion. Metaphor works the same way. The speaker blocks a literal reading by blatant falsity ('Death has shaken out the sands of thy glass') or by blatant triviality ('No man is an island').

Charitable callers infer 'I am not here now' is merely being automatically displayed. Prank recordings deprive the caller of this clue: 'Hello . . . I cannot hear you, please speak up . . . That still is not loud enough . . . '.

If a sentence is merely quoted, the speaker is responsible for accurately reporting what was said, but not for the accuracy of the statement itself. If he asserts the sentence, then the speaker is fully responsible. If a speaker displays a sentence, he assumes an intermediate level of responsibility—as reflected by our intermediate degree of resentment when we are misled by the displayed sentence.

Suppose I make a weather vane. I am not asserting anything when I engrave on the vane's arm 'The wind is blowing this way $\longrightarrow$'. When I put the weather vane into service, the inscription will reliably convey much truth. When I consult the weather vane, I shall not be consulting my own testimony.

Displays let us convey more truth than we can assert. We cannot assert when we are absent or asleep or dead. But we can display sentences that are reliably true.

XII Computer Messages

The reliability of displays can be underwritten by processes that have become technically sophisticated. In the Paleolithic era, hunter-gatherers displayed messages via intermediate speakers or by leaving a sign such as a broken branch to mark a trail. Natural regularities were also exploited (as when trappers use a flag that is raised by the movement of the captured animal).

With the advent of writing, more complicated messages could be left. These still exploit natural regularities. A sign on a door can display the conditional 'If this door is closed, then I am not here now '.

Conjunctions of conditionals can also be displayed. As the number of conditionals increases, we group the connections in a contingency table. For instance, the trouble-shooting guide for my dishwasher lists each symptom along the rows and columns along with diagnoses in the corresponding cells.

When the conditionals become embedded in larger conditionals, a flowchart (such as those printed on tax forms) reduces the clutter. Nowadays many taxpayers buy computer software that 'interviews' them like an accountant.

The scare quotes around 'interview' mark the computer's lack of psychological states. When my 'Turbo Tax' program displays the tax I am to pay, the computer does not believe that this is the amount to be paid. Yet I readily project psychological states on to the computer. I make invidious comparisons between the cheerful warmth of the Turbo Tax persona and the cold impatience of 'Helpline' bureaucrats at the Internal Revenue Service. The program is designed to play to the customer's strength at interpreting of psychological states. Since computers have no psychology, they do not assert anything. Yet the sentences they display are reliably true.

Programmers have some responsibility for a computer's output. The Turbo Tax vendor promises to pay whatever fines the Internal Revenue Service imposes for errors that can be traced to the Turbo Tax software. When a programmed computer displays a false sentence, the programmer is often as deceived as the rest of us. The programmer is not engaged in self-deception. For the most part, programmers are only responsible for what computers do in the way clock manufacturers are responsible for the time displayed by their clocks.

XII Exogenous First Person Reference

Alan Sidelle's appeal to deferred utterances only addresses anomalies concerning temporal indexicals such as 'now'. Epitaphs also challenge the assumption that 'I' must refer to the speaker.

> Stranger by the roadside, do not smile
> When you see this grave, though it is only a dog's,
> My master wept when I died, and his own hand
> Laid me in earth and wrote these lines on my tomb.

Here 'I' refers to a dog and the writer acknowledges in the epitaph itself that he is not the dog.

There are also epitaphs that challenge the assumption that 'us' always refers to a group that includes the speaker. There is a war memorial to commemorate the soldiers of the British 2nd Division who died in the Battle of Kohima in the Second World War. The memorial bears the inscription

> When You Go Home, Tell Them Of Us And Say,
> For Their Tomorrow, We Gave Our Today.

The epitaph was composed by the classicist John Maxwell Edmonds (1875–1958). Edmonds was not among the fallen. He was inspired by the Greek lyric poet Simonides of Ceos (556–468 BC), who wrote after the Battle of Thermopylae in 480 BC: 'Go tell the Spartans, thou that passest by, That faithful to their precepts here we lie.'

The dog epitaph shows that a thought that is normally expressed in the third person ('He died') can be cast, for rhetorical effect, in the first person ('I died'). Exogenous first person reference can prevail against the wishes of the referent. When a prankster places an 'I am a fool' placard on the back of his victim, the 'I' refers to the victim rather than the prankster—despite the fact that the author of the placard is *obviously* the prankster, not the victim.

Greek playwrights used to enact farces over the graves of the illustrious dead. British comics could post a rain-sensitive token of 'It is raining but I do not believe it' on G. E. Moore's headstone in the St Giles Cemetery (in which Wittgenstein is also buried). The inscription would become visible just when it is raining. French comics could do the same with Rene Descartes. His tombstone would sport the reverse cogito: I do not think, therefore, I am not.

The referent of 'I' can be obviously inanimate. In Ayr, Scotland, a southern pier of the Gadgirth bridge bears the inscription: 'I was built by Mr John Steele, of Gadgirth, in 1768.' Since it is common knowledge that bridges do not talk, we do not take the first person reference to be endogenous. (Rhetoricians call this form of personification 'prosopospoeia'.)

The Kohima epitaph involves a transformation from the third person ('They died') into the first person plural ('We died'). The epitaph writer deviates from the standard third person grammar to secure the intimacy of the first person construction.

The first person, present tense is twice as intimate as the third person, future tense. Compare the clinical 'He will die' with the arresting 'I am dead'. Concrete demonstrations are more vivid than descriptions. Thus the epitaph of the architect Christopher Wren does not dryly report that he designed St Paul's Cathedral and is buried therein. His epitaph is an invitation to use your eyes: 'Reader, if you seek his monument look around.'

Some of the dead prefer to keep their distance. They choose grammar that increases social distance. For instance, 'I believe' can be replaced with the more authoritative 'We believe' (intimating group support). Speakers have considerable license. But they can be challenged. When a young minister used 'we' to refer to himself, King Edward VII (1841–1910) rebuked him: 'Only two people are permitted to refer to themselves as "We"—a king, and a man with a tapeworm inside him' (Fadiman 1985, 185).

XIII The Subjectivity of Scheduling

The constraints imposed by grammar are sensitive to background beliefs. St Anselm conveys the atemporality of God in his *Proslogian* with syntax commensurate with his theology and his personal rapport with the Almighty: 'You were not, therefore, yesterday, nor will You be tomorrow, but yesterday and today and tomorrow You *are*.' Similarly, those who think death is not the end of consciousness do say 'I am dead' after an apparently fatal event.

Alan Sidelle assumes that utterances can only be scheduled for release at a *later* date. It is true that we can only control the future. But what matters is the scheduler's *beliefs* about what can be controlled. Consider an eccentric who believes he has constructed a time machine. He believes he can send a small slip of paper back to the eighteenth century at an address of his choosing. He is unsure exactly *when* the message will arrive. To ascertain the precise arrival date, he addresses a message to the curator of the British Museum: 'I do not yet exist but I will later invent a time machine. Please make a note of when you received this message and file it in your archives for my future consultation'. The 'inventor' then strolls over to the British Museum to recover his prenatal message.

XIV Reclassification and Reassembly

The negative part of my paper is a sweeping rejection of conditional assertions and deferred utterances. I reason: if there are conditional assertions, then there are deferred utterances. If there are deferred utterances, then there are postmortem assertions. But postmortem assertions are impossible (by virtue of the Moorean absurdity of statements such as 'I am dead'). Therefore, deferred assertions and conditional assertions are impossible.

But what am I to say about statements that are misclassified into these impossible categories? Compare me to a paleontologist who challenges the reconstruction of fossil bones into an elasmosaurus. The challenger grants that the dinosaur fossils are genuine and interesting. But he argues that the creature, as assembled, is anatomically impossible.

I agree that the specimens furnished by Philip Rhinelander and Alan Sidelle are instructive. I disagree about which lessons are to be drawn from them.

I say first that 'conditional assertions' are not conditionals. They are categorical assertions presented as if they were conditionals. Conditional constructions are politer than flat assertions. If J. L. Austin tells his guest 'There are biscuits in the sideboard if you want them' and there are no such biscuits, then what he said was false—even if his guest did not want the biscuits. Genuine conditionals are never falsified solely by the falsehood of their consequents.

Politeness also leads us to make assertions with the rising intonation pattern of an interrogative. In a similar spirit, we substitute questions for imperatives. When I ask 'Can you pass the salt?' I am not really curious about whether you are able to perform the feat. I am indirectly requesting that you pass the salt to me. That is why it is acceptable to insert 'please': 'Can you please pass the salt?'

A polite way of issuing an imperative is to inquire into the preparatory conditions of obeying that imperative. Similarly, the antecedents of conditional assertions often concern the preparatory conditions for assertion. They orbit Grice's conversational maxims of quantity, quality, relevance, and brevity.

As for Alan Sidelle's examples of 'deferred utterances', I say they fall into two interesting classes. The first are genuine assertions that defer institutional effects; the second are displays.

Assertions may have evolved from displays as our ancestors became more refined consumers of information (Craig 1990). Hearers seek out good informants. They look for some property that will help them to discern informants. This property is knowledge. Once the market for knowledge is recognized, people will begin to advertise themselves as knowers. They begin to assert propositions that purport to reveal their mental state of knowledge.

Displays lack this psychological sophistication but are still a potent source of information. Technological advances have conferred new versatility and reliability on displays. With the advent of computers, the displays seem to be artificially developing into assertions. Alan Turing conjectured that computers would have mental states by the year 2000. His test for whether a computer is thinking is whether it could pass for a human being in a dialogue with interrogators who were trying to sort people from computers just by conversation.

John Searle (1980) objected to Turing's test by imagining himself in the role of the computer. He is given a batch of Chinese symbols and a manual for transforming them into other batches of Chinese symbols. The inputs are the Chinese interrogator's questions and the outputs are Searle's 'answers'. The answers may be good enough to pass Turing's test. But this verbal behavior would not suffice to make Searle a speaker of Chinese. Searle's messages are displays rather than assertions.

The dead cannot make new assertions. Before death, people can set up reliable sentence displays. These sentence displays do not satisfy the psychological prerequisites for being assertions. But displays are often presented as assertions. Switching to the first person and the present tense can magnify the rhetorical effect of this illocutionary guise. Videographers are further enhancing displays. Computers will further magnify the intimacy and the flexibility of displays. But none of this will break the fundamental silence of the dead.

References

Belnap, Nuel, 'Conditional Assertion and Restricted Quantification', Noûs, 4 (1970), 1–13.
Bradley, F. H., 1893 Appearance and Reality (London: Swan Sonnenochein. Corazza, 1893).

Craig, Edward, *Knowledge and the State of Nature: An Essay in Conceptual Synthesis* (New York: Oxford University Press, 1990).

Davidson, Donald, 'The Individuation of Events', in N. Rescher (ed.), *Essays in Honor of Carl G. Hempel* (Dordrecht: D. Reidel, 1969), 217–33.

DeRose, Keith and Grandy, Richard, 'Conditional Assertions and "Biscuit" Conditionals', *Noûs*, 33/3 (1999), 405–20.

Fadiman, Clifton, *The Little, Brown Book of Anecdotes* (Boston: Little, Brown, 1985).

Green, Mitchell, and Williams, John, *Moore's Paradox: New Essays on Belief, Rationality and the First Person* (Oxford University Press, 2006).

Herodotus, *The Histories*, trans. by A. D. Godley (Cambridge, Mass.: Harvard University Press, 1920).

Hardy, G. H., *A Mathematician's Apology* (Cambridge: Cambridge University Press, 1941).

Hetherington, Stephen, 'Lucretian Death: Asymmetries and Agency', *American Philosophical Quarterly*, 42/3 (2005), 211–19.

Kaplan, David, 'Demonstratives', in Joseph Almog, John Perry, and Howard Wettstein (eds.), *Themes from Kaplan* (New York: Oxford University Press 1989), 481–564.

—— 'Quantifying In', *Synthese*, 19 (1968–9), 178–214.

Lewis, David, 'Truth in Fiction', *American Philosophical Quarterly*, 15/1 (1979), 37–46.

Lescarboura, Austin, 'Edison's Views on Life after Death', *Scientific American*, 30 October 1920, 47.

Malcolm, Norman, *Ludwig Wittgenstein: A Memoir* (Oxford: Oxford University Press, 1958).

Parfit, Derek, *Reasons and Persons* (Oxford: Clarendon Press, 1984).

Quine, W. V., *Methods of Logic* (New York: Holt, Rinehart & Winston, 1950).

Searle, John, 'Minds, Brains, and Programs', *Behavioral and Brain Sciences*, 3 (1980), 417–24.

Shore, P., *Rest Lightly: An Anthology of Latin and Greek Tomb Inscriptions* (Wauconda, 1997).

Sidelle, Alan, 'The Answering Machine Paradox', *Canadian Journal of Philosophy* (1991), 525–39.

Sorensen, Roy, 'Self-deception and Scattered Events', *Mind*, 94/373 (1985), 64–9.

Stevenson, C. L., 'Moore's Arguments against Certain Forms of Ethical Naturalism', in P. A. Schilpp (ed.), *The Philosophy of G. E. Moore* (Lasalle, Ill.: Open Court, 1942), 71–90.

Weatherson, Brian, 'Misleading Indexicals', *Analysis*, 62/4 (2002), 308–10.

Williamson, Timothy, 'Knowing and Asserting', *Philosophical Review*, 105/4 (1996), 489–523.

Part III

Moorean Themes in Ethics

9

How is Moorean Value Related to Reasons for Attitudes?

Stephen Darwall

I am using ['Ethics'] to cover . . . the general enquiry into what is good. . . . That which is meant by 'good' is . . . the *only* simple object of thought which is peculiar to Ethics.

(G. E. Moore, *Principia Ethica*)[1]

[T]he fundamental notion represented by the word 'ought' or 'right,' which [ethical] judgments contain expressly or by implication . . .

(Henry Sidgwick, *The Methods of Ethics*)[2]

The whole point for which I am contending is simply this: There is an intrinsic difference, in both origin and mode of operation between objects which present themselves as satisfactory to desire and hence good, and objects which come to one as making demands upon his conduct which should be recognized. Neither can be reduced to the other.

(John Dewey, 'Three Independent Factors in Morals')[3]

G. E. Moore famously claimed in *Principia Ethica* that the idea of good or intrinsic value is the single fundamental ethical idea and that all other ethical notions can be analyzed in terms of it. The right, for example, Moore defined as conduct that maximally promotes the good. ('To assert that a certain line of conduct is, at a given time, absolutely right or obligatory is obviously to assert that more good or less

---

[1] Moore (1993), initially published in 1903. References in the text will include section number.

[2] Sidgwick (1967), initially published in 1907, (25).   [3] Dewey (1998).

evil will exist in the world, if it be adopted than if anything else be done instead' (1993, 77, §17)). And virtue or goodness of character, he defined as 'dispositions to perform actions which are duties', where 'duties are a particular class of those actions, of which the performance has, at least generally, better total results than the omissions'[4] (1993, 221, §103)). And so on for any idea we make use of in genuine ethical judgments.[5]

Moore's claim that the notion of good or intrinsic value is 'common and peculiar' to all ethical judgments comes right at the outset of Principia (1993, 53, §1).[6] The background for Moore's claim was Sidgwick's important chapter on 'Ethical Judgments' which Sidgwick added to The Methods of Ethics in its second edition.[7] Despite the obvious relation between Sidgwick's and Moore's discussions, however, and despite their agreeing that ethical judgments share a fundamental concept that makes them irreducible to any claims of natural or social science, Moore and Sidgwick sharply disagree about what ethics' fundamental concept actually is.

There is, however, much that Moore and Sidgwick agree about otherwise. Both hold consequentialist, indeed, utilitarian normative theories of right, at least as Moore understands utilitarianism. And they agree, as against the naturalist 'inductive' utilitarians of the nineteenth century, including Bentham and Mill, that any ethical doctrine, and hence utilitarianism, can be defended satisfactorily only by respecting ethics' irreducible conceptual core, that is, only by direct ethical judgment or 'intuition' and not on the basis of empirical evidence.[8] Sidgwick puts the point in terms that suggest what Moore will later call the 'naturalistic fallacy'. Ethical claims, Sidgwick says, cannot 'legitimately be interpreted as judgments respecting the present or future existence of human feelings or any facts of the sensible world' (1967, 25). Any judgment that is genuinely ethical must employ the fundamental, irreducible ethical notion, and this is 'essentially different from all notions representing facts of physical or psychical experience' (1967, 25).

---

[4] Moore adds that a virtue can also be a disposition to perform actions 'which would be duties if a volition were sufficient on the part of most men to ensure their performance' (1993, 221, §103).

[5] However, Moore also thought that ethical thinking had traditionally taken some ideas for granted that are actually incoherent or otherwise confused. For example, he held that 'good for someone', if it is taken to refer to anything other than the intrinsic value of something someone has or of his having it, is simply confused (1993, 150–1, §59).

[6] Here is Principia's first sentence: 'It is very easy to point out some among our every-day judgments, with the truth of which Ethics is undoubtedly concerned.' Later in the same paragraph: 'In the vast majority of cases, where we make statements involving any of the terms "virtue", "vice", "duty", "right", "ought", "good", "bad", we are making ethical judgments; and if we wish to discuss their truth, we shall be discussing a point of Ethics' (1993, 53, §1).

[7] Published in 1877.

[8] For this use of 'inductive', see, e.g., Mill, Utilitarianism, ch. I, para. 3. For a discussion of Mill's Utilitarianism that stresses this inductivist strain, see Jacobson (2002).

Moore follows Sidgwick, therefore, in holding that all ethical judgments share an irreducible fundamental concept and in opposing forms of ethical naturalism that, as they both see it, fail to respect this important fact and effectively change the subject from ethics to natural or social science. What's more, Moore characterizes Sidgwick as agreeing with him, perhaps uniquely among all philosophers, about what this core notion is. 'So far as I know', Moore writes, 'there is only one ethical writer, Prof. Henry Sidgwick, who has clearly recognized and stated this fact' (1993, 69, §14). Which fact is this? The 'fact', Moore says, that 'good . . . is indefinable' (1993, 69, §14). However, what Sidgwick actually says about ethics' basic idea is very different, namely, that it is 'the fundamental notion represented by the word "ought" or "right"' (1967, 25). And Sidgwick adds that the 'ethical sense of the term ought' is that of a '"dictate" or "precept"' of reason to the persons to whom it relates' (1967, 34).

This is where our topic begins. Moore believes that the fundamental ethical idea is that of good or intrinsic value. For Moore, therefore, all of ethics is based on the good *at the level of concepts*. As I read him, however, Sidgwick denies this. He takes the fundamental notion involved in all ethical judgments to be *normativity*—the idea of ought or normative reason. Any judgment that is genuinely ethical asserts that some action or attitude is supported (dictated) by normative reasons, that it is an action or attitude someone ought to take or have. It follows that judgments about the intrinsically good are, as Sidgwick sees it, judgments about the warrant, justification, or normative reasons for some attitude. For example, the judgment that something is an 'ultimate good', for Sidgwick, is the judgment that it is intrinsically *desirable*, that there are normative reasons for desiring or aiming at it as an end or that one ought to do so.[9] It follows that ethics can be based on the good at the level of concepts only if all normative reasons for actions and ethical attitudes depend, conceptually, on norms and normative reasons for intrinsic desire.

The question naturally arises, therefore, whether intrinsic value as Moore conceives it is a normative notion. What is the relation between Moorean intrinsic value and reasons for actions or attitudes? Sidgwick's is a 'buck-passing' view.[10] What we say in making an ethical judgment is that there are normative reasons for some action or attitude; the ethical property we attribute—being good, for example—is not itself a further reason. But what about intrinsic value as Moore conceives it? How, exactly, does it relate to normative reasons?

Now, in one way, Sidgwick's proposal may seem too broad. Is ethics the only normative subject? What about epistemology—the theory of what we should believe?

---

[9] 'It would seem then, that if we interpret the notion "good" in relation to "desire", we must identify it not with the actually *desired*, but rather with the *desirable*' (1967, 110−11). And what is desirable is 'what I should [i.e., would] practically desire if my desires were in harmony with reason . . .' (1967, 112).

[10] Scanlon (1998), 41−55.

Or artistic or literary criticism when these involve aesthetic judgments? The most charitable way of reading Sidgwick, however, is to interpret him as saying that the idea of ought or normative reason is a necessary part of any genuinely ethical judgment—that ethics is an inherently normative subject. It is consistent with this that there are other normative subjects, which must be distinguished in some other way.

The most sensible method of distinguishing them is by looking to what their respective normative reasons are reasons *for*, that is, to the distinctive attitudes to which their respective norms or oughts apply. If the question is what we should, or have reason to, believe, then we are in epistemology. But if the question is what we should, or have reason to, desire as an end, esteem, or do, then we are in ethics. And so on. This line drawing doesn't matter very much in itself. What really matters are substantive normative questions like: what do we have reason to do? What do we have reason to aim at for its own sake? What should we want for someone insofar as we care for her? What traits should we esteem or admire? What claims or demands should we recognize? And, more systematically, what are the relations between these different questions?

In what follows, I shall be considering this basic disagreement between Moore and Sidgwick about the fundamental concept common to all ethical judgments. Here I shall take Sidgwick's part. We can adequately appreciate the normativity of ethics only if we see ethical judgments as normative for attitudes, as guiding thought about what *to* desire, esteem, and do. I shall then use this debate to frame some points about the distinctive normative character of *morality* that, as I see it, neither Moore nor Sidgwick fully grasped. Here I shall argue that they both failed to appreciate the distinctive sense of moral demand that is in play when we hold one another morally responsible, and, consequently, the distinctive character of normative judgments concerning the attitudes through which we hold one another responsible and address moral demands to each other.

In the first vein, I shall follow Frankena in arguing that Sidgwick's insight confronts Moore with a dilemma.[11] Either Moorean intrinsic value is not a normative notion or, if it is, then, as Sidgwick believes, it must be what there is reason to desire or aim at as an end. If Moore grasps the first horn, he must then accept that the judgment that something is good still leaves open the question of whether there is any reason to desire or take any attitude toward or action regarding it, in which case it will be hard to see how judgments of intrinsic value are themselves ethical judgments. But if Moore grasps the second horn, he must deny that intrinsic value is a simple, unanalyzable idea. The idea of the good will be composed rather of the more fundamental idea of ought or normative reason conjoined with the idea of valuing or desiring something as an end.

---

[11] Frankena (1942, 93–110). For a discussion of this article, see my (1997, 685–705).

A Sidgwickian critique of this sort holds, effectively, that Moore fails to appreciate what intrinsic value must be if it is to be normative. Normativity for some attitude or other must be involved. I believe, however, that both Moore and Sidgwick significantly underrate the range of attitudes that are central to ethical thought. In addition to desire, there are also: esteem, respect (in a sense different from esteem, that is, recognition or acknowledgment), benevolent concern (which involves a distinctive form of desire, namely, desiring something for someone for that person's sake), and a number of others, including some that I shall argue are especially central to our idea of morality.[12] Conjoining the idea of ought or normative reason with these different attitudes gives rise to a plurality of distinct ethical ideas that an adequate ethical philosophy must link together in some coherent fashion.[13] The desirable is what we ought to desire (perhaps from some point of view or other); the estimable is what we ought to esteem; authority or dignity is what we ought to respect; a person's good is what we should want for her sake; and so on.[14] None of these attitudes can, I believe, be reduced to or constructed out of any of the others. It will follow that neither can any of their respective normative notions—the desirable, the estimable, authority or dignity, and so on—be reduced to or constructed completely out of any that relate to the other attitudes.

As against Moore, Sidgwick thinks that the right cannot be defined in terms of the good, but he none the less agrees with Moore that the good is prior to the right (to do) at the level of *normative* ethical theory. Sidgwick does hold, again, that the concept of good involves the more fundamental concept of ought or right. But it is the concept of what we ought (or it is right) to *desire* or aim at as an end, not the concept of what we ought (or what it is right) to *do*. Nevertheless, although the right does not depend on the good at the level of concepts, Sidgwick does believe as a matter of fundamental ethical intuition that what it is right to do is always what will bring about the most intrinsically valuable (desirable) outcomes.

Sidgwick's defense of consequentialism is an improvement over Moore's in two ways. First, it defends consequentialism as an explicitly normative doctrine and not as an empty tautology. And second, it has the resources to appreciate adequately the conceptual space between norms and normative reasons for desiring outcomes, on the one hand, and norms and normative reasons for *action*, on the other.

---

[12] For the distinction between appraisal (esteem) respect and recognition respect, see my (1977, 36–49).

[13] For a systematic defense of the plurality of ethical ideas (or values, as she puts it) along these lines, see Anderson (1993).

[14] I defend this view of welfare in my (2002). The desirable can also be further subdivided into the desirable for different points of view—say, from the perspective of concern for the person for her own sake (her welfare), from the agent's own point of view (value to or for her), from an impartial point of view, from some intersubjective point of view, and perhaps, as Sidgwick says, 'from the point of view . . . of the universe' (1967, 382).

Even so, I shall also argue that Sidgwick's defense of a consequentialist theory of moral right cannot succeed because, I shall claim, it fails to appreciate the conceptual connection between moral right and wrong, on the one hand, and norms for distinctive moral attitudes that are quite different from and independent of desire, on the other. It therefore does not recognize the relevance to claims of moral right and wrong of normative features that are quite different from the desirable, even from what is desirable from some objective or impartial point of view (Sidgwick's 'point of view of the universe'). Sidgwick shares with Moore, albeit at a different level, an essentially instrumental conception of action that fails to appreciate the ways in which action can realize forms of *relationship*, for example, to express *respect* or recognition of claims or demands that we take ourselves to have the authority or moral standing to address to one another. Sidgwick fails to see, I shall argue, how claims of right and wrong are normative for the attitudes through which we hold one another and ourselves morally *responsible* and that therefore mediate relations between members of a mutually accountable moral community.

So although Sidgwick gives us a promising way to understand the normativity of ethical thought in general, I shall argue that he and Moore both fail to appreciate the distinctive normativity of the moral in particular. Sidgwick sees that ethical judgments invariably make normative claims about attitudes, but he fails to grasp which attitudes are distinctively implicated in judgments of moral right and wrong. What is morally wrong is, as a conceptual matter, what there is warrant (normative reason) to hold someone responsible for and blame him for doing, if the person lacks adequate excuse. As Mill said 'we do not call anything wrong', unless we think it is something for which we appropriately hold people responsible.[15] And for this, as Strawson influentially pointed out, consequentialist considerations are simply reasons of the wrong kind.[16] What is relevant in contexts of responsibility are not norms for desire, hence the value of outcomes, but rather normative reasons for distinctive 'reactive attitudes' like resentment, indignation, and guilt, through which we hold others and ourselves responsible, hence blameworthiness. Putting these two points together gives us that what we are morally obligated to do is what we are morally responsible or accountable to one another for doing, hence what we ought to hold one another to through Strawsonian 'reactive attitudes'. It will follow that if consequentialism is to be defended as a theory of moral right, it will have to be made clear exactly how the desirable bears on what we can warrantedly demand of one another through such attitudes.

[15] See also Adams (1999, 238); Brandt (1979, 163–76); Gibbard (1990, 42); and Skorupski (1999, 142. ch. 5, para 14).

[16] Strawson (1968).

I Moorean Intrinsic Value and Normativity

I have presented Moore's and Sidgwick's views on the irreducible core of ethical judgments as though they were clearly in disagreement. However, there are places in *Principia* where this can seem far from clear. For example, in the very paragraph in which Moore refers to Sidgwick with approval as the only ethical writer to have 'clearly recognized and stated' that 'good' is indefinable, Moore apparently *identifies* his own indefinability thesis with Sidgwick's claim that ' "ought" is unanalysable'. Moore points to a passage in *The Methods of Ethics* in which Sidgwick takes Bentham to task for defining 'right' as 'conducive to the general happiness'.

I will only quote one instance, which will serve to illustrate the meaning and importance of this principle that 'good' is indefinable, or as Prof. Sidgwick says, an 'unanalysable notion'. It is an instance to which Prof. Sidgwick himself refers in a note on the passage, in which he argues that 'ought' is unanalysable. (1993, 69, §14)

This passage is puzzling in two different ways. Why does Moore think that his claim that 'good' is unanalyzable is the same as Sidgwick's claim that 'ought' is unanalyzable? And why does Moore give as an instance of the claim that 'good' is unanalyzable one in which Sidgwick rejects a proposed analysis of 'right'? After all, on Moore's own view, 'right' *is* analyzable. According to Moore in *Principia*, 'right' just means action having the property that 'more good or less evil will exist in the world, if it be adopted than if anything else be done instead of the ones available to the agent'. Granted, this is not a naturalistic analysis, but Moore is still quite clear that it is an analysis. Moore is an intuitionist about the good precisely because he believes that good's being a simple and unanalyzable concept and property entails that no reasons can be given for any judgment of intrinsic value. But Moore rejects deontological intuitionism on the grounds that judgments of right *can* be analyzed. Unlike questions about intrinsic good, the question ' "What is a man's duty under [certain] circumstances?" ... [is] capable of further analysis'. A correct answer to it 'involves both judgments of what is good in itself and causal judgments' (1993, 76, §17).

Why does Moore confuse Sidgwick's claim about the unanalyzability of 'ought' or 'right' with his own about the unanalyzability of 'good'? A clue is that Moore takes 'is good in itself' and 'has intrinsic value' to be synonymous with 'ought to exist for its own sake' (1993, 34, Pr). This last phrase looks normative, but is it really? Sidgwick says that the 'ethical sense of the term is a "dictate" or "precept" of reason to the persons to whom it relates'[17] (1967, 34). This means that when the 'ethical sense of the term ought' is involved, it is within an implicit structure:

---

[17] This passage directly concerns practical oughts, but this is incidental to the 'stricter ethical sense of the term "ought" ', which Sidgwick says 'is the sense in which the term will always be used in the

(1) *S* ought to *Y X*,

where *Y* is some attitude (understood broadly to include intention and action) that *S* should bear toward *X*. For Moore, however, good is a simple property. The claim that *X* ought to exist for its own sake must therefore be understood as the claim that *X* has the simple property of oughting to exist for its own sake.

We can put the points of the last paragraph in the language of normative reasons, by saying, first, that for Sidgwick, ethical claims always have the implicit structure:

(2) There are normative reasons for *S* to *Y X*,

that is, reasons for *S* to bear attitude *Y* to *X*. The claim that pleasure is an ultimate good, or that it is desirable as an end, is therefore the claim that there are normative reasons for someone (anyone) to desire pleasure as an end. The Moorean claim, however, is that the existence of reasons for *X* to exist for its own sake is a simple property of *X*.

But is this idea really intelligible? We can say of something that it ought to exist, or say of an event that it ought to happen, in one sense, and simply mean that its existence or happening follows from the laws of nature and initial conditions (as we believe them to be), as in, 'the car ought to start'[18]. In this sense, we can also say that there are reasons for something to exist or happen. But there is nothing ethical or normative in such a statement; the reasons are not normative reasons. They are not reasons *in favor* of its existing. What could reasons in favor of something's existing be other than reasons that count in favor of wanting it to exist, or valuing its existence in some way? It is very hard to see what ethical ought can be expressed by '*X* ought to exist for its own sake' other than that someone ought to value or desire *X*'s existing for its own sake, or make its existence her end.

Again, Sidgwick understands ultimate good as the desirable, as what there is normative reason for someone (or anyone) to desire. When Moore criticizes Mill's 'Proof' that pleasure is the only good, however, he doesn't object to Mill's identifying the good with the desirable. It is only when Moore takes Mill's analogy between the desirable and the visible to commit Mill to interpreting the desirable as what *can* be desired, that he charges Mill with the naturalistic fallacy—indeed, with 'as naïve and artless a use of the naturalistic fallacy as anybody could desire'! (1993, 118, §40). What Mill should have realized, Moore says, is that 'desirable means simply what *ought* to be desired or *deserves* to be desired' (1993, 118, §40). Then, to confound matters even further, Moore adds that 'desirable' means the same as ' "what it is good to desire" ' (1993, 119, §40).

But Moore can't believe both that 'desirable' means good *and* that it means what it is good to desire, because 'good' would then mean the same as 'good to desire,' which

present treatise, except where the context makes it quite clear that only the wider meaning—that of the political "ought"—is applicable' (1967, 34 n.).

[18] On this point, see Wertheimer (1972).

is impossible.[19] Good is a simple idea, Moore thinks, but the idea of what it is good to desire is complex. A simple idea cannot be identical with a complex idea of which it is itself a part. Moreover, the claim that something is desirable in the sense of warranting desire, of there being normative reasons *to* desire it, is plainly different from the claim that it would be *good* to desire it. It may indeed be good to desire what is desirable, but if so, this is a further fact. In many cases, we might even say that it would be good to desire something *because* it is desirable.[20] Sidgwick would understand such cases as ones where, because X is something we ought to desire (is desirable), we ought to desire that we desire X. Here X's being desirable and its being desirable that we desire X are plainly different facts.

How can we make consistent sense of what Moore says here? Moore must mean that being good and being desirable are *different* ethical notions: the simple unanalyzable idea of good and the complex idea of what it is good to desire. When he says that 'desirable' means what ought to be desired *and* that it means what would be good to be desired, he must mean something similar to what he meant in saying that 'is good in itself' and 'ought to exist for its own sake' mean the same. (And he must really deny that 'good' means the same as 'desirable.') The sense in which something that is desirable ought to be desired for Moore can only mean that *the state of its being desired ought to exist.* But again, it is hard to see how to understand this as an intelligible normative claim. We can well enough understand Sidgwick's idea that for something to be desirable is for there to be reasons to desire it, and similarly for claims that are normative for other attitudes. For Moore, however, 'ought' figures in ethical judgments only as a rough synonym for 'good,' as in 'ought to exist', which Moore takes to be identical with 'good to exist'. Such claims are simply not normative in our familiar contemporary sense; they do not analytically entail reasons *for* anyone *to* take or have an attitude toward anything, or reasons *on the basis of which* anyone might have an attitude towards anything. They do not concern what should *guide* thought or action. If they are guides at all, they are guides to the world or, perhaps, to possible states of affairs—as if, fantastically, possible states might be guided by them in considering whether or not to become actual.

Typically, of course, we form desires for things or for possible states by attention to features that we take as reasons for desiring them.[21] But it is also possible to form

---

[19] Thus 'X is good' = 'X is good to desire' = 'X is good to desire to desire' = 'X is good to desire to desire to desire', etc. Even if these are all equivalent, they clearly don't mean the same.

[20] Compare here Thomas Hurka's idea that loving the good is also intrinsically good (2003). This is a substantive ethical thesis only because something's being worthy of being loved and its being good to love it are different facts. It is good to love that which is worthy of being loved *because* it is worthy of being loved.

[21] On this point, see, e.g., Bond (1983); Dancy (2000); Darwall (1983); Pettit and Smith (1990, 565–92); Scanlon (1998, 41–55).

a desire for something, not on the basis of specific reasons, but just on the grounds that it is desirable, that there are reasons of some kind or other for desiring it. Just as one can come to believe something because one trusts someone else's word that it is true, so also can one come to desire something by taking someone's word that it is good. But it is simply not possible (I am tempted to say, not metaphysically possible), to form a desire for something for the reason or on the basis or ground that it would be good to have the desire. The only desire one can have on the basis of this thought is the desire to have this desire.

We should collect results. Whereas Sidgwick holds that ethical judgments are always normative judgments, concerning normative reasons or oughts for attitudes, Moore holds that ethical judgments always concern what has the simple unanalyzable property of intrinsic good, of being such as ought to exist for its own sake. But what normativity can ethical judgments then have, as Moore conceives them? They are clearly not *explicitly* normative for attitudes in the way that Sidgwickian ethical judgments are. But might the fact that something is intrinsically valuable not still necessarily be a reason for someone to take some attitude toward it, say, to desire or to aim to bring it about for its own sake?

Frankena argued that Moore is confronted with a dilemma (Frankena 1942). Either intrinsic value judgments are normative or they are not. If they are normative in the way that Sidgwick supposed, then good cannot be a simple property. On Sidgwick's view, something's being intrinsically valuable is its being such that there are reasons to value, say to desire, it for its own sake. Intrinsic value is thus a complex property that includes the more fundamental idea of ought or normative reason as a part. And something similar holds for any ethical notion; all are complexes composed of ought and some attitude or attitudes.[22] But if, on the other hand, something's being good still leaves the question open whether there is any reason to desire or take some other attitude with respect to it, then it is hard to see why the judgment that something is good is an ethical judgment. It could, of course, be relevant to an ethical judgment, but many naturalistic judgments are relevant to ethical judgments. What's more, Frankena argued, Moore implicitly relies upon the conceptual connection between intrinsic value and normativity in his arguments against any naturalistic reduction of good. After all, what really does the work in Sidgwick's arguments to the same effect, for example, the one against Bentham that Moore cites so favorably, is that, as Sidgwick puts it, the idea of ought or normative reason is 'essentially different from all notions representing facts of physical or psychical experience' (1967, 25). What gives the open question argument whatever plausibility it has is that any naturalistic description of a thing apparently leaves it logically open whether there is any reason *to* desire, seek, or take any other attitude toward that thing. So if Moore rejects Sidgwick's analysis, he

----

[22] See also Ewing (1939, 1–22).

may be abandoning his strongest argument against naturalistic reduction of ethical concepts.

I find this Frankena/Sidgwick attack on Moore convincing. However, Moore has a reply. In Moore's scheme, there being reason for someone to have some attitude toward something, its being the case that someone ought to have the attitude, is the same thing as its being *good* that the person have that attitude. Moore can accept, even insist, that the fact of Y's being good is different from the fact that S ought to have attitude X toward Y, for any X. And he can also deny that Y's being good is irrelevant to whether S should have attitude X toward Y. That S should have attitude X toward Y is the same fact as

(3) It would be good that S X Y.

If Y is intrinsically good and if S's Xing (say, desiring) Y will tend to bring Y about, then it *is* the case that S ought to X Y, since it is then the case that it would be good (now, extrinsically or instrumentally) for S to X Y. It is true that this is no *necessary* connection between something's being good and there being any reason to want or have any particular attitude toward it at all. The connection between value and reasons for attitudes is completely *external*, depending entirely on causal facts concerning the relation between having the attitude and the existence of the valuable state. Alternatively, Moore could hold as a normative thesis that it is intrinsically good to desire, love, or value in some other way what is intrinsically good.[23] But this normative fact would still be external to something's being good; it would neither follow from the intrinsic goodness fact nor be part of what constitutes it.

Moreover, Moorean reasons and oughts are external also in another way. On Moore's scheme, when there are normative reasons for someone to have a given attitude, when someone ought to have that attitude, that it is because the state of his having that attitude would be good, one that ought to exist. Strictly speaking, the ought and reasons apply, not to the person, but to the state. The relevant fact is

(4) It ought to be that S Y X.

Any claim like (1) or (2) must thus be understood in terms of one like (3) and (4). The bottom line is that in the scheme of *Principia*, there simply is no place for an *S ought to Y* that cannot be reduced to *it ought to be that S Y*, that is, an ought to be concerning the having of that attitude.

This makes ethics thoroughly external, in the sense that, according to Moore, ethical thought is never from the standpoint we must take up to think about (that is, deliberate about) what *to* desire, do, or esteem. And reasons for attitudes never come directly from the nature of their *objects*; they come rather from facts about the having

---

[23] As Hurka does in Hurka (2003).

of the attitude.[24] For example, the fact that X is good is never intrinsically a reason to desire X, nor is it, as on Sidgwick's buck-passing view, a fact that entails that there are reasons to desire X. Any reasons for desiring X must concern the value of being in the state of desiring X. But these are not reasons that can guide deliberation about whether to desire X. It is psychically impossible to desire something simply for the reason that it would be good to desire it. That thought can only lead you to desire that you desire it.

To see how implausible Moore's suggestion is, apply it to belief. In thinking about whether to believe p, we weigh reasons for and against believing p by looking for evidence for and against p. Our attention is on the possibility that p, and how things we think true, say, q, r, or s, bear evidentially on that possibility. But if 'S ought to believe p' means the same as 'It would be good that S believe p', where this doesn't reduce to there being reasons of the ordinary evidential kind for S to believe p, then thinking about whether to believe p would have to focus on the value of being in the state of believing p, where the value in question does not itself depend on some prior notion of epistemic value. But here, again, it is impossible to believe something simply on the grounds that it would be good to believe it, that is, unless we smuggle in evidential or object-related reasons for belief into our conception of value.

I conclude therefore that we should follow Sidgwick rather than Moore on the nature of ethical thought. *Principia*'s conception of ethics robs it of the normativity that makes it an important subject. It removes ethics from thinking about what *to* desire, aim at, esteem, and do, and puts it entirely into the observer's mode. It makes ethics concern what should occur in the world in a sense that is putatively independent of what we should wish to occur in the world, and it makes what we should wish to occur a matter of what is such that it would be good for us to wish its occurrence.

II Normativity, Attitude, and Moral Right and Wrong

I have said that Sidgwick's defense of consequentialism is an improvement over Moore's in two ways: it understands consequentialist theories of right as making genuinely normative claims about conduct; and it appreciates the conceptual space between an outcome we ought to desire, including the outcome of a certain action's being done, and being an action we ought to take. Although Sidgwick believes, as a matter of normative doctrine, that the 'objectively right' action is always the act, of those available, that would 'produce the greatest amount of happiness on the

---

[24] In Parfit's terms, they are 'state-given' rather than 'object-given' (Egonsson, Petersson, Josefsson, and Ronnøw-Rasmussen 2001); see also Rabinowicz and Ronnøw-Rasmussen (2004).

whole', and believes that the latter is what we should most desire—the outcome most desirable, 'from the point of view . . . of the Universe'—none the less, unlike Moore, Sidgwick doesn't think that this is an analytic or conceptual truth (1967, 411, 383).[25]

Another important contrast with Moore is that Sidgwick defends utilitarianism as an account of *morally* right conduct. Whereas Moore finds the concept of a person's good problematic, and rational egoism downright incoherent, Sidgwick explicitly distinguishes between a 'prudential' and a narrowly 'moral' species of ethical judgments.[25] Both what is desirable for oneself for one's own sake and the rational dictate to promote it, on the one hand, *and* what is desirable from a disinterested point of view, as well as a distinctively moral injunction to promote that, on the other, are 'moral in a wider sense', since both concern what we ought to do and desire[26] (1967, 25). But the idea of moral duty, with which utilitarianism is traditionally associated, is, Sidgwick holds, moral in a narrower sense that is clearly distinguished 'in ordinary thought'[27] (1967, 25).

This means that we can distinguish conceptually or analytically between the question of practical reason—What action do I have reason to or should I take? (morality in the wide sense)—and the question of moral duty or right—what does morality require of me or what is my moral obligation? (morality in the narrow sense). Of course, it may be that one has (wide) reason to act rightly (conceived narrowly)—maybe always, maybe necessarily. But the ideas of morally right conduct and practically rational conduct are distinct concepts. For example, it may be part of the concept of moral wrong, or at least a presupposition of our practice of charging people with wrongdoing, that an action's being wrong entails that there are conclusive reasons not to do it. But this claim itself involves two different concepts: the concept of being morally required to do something (narrow); and the concept of an action's being something there is reason to do period (wide). It claims that if an action instantiates the first concept, it must also instantiate the second.

---

[25] It is consistent with this that there is a *pro tanto* conceptual relation, namely, that, as a matter of conceptual necessity, what we ought to desire we ought to bring about, other things being equal. When, however, Sidgwick says in bk. III, ch. XIII, that 'it is evident to me that as a rational being I am bound to aim at good generally,—so far as it is attainable by my efforts,—not merely at a part of it', after having claimed that the good of any being is no less good than one's own from an objective point of view' (1967, 382), he is putting this forward as a substantive normative intuition.

[26] I argue that Sidgwick understands the good for someone in these terms in Darwall (2002, 31–43); see also my (2000).

[27] See in this connection Sidgwick's discussion of the 'quasi-jural notions of modern Ethics', which he contrasts with the notions of ancient ethics (1967, 94). Also relevant is Sidwick's remark in the *Outlines of the History of Ethics* that 'in Platonism and Stoicism, and in Greek moral philosophy generally, but one regulative and governing faculty is recognised under the name of Reason—however the regulation of Reason may be understood; in the modern ethical view, when it has worked itself clear, there are found to be two,—Universal Reason and Egoistic Reason, or Conscience and Self-love' (1964, 198).

Now Sidgwick does maintain that the Principle of Universal Benevolence is a dictate of practical reason. His famous 'dualism of practical reason' is that there are two different (and potentially conflicting) intuitions about practical reasons: first, that an agent should aim at and pursue his own greatest good (Prudence); and second, that an agent should aim at and pursue the greatest good of all (Benevolence) (1967, 373–90). But that practical reason recommends seeking the general good no less than it does one's own good does not yet connect the good of all to any distinctive ought of morality in the narrow sense. If it is true that there are good reasons for any rational agent to pursue both his own good and the good of all, that means that this is what any agent morally ought to do *in the wide sense*. Nothing would follow from this about what our moral duties or obligations are *in the narrow sense*. It wouldn't follow that failing to do what is optimific is *morally wrong*.

Any ethical judgment is, for Sidgwick, a species of *normative* judgment: it involves 'the fundamental notion represented by the word "ought" or "right" '. Ethical judgments include claims about normative reasons or oughts for some attitude or other as part of their content. But ethical judgments are not the only normative judgments; to distinguish ethics from, say, epistemology, we must look to the distinctive attitudes these different areas concern. Epistemology concerns norms for belief, and ethics concerns norms for an ensemble of different, but arguably interrelated, attitudes, including for intention (action), desire, concern, esteem, respect, and a number of others.

Similarly, to distinguish different normative judgments *within* ethics, we must look to the distinctive attitudes that are in play. What is desirable, for example, concerns norms or normative reasons for desire. What is desirable from the point of view, of the universe is what it would make sense to want from that perspective. What is desirable from an individual person's point of view is what it would make sense to want from that perspective. And what is desirable *for* a person (i.e., would benefit her or be part of her welfare), which is a distinct concept from the concept of what is desirable from her point of view, is, I have argued elsewhere, what it would make sense to desire *for her for her sake*, that is, out of sympathetic or benevolent concern for her.[28] Likewise, what a person ought to do, in the wide sense, is what there are conclusive normative reasons for her, what she ought, to intend or to do. And so on.

If, consequently, there is a narrow sense of the moral ought, additional to the ought of practical reason (moral ought in the wide sense), it follows that it must be normative for distinctive moral attitudes other than simply for action, considered widely. In this final section, I shall argue that the moral ought (as it is involved in the concept of moral obligation or moral right and wrong), is properly understood in relation to a set of attitudes that implicitly address moral

[28] Darwall (2002).

demands. Roughly, the claim that an action is morally wrong is the claim that the action is something there are normative reasons for members of the moral community to demand that people not do, and to blame and hold them responsible for doing if they so act without adequate excuse. It will follow that to defend consequentialism as a doctrine of moral right, it is necessary to connect claims about the desirable to the idea of moral *demand* in a way that neither Sidgwick nor Moore do. As Dewey observed: 'there is an intrinsic difference, in both origin and mode of operation between objects which present themselves as satisfactory to desire and hence good, and objects which come to one as making demands upon his conduct which should be recognized. Neither can be reduced to the other'.[29]

Now one might certainly seek to defend utilitarianism or some other form of consequentialism in these terms. After all, what I am proposing is a version of the idea that Mill put forward in a famous passage from chapter V of *Utilitarianism*:

We do not call anything wrong, unless we mean to imply that a person ought to be punished in some way or other for doing it; if not by law, by the opinion of his fellow-creatures; if not by opinion, by the reproaches of his own conscience. This seems the real turning point of the distinction between morality and simple expediency. It is a part of the notion of Duty in every one of its forms, that a person may rightfully be compelled to fulfil it. Duty is a thing which may be exacted from a person, as one exacts a debt.   (Mill 1998, ch.V, para. 14)

The connection between Mill's idea and what I am suggesting is that punishment, accountability, moral responsibility, and moral demand are interconnected ideas.[30] Punishment in the sense that Mill (and I) have in mind always involves a form of blame or 'reproach', in Mill's term, and reproach, whether it is expressed to another or to oneself, as in feelings of guilt, involves the address of a moral demand.

Before developing this Millian interpretation of the (narrowly) moral ought, consider Sidgwick's own discussion of attempts to do so. One is 'the suggestion that the judgments or propositions we commonly call moral—in the narrower sense—really affirm no more than the existence of a specific emotion in the mind of the person who utters them', say, 'moral approbation' (1967, 26, 27). Sidgwick rejects this proposal, anticipating Moore's argument against subjectivism, since it would, now in Sidgwick's words, yield the possibility of 'two coexistent facts stated in two mutually contradictory propositions' (1967, 27). Two people who apparently disagree about, say, the morality of abortion, would simply be truly stating the facts of their respective approbation and disapprobation. Sidgwick also considers an idea like Mill's,

[29] See Dewey (1998, 318–19).

[30] Note here again Sidgwick's remark about the 'quasi-jural' character of modern moral notions. See n. 27.

but crucially different: that claims of moral obligation express the proposition that someone is 'bound under penalties to do it; the particular pains being the pain that will accrue to him being directly or indirectly from the dislike of his fellow-creatures' (1967, 29). He agrees with Mill that 'we commonly use the term "moral obligation" as equivalent to "duty"' and that 'this suggests an analogy between this notion and that of legal obligation' in respect of liability to sanction. But he insists that '*S* is morally obligated to *Y*' or 'It would be wrong for *S* not to *Y*' cannot mean the same as '*S* will incur sanctions if she doesn't *Y*' since 'there are many things we judge men "ought" to do, while perfectly aware that they will incur no serious social penalties for omitting them' (1967, 29).[31][32]

After canvassing and rejecting these alternatives for distinguishing morality in the narrow sense, Sidgwick concludes that '"ought," "right", and other terms expressing the same fundamental notion' are 'too elementary to admit of any formal definition' (1967, 32). But Sidgwick seems now to have lost track of his point, since the notion he here points to is the same 'fundamental notion' that characterizes moral judgments in the wide sense. And this notion can't be what distinguishes morality in the narrow sense, since it is common to morality in the wide sense, as it is, indeed, to any normative subject, including epistemology and literary criticism. It should be clear by this point that the possibility that Sidgwick *should* be considering (if I may now use and not just mention this fundamental normative notion) is that the oughts of morality in the narrow sense are to be understood in terms of normative reasons or oughts for the attitudes that are distinctive of narrow morality. More plausible than the idea that an ought of narrow morality states that the person claiming it actually feels moral approbation is the notion that it expresses the proposition or claim that one *should* feel approbation or that approbation is justified or warranted, that is, the notion of the morally *estimable*. More plausible than the idea that claims of moral duty, obligation, and right and wrong assert the likelihood of negative sanction, for example, by Strawsonian 'reactive attitudes', is the notion that they express the proposition or claim that these ways of addressing moral demands would be warranted by relevant normative reasons or oughts—for example, that the concept of being morally wrong is the concept of being worthy of blame, lacking adequate excuse.

---

[31] Sidgwick also notes that there are cases where we think someone ought to do or forbear actions 'without compulsion' (1967, 29). It is not obvious, however, whether he thinks that such acts can be morally obligatory. And, even if we think that people should do what is morally obligatory without the threat of sanctions even so informal as blame and reproach, it wouldn't follow that actions can be morally obligatory without being such that blame or reproach would be *warranted* (supported by normative reasons) unless the person lacked an adequate excuse.

[32] Sidgwick also specifically considers under this rubric the theological voluntarist idea that moral obligation entails divine sanctions.

This Millian idea can be found in a number of recent writers, a list that includes Brandt, Gibbard, Skorupski, and, in a critical vein, Bernard Williams.[33] In conclusion, I want to say something about its role in Strawson's 'Freedom and Resentment' that is especially relevant to the issues at hand. Strawson's landmark article has been very influential in discussions of moral responsibility, but philosophers have mostly failed to appreciate its implications for the subject of moral obligation and theory of the right. Strawson there famously argues, against pragmatic, consequentialist approaches to moral responsibility, that efficacy 'in regulating behaviour in socially desirable ways' is not a justification of 'the right *sort*... for these practices as we understand them' (1968, 74). Rather, our practices of mutual accountability are mediated by 'reactive attitudes', such as resentment, indignation, reproach, blame, guilt, and so on.

Reactive attitudes invariably express demands. To blame someone just is to hold her responsible for failing to meet a moral demand. As Strawson puts it: 'the making of the demand *is* the proneness to such attitudes', and, we might add, vice versa.[34] To think some action is morally obligatory or demanded, and that failure so to act is morally wrong, consequently, is to think that the action is such as to warrant holding someone morally responsible, including by addressing demands through the relevant reactive attitudes, that is, that there are normative reasons for doing so. The right sorts of reasons for holding people responsible are the distinctive normative reasons for the relevant reactive attitudes—oughts for indignation, resentment, blame, and so on. Without some connection to what is normative for these attitudes, considerations of the 'socially desirable' provide reasons of the wrong kind. Norms for reactive attitudes do not follow from norms for desire.

Like Mill, Strawson connects the concepts of moral obligation and moral responsibility. This means that, in order to support claims of moral right and wrong, consequentialist considerations have to be able to be related to norms for reactive attitudes and the authority to make claims and demands.[35] Without such a connection, they will be reasons of the wrong kind for claims of moral obligation also. In my view, the deep idea underlying Strawson's critique is that moral obligation is tied to what I would call the second-personal authority or standing to address

---

[33] Allan Gibbard argues that narrow moral judgments concern norms for 'impartial anger' and guilt (1990, 42); and John Skorupski holds that the concept of moral wrong is tied to warranted blame (1999, 42). Richard Brandt takes a similar view in Brandt (1979, 163–76); see also Shafer-Landau (2003, ch. 7). Also relevant is Baier(1966). One of the most interesting sources, however, is Bernard Williams, who connects his neo-Nietzschean critique of moral obligation to the role of blame in morality. See Williams (1985; 1995).

[34] (1968, 92–3). See also Watson (1987, 263–4); and Wallace (1994, 19).

[35] One way of trying to do that is with an indirect or rule-consequentialism of the kind that Mill favors. Although I can't argue the point here, I believe that this just postpones the problem.

demands to one another. When we charge someone with wrongdoing, we take up a 'second-personal standpoint' and presuppose we both have standing as members of the moral community to address moral demands to one another. As Strawson points out, holding another responsible for wrongs is none the less 'to view him as a member of the moral community; only as one who offended against its demands'.[36] Unlike other critical attitudes such as contempt or disdain, the reactive attitudes that are conceptually connected to moral obligation always involve a form of reciprocal recognition or respect for the other as having a common second-personal standing. The lesson I draw is that the right place to ground a theory of right is the second-personal standpoint, rather than an observer's perspective, from which, for example, we appropriately assess moral character, on the one hand, or from the agent's point of view, on the other.[37]

One way of putting the Sidgwickian critique of Moore we discussed above is that intrinsic value according to Moore is utterly independent of perspective, even that of the universe, and so it entails no normative guidance to someone thinking (first-personally) about what to desire, feel, or do. For Sidgwick, ethical notions are intrinsically normative; they contain the irreducible idea of ought or normative reason as applied to some attitude or other, and so are relevant as a matter of conceptual necessity to the (first-personal) deliberative question of whether to have some attitude or other. But the idea of the normative in general, when applied broadly to action and desire, fails yet to capture narrow moral notions. Here, I have argued, we should learn from Mill and Strawson that the attitudes that are distinctive of moral obligation are those Strawson called 'reactive'. Deliberating about whether to have one or another of these attitudes is first-personal as well; but it is also second-personal. It is an essentially interpersonal perspective of mutually accountable moral agents.

Works Cited

Adams, R., *Fine and Infinite Goods* (Oxford: Oxford University Press, 1999).

Anderson, E., *Value in Ethics and Economics* (Cambridge, Mass.: Harvard University Press, 1993).

Baier, K., 'Moral Obligation', *American Philosophical Quarterly*, 3 (1966), 210–26.

Bond, E. J., *Reason and Value* (Cambridge: Cambridge University Press, 1983).

[36] (1968, 93). This is an important difference between reproach and disdain that is insufficiently appreciated by ethics of virtue, such as Hume's or Aristotle's. It is also the grain of truth in Hegel's famous of idea or a 'right to punishment', that failure to hold someone accountable can be a failure to respect his dignity as a rational person. See Hegel (1991, 126–7).

[37] I develop and defend this idea in Darwall (2006).

Brandt, R., *A Theory of the Good and the* Right (Oxford: Oxford University Press, 1979).

Dancy, J., *Practical Reality* (Oxford: Oxford University Press, 2000).

Darwall, S., 'Two Kinds of Respect', *Ethics*, 88 (1977), 36–49.

——— *Impartial Reason* (Ithaca, NY: Cornell University Press, 1983).

——— 'Learning from Frankena: A Philosophical Remembrance', *Ethics*, 107 (1997), 685–705.

——— 'Sidgwick, Concern, and the Good', *Utilitas*, 12 (2000), 291–306.

——— *Welfare and Rational Care* (Princeton, NJ: Princeton University Press, 2002).

——— *The Second-person Standpoint: Morality, Respect, and Accountability* (Cambridge, Mass.: Harvard University Press, forthcoming).

Dewey, J., *The Essential Dewey*, V. n. 2, *Ethics Logic, Psychology*, ed. by L. A. Hickman and T. M. Alexander (Bloomington, Ind.: Indiana University Press, 1998), 318–19.

Ewing, A. C., 'A Suggested Non-Naturalistic Analysis of Good', *Mind*, 48 (1939), 1–22.

Frankena, W., 'Obligation and Value in the Ethics of G. E. Moore', in Paul A. Schilpp (ed.), *The Philosophy of G. E. Moore* (La Salle, Ill: Open Court, 1942).

Gibbard, A., *Wise Choices, Apt Feelings* (Cambridge, Mass.: Harvard University Press, 1990).

Hegel, G. W. F., *Elements of the Philosophy of Right*, ed. by Allen W. Wood and Hugh B. Nisbett (Cambridge: Cambridge University Press, 1991).

Hurka, T., *Virtue, Vice, and Value* (Oxford: Oxford University Press, 2003).

Jacobson, D., 'J. S. Mill and the Diversity of Utilitarianism', *Philosophers' Imprint*, 3 (2002), *www.philosophersimprint.org*

Mill, J. S., *Utilitarianism*, ed. by Roger Crisp (Oxford: Oxford University Press, 1998).

Moore, G. E., *Principia Ethica*, rev. edn. with the preface to the (projected) 2nd edn. and other papers, ed. with intro. by Thomas Baldwin (Cambridge: Cambridge University Press, 1993).

Parfit, D., 'Rationality and Reasons', in Dan Egonsson, Bjön Petersson, Jonas Josefsson, and Toni Ronnøw-Rasmussen (eds.), *Exploring Practical Philosophy: From Action to Values*, (Aldershot: Ashgate Press, 2001).

Pettit, P., and Smith, M., 'Backgrounding Desire', *The Philosophical Review*, 99 (1990), 565–92.

Rabinowicz, W., and Ronnøw-Rasmussen, T., 'The Strike of the Demon: On Fitting Pro-attitudes and Value', *Ethics*, 114 (2004), 391–423.

Scanlon, T. M., *What We Owe to Each Other* (Cambridge, Mass.: Harvard University Press, 1998).

Shafer-Landau, R., *Moral Realism: A Defence* (Oxford: Oxford University Press, 2003).

Sidgwick, H., *Outlines of the History of Ethics for English Readers*, 6th edn. (Boston, Mass.: Beacon Press, 1964).

——— *The Methods of Ethics*, 7th edn. (London: Macmillan 1967).

Skorupski, J., *Ethical Explorations* (Oxford: Oxford University Press, 1999).

Strawson, P. F., 'Freedom and Resentment', *Studies in the Philosophy of Thought and Action* (London: Oxford University Press, 1968).

Wallace, R. J., *Responsibility and the Moral Sentiments* (Cambridge, Mass.: Harvard University Press, 1994).

Watson, G., 'Responsibility and the Limits of Evil: Variations on a Strawsonian Theme', in F. D. Schoeman (ed.), *Responsibility, Character, and the Emotions: New Essays in Moral Psychology*, (Cambridge: Cambridge University Press, 1987).

Wertheimer, R., *The Significance of Sense: Meaning, Modality, and Morality* (Ithaca, NY: Cornell University Press, 1972).

Williams, B., *Ethics and the Limits of Philosophy* (Cambridge, Mass.: Harvard University Press, 1985).

—— 'Internal Reasons and the Obscurity of Blame', in *Making Sense of Humanity* (Cambridge: Cambridge University Press, 1995).

10

Moorean Moral Phenomenology

Terry Horgan and Mark Timmons

Inquiry into the what-it-is-likeness of concrete moral experience—moral phenomenology—has not generally been part of moral philosophy as practiced in the analytic tradition at least since G. E. Moore's 1903 *Principia Ethica*.[1] Although there have been a few exceptions—including, most notably, Maurice Mandelbaum's 1955 *The Phenomenology of Moral Experience*—and although analytic philosophers since Moore do sometimes appeal to considerations having to do with the what-it-is-likeness of concrete moral experience, nevertheless one finds almost nothing in this tradition that makes moral phenomenology an extended topic of inquiry.[2] We maintain that this should change—that an adequate ethical theory (including both normative ethics and metaethics) ought to be partially grounded on an adequate phenomenology of moral experience.

However, even if Moore and post-Moorean analytic moral philosophy did not pay much attention to moral phenomenology, one should not conclude that the works of Moore and others are not of phenomenological significance; far from it. In particular,

---

[1] For a useful discussion of this trend within the utilitarian tradition, see Dallas Willard, 'Utilitarianism and Phenomenology', in John J. Drummond and Lester L. Embree, (eds.), *Phenomenological Approaches to Moral Theory* (The Netherlands: Kluwer Academic Publishers, 2002).

[2] Another notable exception is Bernard Williams, whose phenomenological observations about moral regret have been influential. See, e.g., 'Ethical Consistency' and 'Consistency and Realism', both reprinted in his *Problems of the Self* (Cambridge: Cambridge University Press, 1973). It is also worth noting that moral phenomenology is beginning to receive some attention by philosophers. Two very recent examples are Carla Bagnoli, 'Phenomenology of the Aftermath: Ethical Theory and the Intelligibility of Moral Experience', in Sergio Tenenbaum (ed.), *Moral Psychology*, (Amsterdam and New York: Rodopi, forthcoming), and Peter Railton, 'Normative Guidance', in Russ Shafer-Landau, *Oxford Studies in Metaethics*, Vol. 1 (Oxford: Oxford University Press, 2006).

Moore's open question argument has phenomenological significance, we maintain, and ought to be reflected in an adequate phenomenological characterization of moral experience. Explaining this remark is the main task of the present paper. Specifically, our aim is to focus on a certain type of moral experience that is intended to capture what we take to be the fundamental lesson of Moore's open question argument: the ineliminability and irreducibility of moral normativity. The result will be a decidedly Moorean moral phenomenology, even if Moore himself might not have endorsed our particular version of it.

Our plan is to begin in the next section with some remarks about moral phenomenology, followed in section II by a few observations about Moore's lack of explicit attention to the what-it-is-likeness of moral experience. Then, in section III, we turn to those aspects of Moore's metaethical position that we claim ought to be reflected in an adequate moral phenomenology, which we then (in section IV) incorporate into a phenomenological account of a central type of moral experience—experiences of moral obligation. In section V, we briefly consider the bearing of facts about moral phenomenology on the metaethical question of moral realism—a topic which, as we shall explain, requires greater attention than many have thought. Section VI is our conclusion.

I Moral Phenomenology

By 'moral phenomenology', we mean something narrower than the range of features to which this expression is sometimes applied. Used very broadly, the 'phenomenology' associated with moral thought and discourse includes all of those deeply embedded features of moral thought and discourse including not only (1) the what-it-is-likeness of concrete moral experiences, but (2) features having to do with the grammar and logic of ethics, and (3) certain 'critical practices' including, for instance, the fact that people engage in what seem to be genuine moral disagreements. We do not mean to say that these features of moral thought and discourse lack a phenomenology (i.e., a what-it-is-likeness aspect) or lack phenomenological significance. For instance, since there is a what-it-is-likeness to inferring generally, there is a what-it-is-likeness to making moral inferences. But we take the phenomenology of concrete moral experiences—for instance, the what-it-is-likeness of judging that, in the circumstances one now faces, one ought to perform such and so action—to be of primary importance in developing a moral phenomenology. First person judgments of moral obligation are not the only type of concrete moral experience, of course—and among the types of such experience, we do not wish to commit ourselves here to the claim that such judgments are phenomenologically more basic than, say, experiences of judging the worth of someone's character. However, our focus in this paper will concern the what-it-is-likeness of those moral experiences that involve judging that one morally ought or ought not to perform some action in the circumstances one is presently in. To sharpen our focus, we need to engage in a bit of taxonomy.

Across the range of concrete moral experiences there are significant differences that merit distinguishing such experiences into distinct types. One important distinction is between moral experiences that include making or having a moral judgment—call them *judgment-involving* moral experiences—and moral experiences that do not include the making or having of a moral judgment—call them cases of *ethical comportment*.[3] Each of these types of moral experience calls for a brief explanation.

The main point we wish to make about judgment-involving moral experiences is that as we are using the term 'judgment', a moral judgment is simply an occurrent psychological state with moral content. Given this fairly broad usage, such a state that occurs spontaneously as a result, say, of viewing an act of violence counts as a moral judgment, even though no process of deliberation preceded coming to have or make the judgment—i.e., even though no process of deliberative judg*ing* was involved. So, as we are using the term 'judgment', moral judgments could be arranged on a continuum with cases in which one reaches a moral conclusion as the result of long, thoughtful deliberation on one end and cases in which one finds oneself spontaneously thinking, for example, that the action one is witnessing is morally wrong, on the other. And, of course, in between these is a range of cases involving more or less deliberation that precedes one's forming, or finding oneself undergoing, a moral judgment.

Cases of ethical comportment, then, include cases in which one responds in a morally appropriate way on some occasion—say, by spontaneously extending a helping hand to someone who is about to slip on wet pavement—but where the experience does not involve making or having a moral judgment. We recognize that the issue of whether a moral judgment is involved in such cases of spontaneous action is delicate, but here all we wish to do is to acknowledge the prima-facie phenomenological case for recognizing such cases. Since our focus is on a species of judgment-involving moral experience, we may set aside this (possible) type of moral experience.[4]

---

[3] We borrow this term from H. I. Dreyfus and S. E. Dreyfus, 'What is Morality? A Phenomenological Account of the Development of Ethical Expertise', in D. Rasmussen (ed.), *Universalism vs. Communitarianism* (Cambridge, Mass.: MIT Press, 1990).

[4] We suspect that virtually all cases of what the Dreyfus brothers call comportment really are judgment-involving, even though these judgments are spontaneous rather than deliberative—and even though they often issue in spontaneous action too. Non-judgment-involving ethical comportment

More important for present purposes is a division within the category of judgment-involving moral experiences. Here, we follow Mandelbaum (1955, 45) in distinguishing *direct* moral experiences of obligation from *removed* experiences of obligation and value. Direct moral experiences are what Mandelbaum calls 'reflexive' experiences of obligation, and essentially involve what he describes as a felt demand:

It is my contention that the demands which we experience when we make a direct moral judgment are always experienced as emanating from 'outside' us, and as being directed against us. They are demands which seem to be independent of us and to which we feel that we ought to respond (1955, 54)

There are two important elements of direct moral experiences that Mandelbaum is calling attention to in this passage. First, the felt demand in question is experienced as a kind of vector force with an origin and a direction: phenomenologically, one experiences it as having its origin in the 'outside' circumstances and whose force is directed toward oneself. Second, as Mandelbaum says, these demands, phenomenologically emanating as they do from the outside circumstances in which an agent finds herself, are experienced as having an 'independent' authority because they have their source in features of the circumstances rather than in the agent's desires. This sort of authoritative independence grounds the sense of objectivity we take our direct moral experiences to have. (Below, we provide an example meant to illuminate these elements.)

These first-person, reflexive, judgment-involving moral experiences are contrasted with cases in which one morally judges from the perspective of an essentially removed third-person observer. For example, cases in which one judges the conduct of one's past self or that of someone else (removed judgments of obligation) and cases in which one judges one's own character (past or present) or the character of others (examples of judgments of moral value) are cases where one, in effect, assumes the perspective of an observer and passes judgment on action and character. One essential phenomenological difference between direct and removed moral experiences is the 'stirredupness and pressures' (1955, 127) which are present in the former but absent in the latter.[5]

Within this taxonomy, then, our focus is the phenomenology of direct judgment-involving moral experiences. Here is a relatively uncomplicated example that the

---

would be something like involuntary, reflexive, bodily movement which is none the less experienced (perhaps after the fact) as morally appropriate—an extreme case of comportment.

[5] Mandelbaum has additional things to say about the contrast between direct and removed moral judgments. For more on the contrast between direct and removed experiences of *obligation* (rightness) see *Phenomenology*, 127, and for more on the contrast between direct moral judgments and removed experiences of *value*, see *Phenomenology*, 135.

reader may recognize, and that will illustrate the sort of moral experience we have in mind.

It's Friday, the last day of the semester before finals and you arrive at the department headed for your office bright and early. In past weeks, you have been working furiously on a paper due yesterday which you managed to send off at the eleventh hour. As you walk through your building toward your office, you are experiencing a sense of calm as you reflect with relief on what you've managed to accomplish during the semester: a paper just completed and sent off, a large introductory course with 200 students that for you was a new preparation with many hours spent working up slide presentations, meeting every other week with teaching assistants, a departmental hire—not to mention the damaged roof at home and the time spent wrangling with insurance agents, scheduling repairs, training Sophie, your new Lab puppy, and so on. Over the past two weeks, you have had to ignore some things, including a flood of email which you plan to spend the morning sorting through. You really should not have ignored as much email as you did, but you find dealing with email a huge distraction, so, on occasion, you have to take draconian measures and ignore the urgent in order to tackle the truly important projects and tasks. Dealing with your inbox ought to take about three hours you think, then it's home again to pack for a short, much needed, vacation. The teaching assistants are giving the final examination on Monday, you'll be back to submit final grades the following Friday. With email out of the way, you will be able to relax. Ah, sometimes life is good; as you unlock your office door, you now feel positively cheery.

Ready to work, you turn on your computer and as always your weekly calendar pops up. You are about to minimize it when you notice an entry for today at 8:30 (in about half an hour)—and you now remember. Many weeks ago (so it seems) you made an appointment with a struggling student who had asked you to help him go over comments he had received from one of your TAs on his most recent paper. You allow students to re-write papers, and this one is due no later than Monday's final exam period. Your cheery mood is replaced by a mild sinking feeling as you begin to realize how much time it will likely take to provide useful help to this student. For one thing, you will need to re-read his paper, and you can predict that meeting with *this* student is going to take quite a while. You could, of course, close your door, turn out the light, and just not answer the 8:30 knock. You feel ever so slightly tempted as you ask yourself whether the student will *really* benefit from the session, whether he just *might* pass anyway, whether he will be angry if you do not make yourself available . . . But you did arrange to meet the student, the student is in danger of failing, it is the student's last chance to meet with you . . . You feel the press of these competing demands, but think that you really ought to help the student. With a deep sigh, you begin clearing the books from a chair so your student will have a place to sit and then pick up his paper and begin to read.

This example meets the above-mentioned characterization of Mandelbaum's direct moral judgments of obligation: (1) the agent experiences a felt demand directed at her to engage in certain activities whose origin or source is experienced as coming from the 'external' circumstances (as she takes them to be); and (2) this felt demand is experienced as having a kind of authority that provides a basis for the sense that such demands are objective.[6]

II Moral Phenomenology and Moore

One certainly does not find any such descriptions of moral experience in the writings of Moore. He does refer to 'what is before our minds'—something to be determined by direct 'inspection'—when he discusses the issue of defining 'good' and when he presents his open question argument in defense of the claim that this term cannot be defined (see, for example, 1903, §8, 60, §13, 67−8).[7] One might construe these remarks as having to do with the phenomenology of grasping or understanding concepts, but they are not about the phenomenology of concrete moral experience.

Moore also makes claims about the contents of certain kinds of moral judgments. For instance, he writes: 'Whenever we judge that a thing is "good as a means," we are making a judgment with regard to its causal relations: we judge *both* that it will have a particular kind of effect, *and* that that effect will be good in itself' (1903, §16, 73). One might interpret this remark as phenomenological—an attempt to report what is going through one's head when one makes a judgment about positive instrumental value. But there are other remarks Moore makes about what one is asserting when one makes certain other types of moral claims that are probably not best construed as phenomenological. For instance, he claims that 'to assert that a certain line of conduct is, at a given time, absolutely right or obligatory, is obviously to assert that more good or less evil will exist in the world, if it be adopted than if anything else be done instead' (1903, §17, 77). Interpreted as a remark about phenomenology that is supposed to be common to people's deontic moral judgments, this claim is extremely dubious at best. For one thing, considerations of the comparative values of the consequences of alternative lines of action (which is what Moore is here talking about) are probably not often part of the phenomenology of most people when they judge, for example, that they ought to show gratitude toward someone who has done them a huge favor. And the same goes for other 'special' obligations that focus on past actions

---

[6] This characterization, as we shall see below in section IV, is only a partial phenomenological description of direct judgment-involving moral experiences.

[7] All references to Moore's *Principia* include the section number followed by page number(s) from the 1993 revised edition.

of oneself and others.[8] Indeed, Mandelbaum (1955, 99–105) argued that the sort of consequentialist phenomenology that Moore's remark might suggest is not even an adequate description of the common phenomenology of moral judgments generally, even in those cases where one takes into account the actual or intended states of affairs associated with actions. Thus, the quoted remark from Moore is probably best understood as a claim about what one is committed to claiming (given the correctness of Moore's brand of consequentialism) in making such a claim. And, so interpreted, the remark is officially non-committal about the phenomenology involved in thinking that a line of conduct is absolutely right or obligatory.

So, even if one looks hard at Moore's writings for signs of any phenomenological description of moral experience, one finds very little. Why is this?[9] After all, one would think that moral experiences are an important source of information that would bear on questions of the content, status, and, hence, justification of moral judgments.

One obvious reason Moore might have had for thinking (if he did so think) that moral phenomenology was not important for ethical inquiry is his rejection of all versions of ethical naturalism, understood as attempts to define fundamental moral terms in an exclusively naturalistic vocabulary. Moore famously argued that 'good' (which he took to be fundamental in ethics) and the concept this term expresses cannot be defined—and, in particular, that it is always fallacious to attempt to define it via the 'natural' terms and concepts featured in the sciences. Phenomenological description is a matter of descriptive moral psychology, and Moore considered the subject-matter of psychology to be something 'natural' (1903, §26, 92). So, just as Moore thought that facts about biological fitness (in terms of which Spencer tried to define the notion of 'better than') are irrelevant for understanding the primary subject-matter of ethics (namely, goodness), so he would have thought the same thing about trying to define basic moral terms and concepts by terms and concepts from psychology. Thus, the idea that considerations of psychology are irrelevant to the task of understanding the concept of goodness—a task that he held is basic for the enterprise of ethical theorizing—is one possible explanation for the fact that Moore was not concerned with moral phenomenology.[10]

---

[8] According to W. D. Ross, *The Right and the Good* (Oxford: Oxford University Press, 1930), 27, basic prima-facie duties of special obligation include fidelity, gratitude, and reparation.

[9] The question is particularly interesting since, as Willard, 'Utilitarianism and Phenomenology', explains, some of Moore's philosophical predecessors in the utilitarian tradition, including Hume, Mill, and Sidgwick, developed their views in light of phenomenological considerations.

[10] Moore did, however, think that 'natural' causal facts about the consequences of actions are relevant for answering questions about the rightness and wrongness of actions. In *Principia* he defines 'right action' (in the sense of obligatory action) partly in terms of intrinsic value (§17, 77). And so, to be justified in believing of some action that it is right, one needs to know which sorts of possible consequences have intrinsic value (something known by intuition) and also which consequences

There is another possible source of skepticism about the importance (if not the relevance) of matters of moral phenomenology that is worth mentioning here. One might think that all of the really philosophically interesting and important features of moral thought and discourse have to do with the meanings of ethical judgments (and the logical relations among them) and that considerations of moral experience—the what-it-is-likeness of thinking, deliberating, judging, and reacting that constitute such experiences—are irrelevant for getting at meaning and logic.

This contention is worthy of an extensive reply that would require engaging in phenomenological description of moral experience and showing the ways in which it is indispensable for ethical inquiry. We obviously cannot undertake this project here, so we shall simply offer a few brief remarks in reply, about how moral phenomenology seems to bear importantly on issues in metaethics.

First, we follow Mandelbaum (1955, 115–26) in holding that traditional non-cognitivism (typically presented as an account of the meanings of moral terms and concepts) is problematic because it is at odds with moral phenomenology. According to one type of non-cognitivist view, making or coming to have a moral judgment is a matter of having a non-cognitive attitude directed toward the object of evaluation. The sort of phenomenology at least suggested by this sort of view is one where an individual is aware of or focused on some (actual or possible) descriptive state of affairs and this prompts in her a pro- or con-attitude, which is then experienced as the source of the moral judgment. But this description of moral experience is not faithful to the phenomenological facts; it seems to have these facts backwards. For instance, my feeling of moral outrage, directed toward some object of evaluation, appears to me (at least upon reflection) to be prompted by, or result from, my judging that the object in question is outrageous. Arguably, in at least many cases, one experiences some action, in virtue of its nature, as calling for a certain reaction, and one experiences the reaction as prompted by, and a response to, the nature of the act. If this is right, then the non-cognitivist view (at least the version under consideration) is not faithful to moral phenomenology. This is not supposed to be a knock-down objection to the sort of non-cognitivism under discussion, but it does illustrate how facts about moral phenomenology can be brought to bear on philosophical views about the meanings of moral terms and the concepts they express.[11]

---

various alternative actions will produce if performed. In his 1912 *Ethics* (Oxford: Oxford University Press), Moore gave up this definition of 'right' but still maintained that, as a matter of substantive fact, the rightness of an action is entirely determined by the intrinsic value of its consequences together with causal facts about the consequences of actions.

[11] We do not think that what are now called 'expressivist' metaethical views (descendants of traditional non-cognitivism) need be in tension with facts about moral experience. For instance, Blackburn's quasi-realist form of expressivism and our own cognitivist version of expressivism claim

The phenomenological observation just noted is an instance of a general feature of moral experience that is one driving force behind realist views in metaethics, namely, the sense that one experiences obligation and value as something 'external' to oneself, and thus as something objective. In relation to direct moral experiences, we have already noted Mandelbaum's observation (quoted earlier) that in judging that one ought or ought not to perform some action, one typically experiences a felt demand that 'we experience as emanating from "outside" us, and being directed against us' (1955, 54). So, not only is moral phenomenology a basis for objecting to certain metaethical positions (for example, non-cognitivism), it can seem to positively favor others (for example, moral realism).[12]

Having noted some possible reasons why Moore thought (or might have thought) that moral phenomenology is not relevant to the main tasks of ethical inquiry, and having offered some prima-facie evidence to the contrary, let us turn to what we maintain is of phenomenological significance in Moore's metaethics.

III The Lesson of the Open Question Argument

As we have said, the fact that Moore says little or nothing about the phenomenology of concrete moral experience does not mean that his metaethical views are not of phenomenological import. Moore presented his open question argument as an exercise in conceptual investigation: against attempts to define fundamental moral terms (and the concepts they express) in 'natural' or 'metaphysical'—and thus in non-normative—terms (and concepts), Moore asks his readers to pose certain questions (based on whatever putative definition is under consideration) which, if the definition is correct, ought to strike the reader (once she has brought the concepts clearly before her mind) as a closed question. If 'good' just means 'more highly evolved', then the questions: (1) X is good, but is it more highly evolved? and (2) X is more highly evolved, but is it good? ought to strike any competent English-language speaker as having obviously affirmative answers—obvious given one's understanding of the concepts involved in the questions. Except for the phenomenology of grasping or understanding terms and concepts (involved in the process of 'bringing before one's mind'), how is Moore's open question argument of phenomenological significance?

not to be at odds with the phenomenological facts of ordinary moral experience. See Blackburn, *Essays in Quasi-Realism* (Oxford: Oxford University Press, 1994); and T. Horgan and M. Timmons, 'Cognitivist Expressivism', in T. Horgan and M. Timmons (eds.), *Metaethics after Moore* (Oxford: Oxford University Press, 2006).

[12] Whether the appeal to moral phenomenology really does favor some version or other of moral realism is a delicate issue which we take up briefly in section V of this paper.

Our answer to this question involves two claims. First, we follow a standard line of interpretation of the lesson of Moore's argument, according to which its import is that moral terms and concepts are *normative*—in the sense that judgments involving them are *reason-providing*.[13] Second, we claim that the irreducible normative character of moral terms and concepts has an experiential counterpart in one's concrete moral experiences: concrete moral experiences involve, as a constitutive aspect of their nature, the experience of normativity. In the remainder of this section, we focus on the first point about normativity, and in the next section we take up the second point about normativity as an aspect of moral phenomenology.

To focus thinking, let us distinguish a number of central theses in Moore's metaethics, beginning with what we are taking to be the general upshot of the open question argument.

> *Moral normativity*: Basic moral terms and concepts are at least partly normative in the sense that judgments containing them express fundamental reasons for engaging in some action or responding with some attitude with respect to the item being evaluated.

In addition to this thesis, Moore held a certain view about the conceptual interconnections among types of ethical terms and concepts. As noted above, in *Principia*, he defines the rightness (oughtness) of actions in terms of intrinsic value: '[T]he assertion "I am morally bound to perform this action" is identical with the assertion "This action will produce the greatest possible amount of good in the Universe" ' (1903, §89, 197). And, similarly, for the concept of virtue: 'a virtue may be defined as an habitual disposition to perform certain actions, which generally produce the best possible results' (1903, §103, 221). We may sum this up in the following thesis:

Goodness is basic: The concept of intrinsic goodness is the basic concept in ethics: all other ethical concepts, including those of rightness and virtue, are to be understood partly in terms of the concept of intrinsic goodness.[14]

If one embraces both the moral normativity thesis and the thesis that goodness is basic, then a consequence is this:

Fundamental normativity of goodness: The concept of intrinsic goodness is the fundamental normative concept in ethical thought: that something is intrinsically good provides a fundamental reason for responding (in action or attitude) to it in some way.

---

[13] Here is how William Frankena in his 'Obligation and Value in the Ethics of G. E. Moore', in Paul A. Schilpp (ed.), *The Philosophy of G. E. Moore* (La Salle, Ill.: Open Court, 1942) puts the point: '[T]o my mind, what makes ethical judgments seem irreducible to natural or to metaphysical judgments is their apparently normative character' (102).

[14] As explained above in n. 10, Moore eventually gave up his claim that obligation and rightness can be reductively *defined* in terms of the concept good. He nevertheless still held that goodness is more basic than rightness, and so continued to hold the thesis that goodness is basic.

Among those philosophers who accept the moral normativity thesis, there is dispute over the basicness of goodness thesis and, hence, dispute over the fundamental normativity of goodness thesis. Those who challenge the former typically claim that the concept of ought is the most basic normative concept in ethics.[15] We do not wish to weigh in here on this issue. Rather, we wish to place emphasis on the moral normativity thesis in developing a moral phenomenology, and to remain neutral about both (1) the thesis of the basicness of goodness; and (2) whether or not reasons for action and attitude are provided at all by considerations of intrinsic value. A *robust* Moorean moral phenomenology would embrace both the moral normativity thesis and the thesis of the basicness of goodness, whereas a more *modest* Moorean moral phenomenology would embrace the moral normativity thesis and remain neutral about the basicness thesis. It will be enough for our purposes to sketch a modest Moorean moral phenomenology.

IV   Toward a Moorean Moral Phenomenology

We have been saying that we wish to preserve the lesson of Moore's open question argument in presenting an adequate moral phenomenology of judgment-involving direct experiences. But there is another Moorean element we wish to preserve: direct moral judgments are genuine *beliefs*. So in order to accomplish the task of developing the rudiments of a Moorean moral phenomenology, we will proceed to do the following.

(1) Make a case for the claim that direct ought-judgments are genuine beliefs by investigating the phenomenology of belief and arguing that these judgments exhibit that phenomenology. In so doing, vindicate the cognitivist element of Moore's view.

(2) Call attention to how such beliefs are typically embedded in an overall experience that is psychologically complex: the felt demand (described above) that is characteristic of direct moral judgments is phenomenologically grounded in one's experiencing certain actions or attitudes as fitting or

---

[15] See, e.g., A. C. Ewing, *The Definition of Good* (New York: Macmillan, 1947). Granted, Moore held that the concept of intrinsic value is synonymous with the concept of what *ought to be or exist for its own sake*. See *Principia*, preface, 34, §13, 68, §68, 166, §69, 169, §70, 170. But some of Moore's critics have argued that Moore's conception of intrinsic value as a simple, non-relational property, even understood as equivalent to the concept of what ought to exist for its own sake, is incompatible with what we are calling the normativity of goodness thesis. See, e.g., W. Frankena, 'Obligation and Value', and Stephen Darwall, 'How Should Ethics Relate to (the Rest of) Philosophy?: Moore's Legacy', in T. Horgan and M. Timmons (eds.), *Metaethics after Moore* (Oxford: Oxford University Press, 2006).

unfitting (depending on whether one experiences an action (or an attitude) as demanded by or prohibited by the circumstances in which one is placed).

(3) Call attention to the fact that the experiences of fit and unfit, which are the normative core of moral judgments, have a sui generis, irreducible element even though they also involve interesting structural complexity.[16]

We now proceed to take each of these points in order.

i The Phenomenology of Belief and Direct Ought-judgments

Occurrent beliefs, we claim, have a phenomenology: there is something it is like to occurrently believe something.[17] They also have other features *qua* beliefs: they are semantically assessable (one can ascribe truth and falsity to their contents) and they have a functional role to play in the overall psychological economy of agents. In a previous article (Horgan and Timmons, 2006b) we have explored these generic features of belief, making a case that moral judgments are, indeed, a type of belief. But here we can afford to focus exclusively on the phenomenological dimension of belief generally and moral belief in particular.[18]

We wish to call attention to five interrelated features of the what-it-is-likeness of occurrent belief generally (its phenomenology), making a case as we go that each of these features is possessed by direct moral judgments. The phenomenological features of occurrent belief include: (1) psychologically 'coming down' on some issue (2) through which one classifies or sorts something into one or more categories (3) that is typically experienced as involuntary and in which (4) one experiences the coming down in this way as a cognitive response to some consideration that is (at least peripherally) experienced as a sufficient reason for the categorization, and also (5) as a judgment that is apt for assertion and hence is naturally expressible by a declarative sentence in language. We now proceed to take up these elements in order, illustrating

---

[16] In our discussion of the open question argument, we did not mention Moore's claim that the concept of goodness (and the corresponding property) is *simple*. We think that issues of unanalyzability, simplicity, and the lesson of the open question argument are muddled in Moore—as he himself noted in his 'Preface to the Second Edition' to *Principia*, unpublished until Baldwin's 1993 edition of Moore's book. We note here that it is possible to read Moore's texts in a way that would allow him to embrace these three points while also maintaining that the fundamental notion in ethics is simple. That is, his texts might allow for the idea that fittingness is a primitive, irreducible relation and in *that* sense it is simple, though allowing that (1) its relata are often complex, and (2) fittingness *facts*, because they are relational facts, are structurally complex.

[17] So did Hume. See Hume's appendix to *A Treatise of Human Nature* (Oxford: Oxford University Press, 1739), 628–9.

[18] The following remarks reflect what we say in T. Horgan and M. Timmons, 'Cognitivist Expressivism', 263–5.

each of them first in connection with descriptive beliefs and then in connection with direct moral judgments.

(1) I glance up from my computer and see my dog chewing an old tennis shoe. In so doing, I 'come down' on the issue of what she is chewing. Here the experience of coming down is spontaneous: I do not need to think about what she is doing, rather I just see what she is doing—which immediately prompts the corresponding thought. But often my coming down on some issue requires more or less thought, as when I ponder the evidence and then come down on some issue. I glance up, see my dog chewing away with her back to me, I think for a few moments about what she could be chewing and, remembering that the only item available to her is her favorite toy, I come down on the matter of what she is chewing: she is chewing her favorite toy.

Next, consider all-things-considered direct ought-judgments. In some cases, one finds oneself spontaneously coming down on the matter of what one ought to do given what one is currently experiencing. Seeing that a nearby child has lost her footing and slipped into the deep end of a swimming pool, one spontaneously judges that, one ought to pull her out. In other cases, of course, coming down on some issue is preceded by some amount of reflection, as when one judges that, in the midst of a conversation, one ought to withhold a certain comment that might wrongly be taken as an insult. Direct ought-judgments, then—like beliefs about matters of non-moral, descriptive fact—involve as part of their phenomenology the experience of coming down on some issue.

(2) Of course, many non-belief psychological states also involve the experience of coming down, as, for example, when one forms an intention to get a beer from the fridge. Intentions are, like beliefs, psychological states in which one comes down on a matter of what to do, but arguably intentions are not themselves beliefs. The sort of coming down that does distinguish beliefs from intentions involves the experience of categorizing or sorting the item(s) being thought about. Presumably, intending to get a beer from the fridge is partly based on one's belief that there is a beer there, and in having this belief one is categorizing a beer as belonging in the 'being in the fridge (currently)' category. In the case of non-moral descriptive beliefs, things get sorted into descriptive categories by the use of category-concepts that purport to represent some worldly object-kind or some property.

Similarly, when a person judges of some action that she ought to do it, she experiences her coming down morally as involving the classifying or categorizing the act in question as being *something to be done by her*. And this same sort of phenomenological feature is typically present in what we have called removed moral judgments as well—for instance, where one judges of someone else that their action was *something to be done by them*.

(3) Beliefs are most often involuntary. This feature of the phenomenology of belief is implicit in how we have described our previous examples. In glancing up from my computer and looking across the room, my belief that the dog is chewing a shoe is (at least in normal frames of mind) involuntary. I can, of course, withhold belief about how things are—for example, when (owing to past experience) my seeing what looks like water further down the highway no longer prompts me to spontaneously believe that there is water in that place. Involuntariness is also characteristic of beliefs that result from deliberation and reflection: the evidence seems to compel (at least in many cases) a particular verdict which one experiences as involuntary.

Clearly, direct ought-judgments are normally experienced as involuntary in roughly the same way as are experiences of non-moral beliefs. One finds oneself being psychologically compelled to judge, for example, that one ought to rush to assist an elderly person who is losing his balance and about to take a bad tumble. And this same involuntary character of the phenomenology of moral judgment is also clearly present (in most cases) where one mulls over her present circumstances and comes to think that she really ought to open her door and prepare for her 8:30 meeting with the student. Psychologically, the all-things-considered ought-judgment is experienced as 'forced' by the particulars of the circumstances (as she takes them to be); it is experienced as involuntary.

(4) Beliefs about non-moral matters of fact are further experienced as grounded in considerations that serve as sufficient reasons for the belief in question. My occurrent belief about my dog and her chewing is grounded in my perceptual awareness, which I (implicitly) take to be a sufficient basis for my belief that she is chewing an old tennis shoe. My perceptually grounded belief is here experienced as grounded in the authority of reasons provided by my visual experience. Similar remarks apply to beliefs about non-moral (non-evaluative) matters—for instance, when I come to a belief about who ate the last brownie, on the basis of strong circumstantial evidence.

Occurrent, first-person judgments of moral obligation are likewise grounded in the authority of reasons. In judging that one ought to rush toward the elderly person about to fall, one experiences this judgment as grounded in what one takes to be morally salient features of the situation that are perceptually manifest: the person is frail-looking and is losing his balance, no one else is nearby, and so on. And, of course, the same is true (and even more obvious) in cases where one deliberates about what to do, and after weighing everything up, comes to judge that (all things considered) she ought to do this or that action.

(5) Finally, ordinary descriptive beliefs are naturally experienced as apt for assertion in sentences in the declarative mood. The same holds for moral judgments generally and direct ought-judgments in particular. In giving voice to her thought, the teacher affirms (out loud to herself) that she ought to keep the appointment. Here, the

relevant psychological state is a categorizing, coming-down state that is not willfully imposed as when one forms an intention to do some action. Rather, the teacher's judgment that she ought to keep the appointment is experienced as demanded by sufficient reasons. This kind of involuntary, reason-based categorizing judgment is naturally expressible by an act of assertion—i.e., by uttering a declarative sentence.

So, reflection on the what-it-is-likeness of uncontentious cases of belief—non-moral, descriptive belief—reveals a number of interrelated phenomenological features of belief which are also possessed by moral judgments generally and direct ought-judgments in particular. Of course, as mentioned above, there is more to being a belief than its phenomenology: there are also considerations of semantic assessibility and of functional role. And, as noted, elsewhere we have argued that moral judgments do, indeed, possess these further belief-characterizing features. All of this, we submit, favors a cognitivist construal of moral judgments—Moore was right about this much: moral judgments are beliefs.[19]

ii The Experience of Fittingness as Phenomenologically Basic

So far, in developing a Moorean moral phenomenology of judgment-involving direct moral experiences, we have made two principal observations. First, such experiences are characterized by a felt 'reflexive' demand on the part of the agent, which is experienced as a kind of force whose origin is 'external' to the agent and directed against the agent. Second, the moral judgments involved in such experiences—judgments of the form, *I ought/must/should do (not do) A*—are experienced as beliefs. But now one may ask whether there is anything that is experienced as a *basis* for this kind of felt demand and the associated moral ought-judgment.

Mandelbaum (1955, 59–71) posed just this question, and he claimed that the phenomenological basis of direct moral judgments is the 'apprehension' of the relationship of some action's being 'fitting' or 'unfitting' to the circumstances facing the agent. To explain this, let us first say something about these relations and then explain how, at least on Mandelbaum's view, experiences of them are phenomenologically basic.

The experiences of fit and unfit involve the relationship between some circumstance (or situation) that the agent currently faces (at least as she takes them to be) and some possible action on her part of which she is aware. To return to our earlier example of

---

[19] But to say this is not, on our view, to say that moral beliefs are descriptive beliefs—beliefs whose overall content is a *way-the-world-might-be* content. Our above characterization leaves this open. Elsewhere in Horgan and Timmons, 'Cognitivist Expressivism' and 'Nondescriptivist Cognitivism: Toward a New Metaethic', *Philosophical Papers* 29 (2000), 121–53, we argue that they are not best interpreted as descriptive. We return to this matter of the descriptivity of moral beliefs below in section v.

the felt demand on the instructor to meet with her student, her circumstances include such considerations as her having agreed to meet the student, that the agreed-upon time is near, that it is the student's last opportunity to meet with her, and so forth. These features of her present circumstance 'call for' an action (or series of actions) on her part: the actions of opening her door, clearing off a chair for the student, getting out the student's paper and reading it, and so on, are experienced by her as a fitting, indeed the most fitting, series of actions for her to perform in her circumstances. Other, alternative courses of action are experienced by her as unfitting or less fitting (and as all-things-considered unfitting).

This experience of some action fitting or not fitting one's present circumstances is, evidently, what phenomenologically grounds the experience of a felt objective demand—a demand that is reflected in the associated ought-judgment. In the example under discussion, it is the instructor's sense of the circumstances *calling for* a series of actions and, correlatively, an envisioned series of actions being most appropriately *suited to* the circumstances that prompts the felt demand to engage in the series of envisioned actions. Two phenomenological observations are worth making here. First, as we have already noted, the sense that some set of 'external' circumstances are experienced as *themselves* calling for an action, independently of the desires or aversions one may have toward elements of those circumstances, provides the phenomenological basis of the felt *objectivity* of the demand. Second, this sense of circumstances calling for some action reflects a lately noted feature of the phenomenology of moral belief, namely, that such beliefs are experienced as being grounded in the authority of reasons—considerations that one takes to objectively demand a certain course of action.

Thus, to sum up: judgment-involving direct moral experiences involve three phenomenologically salient elements: (1) a felt reflexive objective-seeming demand; (2) an ought-belief; and (3) an experience of fit or unfit. And what we have just noted is that the first two elements are phenomenologically grounded in the third. But one should be careful here about how one understands talk of phenomenological grounding. In articulating these elements (largely following Mandelbaum), we have, in effect, teased apart aspects of a unified kind of experience. We do not mean to suggest that direct moral experiences of these elements must be temporally segmented and causally ordered—that one *first* apprehends something's being fitting or unfitting and *then* experiences this apprehension as *causing* one to make a moral ought-judgment which one *then* experiences as *causing* one to experience a kind of affective pressure to do or not do something. Rather, the phenomenology is typically seamless, in that these elements are fused together: the experience of reacting to some situation with the thought that one ought to perform some action is mixed with the felt demand coming from the circumstances and being directed at oneself.

iii Sui Generis Moral Normative Experiences

Having spelled out the rudiments of a phenomenology of judgment-involving direct moral experiences, let us now return to the issue of how our view is Moorean. We have claimed (along with others) that the lesson of the open question argument is the idea that moral terms and concepts are irreducibly normative—that they concern the idea of there being *reasons* for or against acting or for or against reacting; that some considerations 'call for' certain responses and, correlatively, certain responses are 'called for' by various considerations. Those responses 'called for' are fitting and sometimes most fitting, and those responses 'uncalled for' are unfitting. The irreducibility of these concepts is to be understood as the fact that they cannot be defined or adequately characterized without the use of normative concepts. But irreducibility in this sense does not entail a *kind* of metaphysical brute monadic simplicity that Moore perhaps thought was possessed by the property of intrinsic goodness. However, there is a sense in which the concept of fittingness, despite being relational, does involve a kind of simplicity—a point we mentioned in note 16, but is worth emphasizing here. That is, one can sensibly claim that the very idea of fittingness is of an irreducibly simple relation and thus a primitive normative notion. But saying this is compatible with this concept picking out a relation whose relata are often complex, and with the fact that fittingness *facts* are themselves complex. That fittingness is simple in this way is enough to justify the claim that this concept is *sui generis*. Rather than attempting to define or reduce the concept of fittingness, one explains it by clarifying the items involved in this relational notion, and also by calling attention to various instances of it—i.e., experiences of contemplated actions being fit or appropriate, unfit or inappropriate, in relation to a contemplated set of circumstances. There is something that it is like to experience an action as something demanded of you given your understanding of your circumstances, and this particular normative what-it-is-likeness—the sense of fit and unfit—is experientially *sui generis*.[20]

So Moore was right about the ultimate irreducibility of moral concepts, but he might have done better to focus on the closely related concepts of ought, normative

---

[20] Here it is appropriate to note what Moore said about fittingness judgments: 'by saying that a certain relation between two things is fitting or appropriate, we can only mean that the existence of that relation is absolutely good in itself . . . ' *Principia*, 152. If to say that a relation between two things is fitting just means that the relation between them is intrinsically good—by which we take it that Moore means to say that a specific relational *fact* is fitting (e.g., the fact that a contemplated act would bear the relation 'performed in' to certain specific circumstances)—then one might embrace both the moral normativity thesis and the thesis of goodness as basic. This could serve as a basis for developing a moral phenomenology that would yield what we called earlier a robust Moorean view of moral experience. According to this robust view, fittingness is not a normative concept that is distinct from, and more basic than, goodness. Rather, experiences of fittingness are themselves really just experiences of the absolute intrinsic goodness of certain relationally characterizable (actual or potential) states of affairs.

reason, and fittingness as at the heart of this irreducibility. Moreover, the conceptual irreducibility that moral concepts enjoy is reflected in the sorts of concrete moral experiences that we have been describing—experiences that we clearly have.

We conclude this section by noting some historical resistance to Moore's own moral metaphysics—resistance that is naturally construed as grounded in introspective attention to moral phenomenology. In evaluating Moore's claim that the property goodness is a *simple* non-natural property, it is standard to raise metaphysical queerness worries that Mackie (1977, ch. 1) famously pressed against Moore and the realist tradition in ethics generally. Such worries are partly grounded in considerations of moral phenomenology. Toward the end of his 1937 'The Emotive Meaning of Ethical Terms', C. L. Stevenson raises the worry that his emotivist construal of moral terms does not capture what moral judgments are about—namely a (presumably) simple moral property—and thus does not capture the idea that moral judgments are supposed to be responsive to moral truths. He writes in response to this complaint:

I can only answer that I do not understand. What is this truth to be *about*? For I recollect no Platonic Idea, nor do I know what to *try* to recollect. I find no indefinable property, nor do I know what to look for (1937: 30).

Now one might attribute this response to Stevenson's strong empiricist leanings, but the rationalist A. C. Ewing makes a similar remark in his 1947 *The Definition of Good*. In challenging attempts to reduce moral terms and concepts to 'natural' terms and concepts, Ewing complained that 'the philosophers who give naturalistic definitions of ethical terms, do not, despite their predeliction for empiricism, commend their conclusions as the direct result of a plain empirical investigation of our moral experience . . .'. (1947: 44) He then goes on to note that perhaps the best argument against a naturalistic account of ethical terms is that, 'if goodness were, as Moore claimed, a simple property, it is strange that nobody has discovered this until the time of Sidgwick. If we were aware of such a simple property or concept, must we not know that we are aware of it?' (1947: 45). Ewing concludes that people do not experience the sort of simple property often associated with Moore's view. He also offers a non-naturalistic definition of intrinsic value in terms of the concept of ought, which he further analyzes in terms of fittingness. So in cases where one judges of some action that it is intrinsically good, Ewing claims, 'There are various psychological characteristics, for example, the direction of the will to a certain end, and there are non-natural characteristics based on these, of being an action which ought to be done and of being a fitting object of admiration, but besides these there is no further quality of goodness that I can detect' (1947: 157).

One finds a similar phenomenological reaction in Frankena's contribution to the Schilpp volume on Moore's philosophy: 'I cannot discover in the things which may be considered to be good in themselves any simple quality of goodness in addition to their non-ethical qualities and the property of being right for an appropriate agent to pursue or produce' (1942, 108).

All three authors—Stevenson, Ewing, and Frankena—are offering phenomenological arguments against what was apparently Moore's moral metaphysics of intrinsic value. Clearly these phenomenologically based reactions are out of place when one focuses on experiences of fit and unfit, and one embraces only a *modest* Moorean phenomenology. Indeed, experiences of actions being fitting are common and not confined to moral experiences. For example, one responds to certain social situations with a sense of what would and would not be fitting from the point of view of custom and etiquette. One also has experiences of prudential fittingness—what would be fitting in relation to one's own welfare. Epistemological fittingness of certain beliefs relative to certain evidence is yet another example. The list can be extended.

V Moral Phenomenology and Moral Realism

At this point the attentive reader may be thinking or sensing that the Moorean moral phenomenology we have been describing cries out for some discussion of its bearing on questions of moral metaphysics. If direct, judgment-involving moral experiences have as an essential part of their phenomenology a sense of some action's fitting or not fitting the circumstances, and if the associated felt demand is experienced as having its source in the external circumstances, then don't such experiences have intentional content that involves fittingness as an objective, in-the-world, *relational property*? Don't these experiences thereby purport to represent objective, in-the-world, *moral facts*? If, furthermore, one takes one's experiences of the world as providing presumptive evidence for how the world really is, then doesn't the phenomenology of moral experience (at least direct moral experience) provide a presumptive reason to favor moral realism? And, if so, aren't views that deny the reality of such putative normative properties forced to embrace a form of the error theory?

In the space remaining we will not be able to address these questions with the philosophical care they deserve. Instead, we will simply indicate, in a series of rapid-fire remarks, how we view the issue of the bearing of Moorean moral phenomenology on questions about moral metaphysics, leaving a full defense of our position for elsewhere.

The question. The question at hand is whether or not the presentational content of one's moral phenomenology is the presentation of objective moral properties being instantiated in the world—and/or the presentation of objective moral relations being instantiated. The question is whether one's moral phenomenology has *descriptive purport*—whether, that is, the moral judgments embedded in moral experience purport to represent some worldly state of affairs that involves the instantiation of a moral property or a moral relation by some worldly item or items.

Our core non-descriptivist contention, and two related claims. Our core contention is that the answer to this question is No—even if one construes realism broadly enough to include 'dispositionalist' accounts of moral properties that would construe them on analogy with colors and other secondary qualities. The Moorean moral phenomenology we have described—what can be regarded as a common 'base-level' phenomenology—does not carry descriptive purport.[21] To this, we would add two supplemental claims. First, the answer to the question whether moral phenomenology has descriptive purport is *not introspectively manifest*; i.e., one cannot readily determine, just on the basis of introspective attention to one's own moral phenomenology, the answer to this question. Second, it is very easy to form the mistaken belief that a Yes answer to the question of descriptive purport *is* introspectively manifest—and thus to form the belief (seemingly on secure introspective grounds) that the answer is indeed Yes. For, the very features of moral phenomenology that constitute the what-it-is-like of occurrent *belief*—the aspects of involuntary, external-reason-based, categorizing, 'coming down' on an issue (as described in section IV.i above)—are features that make it easy to construe one's own involuntary moral categorization-judgment as a representation of a state of affairs consisting of the in-the-world instantiation of a moral property or relation. But that is an over-interpretation of the belief-ish aspects of moral phenomenology.

Appeals to grammar. Appeals to the so-called realist-seeming grammar of moral discourse do not help the realist's presumptive case based on moral phenomenology. That is, one might be tempted to argue that moral thought and discourse is expressed in declarative sentences in which such predicates as 'is wrong', 'is right', 'is good', 'is bad' are employed—thus strongly suggesting that sentences featuring them are used to attribute properties to objects of evaluation. Add to this grammatical observation the thought that the grammar reflects something about moral experiences, and one might be tempted to conclude that moral experiences have descriptive purport. But the argument here moves too quickly. To borrow an example from Michael Smith (1988), the predicate, 'is nauseating' functions grammatically just like many other

---

[21] Of course, there may be *further* aspects of the moral experiences of some individuals that do carry descriptive purport, but this does not affect our present point about what we are calling 'base-level' moral experience. Some people's overall moral phenomenology may well be somewhat colored by their beliefs, perhaps in such a way that beliefs about the existence of objective moral facts can imbue moral experience itself with objective purport. But that would be a belief-induced 'overlay' of phenomenological descriptivity, superimposed upon non-descriptive base-level moral phenomenology.

moral and non-moral predicates—as, for example, when someone thinks or says, 'That painting is nauseating'. But people do not suppose that this form of expression is deeply revealing of some aspect of their phenomenology—that their experiences and the associated judgments about what is and is not nauseating have descriptive purport. Those wishing to appeal to moral phenomenology to make a presumptive case for moral realism must find something else besides surface grammar to make their case. Indeed, on our view, given the belief-ish nature of moral judgments, the indicative mood is a natural linguistic vehicle for expressing these judgments—whether or not they are descriptive in their overall content.

Appeals to belief. But doesn't the belief-ish nature of moral judgments—featured in judgment-involving moral experiences—itself provide strong prima-facie reason to favor a realist moral metaphysics? After all, isn't it constitutive of a psychological state's being a genuine *belief* that it has descriptive purport—that it represents the world as being a certain way? Here, again, our response is negative. In other writings we have argued for a conception of belief according to which (1) a belief is a *commitment state* with respect to one or more descriptive contents; and (2) there are two distinct logically basic species of belief, namely, 'is-commitment' and 'ought-commitment'. On our view, that a psychological state is a belief state does not entail that its overall content is descriptive content. Moral ought-judgments, we claim, are a species of non-descriptive belief—they involve a distinctive sort of commitment directed toward some non-moral descriptive possible state of affairs—an ought-commitment, *vis-à-vis* a way the world might be. On our view, then, when one sincerely thinks or says 'I ought to express gratitude toward Jones', one thereby expresses an ought-commitment directed toward the possible states of affairs, *my expressing gratitude toward Jones.* So we deny that because judgment-involving moral experiences involve making or having moral beliefs, one must embrace a realist moral metaphysics. (For an elaboration and defense of this view, see Horgan and Timmons 2000, 2006b.)

Appeal to an is/seems distinction. Another route for trying to go from moral phenomenology to a presumption in favor of moral realism is to argue that moral experiences permit a distinction between what *seems* to be the case, morally speaking, and what really *is* the case. In this way they might be thought to resemble experiences of color and stand in contrast to experiences of nausea. Pursuing the apparent analogy between color experiences and color judgments on the one hand and moral experiences and judgments on the other would take us deep into the heart of the question under consideration, and is beyond the scope of this paper. We will simply make one observation that leads to the next and final point we wish to make. It would appear that someone who denies the descriptive purport of moral phenomenology can easily draw an is/seems distinction by pointing to the fact that, to make this distinction, it is sufficient if one can make sense of certain modal claims such as, 'Although it seems to me that I ought to help her with that project, *I might be mistaken.*'[22] If, as we think, those who deny the descriptive purport of moral experience can make sense of such modal remarks about one's own possibly being in error, then the mere appeal to the facts of moral phenomenology to support moral realism does not go through. We concede that an important burden on moral irrealism is to make plausible sense of the is/seems distinction and of the thought, 'I could be mistaken'. But we claim that this burden can be met, and if we are right about this, then the fact that moral phenomenology admits of an is/seems distinction does not show that it has descriptive purport.

Upshot. We maintain that the facts of moral phenomenology do not favor realist over irrealist views in ethics; to think otherwise is to try to make the phenomenology do too much. Rather, questions about realism vs. irrealism will require that various theoretical considerations be brought to bear on matters of moral metaphysics. Returning for a moment to our Moorean moral phenomenology featuring the idea of fittingness, we maintain that this sort of phenomenological description does favor the idea that morality is in some sense objective. In cases of judgment-involving direct experiences of obligation, one does experience the circumstances which one confronts as 'calling for' a certain action. But how to understand this phenomenology, as it is related to questions of moral metaphysics, is a subtle and complex matter, and is not something that can be easily 'read off' from what is manifest in the phenomenology itself. We contend that, even though the moral phenomenology we have described is indeed objective in the sense lately noted, it does not purport to represent fittingness as a relation that is 'out there' in the fabric of reality, a relation that obtains or does not obtain completely independently of one's own reactive attitudes. Experiences of fit and unfit being independent of one's desires and preferences, as they surely are, is one thing; but complete independence of one's own fittingness-sensibility is quite another.[23]

VI Conclusion

Our main task has been to sketch a decidedly Moorean moral phenomenology. After explaining what we mean by the phenomenology of concrete moral experience, we

---

[22] See, e.g., S. Blackburn, 'Errors and the Phenomenology of Value', in *Essays in Quasi-Realism* (Oxford: Oxford University Press, 1994); M. Timmons, *Morality without Foundations*, ch. 4, and T. Horgan and M. Timmons, 2000 and 2006a.

[23] On this point, see T. Horgan and M. Timmons, 'Moral Phenomenology and Moral Theory', 'Cognitivist Expressivism', and S. Kirchin, 'Ethical Phenomenology and Moral Realism', *Ethical Theory and Moral Practice* 6 (2003), 241–64.

proceeded to discuss what is often taken to be the main lesson of the open question argument—namely, the idea that moral concepts are ineliminably and irreducibly normative. Here, on the basis of reflection on the nature of normativity, we concluded that the notion of fittingness is arguably the fundamental normative notion in ethical thought and discourse. Our goal, then, was to sketch a phenomenology of certain moral experiences—experiences of what Mandelbaum calls direct moral obligation—that reflects the normative lesson of Moore's open question argument. In doing so, we followed the lead of Mandelbaum in proposing that direct moral experiences involve a felt 'reflexive' demand that is phenomenologically grounded in an apprehension of the fittingness of an action to a situation. It is this normative apprehension—a *sui generis* element of direct moral experience—that reflects the lesson of the open question argument. Finally, questions about moral phenomenology are thought to be relevant to questions in metaethics, including questions about moral metaphysics. And so, in the penultimate section, we claimed (although we did not fully argue) that the facts of moral phenomenology are non-committal with regard to the issue of moral realism vs. irrealism. But in saying this we do not mean to claim that considerations of moral phenomenology do not have much bearing on other metaethics questions and on questions in normative ethics. We have noted, for instance, that Moorean moral phenomenology bears quite directly on questions of ethical objectivity, and that it tells against traditional non-cognitivism. Pursuing the connections between moral phenomenology and other issues in ethics is something befitting another occasion.[24]

Works Cited

Bagnoli, C., 'Phenomenology of the Aftermath: Ethical Theory and the Intelligibility of Moral Experience', in Sergio Tenenbaum (ed.), *Moral Psychology, Poznan Studies in the Philosophy of the Sciences and Humanities*, vol. 94 (Amsterdam and New York: Rodopi, forthcoming).

Blackburn, S., 'Errors and the Phenomenology of Value' (1985), repr. in S. Blackburn, *Essays in Quasi-Realism* (Oxford: Oxford University Press, 1994).

Darwall, S., 'How Should Ethics Relate to (the Rest of) Philosophy?: Moore's Legacy', *Southern Journal of Philosophy* 41 (2003), 1–20, suppl. vol. repr. in T. Horgan and M. Timmons (eds.), *Metaethics after Moore* (Oxford: Oxford University Press, 2006).

Dreyfus, H. I., and Dreyfus, S. E., 'What is Morality? A Phenomenological Account of the Development of Ethical Expertise', in D. Rasmussen (ed.), *Universalism vs. Communitarianism* (Cambridge, Mass.: MIT Press, 1990).

---

[24] We pursue them further in T. Horgan and M. Timmons, 'What Can Moral Phenomenology Tell us About Moral Objectivity?', 'Prolegomena to a Future Phenomenology of Morals', *Phenomenology and the Cognitive Sciences* 7, special issue ed. by Uriah Kriegel (forthcoming, 2008).

Ewing, A. C., *The Definition of Good* (New York: Macmillan, 1947).

Frankena, W., 'Obligation and Value in the Ethics of G. E. Moore', in Paul A. Schilpp (ed.), *The Philosophy of G. E. Moore* (La Salle, Ill.: Open Court, 1942).

Horgan, T., and Timmons, M., 'Nondescriptivist Cognitivism: Toward a New Metaethic', *Philosophical Papers* 29 (2000), 121–53.

_____ 'Moral Phenomenology and Moral Theory', *Philosophical Issues* 15 (2005), 56–77.

_____ 'Morality without Moral Facts', in J. Dreier (ed.), *Contemporary Debates in Moral Theory* (Oxford: Blackwell, 2006a).

_____ 'Cognitivist Expressivism', in T. Horgan and M. Timmons (eds.), *Metaethics after Moore* (Oxford: Oxford University Press, 2006b).

_____ 'Prolegomena to a Future Phenomenology of Morals', *Phenomenology and the Cognitive Sciences* 6, speical issue ed. by Uriah Kriegel (forthcoming, 2007).

_____ 'What can Moral Phenomenology Tell us About Moral Objectivity?', *Social Philosophy and Policy*, issue on: 'Objectivism, Subjectivism, and Relativism in Ethics' (forthcoming, 2008).

Hume, D., *A Treatise of Human Nature* (Oxford: Oxford University Press, 1739).

Kirchin, S., 'Ethical Phenomenology and Moral Realism', *Ethical Theory and Moral Practice*, 6 (2003), 241–64.

Mackie, J. L., *Ethics: Inventing Right and Wrong* (New York: Penguin Books, 1977).

Mandelbaum, M., *The Phenomenology of Moral Experience* (Glencoe, Ill.: The Free Press, 1955).

Moore, G. E., *Principia Ethica* (1903), rev. edn., ed. by Thomas Baldwin (Cambridge: Cambridge University Press, 1993).

_____ *Ethics* (Oxford: Oxford University Press).

Railton, P., 'Normative Guidance', in Russ Shafer-Landau (ed.), *Oxford Studies in Metaethics*, Vol. 1 (Oxford: Oxford University Press, 2006).

Ross, W. D., *The Right and the Good* (Oxford: Oxford University Press, 1930).

Smith, M., 'Objectivity and Moral Realism: On the Significance of the Phenomenology of Moral Experience' (1988), repr. in M. Smith, *Ethics and the A Priori* (Cambridge: Cambridge University Press, 2004).

Stevenson, C. L., 'The Emotive Meaning of Ethical Terms', *Mind* 46 (1937), 14–31.

Timmons, M., *Morality without Foundations* (Oxford: Oxford University Press, 1999).

Willard, D., 'Utilitarianism and Phenomenology', in John J. Drummond and Lester L. Embree (eds.), *Phenomenological Approaches to Moral Theory* (The Netherlands: Kluwer Academic Publishers, 2002).

Williams, B., 'Ethical Consistency', *Proceedings of the Aristotelian Society* (1963), supp. vol., 39, repr. in his *Problems of the Self* (Cambridge: Cambridge University Press, 1973).

_____ 'Consistency and Realism', *Proceedings of the Aristotelian Society* (1965), supp. vol., 40, repr. in his *Problems of the Self* (Cambridge: Cambridge University Press, 1973).

11

Open Questions and the Nature of Philosophical Analysis*

Richard Fumerton

Moore was one of the most influential philosophers in the first half of the twentieth century. With influence comes controversy. His defense of common sense against the challenge of skepticism, for example, earned both strong support and ridicule. In the field of ethics, he is still probably viewed as the paradigmatic objectivist—a philosopher who grounds knowledge of all ethical truths in a foundation of self-evident truths describing the objective and intrinsic value of various sorts of states. But just as his epistemology is arguably best known for a negative thesis—his rejection of skepticism, so also his ethics is arguably best known for a negative thesis—his rejection of all attempts to analyze the property of being intrinsically good. His famous open question argument is still cited by some as the decisive objection to all attempts at defining value in naturalistic terms. The interest of the argument, however, goes far beyond its implications for one's analysis of ethical concepts. The argument forces one to think carefully about fundamental metaphilosophical issues concerning the nature of analysis—indeed the very subject-matter of philosophy.

In this paper I want to revisit the argument. While there is, I believe, no version of the open question argument that could possibly be good, there are, I also believe, important lessons to be learned from a careful evaluation of both the original argument and more recent arguments into which it seems to have morphed. In Section I, I shall revisit familiar ground in an effort to critically reconstruct the open question argument from Moore's text. In Section II, I shall consider and reject

* I'd like to thank my colleague, Diane Jeske, for comments on an earlier draft of this paper.

attempts to identify the flaw in Moore's argument by modeling philosophical analysis in general, and ethical analysis in particular, on the kind of informative identity claims one encounters in science. I shall then return in Section III to the way in which one can respond to the argument presupposing the more traditional framework of philosophical analysis as meaning analysis. Finally, in Section IV I shall make a brief observation about what seems to me to be a resurgence of open question reasoning in connection with both naturalistic analyses of ethical judgments and naturalistic analyses of reasons for acting.

I The Open Question Argument

For all of their emphasis on careful critical evaluation, philosophers have a nasty habit of treating certain famous arguments as having decisively settled controversies even when the arguments in question are neither uncontroversial nor often even clearly stated. Sellars, for example, is widely credited with exposing the myth of the given. But his arguments, such as they are, tell at best only against certain very idiosyncratic and careless statements of the doctrine. It is gospel, according to his followers, that Wittgenstein has decisively refuted the possibility of a private language. But I've never even been able to formulate a version of the private language argument that wouldn't be equally telling against the possibility of a solitary linguist, and it is a brave soul who wants to argue against the possibility of there existing just one individual capable of representing his world. Very few arguments have been as influential as Moore's open question argument, but it is terribly difficult to find even a coherent version of the argument in Moore's text. And the contemporary caricature of the argument, one Moore himself may have accepted, is decidedly problematic.

What people call the open question argument is introduced by Moore to eliminate the possibility that one can define intrinsic value. Given that he thought there were only three alternatives—intrinsic goodness is simple and indefinable; it is complex and definable; or our talk of such goodness is meaningless—Moore was convinced a successful argument against all definitions of intrinsic value would naturally lead his audience to embrace his view. Ironically, perhaps, the non-cognitivists who arrived on the metaethical scene later were often eager to embrace Moore's attack on naturalism. Convinced that he had overlooked the possibility that 'good' was meaningful without being descriptive, they were happy to concede that attempts to identify being good with natural properties are doomed to failure.

But what precisely is the open question argument? Moore is usually taken to have presented *something* like the following. Take any proposed definition of intrinsic goodness, for example, 'is good in itself' means 'is desired as an end by most people' (hereafter, for ease of exposition, abbreviated as 'is good' means 'is desired'). We can then employ a simple *modus tollens* to refute the definition:

(OQ1)

(1) If 'is good' just means 'is desired' then to ask whether what is desired is good is the same as to ask whether what is desired is desired (or whether what is good is good).

(2) But to ask whether what is desired is good is not the same as to ask whether what is desired is desired.

(And here we have a sub proof for premise 2: the former question is significant or open; the latter is trivial or closed. For all x s and y s, if x = y, then whatever is true of x is true of y and vice versa [The first half of Leibniz's Law]. There is something that is true of the one question that isn't true of the other, so the questions are not the same.)

Therefore,

(3) 'Is good' doesn't mean 'is desired'.

Reflecting on the structure of the argument should convince one that if it is successful against this definition of 'good', a similar argument should work against any other proposed definition of 'good'.

As I said, Moore is usually thought to have endorsed something like the above argument. But, as I also indicated, it is painfully difficult to come up with a passage in the text that clearly presents the argument. To be sure, the following passages from *Principia* might suggest it:

(I) The hypothesis that disagreement about the meaning of good is disagreement with regard to the correct analysis of a given whole, may be most plainly seen to be incorrect by consideration of the fact that, whatever definition be offered, it may be always asked with significance of the complex so defined, whether it is itself good. To take, for instance, one of the most plausible, because one of the more complicated, of such proposed definitions, it may easily be thought, at first sight, that to be good may mean to be that which we desire to desire. Thus if we apply this definition to a particular instance and say 'When we think that A is good we are thinking that A is one of the things which we desire to desire', our proposition may seem quite plausible. But if we carry the investigation further and ask ourselves 'Is it good to desire to desire A?' it is apparent, on a little reflection, that this question is itself as intelligible as the original question 'Is A good?' ... But it is also apparent that the meaning of this second question cannot be analyzed into 'Is the desire to desire A one of the things that we desire to desire?': we have not before our minds anything so complicated as the question 'Do we desire to desire to desire to desire A?' (15–16)

(II) And thus it is very easy to conclude that what seems to be a universal ethical principle is in fact an identical proposition; that if, for example, whatever is called 'good' seems to be pleasant, the proposition 'Pleasure is the good' does not assert a connection between two different notions but involves only one, that of pleasure . . . But whoever will attentively consider with himself what is actually before his mind when he asks the question 'Is pleasure (or whatever it may be) after all good?' can easily satisfy himself that he is not merely wondering whether pleasure is pleasant.   (16)

Both passages are, however, problematic. In I, the question that should be trivial when we substitute the proposed definition of 'good' for 'good' actually becomes too *complicated*. It certainly isn't trivial to ask whether we typically desire to desire to desire to desire some A. But then it also isn't trivial to ask whether it is good that something is good. I don't even know what the answer to the second question might be—indeed, it sounds like it might involve a category mistake. In II, we do get what is *supposed* to be a trivial question when we replace 'good' with its proposed definiens, but the question *isn't* trivial. Again, I'm not at all sure that *pleasure* is pleasant. Golf, tennis, interesting conversation, and fine wine are all pleasant. But is pleasure pleasant? From the fact that 'is good' means 'is pleasant' it doesn't follow that either the proposition that pleasure is good or that the proposition pleasure is pleasant is trivial. Still, when Langford (1942) attributes something like OQ1 to Moore, Moore seems to go along with Langford's characterization of the argument. And it might not be that difficult to suppose that Moore simply mangled the argument a bit in II. He might well have meant to suggest that if 'is good' means 'is pleasing', then to ask whether what is pleasing is good should be the same as to ask whether what is pleasing is pleasing, where, again, these questions seem to be quite distinct, in part because the latter is trivial in a way in which the former is not.

Let's suppose that OQ1 above is at least in the neighborhood of Moore's intended argument. How could any analytic philosopher have taken the argument seriously? Analytic philosophers are in the *business* of coming up with interesting and informative philosophical analyses. First-year undergraduates can see that if OQ1 successfully refutes analyses of 'good', a similar argument will be equally effective against all analyses. Moore himself thought that analysis was an important part of philosophy and he surely thought that the analyses he worked hard to provide were significant—even if, to be successful, they would have to be analytically equivalent to trivial tautologies. At the time he wrote *Principia Ethica*, for example, Moore was convinced that one could identify right action with action that maximizes value. He presumably wouldn't be amused by a deontologist who attempted to refute the analysis by pointing out that to ask whether the right thing to do is always that action which maximizes value is surely more significant than to ask whether the right thing to do is always the right thing to do.

To assert that there must be something wrong with the argument is not, however, to identify its flaw. In Fumerton (1990) I suggested that the argument is simply ambiguous as between the following two readings:

(OQ2):

(1a) If 'is good' means 'is desired' then the question 'Is what is desired good?' is the same as the question 'Is what is desired desired?'

(2a) The question 'Is what is desired good?' is not the same as the question 'Is what is desired desired?' (Proof: one is significant; the other, trivial).

Therefore,

(3a) 'Is good' doesn't mean 'is desired'.

(OQ3):

(1b) If 'is good' means 'is desired' then the question 'Is what is desired good?' *has the same meaning as* the question 'Is what is desired desired?'

(2b) These questions don't have the same meaning. (Proof: one is significant; the other, trivial).

Therefore,

(3b) 'Is good' doesn't mean 'is desired by most people'.

OQ2 is a pathetically bad argument. Premise (1a) is uncontroversially false. When we talk about the significance or triviality of a *question*, it is tempting to think that we are discussing a linguistic entity—in one clear sense questions are pieces of language. But even if 'is good' just means 'is desired' one obviously can't substitute the one term for the other in a sentence and still have the same *sentence*. If one needed a more formal statement of the problem, it is that one cannot substitute what appear to be synonymous expressions within quotes.[1] Premise (2a) is true and one can prove it by pointing out that the one question is more significant than the other. But one could just as well prove it by pointing out that the word 'desired' appears twice in the one question but only once in the other!

OQ3 looks as if it might be in better shape. If 'is good' does mean 'is desired' then it is entirely plausible to suppose that the question 'Is what is desired good?' should have the same meaning as the question 'Is what is desired desired?' To be sure, we are substituting synonyms within quotes again, but the substitution is supposed only to preserve the *meaning* of the sentence in which the substitution took place. We are relying on the presupposition that something like a compositional theory of meaning

---

[1] I say what *appear* to be synonymous expressions, for if Quine was right (and I think he was) it is simply false to suppose that the *word* 'good' even appears in the word ' "good" ' or the sentence ' "Is what is desired good?" ' I'll continue to talk, however, as if there were a possibility of replacing a word with its synonym within quotes.

is correct—the meaning of a sentence is a function of the meaning of its linguistic parts and synonymous parts would make the same contribution to that meaning. The principle may not be uncontroversial, but it surely has prima-facie plausibility. The problem with OQ3, however, is the second premise, or, more accurately, the sub-proof for the second premise. Can one establish that two questions don't have the same meaning by pointing out that one is significant while the other is trivial?

The first thing to note in answering this question is that we can no longer appeal to Leibniz's Law. As we saw in our discussion of OQ2, we can settle the issue of whether one question is identical to another by finding a property of the one that is not a property of the other. But numerically distinct linguistic items may still have the same meaning. Still, it might be tempting to suppose that if a competent speaker of English takes one question to be significant and another trivial, the questions must have different meanings. After all, if someone *understands* both questions, that person knows what the questions mean, and reflecting on that meaning should result in treating the respective questions as having the same sort of significance. Now I think this reasoning is flawed even if we restrict ourselves to a very traditional conception of analysis as the search for analytic truths. But before we investigate the matter further, we should note that some who are critical of the open question argument seem to concede that the argument should force us to a different conception of analysis—one that understands analysis as the attempt to discover an informative identity claim. On the most extreme of such views, the suggestion is that we model philosophical analysis on scientific analysis of the underlying structure of so-called natural kinds. Such a conception of analysis might initially strike one as very much in the spirit of Moore's own emphasis on ontology rather than language.

II The Open Question Argument and Philosophical Analyses as Informative Identity Claims

OQ2 and OQ3 both treat the open question argument as fundamentally concerned with whether the expression 'is good' has the same meaning as some other expression, say 'is desired'. But Moore himself makes very clear that he would like to leave the level of language as soon as possible. In stressing that he is not interested in verbal definition, Moore emphasizes that he is concerned 'solely with that object or idea, which I hold, rightly or wrongly, that the word is generally used to stand for' (6). He goes on to say that his purpose is to discover 'the nature of that object or idea'. Like many of his contemporaries, and in a quite different way, like more recent philosophers influenced by direct reference theories, Moore thought that when doing analysis it was important to leave language behind and focus one's attention on concepts or properties. For Moore the two were intimately connected, for one's concept or idea of a property is just the property 'before' or 'in' mind. So it is not initially implausible to suppose that Moore would not appreciate either OQ2 or OQ3 as 'helpful' clarifications of his argument. We were never supposed to be comparing linguistic items. We were instead supposed to be comparing the meanings of such items—propositions and whatever the propositional counterpart to a linguistic question is. So Moore's talk of philosophical definition might be better understood in terms of talk of informative identity claims. Put in terms of concepts and propositions, then, an open question argument might look as follows:

(OQ4)

(1) If the concept of being good is identical with the concept of being desired, then the proposition that what is desired is good would be identical to the proposition that what is desired is desired.

(2) These propositions are not identical—one is significant, the other trivial.

Therefore,

(3) Being good is not identical with being desired.

Again, because concepts, for Moore, are just properties before consciousness, one might restate the argument in terms of properties and facts (the truth makers for propositions):

(OQ5)

(1) If the property of being good is identical with the property of being desired, then the fact that what is desired is desired would be identical with the fact that what is desired is good.

(2) These facts are not identical—one is significant, the other trivial.[2]

Therefore,

(3) Being good is not identical with being desired.

The difficulty with both OQ4 and OQ5 might seem to lie with the presupposition that philosophers can easily 'leave language behind' and contemplate the ideas or content that such language expresses. The presupposition is highly problematic. We can successfully use language to refer to both things and properties, but such successful reference does not ensure knowledge of the nature of that to which we refer. I shall argue in Section III that our meaningful use of an expression does not even ensure

---

[2] It is not entirely clear that one can speak of a fact as significant or trivial. To be sure, we sometimes talk this way. We say of some facts that they are surprising or interesting, but it may well be that on analysis we would be more comfortable understanding that which is surprising or interesting as the corresponding truth that we discover.

that we know what the meaning of that expression is. Both these concessions should be carefully distinguished, however, from another equally correct observation: there are obviously true and informative identity judgments. Some philosophers who take seriously the direct reference theorist's slogan that meaning is reference will argue that there is a *sense* in which genuinely informative identity claims say the same thing as uninformative, trivial identity statements. So, for example, the direct reference theorist will argue that it is true, and *informatively* true, that water is H_20, and this is so even though for it to be true, water must be strictly, and even necessarily, identical with H_20. Heat is molecular motion. The discovery of this truth was a genuine scientific advance even though *in a sense* the truth says no more about the world than does the truth that heat is heat.[3]

Here, however, I believe that it is easy for philosophers eager to reject the open question argument and the significance/triviality test for the success of an analysis to draw radically mistaken conclusions about the nature of analysis. Moore himself would have nothing to do with any attempt to model philosophical analysis on the scientific 'analyses' of heat or water,[4] and while I am in an increasing minority, I'm convinced that about this he was right. Direct reference theorists have always had a terrible time trying to explain how their slogan that the meaning of an expression is its referent can be reconciled with the informative character of identity claims. Before Kripke (1980), Russell, of course, dominated analytic thought about informative identity claims.[5] Where we have informative identity claims, Russell argued, it is always because one or both of the terms flanking the identity sign has the meaning of a definite description. When successful, a definite description picks out some object or property via a uniquely exemplified property of the object or a uniquely exemplified second-level property of the property. There is no mystery as to how we might find informative the claim that the sole thing that is F is also the sole thing that is G.

The direct reference theorist has no alternative but to borrow *something* from the Russellian position if the theory is to have any hope of accommodating the informative character of identity claims.[6] So Kripke and his followers concede, for example, that it is often in virtue of 'reference fixing' definite descriptions that we successfully send our pure referring terms out on their referential mission. The claim is that the reference fixers can do their job without *defining* the referential term. Through the

---

[3] I stress 'in a sense'. The two propositions may be logically equivalent according to direct reference theorists but the direct reference theorists obviously need to do *something* by way of explaining the difference in information conveyed by the statements.

[4] Remember Moore's own quick dismissal of any attempt to understand being yellow in terms of physical properties such as reflecting or absorbing light.

[5] Beginning with his classic discussion of the problem in Russell (1903).

[6] Howard Wettstein (2004) argues that the direct reference theorists concede too much to the Frege/Russell view of reference.

use of a description like 'the cause of sensation S' we target something whose nature we can empirically investigate. Similarly, causal theorists insist that by inheriting an expression from someone else who successfully uses the term to refer, we can piggyback on such reference and use the term ourselves to pick out the same object or property, an object or property whose nature we can investigate.

I have argued elsewhere (1989) that Russellians can always successfully steal whatever plausible insights direct reference theorists bring to their views. So-called reference-fixing definite descriptions should be viewed as synonymous with the terms whose reference they fix, and one can handle the now familiar modal objections with appropriate *de re/de dicto* distinctions and plausible postulation of semantic rules about how modalities are to be understood in sentences containing names and predicate expressions. One can also steal whatever is plausible in a *causal* theory and take the very definite descriptions that the causal theorist gives in attempting to identify the necessary and sufficient conditions for a term's referring as the descriptions that capture the meaning of the term in question—a meaning that might be very difficult to discover (more about this in Section III).

I can't try to convince you of all this here, but painting with a very broad stroke, I want to suggest that there are always two fundamentally different ways of thinking about things or properties. One can think about them *directly*, or one can think about them *indirectly*. When one thinks of a thing or property indirectly, one thinks of that thing or property by thinking about some property that one takes the thing or property to exemplify uniquely. So there is a sense in which I can think indirectly of my aunt's favorite color without knowing what that color is. I am thinking of the color as whatever it is that has the property of being my aunt's favorite. I can think of Jack the Ripper as the guy who killed those prostitutes in London near the turn of the century, and I can do that without in one perfectly clear sense knowing who Jack the Ripper is. Just as foundationalists in epistemology are convinced that one must end a threatening regress of justification, so also it is tempting to suppose that one must end a threatening regress of representation. We can think of some things—perhaps almost everything—through thinking of some other thing. But not all thought can be parasitic in this way on other thought. There must be some things one thinks of, one represents, directly. I am inclined to think that this 'foundationalism' of representation crosses internalist/externalist controversies over content, and direct/indirect theories of reference. Even if reference fixing were an intelligible concept, one must surely concede that one's ability to fix the reference of an expression using a definite description is parasitic upon one's successfully referring to at least the properties picked out by the predicate expressions in the definite description. To be sure, one may pick out those properties in turn through still other reference-fixing definite descriptions, but the regress must end. If our reference is somehow parasitic upon causal chains extending back to successful reference by others, that simply pushes the problem back to whatever generates initial successful reference. We need to figure out how someone earlier in the causal chain achieved successful reference in order to block a threatening regress.

If we accept the distinction between direct and indirect thought, it is tempting to suppose that we find an identity claim informative only when one or more of the thoughts expressed by the terms flanking the identity sign are only indirect. When we grasp *directly* a property F, and a property G, for example, it is difficult to see how one could fail to grasp either that F and G are one or that F and G are two.[7] At least this is so if grasping is to be understood the way philosophers like Moore and Russell understood it. If one could give a fully naturalistic account of both direct and indirect representation (as, for example, Dretske tries to do[8]), it may still be possible for one to represent directly a property F and a property G without realizing that the object of one's thought is one property, not two. That feature of externalist and naturalistic accounts of the referent of thought, however, might be taken to be a *reductio* of the view if one presupposes that one has unproblematic introspective access to the content of one's thoughts.[9]

Moore would have nothing to do with attempts to model an informative philosophical identity claim about the property of being good on informative scientific claims about the nature of water or heat. He was convinced that one's grasp of both goodness and most of the natural properties with which philosophers have tried to identify it was direct, direct in a way that made it possible simply to hold both properties directly before the mind. And, indeed, it is more than a bit puzzling to find some contemporary moral realists attempting to defend naturalistic accounts of goodness by trying to treat goodness as a property of which we have initially only an indirect grasp—an indirect grasp which, through empirical investigation, can evolve into an understanding of its true underlying nature. We grasp goodness, we might be told, as that which satisfies deep human needs, or as that which causes people to flourish (other things being equal).[10] I take it that the idea must be that we have a

---

[7] This is, of course, the basis behind Kripke's rejection of physicalism. He thought that we had a kind of direct or immediate access to a property like pain, an access that precludes discovering empirically that pain is something like a brain state. He forgot, however, that one's access to brain states might be indirect, and all that one needs is one 'indirect thought' to allow for the possibility of empirically informative identity claims.

[8] His project of naturalizing representation is ongoing, but Dretske (1995) gives one as good a feel for the project as any of his other works.

[9] See Fumerton (2003) for one version of such an argument.

[10] Although I have in mind the so-called 'Cornell realists', I would concede that this is a gross oversimplification of the views of philosophers like Brink (1989), Sturgeon (1988), and Boyd (1988). But the truth is, when I try to understand their views, I have a very difficult time figuring out what is supposed to be analogous to, for example, 'the cause of sensation S' in the case of our indirect access to heat, or 'the underlying structure of that which presents a certain clear, odorless appearance' in the

relatively more direct grasp of needs or flourishing but have only (at least initially) an indirect grasp of goodness. But we know full well why we're interested in all this 'need'/'flourishing' talk when it comes to goodness. We think that the satisfaction of human needs is *good*. The idea of something's flourishing is not even a very well disguised way of talking about something's developing in a *good* way. When thrashing about for reference-fixing descriptions, we know that our naturalist, inspired by direct reference theories, is guided not only by a prior understanding of goodness but also by a particular view about what things have that property.

Again, let me stress that I am not denying the obvious truth that there are informative identity statements made about both things and properties. Both things and properties have indefinitely many properties, and we may latch on to a thing or a property by forming the thought of the thing or property that uniquely has certain properties. Having formed such a thought, we can be interested in investigating further the nature of that thing or property singled out. But notice that in the paradigm of scientific investigation that is supposed to serve as our model, we are not primarily worried about a language/world connection. There is this stuff—we call it 'water'. But, whatever it is called, we can wonder about its microstructure. We can wonder what 'hidden' properties the stuff that presents a certain appearance has. To employ this model in trying to understand our search for the analysis of a property like good, it would have to be plausible to suppose that we get the property of goodness before us through some property it uniquely exemplifies and then conduct an empirical search for its hidden nature. The properties that are candidates for serving as the contents of our ethical judgments are not properties that are 'hidden' in this way. To be sure, *that they are the properties that are the referents of our moral predicate expressions* is not something to which we have unproblematic access. I shall try to explain this in more detail shortly. But there is no reason to suppose that the *property* of goodness has a nature that is somehow hidden from us until we complete a successful empirical inquiry.

Moore isn't going to be, and shouldn't be, impressed by those philosophers who think that he failed to recognize the nature of non-trivial identity claims. Moore thought that we have a direct grasp of goodness that would make almost comical the idea that *empirical* investigation might reveal its true nature. But precisely because Moore thought that one could have a direct grasp of both goodness and various candidates for its *definiens*, one might suppose that the open question argument should have been recast simply as a phenomenological argument. And some of Moore's comments suggest that he *does* have something like a phenomenological appeal in mind. Consider, for example, the following:

case of water. In a later work, Brink (2001) says at least some things that suggest he might be more amenable to a naturalism understood as the kind of conceptual analysis I discuss later in this paper.

Everyone does in fact understand the question 'Is this good?' When he thinks of it, his state of mind is different from what it would be, were he asked 'Is this pleasant, or desired, or approved?'

He goes on to assert that 'Everybody is constantly aware of this notion [goodness], although he may never become aware at all that it is different from other notions of which he is also aware' (16–17).

Moore seems to think that one's meaningful use of, and one's understanding of, a term like 'is good' is accompanied by a unique state of mind, one that is different from the state of mind one is in when one uses or understands an expression like 'is desired'. The relevant states of mind constitute the meanings of the expressions. While he says that one may not grasp that the two states of mind—the two thoughts—are different, the implication is that one need only introspect carefully to discover the difference and to end once and for all speculation that the meaning of 'is good' (the thought it expresses) is the same as the meaning of (the thought expressed by) 'is desired'. One can simply find phenomenologically that the thoughts are different. By contrast, one assumes that Moore believed that if one compares the thought expressed by 'is right' with the thought expressed by 'maximizes value', one will discover relatively easily that there is but one thought expressed both by 'Right action is action that maximizes value' and 'Right action is right action'. With this as background let's return to OQ3 and an evaluation of the triviality/significance test for sameness of meaning.

III The Open Question Argument and More Traditional Conceptions of Analysis

As I indicated, I don't think Moore would have anything to do with treating informative philosophical analysis as something we should model on informative scientific discoveries, such as that water is H_2O or that heat is molecular motion. Moore clearly drew an analytic/synthetic distinction, and equally clearly wanted the statement of a correct philosophical analysis to be the expression of an analytic truth. In short, I do think that the only argument that would have worked for Moore is something like OQ3.

In our preceding discussion we looked at least superficially at what seems to be a presupposition of Moore's theory of meaning. Like almost all of his predecessors and contemporaries, Moore thought language has meaning, has the capacity to represent, only in so far as it goes proxy for thought that has content. Indeed, if you understand an expression like 'is good', you have before your mind the property of being good. If you understand an expression like 'is desired', then you have before your mind the property of being desired. When you grasp these properties directly (not through some metaproperty they are taken to exemplify uniquely) it should be relatively simple to compare them and discover that they are distinct. It is no wonder that Moore thought that if the question 'Is what is desired good?' is significant, then it expresses a different thought from the trivial question 'Is what is desired desired?' If you were to understand the respective questions the same way, you should be in precisely the same state of mind. Since the one question leaves you more perplexed than the other, the states of mind expressed must be different.

We still know that if philosophical analysis can result in interesting and informative analytic truths, there must be something wrong with the above reasoning. Moore, himself, should have realized that there is something strange about the argument. It is far too powerful. We are fairly certain that the flaw lies in the sub-proof for (2b), but what precisely has gone wrong? The direct reference theorist had an answer—meaning is reference and the referents of our expressions, including our predicate expressions, can be epistemically hidden from us. But we needn't embrace a direct reference theory or the slogan that meaning is reference in order to diagnose correctly the flaw in the argument. It seems to me that the fundamental problem lies in the assumption that when we use meaningfully, or when we understand, an expression, there is some occurrent state of mind we are in, a state of mind that constitutes the meaning of the expression. If anything like that assumption were true, philosophical analysis wouldn't be as difficult as it is. It simply isn't nearly as easy as Moore implies to leave language behind and focus our attention on the thought that gives that language life. Consider any philosophically interesting concept. Get before your mind, for example, the properties of causing, knowing, having epistemic justification, being morally right. What happens when you try to comply with the instruction? Either not much of anything, or a congeries of very particular images. If we try to get before our minds causation, for example, we might, as Hume did, think of a billiard ball striking another billiard ball. Or we might imagine various claims we make about one thing's causing another. But neither of these would be to get before our minds the abstracted property of causing. The thought of one billiard ball's striking another contains indefinitely many details, most of which are quite irrelevant to the causal relation. The problem is not that the relational property of causing is hidden. It is presumably there somewhere in the incredibly complex array of non-relational and relational properties exemplified by the billiard balls that came into contact. The problem is in isolating the property or properties that the word 'causes' picks out.

For properties of the sort that most interest philosophers, it is not even clear that we can easily identify correct paradigms of entities that exemplify the property. It is notoriously difficult to get two philosophers to agree on examples of what is intrinsically good or bad, for example. Some will insist that it is all and only pleasures that constitute the intrinsically good. Others insist that there are states besides pleasures that are intrinsically good. And still others deny that all pleasures are intrinsically good. So what *is* our goal when we try to figure out what we mean by a term like 'good?' The short answer is that we are trying to uncover the semantic rules we follow when using the term, where one follows a semantic rule governing an expression in virtue of having complex linguistic dispositions to regard the expression as the correct way to describe hypothetical situations.[11]

Uncovering the semantic rules one follows, and uncovering the relevant linguistic dispositions that constitute following those rules, is no easy task. It requires employment of the classic thought experiments that have been the stock-in-trade of philosophers for well over two and a half thousand years. By reflecting on various hypothetical situations, you might become convinced that you use 'know', for example, to describe all and only those situations in which you are relatively certain of a true proposition, where that certainty is based on very strong evidence. A Gettier can come along, however, and convince you in short order that this is not the semantic rule you follow when using the expression 'know'. You find that you don't have the linguistic disposition you thought you had. Uncovering semantic rules is at least as difficult as coming to know the syntactic rules one follows in speaking a language. At a very early age, children follow very complex syntactic rules in speaking English. But they couldn't begin to tell you what those rules are. The sad truth is that most college graduates today can't tell you the syntactic rules of English, even though many are pretty good at following those rules.

So we don't need to model philosophy on science to understand how successful philosophical analyses can be interesting and informative. Moore's mistake was in thinking that philosophical analysis is something we can engage in after leaving language behind. Conceptual analysis really is *essentially* about a word/world fit. Scientific analysis, by contrast, *can* leave meaning behind and concentrate on an empirical investigation into the nature of reality. To understand how investigation into meaning can be informative, to understand how we can learn about the meaning-rules that tie words to the world, we need nothing more complicated than the distinction between *following* a rule and *knowing* what rule it is that one follows. If 'is good' did mean 'is desired' (it doesn't, of course), then it would be analytic that what

---

[11] For a more detailed attempt to develop this conception of philosophical analysis, see Fumerton (1983). As I indicated in an earlier note, while Brink (1989) seems to be attracted to the 'scientific model' of philosophical analyses of value terms, Brink (2001) seems to suggest a position that is much closer to the one I am defending here. In trying to identify the natural properties that regulate our use of moral terms, he suggests that moral terms 'refer to properties that regulate not just actual usage, but also counterfactual or hypothetical usage—in particular, the way speakers would apply terms upon due reflection in imagined situations and thought experiments' (168). While I agree with this, I would argue that it is through evaluating the truth of such counter-factuals that one uncovers the *semantic* rules we follow, rules the existence of which ground correct *meaning* analysis.

is desired is good, and the meaning of the sentence 'What is desired is good' would be the same as the meaning of the sentence 'What is desired is desired'. One might not *realize* that the sentences have the same meaning, however. The sentence 'What is desired is desired' has an interesting feature that the sentence 'What is desired is good' lacks. One can discover the truth of the first sentence simply by reflecting on its *form*. As long as one understands predication, and certain rules concerning the fact that a term's placement in a sentence doesn't generally affect its meaning, one knows that if the statement means anything at all, it is true. What is desired is desired; quarks are quarks; electromagnetic fields are electromagnetic fields. I know that all these *sentences* express truths even though I really don't have the faintest idea what a quark or an electromagnetic field is. I needn't worry about the meaning of such terms to assure myself that if the sentences are meaningful they are true. I do have to think about the meaning of the terms contained in the sentence 'What is desired is good' in order to assess its truth. And I have to think long and hard about the meanings of the terms contained in that statement to discover the *modal* status of the truth expressed. These considerations should be sufficient to dispose of significance/triviality tests for sameness of meaning.

IV   A New Form of the Open Question Argument?

One might suppose that criticizing Moore's open question argument is at best an interesting exercise in the history of philosophy. As I tried to make clear, I believe that the exercise has important implications for the way in which one thinks of philosophical analysis. While it should always have been obvious that there is something wrong with the open question argument, it is important to diagnose its flaws correctly. In particular, it is important to realize that one needn't abandon traditional conceptions of philosophy as armchair conceptual analysis in order to deal with the argument.

I said that it should have been obvious from the moment the open question argument was first presented that there was something wrong with it. But I'm not sure the argument ever did receive the unqualified rejection that it deserved. I still hear people dismiss various naturalistic analyses of both 'good' and 'right' by appealing to what Moore 'established' using the open question argument. Furthermore, there is another increasingly common complaint against certain forms of naturalism in value theory that bears a striking resemblance to the open question argument. One might call it the argument from 'normativity'. Korsgaard and her followers, for example, often seem to reject naturalistic analyses of what one ought to do, or what one has reason to do, on the grounds that such analyses fail to capture the *normativity* of such judgments.[12] The Humean argues, for example, that one has a reason to do X in virtue of the fact that one realizes that X will or might lead to some Y that one desires as an end. Such a Humean might go on to identify *what one ought to do, all things considered* with *what maximizes satisfaction of desire* (or more plausibly what maximizes expected utility). The critic then protests that it is surely an *open question* whether one ought to be moved by the desires one finds oneself with—i.e., whether reason requires that desires move one in that way. One can surely ask oneself whether reason might dictate, or at least allow, that one not have certain goals or ends, and if one reaches such a conclusion one should surely reject the view that contingent facts about what one happens to desire can *define* what one ought to do. It certainly seems that one can entertain questions about not only how to act but with what ends one ought to act. When the smoke clears, however, I worry that this sort of argument is just Moore's old open question argument disguised with talk of normativity.

What does it mean to say of a judgment that it has normative force? What makes a claim normative? In the final analysis, I am not sure that talk of normativity is anything other than talk about what one ought to do or what one has reason to do. It is surely *controversial* to claim that one has reason to do X solely in virtue of the fact that X will bring about some state of affairs that one desires intrinsically. *Any* analysis of what one has reason to do will be controversial. It is controversial to claim that reason requires one to pursue that which is objectively and intrinsically good (if there is such a thing). It is controversial to claim that reason requires one to respect the goals of others. Philosophers have been arguing about such matters for thousands of years, and they don't seem to be in any danger of reaching a consensus soon. But the Humean, for example, should surely be unmoved by the critic who simply points out that it is an open (significant) question as to whether one ought to pursue one's subjective goals or ends. We need to remember the lesson we learned from the flaw in Moore's original open question argument. One simply can't take seriously the controversial character of a claim about what constitutes necessary and sufficient conditions for moral/rational action as a reason for rejecting the proposed analysis.

Works Cited

Boyd, Richard, 'How to be a Moral Realist', in Geoffrey Sayre-McCord (ed.), *Essays on Moral Realism*. Ed. Geoffrey (Ithaca: Cornell University Press, 1988), 181–228.

Brink, David, *Moral Realism and the Foundation of Ethics* (Cambridge: Cambridge University Press, 1989).

[12] I have in mind Korsgaard (1996) and (2002). The interpretation of Korsgaard's views is a difficult matter, and I am not suggesting that she herself would endorse anything as crude as this characterization of her rejection of various descriptivist and naturalistic analyses of reasons for acting.

_____ 'Realism, Naturalism and Moral Semantics', *Social Philosophy and Policy* 18 (Summer 2001), 154–76.

Dretske, Fred, *Naturalizing the Mind* (Cambridge, Mass.: MIT Press, 1995).

Fumerton, Richard, 'The Paradox of Analysis', *Philosophy and Phenomenological Research*, 32 (1983), 477–97.

_____ 'Russelling Causal Theories of Reference', in Wade Savage and C. A. Anderson (eds.), *Rereading Russell* (Minneapolis: University of Minnesota Press, 1989), 108–18.

_____ *Reason and Morality* (Ithaca, NY: Cornell University Press, 1990).

_____ 'Introspection and Internalism', in Susana Nuccetelli (ed.), *New Essays on Semantic Externalism, and Self-Knowledge* (Cambridge, Mass.: MIT Press, 2003).

Korsgaard, Christine, *The Sources of Normativity* (Cambridge: Cambridge University Press, 1996).

_____ *Locke Lectures* (2002), Korsgaard's web site.

Kripke, Saul, *Naming and Necessity* (Cambridge: Cambridge University Press, 1980).

Langford, C. H., 'Moore's Notion of Analysis', in P. A. Schilpp (ed.), *The Philosophy of G. E. Moore* (LaSalle, Ill: Open Court, 1942), 319–42.

Moore, G. E., *Principia Ethica* (Cambridge: Cambridge University Press, 1903).

Russell, Bertrand, 'On Denoting', *Mind*, 14 (1903), 479–93.

Sturgeon, Nicholas, 'Moral Explanations', in *Essays on Moral Realism*.

Wettstein, Howard, *The Magic Prism* (Oxford: Oxford University Press, 2004).

12

Desiring to Desire: Russell, Lewis, and G. E Moore[1]

Charles R. Pigden

I Moore's Warning

'I am the person Moore warned you against,' joked David Lewis[2] before reading his now famous paper, 'Dispositional Theories of Value', to the Aristotelian Society in 1989.[3] The alleged warning occurs in §13 of *Principia Ethica*,[4] the crucial passage in which Moore expounds the Open Question Argument. 'To take, for instance one of the more plausible, because one of the more complicated of such [naturalistic] definitions,

---

[1] This paper is dedicated to the memory of David Lewis.

[2] So I was told by an ear-witness, though Lewis himself had no recollection of the remark. However, he certainly subscribed to the sentiment. 'The position defended is similar to the one that G. E. Moore chose as the target for his "naturalistic fallacy" argument.' See David Lewis, *Papers in Ethics and Social Philosophy* (Cambridge: Cambridge University Press, 2000), 2.

[3] David Lewis, 'Dispositional Theories of Value', *Proceedings of the Aristotelian Society Supplementary Volume*, 63 (1989), 113–37; repr. in David Lewis, *Papers in Ethics and Social Philosophy* (Cambridge: Cambridge University Press, 2000), 68–94. Henceforward, DTV II with page references both to the original and to the reprint.

[4] G. E. Moore, *Principia Ethica*, rev. edn., ed. Thomas Baldwin (Cambridge: Cambridge University Press, 1993). Henceforward, *PE*. On the whole, I give section rather than page references to accommodate those with earlier editions.

it may easily be thought, at first sight, that to be good may mean to be that which we desire to desire' (*PE*, §13). But plausible as it may be, Moore goes on to contend that this definition is false, since it is possible to wonder whether what we desire to desire is good. If 'good' *meant* 'what we desire to desire', the question 'Is what we desire to desire good?' would be a silly question since the answer would be very obvious—'Yes'. Since the question is open and the answer is *not* obvious to every competent speaker, the definition cannot be correct.

Now Moore's 'warning' certainly *applies* to Lewis, since he develops an analysis of value as what we are ideally disposed to desire to desire (an analysis which would fall foul of the Open Question Argument if that argument were sound). But Moore can hardly have had Lewis in mind when he penned this notorious passage in the early 1900s. Since he gives no citations, it is tempting to suppose that Moore plucked his opponent out of thin air. But, in fact, the person Moore warned us against was neither David Lewis nor Mr Nobody but Bertrand Russell. For the definition of 'good' selected for dissection is precisely the definition suggested by Russell in 'Is Ethics a Branch of Empirical Psychology', a paper read to the Apostles in 1897.[5] (*RoE*, 71−8/*Papers* 1, 100−4.) 'The criterion [of morality] must be supplied, therefore, by the contrast between ideal and actual desires, by the contrast between the desires we desire and desires we dislike.' Moore does not just criticize Russell's definition in 'Is Ethics a Branch of Empirical Psychology?'—he criticizes the chief thesis of Russell's paper, namely that ethics is indeed a branch of empirical psychology. This thesis follows fairly obviously from the definition, since if 'good' means what we desire to desire, to find out what is good we need to ascertain what we desire to desire, which is a matter of psychological fact. And since [normative] ethics largely consists in the enquiry into what is good, ethics becomes a 'matter for purely psychological investigation' (*RoE*, 78/*Papers* 1, 104). The conclusion follows whether goodness consists in what *we* (the community, reasonable people, or whatever) desire to desire (which is roughly Lewis's line), or whether goodness *for each individual* consists in what *that person* desires to desire (which is what Russell seems to suggest). Moore is very severe with this sort of thing. Naturalism, he says, consists in fixing on some natural property and then supposing that 'to be "good" *means* to possess the property in question . . . thus replacing Ethics by some one of the natural sciences'. 'In general', explains Moore, 'Psychology has been the science substituted, as by J. S. Mill' (*PE*, §26). Moore does not add 'and by Mill's secular godson, Bertrand Russell', presumably because the substituting was done in a confidential paper read to a secret society (the Apostles). Moore was very scrupulous about keeping the Society secret, so much so that he was worried about discussing its doings by postcard (see

---

[5] Most of the works of Russell referred to in this paper are collected in Charles R. Pigden (ed.), *Russell on Ethics* (London: Routledge, 1999), henceforward *RoE*. References are to *RoE* and to the relevant volumes of *The Collected Papers of Bertrand Russell* (abbreviated, for example, as *Papers* 1).

Griffin (2002, 186)). But the consequence was that until very recently, nobody realized that at least *one* of Moore's targets in *Principia Ethica* was Bertrand Russell.

I have two aims in this paper. In §§II–IV, I contend that Moore has *two* arguments (not one) for the view that that 'good' denotes a non-natural property not to be identified with the naturalistic properties of science and common sense (or, for that matter, the more exotic properties posited by metaphysicians and theologians). The *first* argument, the Barren Tautology Argument (or the BTA), is derived, via Sidgwick, from a long tradition of anti-naturalist polemic. But the *second* argument, the Open Question Argument proper (or the OQA), seems to have been Moore's own invention and was probably devised to deal with naturalistic theories, such as Russell's, which are immune to the Barren Tautology Argument. The OQA is valid and not (as Frankena (1939) has alleged) question-begging. Moreover, if its premises were true, it would have disposed of the desire-to-desire theory. But, as I explain in §V, from 1970 onwards, two key premises of the OQA were successively called into question: the one because philosophers came to believe in synthetic identities between properties; and the other because it led to the Paradox of Analysis. By 1989 a philosopher like Lewis could put forward precisely the kind of theory that Moore professed to have refuted with a clean intellectual conscience. However, in §§VI–VIII I shall argue that all is not lost for the OQA. I first press an objection to the desire-to-desire theory derived from Kripke's famous epistemic argument. On reflection, this argument looks uncannily like the OQA. But the premise on which it relies is weaker than the one that betrayed Moore by leading to the Paradox of Analysis. This suggests three conclusions: (1) that the desire-to-desire theory is false; (2) that the OQA can be revived, albeit in a modified form; and (3) that the revived OQA poses a serious threat to what might be called *semantic naturalism*.

II Moore's Two Arguments

Though Moore managed to convert Russell to non-naturalism (*RoE*, 73, 75–104), there is reason to suspect that the desire-to-desire theory continued to be a worry. It is not always noticed that Moore has not one but *two* distinct arguments against naturalism, the Open Question Argument and the Barren Tautology Argument.[6] The first contends that 'good' cannot be synonymous with any naturalistic predicate 'X' since 'Are X things good?' is a significant or open question for every 'X'. The second

---

[6] It seems to me that the discussion of Moore in Darwall, Gibbard, and Railton's justly famous 'Towards *Fin de Siecle* Ethics: Some Trends', *The Philosophical Review*, 101 (1992), 115–89, is vitiated by a failure to distinguish clearly between the Open Question Argument and the Barren Tautology Argument.

contends that 'good' cannot be synonymous with any naturalistic 'X', if 'X things are good' is supposed to be a reason for action rather than a 'barren tautology'. The first is set forth at *PE*, §13, whilst the second crops up at *PE*, §11, though variants of it recur throughout the first four chapters (*PE*, §§14, 24, 26). Russell (who was rather more succinct than Moore) summarizes it thus:

Chapter II, on *Naturalistic Ethics*, discusses theories which hold that the only good things are certain natural objects, in so far as these theories are advocated as derivable from the very meaning of *good*. It is shown that such theories always confuse good, in its correct and indefinable sense, with the sense which they assign to it by definition. For example, Evolutionist Ethics are apt to argue that *good* means *more evolved*, and on this to base practical recommendations. Yet, if their contention were correct, no practical consequences could follow. We ask: Why should I prefer this to that? And they reply: Because the more evolved is the better. But if they were right in the reason they give for thinking so, they have only said that the more evolved is the more evolved; and this barren tautology can be no basis for action. The meaning of two phrases cannot be the same, if it makes any difference whether we use one of them or the other; and, applying this test, it is easy to see that *more evolved* does not mean the same as *better*.   (*RoE*, 100/*Papers* 4, 572.)

More formally, we can restate the argument as follows:

(1#) For any naturalistic or metaphysical 'X', if 'good' meant 'X', then (i) 'X things are good', would be a barren tautology equivalent to (ii) 'X things are X', or (iii) 'Good things are good'.

(2#) For any naturalistic or metaphysical 'X', if (i) 'X things are good', were a barren tautology, it would not provide a reason for action (i.e., a reason to pursue or promote X-ness).

(3#) So for any naturalistic or metaphysical 'X', *either* (i) 'X things are good', does *not* provide a reason for action (i.e. a reason to promote X-ness), *or* 'good' does not mean 'X'.

To put the point another way:

(3#′) For any naturalistic or metaphysical 'X', *if* (i) 'X things are good', provides a reason for action (that is, a reason to promote X-ness), *then* 'good' does not mean 'X'.

In other words, if you want the basic principles of your naturalistic ethic to be true by definition, they can't at the same time be action-guiding. (Note: this argument does not entail or presuppose that factual considerations cannot provide reasons for action.)

This is, I think, the *real* argument for the naturalistic fallacy, since it suggests that *most* naturalists actually commit an intellectual mistake that can reasonably be described as a fallacy—they propound as a reason for action some such principle as 'X things are good', or even 'Only X things are good', and then try to defend it by claiming that it is some sort of analyticity, 'the very meaning of the word', etc. (See Prior, 1949, chs. 1 and 9; and *PE*, 11, 24.) But this is to subvert the action-guiding power of their original pronouncement. It cannot *both* be that 'X things are good', is analytic (and thus secure from all shocks) *and* that it provides a reason for promoting X-ness. To suppose that it can, or to propound such an inconsistent view, is to make a mistake in reasoning that might reasonably be dubbed 'the naturalistic fallacy'.

But, on this reading, not all forms of naturalism are fallacious. In some cases the suggested 'X' is not supposed to denote a property that its proponent wants to see promoted. Rather the 'X' constitutes an *analysis* of 'good' which is designed to explain why thinking something good provides (or might provide) some sort of motive to promote it. The analysis is supposed to forge a conceptual connection between moral belief and action. Moore's Russell-derived example of 'what we desire to desire' provides a case in point. When Russell and (later) Lewis claim that goodness (or value) is what we desire to desire, this is not because they have a special yen for what we desire to desire and think that by calling it 'good' they can get people to maximize it. Rather, they think that if we construe 'good' as what we desire to desire, we can see why people have a rational motive to promote what they believe to be the good. If we desire what we desire to desire (which we don't always do), then we will have a desire (and, hence, a rational motive) to promote what we believe to be good. The aim of the proposed analysis is not action but understanding, specifically an understanding of the 'conceptual connection between value and motivation' (DTV II, 113/69). Thus Russell and Lewis would be willing to concede that 'What we desire to desire is good', *is* a barren tautology, in the sense that it is unlikely to beget anything very spectacular in the way of action. But though it is an analytic truth and hence, if you like, a tautology, it is fruitful rather than barren when it comes to understanding the action-guiding power of 'good'.

Remember that the conclusion of the Barren Tautology Argument is a (quantified) conditional:

> (3#′) For any naturalistic or metaphysical 'X', *if* (i) 'X things are good', provides a reason for action (i.e. a reason to promote X-ness), *then* 'good' does not mean 'X'.

And it is quite consistent with (3#′) that 'good' means 'X' for some naturalistic or metaphysical 'X' *so long as* (i) 'X things are good' (or 'Good things are X') does *not* provide a reason for action (in the sense of a reason to promote X-ness).

But this means that the Barren Tautology Argument is a much less powerful engine against naturalism than is commonly supposed. It is not just the Russell/Lewis theory that escapes the net. The Hutcheson/Hume theory (that value consists in a disposition to excite the approbation of a suitably qualified spectator),[7] the Michael Smith theory (that rightness is what we would desire ourselves to do if we were fully rational),[8] even the Hobbes/Locke/Paley theory (that rightness consists in obedience to some Authority—God, the Sovereign, or even the Beau Monde)[9]—*all* of them are immune to the Barren Tautology Argument. This is most surprising in the case of Hobbes/Locke/Paley, but all three could concede that 'Obeying the Authority is right', is a barren and unmotivating tautology, since each supplies *another* motive for obeying the Authority—the fear of punishment or, in the case of the Beau Monde, the fear of ridicule and ostracism. At all events, we are a long way from a simple and unanalyzable property of goodness, which is what Moore wants to establish.

III Why the Open Question Argument?

Now, I am not sure how clearly Moore distinguished between his various arguments or if he was fully aware of how far they succeed. But the above analysis suggests an interesting speculation. We know that the BTA was developed *before* the OQA, since *PE*, §11 (which contains the Barren Tautology Argument) dates back to Moore's 1898 draft 'The Elements of Ethics', whereas *PE*, §13 (which contains the Open Question Argument) was written rather later. (See *PE*, revised edn., 312–13.) There are, indeed, hints of the OQA in the *Elements of Ethics*, but so far as I can see they are only hints. In fact, the BTA is cribbed (with due acknowledgment) from Sidgwick's *The Methods of Ethics*. Now, it may be that Moore realized that the BTA does not do everything that he wanted. It points to a fallacy committed by many naturalists and it shows that you cannot found an action-guiding ethic upon a mere definition. But it does not exclude *all* forms of naturalism. In particular, it does not exclude the definition suggested by Russell, that 'good' means what we desire to desire. For this definition is not *intended* to provide a reason for action but to explain why goodness is a property which furnishes us with such reasons. *If* he realized this (and it is a pretty big 'if'), Moore *may* have been driven to invent the OQA in order to deal with naturalistic definitions such as this. For the OQA (if sound) would dispose of *all* brands of naturalism including the kind of theory propounded by Russell and Lewis. If this is correct, Russell's intervention may have forced Moore to move from the BTA to the OQA, which, despite one or two vague anticipations, seems to have been his own invention. (The final chapter of Prior (1949), 'The Naturalistic Fallacy—the History of its Refutation', which deals at some

---

[7] See the extracts from Hutcheson and Hume in D. D. Raphael (ed.), *The British Moralists 1650–1800*, 2 vols. (Oxford: Oxford University Press, 1967).

[8] See Michael Smith, *The Moral Problem* (Oxford: Blackwell, 1991).

[9] Again, see Raphael (1967) for relevant extracts.

length with the anticipations of Moore, is exclusively concerned with the BTA.) Indeed, Russell's intervention might explain the long delay in the publication of *Principia Ethica*, which did not come out until 1903, even though Moore had a pretty good first draft by 1898. Perhaps it took Moore a long time to come up with an adequate response. The flaw with this proposal is that Russell propounded his definition in 1897, *before* Moore wrote *The Elements of Ethics*. But it might have taken Moore a while to realize that the BTA could not deal with this particular threat.

IV The Open Question Argument Stated

It may be useful at this point to state the OQA a little more precisely. The OQA (*PE*, §13) rests on three premises.

> (1) 'Are X things good?' is a significant or open question for any naturalistic or metaphysical predicate 'X' (whether simple or complex).

'Every one does in fact understand the question'; it is 'intelligible', it can be 'asked with significance' and 'we can understand very well what is meant by doubting' the answer (*PE*, §13). Such questions would *not* be 'significant' (in Moore's sense) if an understanding of the words involved were enough for an affirmative answer. This is the case with 'Are X things X?', 'Are good things good?', and 'Are bachelors unmarried?', where the questions posed are, in effect, interrogative tautologies. But since 'Are X things good?' *is* 'significant' for any 'X' (indeed 'significant' for 'every one' by which Moore would appear to mean all competent speakers), it follows that an understanding of the words involved (which is shared by all competent speakers) does not suffice for an affirmative answer.

> (2) If two expressions (whether simple or complex) are synonymous, this is evident on reflection to every competent speaker.
>
> (3) The meaning of a predicate or property word is the property for which it stands. Thus if two predicates or property words have distinct meanings, they denote distinct properties.

From (1) and (2) it follows that

> (4) 'Good' is not synonymous with any naturalistic or metaphysical predicate 'X' (or 'goodness' with any corresponding noun or noun-phrase 'X-ness').

If 'good' *were* synonymous with any predicate 'X', then this would be evident on reflection to every competent speaker, and the question 'Are X things good?' would not be open or significant for that particular 'X'. Thus, the fact that 'Are X things good?' is significant or open for every 'X' shows that 'good' is not synonymous with any such predicate. But sub-conclusion (4) does not give Moore everything he wants. It states that the word 'good' is not synonymous with any natural predicate, not that goodness itself is not identical with any natural or non-moral property. It is tantamount to what I call the semantic autonomy of ethics, the thesis that moral words are not susceptible to a naturalistic definition (see Pigden (1991)). It is therefore incompatible with semantic naturalism, which is precisely the thesis that the moral can be reduced to the non-moral by means of definitions, i.e., by establishing that 'good' (or whatever) means the same as some (presumably complex) naturalistic predicate. Moore, however, professes a lofty disdain for mere semantics. 'Verbal questions are properly left to the writers of dictionaries and other persons interested in literature; philosophy, as we shall see, has no concern with them' (PE, §2). He has bigger fish to fry. He wants to establish what I call the ontological autonomy of ethics, the thesis that for moral judgments to be true there must be a realm of distinctively moral facts and properties, of which goodness is the chief. Nevertheless, sub-conclusion (4) is not without importance, since if it is true, the Russell/Lewis theory is false. For Russell and his unwitting disciple David Lewis are both semantic naturalists. Lewis is quite explicit about this. His theory, he says is 'naturalistic [i.e., semantically naturalistic] since it advances an analytic definition of value' (DTV II, 113/68). But so, too, is Russell's. 'Unless, therefore, the good can be defined otherwise than in terms of desire, ethics, properly studied, must always remain . . . purely a branch of empirical psychology' (RoE, 75/Papers I, 102). In Russell's view the good can't be defined otherwise than in terms of desire, which means that ethics is indeed a branch of empirical psychology. But the point is that it is a definition, a purported analysis of the concept 'good', that is supposed to do the trick. But, important as it is for Moore to refute the likes of Bertrand Russell, he wants to go one better. He wants to go beyond the word 'good' to the property for which it stands. How does he get from semantic autonomy (a predicate, 'good', that cannot be defined in terms of the non-moral) to ontological autonomy (a non-natural property of goodness that cannot be identified with anything non-moral)? By appealing to premise (3), the thesis that the meaning of a predicate is the property that it denotes and thus that if two predicates have distinct meanings they stand for distinct properties. Moore certainly believed in properties at the time he wrote Principia, and then, and thereafter, he seems to have subscribed to a 'one-level' theory of meaning according to which the meaning of a word is the thing it denotes (see Baldwin (1990, 39–50, 203) and Hylton (1990, 140–1)). Premise (3) provides the bridge between semantics and ontology.

From (3) and (4) it follows that

(5) Goodness is not identical with any natural or metaphysical property of X-ness.

Since 'good' has a distinct meaning from every naturalistic or metaphysical predicate 'X', it denotes a distinct and non-natural property. And this is precisely what Moore set out to prove.

V The OQA Discredited

Premises (1), (2), and (3) suffice to prove Moore's point. But premise (3) is highly questionable. Bob Durrant (1970) was perhaps the first to point out: (a) that Moore's argument requires some such premise if it is to succeed; but (b) that the assumption depends upon a purely referential theory of meaning according to which there is nothing more to the meaning of a predicate than the property for which it stands. Once we admit that, non-synonymous predicates can refer to the same property (just as non-synonymous names can refer to the same thing), Moore's argument for (5) collapses and he is reduced to sub-conclusion (4). 'Good' may not be synonymous with any naturalistic predicate 'X' (whether simple or complex) but this does not prove that goodness is not identical with some naturalistic property of X-ness. We can no longer proceed from an unanalyzable and non-natural *predicate* 'good' to an unanalyzable and non-natural *property* of goodness. Cornell realists rejoice in this fact and happily propound synthetic identities between moral properties and others analogous to the celebrated identity between water and H_2O. We can have moral truth without either metaphysical spooks or implausible attempts to give a naturalistic definition of the word 'good'.

Nevertheless, sub-conclusion (4) is not without importance, since it suggests the *semantic* autonomy of ethics, the thesis that morals words are not susceptible of naturalistic definition. It is, therefore, incompatible with *semantic* naturalism, which claims that the moral can be reduced to the non-moral *by definition*, i.e., by establishing that 'good' *means the same* as some naturalistic predicate 'X'. Thus if sub-conclusion (4) is correct, the Russell/Lewis theory is false.

But sub-conclusion (4) depends upon premise (2). And premise (2) is false. For it leads straight to the Paradox of Analysis, a problem that Moore recognized but did not succeed in solving. The Paradox first appeared in a paper by Langford (1942) but was probably discovered by Moore himself (Baldwin (1990, 208)). The Paradox is that conceptual analysis (which was Moore's stock-in-trade) is either useless or productive of falsehoods. For suppose the *analysandum* (the expression to be analyzed) means the same as the *analysans* (or analyzing phrase). Then by (2) this will be evident to every competent speaker and the analysis will teach us nothing new. Suppose, on the other hand, that the analysis teaches us something new, i.e., that it is *not* evident on reflection to every competent speaker. Then, again by (2), the analysis is false. For if it is not evident to every competent speaker that the *analysans* and the *analysandum* share the same meaning, then they won't share the same meaning and the analysis will be false (Baldwin (1990, 210–11); Pigden (1991, 427); Darwall, Gibbard, and Railton (1992, 115)). If conceptual analysis is to be a worthwhile enterprise, one *capable* of turning up new and interesting truths, premise (2), which generates the Paradox had better be false. And it *is* false, since it presupposes that our concepts are transparent to us. This is a point now widely recognized. Baldwin, for instance states that what I call premise (2) relies on 'the Cartesian conception of the content of thought as transparently available to the subject' (1990: 210–11), whilst Darwall, Gibbard, and Railton talk of 'assumptions about the transparency of concepts and the obviousness of analytic truth' (1992: 115). Moore, therefore, is in the embarrassing position of relying on an assumption which, if true, would have sabotaged his philosophical career. It is an assumption that anyone who believes in the possibility of conceptual analysis—from Moore and Russell through to David Lewis and Frank Jackson—must reject. What is analytic isn't always obvious. Hence the fact (if it be a fact) that 'Are X things good?' is an open question for every naturalistic or metaphysical 'X' does not prove that 'good' is not synonymous with some such 'X'.

Thus the Open Question Argument has collapsed. It relied on three premises, (1), (2), and (3). Premise (3) was shot down in the 1970s, first by Bob Durrant and subsequently by others such as Putnam (1981, 205–11). This opened the way for brands of naturalism such as Cornell Realism, which rely on synthetic identities. It was a liberating thought that you can have moral truths without resorting to non-natural properties or dubious conceptual analyses. But the deletion of premise (3) still left the OQA able to limp along as a disproof of semantic naturalism. But somewhere around 1980 people began to realize that premise (2) 'the publicity condition', leads to the Paradox of Analysis and therefore had to go. The first person to make this point was Casimir Lewy in a paper published as far back as 1964. But, despite the most memorably bizarre set of lecturing mannerisms that I have ever encountered, Lewy was not a philosophical superstar, and his paper went largely unnoticed. I heard the point first from the lips of David Lewis in 1981 (though at the time I did not understand what he was getting at). Not surprising, then, that Lewis went on to reinvent a version of the desire-to-desire theory that the OQA was devised to disprove. The wheel had come full circle.

VI G. E. Moore Redux?

At the moment Moore seems to be in a pretty bad way while Russell and Lewis are laughing. The BTA does not work against the desire-to-desire theory, whilst the

OQA, which was probably invented to dispose of it, relies on three premises, two of which are false. Moore made his name with an argument, which, if it were sound, would have made mincemeat of much of his subsequent philosophy. But it was one of Lewis's pet theses that knock down refutations are rare to non-existent in philosophy. In the latter part of this paper I shall be illustrating this thesis by arguing that there is something to be said for the OQA—though in a suitably amended form, of course.

VII Colors, Values, and the Epistemic Argument

As the title suggests, Lewis's version of the desire-to-desire theory is a *dispositional* theory of value. It stands in a long tradition which represents value properties as akin to secondary properties, and construes secondary properties themselves as dispositions to cause certain effects in us.[10] I want to consider an argument of Kripke's—the epistemic argument—that can be deployed to show that neither colors nor values should be understood as dispositional properties. It is my contention that the argument fails with respect to colors but succeeds with respect to values. Thus this semi-successful argument tends to show that goodness, *unlike* yellow, is *not* a secondary property, and, hence, that Lewis's desire-to-desire theory is false. Furthermore, the successful argument turns out to be a variant of the OQA.

The principal purpose of Kripke's *Naming and Necessity* is to argue that proper names are—at least typically—rigid designators and that they lack sense. But one of his subsidiary purposes is to argue against a dispositional account of secondary properties and, more specifically, colors (Kripke (1980, 140 n)). In Kripke's view, color terms such as 'yellow' are also rigid designators, and, like proper names, they too lack sense. 'Yellow' denotes yellowness, but *not* by abbreviating some such description as 'that (manifest) property of objects that causes them, under normal circumstances to be seen as yellow (i.e., to be sensed by certain visual impressions)'. That description fixes the reference but not the sense of 'yellow', since the word 'yellow' has no sense to fix. In my view Kripke is wrong about this. But I am not going to discuss the matter in detail. I am just going to focus on *one* of his arguments, the epistemic argument. We shall first apply the argument to names, then to color terms, and finally to 'good'.

---

[10] There are hints of this in Shaftsbury, but Frances Hutcheson (1694–1746) was probably the first philosopher of modern times to produce a well-worked out account of moral properties as secondary qualities. He found a distinguished, if heterodox, disciple in Hume. See Raphael (1967) for relevant extracts.

(1*) If 'Shakespeare' meant 'the actual[11] author of *Hamlet, Othello*, etc.', then it would be analytic that Shakespeare (if he existed) was the actual author of *Hamlet, Othello*, etc.

(2*) But it is not analytic that Shakespeare (if he existed) was the actual author of *Hamlet, Othello*, etc.

(3*) So 'Shakespeare' does not mean 'the actual author of *Hamlet, Othello*, etc.' (Salmon (1981, 27–9).

I have no comment to make about this argument, which seems completely convincing, at least with respect to the vast bulk of proper names. Can it be adapted to show that words like 'yellow' are senseless and should not be subjected to a dispositional analysis?

(1**) If 'yellow' meant 'that property, if it exists, that given our actual optical propensities, excites yellow sensations under normal circumstances', then it would be analytic that given our actual optical propensities, yellow, if it exists, excites yellow sensations under normal circumstances.

(2**) But it is synthetic not analytic that given our actual optical propensities, yellow, if it exists, excites yellow sensations under normal circumstances.

(3**) So 'yellow' does not mean 'that property, if it exists, that given our actual optical propensities, excites yellow sensations under normal circumstances'.

I deny the second premise. It is *not* a matter of synthetic fact that yellow (if it exists) actually excites yellow sensations, but something we learn with the language. What *is* synthetic is that things with a certain range of surface microstructures and reflexive propensities excite yellow sensations. But this I can happily admit. Indeed it paves the way for a synthetic identity between instances of yellow and the microstructural properties which excite the sensations. In *this* case the epistemic argument fails.

So much for 'yellow', what about 'good'?

(1***) If 'good' meant what Lewis thinks it means, then it would be analytic that what we are actually, ideally disposed to desire to desire is good.

(2***) But this is, if true, a matter of synthetic fact.

(3***) Accordingly the analysis is false and goodness is not a secondary property.

---

[11] As is well known, Kripke's *modal* argument (to the effect that names and other terms lack descriptive content) can be neutralized if we rigidify the terms in question with the aid of some well-placed 'actuals and 'actuallys'. It seems to me that 'yellow' and 'good' are both used rigidly, which means that an 'actually' must be read into them. For ease of exposition, I have given 'Shakespeare' the same treatment. See Nathan U. Salmon, *Reference and Essence* (Oxford: Blackwell, 1982), 26 ff. and Lewis, DTV II, 132–3/88–9.

In the case of yellow I denied the second premise—that it is synthetic that if there is such a thing as yellow, it is what actually arouses yellow sensations in us. But this will not wash with good. For it is quite conceivable that what ideal human beings actually value is mostly bad. We can imagine Luther's opinion of Lewis's theory. The idea that the desires of unregenerate human beings should be a guide to the good would strike him as ridiculous. The whole project of converting oneself into an ideal desirer smacks of the impious vanity of the damned. For Luther our second order desires (whether idealized or not) would be like reason—the Devil's whore (see Luther (1957, 46)). The King of Brobdingnag, after hearing a somewhat slanted catalogue of human achievements, told his pet human that despite the high regard he felt for him it was obvious that mankind (well actually Englishmen) were 'the most pernicious race of little odious vermin that nature has ever suffered to crawl upon the face of the earth' (Swift (1967, 173)). Is it likely that the desires of such contemptible creatures, even the best of them, will indicate what goodness is? Won't they rather give an absurdly high ranking to the interests of their own noxious species? Now I do not *agree* with Luther and the King of Brobdingnag (except in my most jaundiced moments). But their views embody no manifest contradiction. If it *is* analytic that 'What we humans ideally desire to desire is good', it is certainly not an obvious analyticity.

Isn't the epistemic argument just the Open Question Argument all over again? After all, the OQA was that 'good' cannot mean 'X' because we can conceive of something being X without it's being good. (That is why the question 'Are X things, good?' makes sense or can be sensibly asked). We cannot in the same way conceive of someone as a bachelor without conceiving of him as an unmarried man—not if we know the meanings of the relevant words that is. Now the epistemic argument is very like this. It claims that 'good' cannot be analyzed as what we would be ideally disposed to desire to desire (i.e., it is not analytic that 'What we are ideally disposed to desire to desire is good'). Why not? Because we can conceive that we are ideally disposed to desire to desire something which is not really good. Indeed, we can imagine that it might be bad.

The candid answer to my question has to be 'yes'—the epistemic argument *is* pretty much a rehash of the OQA. Then shouldn't it be discarded? Once we admit that there are unobvious analyticities, the fact that we can conceive of Xs which are not Ys does not demonstrate that 'X' is a mistaken analysis of 'Y'. It might be that we have not thought the matter through. Hypothetico-deductive methods and even empirical research are required to establish non-trivial analyticities. Linguistic intuitions are not enough. Nor are linguistic intuitions enough to *dis*establish an alleged analyticity. Our intuitions may not penetrate to the buried rules and presuppositions that govern our use of language.

Nevertheless, our intuitions about what can and what cannot be conceived are not devoid of probative force. They reflect, albeit imperfectly, our understanding of the concepts we employ. Hence, they can provide evidence for and against analytical hypotheses, though this evidence ceases to be decisive. Now it does seem to me clear that Luther and the King of Brobdingnag could be right, and that what we ideally desire to desire could be wrong. In which case we have evidence, though not conclusive evidence, against the desire-to-desire theory.

Now Lewis (DTV II, 132/88) wants to argue that in this case the intuitive evidence is misleading. My intuitions reflect my superficial thinking not the deep structure of the relevant concepts. If we try to flesh out Luther's story or the story of the King, we see that the hypothesis collapses. We cannot really imagine what it would be like for what we are ideally disposed to value to be wrong. To talk largely of human depravity is not enough. What we need is corroborative detail: a plausible disvalue ideal humans are inclined to value or a value they are inclined to disvalue. Although Swift was about as misanthropic as they come, and although *Gulliver* is from first to last a satire on human nature, he does not manage to provide this. Yahoos, of course, value all sorts of nasty things, but they are far from ideal. Englishmen likewise value things of doubtful worth, such as money, titles, and military renown. But Englishmen, too, can be improved upon; for a start, they could be more disinterested. But what about truly ideal people? Could *ideal* humans be wrongly inclined to value domination—something Swift's repulsive puppets pursue? But although sub-ideal human beings in their fallen state may value domination, this is not something they need desire to desire, nor is it something they *would* desire to desire if the defects which make them less than ideal were removed.

I think Lewis's challenge can be met and corroborative detail supplied. Indeed, it has been supplied in numerous works of science fiction. It is the oldest trick in science fiction's book to present human beings through the eyes of the aliens, and to present them as ridiculous and repulsive. They are greedy, savage, selfish, and stupid, destroying other species and the ecosystems on which they depend. Given space-travel, they will spread through the galaxy like a noxious slime, blighting every planet they touch. They must be stopped! If I pile it on thick enough, I can get you to sympathize momentarily with the extermination of the human race. It is at least conceivable that the destruction of the human race would be a Good Thing from the point of view of the Universe as a whole. But could ideal human desirers be brought to desire this, not just in a moment of ecological frenzy, but as a settled policy? Surely not. Human chauvinism, in the weak form of a tendency to desire our continued survival, is surely part of our make-up and it is not a desire that we desire not to have—not even under ideal circumstances. So the extinction of the human race is a conceivable (if not a plausible) value that ideal human beings would be inclined to disvalue.

Now if we can conceive of what is good and what the best of us are disposed to desire to desire coming apart, this is evidence (though not conclusive evidence) that the one does not constitute an analysis of the other. The epistemic argument may be weaker than Kripke supposes, but in this context, it works after a fashion.

VIII The OQA Amended

But if the epistemic argument works after a fashion, then there is something to be said for the OQA, too, since in this context they come to much the same thing. The OQA failed because premise (2), the publicity condition, had to be rejected. However, even if we reject (2), and with it the assumption that our concepts are transparent to us, it does not follow that Moore's argument is entirely worthless. For there are weaker and more plausible variants of (2) which would take us to probabilistic variants of sub-conclusion (4). Consider, for example:

> (2′) If it is evident to *some* competent speakers that two expressions 'X' and 'Y' are *not* synonymous (since it is not analytic that X is Y), then this is evidence (though not conclusive evidence) that they are not, in fact, synonymous.

This suggests the following reformulation of the OQA, though as reformulated it presupposes not an Open Question but a strong intuition on the part of some speakers that the two expressions do *not* mean the same. Nevertheless we shall call it the OQA*:

> (1′) It is evident to some competent speakers that (so far as our understanding of the words is concerned) a thing could be X without being good.

> (2′) If it is evident to *some* competent speakers that two expressions 'X' and 'Y' are *not* synonymous (since it is not analytic that X is Y), then this is evidence (though not conclusive evidence) that they are not, in fact, synonymous.

> (4′) 'Good' is *probably* not synonymous with the predicate 'X' (or 'goodness' with the corresponding noun 'X-ness').

This argument, the OQA* can be deployed against most naturalistic definitions of the moral predicates, though whether it can be deployed against *all* such definitions is, to coin a phrase, an open question. Furthermore, the argument has to be deployed piecemeal. We no longer have a blanket premise covering *all* naturalistic predicates. Instead, we have a series of specific premises for specific naturalistic predicates 'X', saying that according to some competent speakers a thing could be X without being good. It is no longer enough *not* to believe that the two terms *are* synonymous (which is all that was required for the original OQA). Rather *someone* has to believe that they are *not* synonymous, because they can conceive of a thing's being X without being good. And we can't be sure that (1') will be satisfied for *every* naturalistic predicate 'X'. Thus the revised argument does not constitute a refutation of semantic naturalism but a series of *potential* refutations of *specific versions* of semantic naturalism And even when premise (1') is true for some 'X', the refutation is far from conclusive. Nevertheless, OQA* constitutes an argument schema which can be used to refute—or perhaps, since that's a weaker word, to *discredit*—a wide variety of semantic naturalisms, among them the theory that to be good is to be what we are ideally disposed to desire to desire. This is much less than Moore purported to prove, but it does indicate that he is not quite the undischarged intellectual bankrupt that he once appeared to be.

References

Baldwin, Thomas, *G. E. Moore* (London: Routledge, 1990).

Darwall, S., Gibbard, A. and Railton., P. 'Towards *Fin de Siécle* Ethics: Some Trends', *The Philosophical Review*, 101 (1992), 115—89.

Durrant, R. G., 'Identity of Properties and the Definition of Good', *Australasian Journal of Philosophy*, 48 (1970), 360—1.

Frankena, W. K., 'The Naturalistic Fallacy', *Mind*, 48 (1939), 464—77.

Griffin, Nicholas (ed.), *The Selected Letters of Bertrand Russell, Vol. 1: The Private Years 1884—1914* (London: Routledge, 2002).

Hylton, Peter, *Russell, Idealism and the Emergence of Analytic Philosophy* (Oxford: Oxford University Press, 1990).

Kripke, Saul, *Naming and Necessity* (Oxford: Blackwell, 1980).

Langford, C. H., 'Moore's Notion of Analysis', in P. A. Schilpp (ed.), *The Philosophy of G. E. Moore* (Lassalle: Open Court, 1942), 319—42.

Lewis, David, 'Dispositional Theories of Value II', *Proceedings of the Aristotelian Society, supp. vol.*, 63 (1989), 113—37.

Lewis, David, 'Dispositional Theories of Value', in David Lewis, *Papers in Ethics and Social Philosophy* (Cambridge: Cambridge University Press, 2000), 68—94.

Lewy, Casimir, 'G.E. Moore on the Naturalistic Fallacy', *Proceedings of the British Academy*, 50 (1964), 251—62.

Luther, Martin, *On the Bondage of the Will*, trans. by J. I. Packer and O. R. Johnston (Cambridge: James Clarke, 1957).

Moore, G. E. *The Elements of Ethics*, ed. by Tom Regan (Philadelphia: Temple University Press, 1991).

——— *Principia Ethica*, rev. edn., ed. by Thomas Baldwin (Cambridge: Cambridge University Press, 1993).

Pigden, Charles R., 'Naturalism', in Peter Singer (ed.), *A Companion to Ethics* (Oxford: Blackwell, 1991).

——— (ed.), *Russell on Ethics* (London: Routledge, 1999).

Prior, A. N., *Logic and the Basis of Ethics* (Oxford: Oxford University Press, 1949).

Putnam, Hilary, *Reason, Truth and History* (Cambridge: Cambridge University Press, 1981).

Raphael, D. D. (ed.), *The British Moralists*, 2 vols. (Oxford: Oxford University Press, 1967).

Russell, Bertrand, *The Collected Papers of Bertrand Russell. Vol. 1, Cambridge Essays, 1888—1899*, ed. by K. Blackwell, A. Brink, N. Griffin, R. Rempel, and J. Slater (London: Allen & Unwin, 1983).

———— *The Collected Papers of Bertrand Russell. Vol. 4, Foundations of Logic 1903—05*, ed. by A. Urquhart and A. C. Lewis, (London: Routledge, 1994).

Salmon, Nathan U., *Reference and Essence* (Oxford: Blackwell, 1982).

Sidgwick, Henry, *The Methods of Ethics*, 7th edn. (London: Macmillan, 1907).

Smith, Michael, *The Moral Problem* (Oxford: Blackwell, 1991).

Swift, Jonathan, *Gulliver's Travels* (Harmondsworth: Penguin, 1967).

13

What's Right with the Open Question Argument*

Susana Nuccetelli & Gary Seay

Ethics . . . [is] partly analysis of what's meant by 'good', 'ought', 'right', 'wrong', 'valuable', etc. And *if* certain analyses of these are right, then *other* ethical propositions, ones which aren't analytic, wouldn't be philosophical at all, but belong to psychology, sociology, and the theory of evolution.

G. E. Moore, Lectures on Philosophy, 196

Naturalism: the recognition that it is within science itself, and not in some prior philosophy, that reality is to be identified and described.

W. V. Quine, Theories and Things, 21

I

The substantive issues of moral ontology raised by G. E. Moore's Open Question Argument (*OQA*) are bound up with difficult problems of knowledge, language, and philosophical analysis. Offered as a refutation of ethical naturalism, the *OQA* has been thought to founder on some such problems, as can be seen from the long and varied history of attempted rebuttals it has inspired.[1] In spite of widespread

---

* We wish to thank Stephen Schiffer, Gary Ostertag, Ken Williford, and Fritz McDonald for helpful suggestions that have made this a better paper than it would otherwise have been.
[1] The version of the argument most prominent in chapter 1 of *Principia* has come under fire both from ethical naturalists and non-naturalists, who have criticized it on several counts—including that it is

objections, however, the argument has remained a central point of contention in the naturalism/non-naturalism debate, rivaled in longevity among Moore's most controversial arguments not even by his 1939 'Proof of an External World'. When an argument is as resilient as that, we may suspect that there is something to be learned from trying to determine the source of its enduring appeal, even though much might still be wrong with its original formulation. Here we propose a sympathetic reading of the OQA that neither endorses Moore's moral ontology nor focuses on exegesis.[2] Our qualified defense distinguishes two arguments, OQA_1 and OQA_2, roughly according to the type of reductive ethical naturalism each attempts to undermine. OQA_1 targets any such program grounded in a semantic thesis, OQA_2 any such program grounded in a metaphysical thesis. This distinction is consistent with Moore's own reasoning against what he thought of, in broad terms, as naturalism in ethics, which also points to two independent, though compatible, arguments. Although OQA_2 might at first appear more fundamental, here we devote most of our efforts to the *other* argument, OQA_1, whose scope is often underestimated (cf. Pigden, this volume). If we are right, OQA_1 amounts to a *refutation* of semantic reductive naturalism, a family of doctrines that will be shown to be of greater metaethical significance than sometimes thought. Given OQA_1, OQA_2 can be made out as an independent argument to the effect that there may in fact be *no* good grounds for metaphysical varieties of reductive naturalism.[3]

II

One of Moore's goals with his OQA was to show that the value predicate 'good' is indefinable. Clearly, if 'good' were indefinable, then *a fortiori* it could not be defined in terms of any descriptive predicate standing for a purely natural or metaphysical property, and any version of naturalism *that rested on such definitions* would therefore be false. Yet the indefinability of 'good' would have no tendency to undermine all doctrines of ethical naturalists—though Moore himself seems to have thought that it did disprove them as well. As we shall see later, there is a certain casting of the

---

invalid, that it leads to the paradox of analysis, that it presupposes an inflated moral ontology, and that it begs the question.

[2] Exegetical readings sympathetic to the open question argument can be found in Sylvester (1990) and Ball (1988). For more critical treatments, see Hutchinson (2001), Baldwin (1990), and White (1958).

[3] The achievement of Moore's OQA may be largely that it points to the normativity moral agents associate with evaluative concepts, as recently argued by Scanlon (1998); Stratton-Lake (2002); and Darwall (2006), among others. But we believe that substantiating any such claim requires that we first undertake a charitable construal of Moore's OQA, whether this is reconstructed as deductive or inductive. Cf. Shafer-Landau (2003); Strandberg (2004); Ball (1991); and Snare (1975).

Moorean argument that does refute a semantic brand of ethical naturalism. This relatively modest conclusion, however, is not an obvious consequence of Moore's original argument, which can be reconstructed in a first approximation as follows:

OQA

1 If a certain variety of ethical naturalism is true, then a value predicate such as 'good' is analyzable into a purely descriptive predicate such as 'pleasure maximizing'.

2 If 'good' is analyzable into 'pleasure maximizing', then the question, 'Granted *a* is pleasure maximizing, but is it good?' is closed.

3 But the question, 'Granted *a* is pleasure maximizing, but is it good?' is open.

Therefore,

4 'Good' is not analyzable into 'pleasure maximizing'.

5 Steps (1) through (4) can be iterated for each attempted naturalistic analysis of value predicates into purely descriptive predicates.

Therefore,

6 No value predicates are analyzable into purely descriptive predicates.

Therefore,

7 Ethical naturalism is false.

A number of arguments may result from this *OQA*, depending on how some unclear terms are cashed out. Note, however, that no such arguments could have force against *non-reductive* naturalism in ethics: that is, against a doctrine holding, for example, that evaluative and normative properties supervene on, but are not reducible to, purely descriptive properties. Of course, Moore himself allowed that value properties do (as we would now say) supervene on natural properties. Thus the logical space of theories vulnerable to *OQA* is limited to *reductive* theses of ethical naturalists such as

Semantic Reductive Naturalism (*SRN*)
    Value predicates are analyzable without evaluative or normative remainder into purely descriptive predicates.

Metaphysical Reductive Naturalism (*MRN*)
    Value properties are analyzable without evaluative or normative remainder into purely descriptive properties.

A common motivation for proponents of either of these theses seems to be

Epistemic Reductive Naturalism (*ERN*)
    Ethical inquiry into value properties needs no other justification beyond that attainable through the standard methods of science.

Views such as *ERN* were rejected by Moore, who rightly saw them as challenging the status of ethics as a part of philosophy with a subject-matter and method entirely independent of the natural and social sciences. Such views, which do not entail the repudiation of ethics but rather its assimilation to the sciences, usually fuel theses along the lines of *MRN* or *SRN*. Of the two, only *MRN* entails that value properties are nothing over and above natural properties. *SRN* could not have that consequence unless there were nothing else to the content of the relevant predicates than the properties they denote. Since that would be, in effect, only a highly implausible 'Fido'-Fido theory for those predicates, therefore when more is allowed into their content, *SRN* does not entail *MRN*. It follows that no *OQA* that defeats *SRN* could by itself refute *MRN*.

The two revised versions of *OQA* that we shall present here are in part the products of distinguishing these two theses of reductive ethical naturalism in the above argument. OQA_1 starts out with a premise to the effect that, given *SRN*, a predicate such as 'good' is analyzable (in a way to be spelled out presently) without evaluative or normative remainder into a predicate such as 'pleasure maximizing'. By deploying a Moorean strategy against that thesis, the argument demonstrates that no such analysis is possible. This, together with a premise along the lines of (5) above, entails that no evaluative or normative predicate is analyzable into a purely descriptive predicate or set of predicates—which amounts to demonstrating the falsity of *SRN*. (As sometimes noted, a similar Moorean strategy could also be deployed to show that value predicates are not analyzable into metaphysical predicates such as 'follows the will of God' or 'creates positive karma.')

OQA is also an argument against *MRN*, to the effect that no value property is either identical or reducible to a purely descriptive property or set of properties. A major problem facing the argument for this conclusion is its alleged commitment to a 'Fido'-Fido theory of general terms/concepts. Perhaps it is Moore's own unclarity on the semantic features of general terms that fuels this objection.[4] But, as will be shown, there is a related argument, OQA_2, that doesn't rest on that problematic semantic theory for predicates. On our view, support for OQA_2 stems from the reasons for OQA_1's success—together with the difficulties facing metaphysical varieties of reductive naturalism in accommodating widely accepted intuitions about the modal status of identity statements entailed by their preferred analyses. But before we can examine these arguments, some further points of clarification are in order about Moore's *OQA* above.

---

[4] Although Moore seems to have held, at different times, more than one theory of meaning, there is no evidence that he was a 'Fido'-Fido theorist about predicates. See, e.g., 'Classes and Incomplete Symbols', a selection from a course of lectures given in 1925–6 and later included in Moore (1966). According to Sylvester (1990); and White (1958), at the time of *Principia*, Moore endorsed a concept theory for predicates: namely, the view that a predicate stands for a concept. Cf. Baldwin (1990).

First, in *OQA*, questions of the form, 'Granted *a* is *X*, but is it *Y*?' are offered in order to tease out intuitions about certain equivalences. Let's call any such question 'Moorean' and note that it would admit of two readings, depending on whether we take the intuitions it attempts to elicit to concern the equivalence of predicates or of properties. For, clearly, although it might appear that a question of that sort concerns only the equivalence of the latter, it could also involve that of the former. To find out about a certain conceptual identity, surely one may unambiguously ask, for example, 'Are concepts "*X*" and "*Y*" the same, semantically individuated?' or 'Do predicates "*X*" and "*Y*" have the same meaning?' But an equally effective way to proceed would be by asking, 'Is to be an *X* to be a *Y*?' or 'Is an *X* a *Y*?' After all, imagine a sincere and competent speaker of English, who masters the predicate 'attorney' but is uncertain about its synonymity with 'lawyer'. To find out whether these terms mean the same, that speaker may simply ask, 'Is a lawyer an attorney?' Yet any unequivocal *OQA* should make plain whether it is a conceptual question that is being raised.

However ambiguous the appeal to the Moorean question in the *OQA* above may be, it is clearly part of a *reductio* strategy against a certain doctrine. It constitutes, then, an exercise of philosophical analysis involving a thinker whose intuitions are sought for the issue at hand, similar in this respect to the Gettier counterexamples or Putnam's Twin Earth. In all such cases, the intended thinker is oneself, provided one is a *competent user* of the terms involved and there is no reason to believe that one's intuitions on the topic of concern are *atypical* and therefore irrelevant to the folk conception of them.[5]

A related unclarity undermining *OQA* also concerns its appeal to *analysis*: which of the two philosophical methods standardly designated in that way, the conceptual or the factual, is at work in this argument? Needless to say, although methods of both sorts have been characteristic of reductive programs in philosophy, of the two, it is chiefly conceptual analysis that is associated with *semantic* theses such as analytical behaviorism in philosophy of mind. On the other hand, factual analysis is a strategy typical of metaphysical theses, such as the Strawsonian account of speech acts in terms of speaker-meaning in philosophy of language or Hume's analysis of causation (Mackie 1973). Our reconstructions of Moore's argument also accommodate these two different methods of analysis, since OQA_1 targets the conceptual analyses of semantic naturalists, and OQA_2 the factual analyses of metaphysical naturalists. Thus, where Moore talked equivocally of naturalistic *definition* in both cases, we talk of *content equivalence*—but only in connection with the naturalistic program targeted by OQA_1. On the other hand, the naturalistic program targeted by OQA_2 invokes identifications of value properties with purely descriptive properties.

[5] For more on the purpose of analysis along the lines suggested here, see Mackie (1973); and Jackson (1998).

Regarding conceptual analysis, Moore sometimes denied emphatically that it concerned linguistic expressions, noting that a word may stand for different concepts. He often insisted that his interest was not merely in the words of a public language but in the objects of thought—the notions themselves as they are present to the mind (for example, 1966, 159). But a proper treatment of this subject would require discussion of how words are individuated and of the type/token distinction—both topics that Moore seems not to have developed at all. Even so, he later acknowledged (1942) that he could hardly have made out his arguments without some appeal to linguistic categories, as his use of the word 'predicate' suggests. Here we accept the point first made by Vendler, that when speakers are sincere and competent, what they say is syntactically and semantically parallel to what they think. That is, we accept that, when speakers are sincere and competent, many of their sentence-size utterances convey the contents of their psychological attitudes, as their singular and general terms convey the concepts they entertain. Throughout, then, instances of the Moorean question itself, together with its building blocks, are considered linguistic or mental entities of the standard sorts.

The reductionist programs targeted by Moore's argument involve analyses of predicates/terms/concepts (and properties) of two types: what we may call 'value', which are either evaluative or normative; and 'purely descriptive', which correspond to what Moore himself referred to as 'natural' predicates. In his early work (for example, 1922, 253 ff.), the first group comprises predicates for intrinsic value ('good', 'beautiful', etc.) as well as terms that have 'a fixed relation' to kinds of value that are intrinsic ('right', 'what ought to be done', etc.); the second group includes terms for *natural* properties,[6] some that on Moore's view are intrinsic to whatever possesses them ('yellowness') and some that aren't ('being better fitted to survive'). This, of course, falls short of providing a criterion for the distinction between natural and non-natural properties, a problem that Moore continued to wrestle with long after *Principia* (1922, 1942). On our view, an epistemic criterion might do the best job of drawing the distinction—for example:

---

[6] Criteria for defining a 'natural property' are at best vague in Moore's work. In *Principia*, they consist in any such property's existing in time all by itself and being a 'part' of anything that it characterizes. According to the most adequate metaphysical construal that can be culled from his later labors, a property counts as *natural* if and only if, for any object that possesses it, no description of that object could be complete without a reference to that property, unless it is entailed by one or more other properties listed in a complete description of that object. In 'The Conception of Intrinsic Value', he writes: '. . . intrinsic properties seem to describe the intrinsic nature of what possesses them in a sense in which predicates of value never do. If you could enumerate all the intrinsic properties a given thing possessed, you would have given a complete description of it, and would not need to mention any predicates of value it possessed; whereas no description of a given thing could be complete which omitted any intrinsic property' (1922, 273). Yet, as many have pointed out, this falls short of settling the distinction Moore wishes to make between natural and non-natural properties. On the other hand, the distinction of intrinsic properties/intrinsic values was unsatisfactory from the outset.

Natural Property
> A property counts as *purely natural* or *descriptive* if and only if any claim about whether something has it is defeasible, at least in principle, by empirical investigation alone.

A criterion of this sort seems not only to beg no questions, but to accommodate what naturalists often find most implausible about non-naturalist positions: namely, that they countenance objects, properties, and relations well beyond what could be revealed by even the most complete empirical science. At the same time, our criterion is consistent with Moore's reasons for defending the autonomy of ethics and his related rejection of naturalistic reductions of value properties to psychological, sociological, or biological properties.

III

Freed of some of its baggage, the original *OQA* may now be recast as either *OQA₁* or *OQA₂*, depending on which program of reductive ethical naturalism the argument attempts to undermine, and also on the casting of the Moorean question and the sort of philosophical analysis at work in the targeted program. *OQA₁* targets a program advancing a semantic thesis such as *SRN* above, now recast as holding that value terms are *conceptually* analyzable (in a sense to be determined later) into some purely descriptive terms. *OQA₂* targets a program advancing a metaphysical thesis such as *MRN*, now recast as holding that value properties are *factually* analyzable into some purely descriptive properties. Unlike Moore's *OQA*, however, neither of these arguments is undermined by equivocation. Since it is *OQA₁* that provides initial support for the other argument, let's begin by having a closer look at it.

OQA₁

1 If semantic reductive naturalism is true, then tokens of one's value terms and purely descriptive terms such as 'good' and 'pleasure maximizing' instantiate the same semantic type.

2 If one's tokens of 'good' and 'pleasure maximizing' instantiate the same semantic type, then the question, 'Do my thoughts *that a is pleasure maximizing* and *that a is good* have the same content?' is closed.

3 But the question, 'Do my thoughts *that a is pleasure maximizing* and *that a is good* have the same content?' is open.

Therefore,

4 One's tokens of 'good' and 'pleasure maximizing' do not instantiate the same semantic type.

5 Steps (1) through (4) can be iterated for each attempted conceptual analysis of a value term into purely descriptive terms.

Therefore,

6 Semantic reductive naturalism is false.

If OQA_1's deductive core, (1) through (4), is compelling, then the rest of the argument, which concludes with a generalization against the reductive program it targets, will be in the clear. We shall now show that it is. Crucial to OQA_1's deductive core are the premises that deploy a *reductio* strategy against the targeted thesis: (2) contends that, given the proposed naturalistic analysis, a related Moorean question *would be closed*; while (3) asserts that the question *is open*.

We'll take up the Moorean question first. As noted above, its intended addressee is *oneself* provided that (a) in the vocabularies involved, one is a competent user of the predicates, both the evaluative or normative and the purely descriptive; and (b) one has no reason to think that one is an atypical thinker, likely to give answers unrepresentative of ordinary intuitions about the alleged content equivalence of those predicates. Suppose one is now seriously considering a question of that kind. It seems that any suitable answer would require looking into the two propositional contents one is entertaining not merely *dispositionally* but *occurrently*, and not only *subconsciously* but *consciously*. As is apparent in OQA_1, the Moorean question therefore turns on a *cogito*-like judgment of content: one that consists in a present tense, self-attributed, judgment about whether one's own propositional attitudes (for example, that one is judging *that a is pleasure maximizing* and *that a is good*) are content equivalent. To better capture that *that* is precisely the sort of judgment prompted by the Moorean question, we have recast the question accordingly. We take any qualifying questions to be of the form

CMQ (Cogito-like Moorean Question)

'Are my current judgments *that a is D* and *that a is V* content equivalent?'

—where 'D' and 'V' stand for a general term/concept in each of the aforementioned vocabularies. Since the term/concept 'a' is held constant, therefore *other things are equal* in the content-clauses of any CMQ. It follows that the comparative judgment of content teased out by the question boils down to determining whether general term/concepts 'D' and 'V' are content equivalent in a sense we'll now spell out.

Suppose one is seriously entertaining a certain CMQ and meets conditions (a) and (b) above. A suitable answer would require that one make a comparative judgment of content equivalence by looking into that CMQ's content-clauses: the that-clauses widely taken to count as primary vehicles for individuating the content of whatever propositional attitudes they are used to report. *Contra* Moore, it doesn't really matter whether one entertains such that-clauses in thought only, or also in language (recall we are assuming Vendler's point). The differences among the tokens of a

CMQ's that-clauses may concern the syntactic type and/or the semantic type they instantiate. Of course, any two such clauses that differ syntactically in virtue of being instances of two different syntactic types may none the less have the same content in virtue of instantiating the same semantic type. Naturally, any two that-clauses that instantiate the same semantic type are *content equivalent*. Thus in a *CMQ's* that-clauses, since other things are equal except for the tokens of certain general term/concepts 'D' and 'V,' determining content equivalence amounts to determining whether those tokens instantiate the same semantic type. Given OQA_1's premises (2) and (3), whenever one meets the conditions for being a suitable addressee of the relevant *CMQ*, one is a reliable judge of the putative content equivalence of the two that-clauses one is consciously and occurrently entertaining. That is, the premises require that one could reliably judge that the question is closed whenever a *CMQ's* that-clauses are content equivalent, but that it is open whenever they are not content equivalent.

It is now clear that to undermine the analyses of semantical reductive naturalists, OQA_1 presupposes that competent users of the concepts involved in such analyses can reliably assess claims of content equivalence in answering corresponding *CMQs*. But this boils down to assuming the transparency of mental content: after all, when presented with a *CMQ*, one is supposed to be able to make a self-ascriptive comparative judgment of content right off, by looking into the contents of one's own thoughts prompted by the question. Yet there is tension between transparency and allowing for unobvious analyses, and the latter seems required by the argument in order to avoid the so-called paradox of analysis: the problem that any conceptual analysis, if correct, must be trivial.[7] Given that comparative judgments of content triggered by *CMQs* presuppose the transparency of mental content, in order to avoid the paradox of analysis, proponents of the argument would have to countenance the possibility of unobvious analyses. And once they do that, the appeal to *CMQs* could have no force against semantic theses of reductive naturalism. It appears, then, that if there were such unobvious correct analyses, then premise (2) would be false. *That a is good* might after all be content equivalent with *that a is pleasure maximizing*, even when the question, 'Are my current thoughts *that a is pleasure maximizing* and *that a is good* content equivalent?' remained open for some competent users of the concepts involved. Since at least some such analyses could then be both *correct* and *open* for competent users, OQA_1 would founder in light of the paradox of analysis.

Although it may be thought that proponents of OQA_1 need not worry about a paradox that has already been resolved in more than one way (see, for example, Mackie 1973; Katz 2004), on our view, meeting this objection really amounts to being able to formulate a plausible thesis of the transparency of mental content, one that

---

[7] We are indebted to Ken Williford for this suggestion.

could also be deployed to resolve the paradox of analysis. In fact, nothing stronger than the following is required by the argument:

> Transparency of Mental Content Thesis (*TMC*)
>> Under normal circumstances, first-person comparative judgments of content teased out by *CMQs* amount to a priori knowledge—i.e., to beliefs that are (i) default true and (ii) warranted without empirical investigation.

Now clearly proponents of OQA_1 are not committed to denying the possibility of unobvious analyses. To qualify for a priori knowledge, a true belief need not be *obviously* warranted, but rather warranted *just by thinking*.

At the same time, it is not difficult to see how *TMC* is weaker, and therefore more plausible than an unqualified Cartesian thesis to the effect that one is *always* in a position to know whether any two self-attributed thoughts have the same content. For one thing, *TMC*'s scope is limited to *cogito*-like Moorean questions of the sort featured in OQA_1's premises (2) and (3). Such questions seek to refute attempted naturalistic analyses of value terms/concepts into purely descriptive terms/concepts. Since *other things are equal* in the Moorean question, *TMC* boils down to claiming a plausible privilege for one's assessment of the content equivalence of certain concepts one is competently entertaining, which belong to those two types of term/concept. This thesis leaves open the possibility that, for other types *no* such transparency holds. Thus, *TMC* falls short of entailing that one is always in a position to know whether any two concepts one is entertaining are content equivalent. Furthermore, *TMC* requires 'normal circumstances', which are those meeting the specified conditions (a) and (b) for being an eligible addressee of the question—namely, that one is a competent and typical user of the concepts whose content equivalence one is assessing. Thus, *TMC* commits to neither the infallibility nor the incorrigibility of one's comparative judgment prompted by a *CMQ*. In addition, a case could be made that 'default true', a weak, truth-related immunity required by *TMC,* is a privilege conferred by the first-person grounds available for judgments teased out by *CMQs*. After all, they amount to *cogito*-like thoughts whose privileged-truth status is widely accepted, given first-person authority. As we construe their truth status, although they fall short of being immune to falsity or corrections by others, they are predominantly true or true in the absence of evidence to the contrary—a qualification needed to accommodate those rare occasions where observation and the testimony of others may be necessary, for example, in order to disqualify oneself as a suitable addressee of a certain *CMQ*. But if generally true and warranted non-empirically (i.e., just by thinking) such judgments constitute a priori knowledge—at least in the sense of amounting to *true beliefs warranted without empirical investigation*. In fact, there is now dialectical space to contend that OQA_1's premises are *all* a priori in exactly this sense. If so, then since the argument is valid and non-question begging, it follows that such an epistemic status may transmit to its conclusions. But there is another condition, to which we now turn, that must also be met.

IV

OQA_1's conclusion (4) could inherit an a priori status from the argument's premises, provided that if one can know a priori both that p and that p entails q, then one can also know a priori that q. Yet a principle sanctioning this is weaker than other closure principles, and therefore at least prima facie very plausible. Given this principle, since OQA_1 is a non-question-begging valid argument, the apriority of its conclusion (4) depends entirely on that of supporting premises. Moreover, if (4) is knowable a priori, then since it is clear that premise (5) could be known by philosophical reflection alone, conclusion (6) would qualify as a priori knowledge, too. Thus, support for OQA_1 amounts to showing that premises (1) through (3) can be considered by default true and warranted non-empirically.

Arguably, one could come to know a priori the implication in premise (1). For it appears to be both a true consequence of a semantic thesis such as SRN, and warranted by philosophical theorizing with no empirical investigation necessary. Yet premise (1) is sure to face one objection: has any naturalist ever held a thesis along such lines? Is semantic reductive naturalism a position of any weight in ethics? Skepticism on this count has historically taken the form of doubt about whether anyone really did commit the 'naturalistic fallacy'. Moore, of course, held an inflationary view of the universe of offenders on this score.[8] Yet the list of reductive naturalists willing to advance semantic theses along SRN's lines is by no means short. Bentham famously *defined* 'right action' as 'an action that is conformable to the principle of utility,' insisting that the words 'right', 'wrong', and 'ought' *have meaning* only when interpreted in terms of that principle (1789, ch. 1, §10). Westermarck, with whom Moore takes issue in 'The Nature of Moral Philosophy' (1922, 332), appears to have held that calling an action 'right' or 'wrong' is equivalent to saying that it produces in us certain feelings of approbation or disapprobation. For clear examples of semantic naturalists, however, Moore needn't have looked further than his own contemporaries: R. B. Perry famously wrote that 'x is valuable = interest is taken in x' (1926); and F. C. Sharp presented the following definitions: ' "good" means "desired upon reflection" ' and

---

[8] Sidgwick appears Moore's immediate predecessor in pointing out what might constitute one of the so-called informal fallacies. As often noted, however, there is no agreement on precisely what these are. Moore himself claimed to have found the naturalistic fallacy in Aristotle, the Stoics, Spinoza, Rousseau, Bentham, Kant, Mill, Spencer, and Green (Baldwin(1990), 69). For a more conservative list, see Prior (1949, 104–7).

' "right" means "desired when looked at from an impersonal point of view" '(1928; cited by Frankena 1963, 81). Nor are semantic naturalists absent from the present-day philosophical stage, as can be seen from the work of Frank Jackson, according to whom, in some cases, once a situation has been well described in *nonmoral terms*, certain *ethical sentences* will follow a priori from that description—or, as he puts it, ethical sentences are 'a priori equivalent to and analyzable in terms of nonmoral ones' (2003, 558). Clearly, semantic reductive naturalism is a view in moral philosophy that has had prominent defenders and remains currently a live option.[9] OQA_1's premise (1), then, does not render the argument vulnerable to a straw-man objection.

We can now proceed to the next step of showing the apriority of the conditional in its premise (2). If warranted a priori and *true*, that premise also would qualify as a priori knowledge. That warrant for premise (2) is a priori follows from its being grounded entirely on philosophical theorizing about the cognitive value of a Moorean question involving concepts that would be content equivalent provided the implication of semantic naturalism in premise (1) is true. No warrant of that sort requires empirical investigation. For premise (2) to be true, it should be true that, given its antecedent, the Moorean question in its consequent is not open. As argued above, suitable assessments of the cognitive value of any such question involve first-person comparative judgments of content, which are a priori warranted and default true. If this is correct, then not only does premise (2) come out a priori, but (3) does as well, a premise entirely based on a first-person judgment of content teased out by the Moorean question.

Further support for the contention that answers to such questions are a priori can be found in Moore's own ways of cashing out the cognitive values they aim at eliciting. We may spell out one such way as follows:

> OQ   For any *CMQ* and for any competent user of the predicates involved in it, the
> question is *closed* or *settled* if and only if those predicates are content equivalent,
> and otherwise it is *open* or *unsettled*

Under a certain reading of 'settled'/'unsettled', determining whether a *CMQ* is open appears to hinge on whether or not any suitable answer to that question would be *controversial*, which might require evidence of the sort provided by opinion polls and other procedures of empirical investigation. Needless to say, if judgments about sameness and difference in content prompted by *CMQs* were at least in part warranted only by evidence, then the above argument's premises featuring a question of that sort would fall short of a priori knowledge. Yet 'settled'/'unsettled' also admit of a reading

---

[9] Bertrand Russell and David Lewis may also be added to the list of semantic reductive naturalists. For arguments to the effect that they both attempted naturalistic analyses of the sort rejected by Moore, see Pigden (this volume).

more friendly to the apriority of answers properly teased out by *CMQs*—as captured by another common casting of their two possible values, 'significant'/'non-significant'. This construal is consistent with our contention that proper answers to *CMQs* consist entirely in first-person judgments about the content equivalence of two self-attributed propositional attitudes prompted by any such question. If so, then those answers are default true and non-empirically warranted. They therefore qualify as a priori knowledge.

In invoking these privileges for *cogito*-like thoughts, we are, of course, not alone. As the current literature makes clear, much can be learned about the plausibility of such privileges from philosophers whose theories appear incompatible with them. Rightly fearing that any failure to accommodate these privileges would count as a *reductio* of their own theories, their standard reaction has been to make provisions for accommodation. Cases in point are the content-externalist theories of Tyler Burge and Donald Davidson. Burge has long been at pains to demonstrate that his externalism is, in fact, compatible with what he calls 'the epistemic specialness' of self-knowledge, offering an account of its privileges more ambitious than the transparency of mental content defended here. He writes: 'some present tense self-attributed thoughts about propositional attitude content and type are self-referential, non-contextually self-verifying, and directly and non-empirically warranted' (1996, 92–4). Likewise, Davidson proposed, though perhaps less emphatically, similar privileges for self-knowledge judgments—for example, when he argues

... [although] an interpreter must, if he is to get things right, look to relations between the mind he is interpreting and its environment, this does not prejudice the self-knowledge of the knower ... I say 'I believe the Koh-i-noor diamond is a crown jewel' ... And suppose, as is the case, that I know what the words I have just uttered mean, and that I am making a sincere assertion. Finally, let us suppose that you and I agree on these points ... From these suppositions it follows that I know what I believe, but it does not follow that you know what I believe. The reason is simple: you may not know what I mean. Your knowledge of what my words mean has to be based on evidence and inference ... it does not make sense to suppose I am generally mistaken about what my words mean; the presumption that I am not generally mistaken about what I mean is essential to my having a language—to my being interpretable at all. (1991, 212)

Efforts of these sorts indirectly support our contention that the *cogito*-like judgments elicited by Moorean questions are a priori. Clearly, the view proposed here is consistent with Davidson's claim that the assumption that one is *not generally mistaken* in evaluating the content of one's own propositional attitudes is necessary for our having a language. Furthermore, it is consistent with arguments by Burge (1998) and (more especially) Paul Boghossian (1994) to vindicate the transparency of mental content, on the ground that it is a necessary condition of our being critical thinkers and rational at all. It should also be noted that the truth-related immunity we ascribe to judgments elicited by Moorean questions is weaker than Burge's claim of non-contextual self-verifiability cited above—though, like him, we also take *cogito*-like thoughts, of which Moorean questions are instances, to be warranted non-empirically. But when it comes to the truth-status of such thoughts, our more modest claim is closer to Davidson's: viz., that whenever one meets the conditions for being able to evaluate a certain *CMQ*, then if one considers that the question is open (or closed), that judgment is *default* true, a status that could yet be overriden by countervailing evidence. In any case, if default true and non-empirically warranted, that judgment is then a priori. Knowledge of this sort plainly falls beyond what can ordinarily be challenged by others, whether or not one is able to articulate that that is its normative force.

Given the presumption that qualifying answers to *CMQs* are privileged in these ways, OQA_1's premises (2) and (3) are now established as clearly a priori. Since premises (1) and (5) have already been shown to have that epistemic status too, and OQA_1 is a non-question-begging valid argument presupposing a plausible closure principle, it follows that its conclusions (4) and (6) can be known a priori.

V

Our defense of OQA_1 is incomplete, however, for we still must dispose of some possible objections. Prominent among them is one likely to be raised by direct-reference semanticists—and, more generally, by any content externalists wishing to reject the transparency of mental content, even in the very modest version offered by our *TMC* above. Objections on these counts would likely invoke Pierre-style scenarios (Kripke 1979) thought to raise a paradox, or at least a puzzle, for belief ascription and rationality. Although we need not rehearse here the details of that case, recall that Pierre, a bilingual speaker of French and English, each independently learned, has two occurrent, conscious beliefs that he would sincerely and competently express by uttering 'Londres est jolie' and 'London is not pretty'. By hypothesis unaware that the propositional contents thus expressed are contradictory, Pierre appears altogether rational. From Pierre's own perspective, the only possible epistemic warrant for a knowledgeable comparative judgment of those contents would seem empirical. Furthermore, once we grant that it is the extension of a term that in part determines its content, we appear in a position to run parallel scenarios for propositions containing some general terms/concepts such as 'cat', 'water', and the like.

Here is one: imagine Pierre, now resettled in Wisconsin, periodically undertaking hunting expeditions to nearby states. Suppose that in the presence of a certain animal—say in Minnesota—Pierre has thoughts he would competently and sincerely express by uttering 'That's a woodchuck'; while in Illinois he has thoughts he would also competently and sincerely express by uttering 'That's a groundhog'. *Ex hypothesi*, Pierre fails to notice that groundhogs are woodchucks. To test whether he is able to put two and two together, we meet Pierre in Minnesota, at a moment when he has just competently and sincerely reported the presence of such an animal. We then pose this quasi-Moorean question: 'Granted that is a woodchuck, but is it a groundhog?' Pierre must now make a comparative judgment of content about the two propositional attitudes he is occurrently and consciously entertaining. By hypothesis, however, he is in no position to produce a knowledgeable first-person judgment of that sort.[10] Thus, the transparency of mental content would fail in this scenario. Needless to say, it would also fail in relevantly similar scenarios run for pairs of natural-kind terms/concepts and even of *non*-natural-kind ones such as 'hotdog'/'frankfurter', 'ketchup'/'catsup', 'computer'/'ordinateur', 'pencil'/'crayon', and so on. Since, by hypothesis, Pierre would meet the conditions for being a suitable addressee of quasi-Moorean questions in those cases, his failed comparative judgments of content would seem to lead us straight to the conclusion that no transparency thesis can succeed—and thus neither can OQA_1, our Moorean argument presupposing one such thesis.

Yet more than this will be needed to defeat OQA_1. For, clearly, that would require that Pierre-style scenarios be compelling for propositional attitude contents of the sort relevant to the naturalistic analyses targeted by that argument, which trade on alleged content equivalences between value terms and purely descriptive terms. But could any intuition about the failure of transparency fueled by Pierre-style scenarios also be plausible in the case of propositional-attitude contents featuring predicates relevant to naturalistic analyses? It may be shown that there is no compelling reason in the offing for thinking that it could. In fact, there is considerable agreement that such scenarios are not compelling across the board for general terms/concepts of any type whatsoever. As Kripke (1979, 264–5) notes:

At the moment, at least, it seems to me that Pierre, if he learns English and French separately, without learning a translation manual between them, must conclude, if he reflects enough, that 'doctor' and 'medicin' and 'heureux' and 'happy' are synonymous, or at any rate, coextensive; any potential paradox of the present kind [Pierre-style scenarios] for these word pairs is thus blocked.

Here Kripke seems himself to be upholding the transparency of content for terms of the sort he cites: competent users of such pairs ought to be able to tell by reflection alone whether the predicates involved are content equivalent. Fregeans would, of course, agree that in these cases (and many others) the transparency of the entertained contents remains unchallenged. Even direct-reference theorists such as Putnam (1970)

---

[10] This case also shows that in Pierre-style scenarios nothing hinges on translation.

would concede Kripke's claim, offering among salient counter-examples to Pierre-style scenarios 'bachelor', 'sister', 'triangle', and other 'one-criterion' generalized terms, whose definability or analyticity has never been an issue for direct-reference semanticists and content externalists. It appears, then, that no matter which of the available semantic theories will turn out to be the end-of-the-day theory of content for general terms/concepts, there is current consensus that the transparency of mental content must be assumed for a great number of such terms/concepts.

We now seem to have a principled way of distinguishing propositional contents for which transparency could fail from those for which it couldn't. Such a criterion is simply *vulnerability to Pierre-style scenarios*. This would not only be accepted by some Fregeans but also beg no question against reasonable direct-reference semanticists and content externalists who are none the less willing to jettison an unqualified thesis of the transparency of mental content. Clearly, they could still maintain that transparency fails for externally determined propositional-attitude contents while it obtains for contents that are internally individuated. The former are of the sort vulnerable to Pierre-style scenarios; the latter are not.

To complete our defense of OQA_1, we next need to determine how the predicates at issue in naturalistic analyses compare with the predicates so far considered. Are they similar to Pierre-style-scenario-vulnerable general terms/concepts such as 'woodchuck' and 'water'—or to Pierre-style-scenario-resistant ones such as 'happy' and 'bachelor'? Clearly, what works for 'happy' also works for 'pleasant', and many other predicates featured on the right-hand side of naturalistic analyses. But once we agree that a term such as 'happy' or 'pleasant' resists Pierre-style scenarios, we are committed to holding that any value term that is content equivalent with it would likewise resist such scenarios.

That is, given the consensus that those scenarios are blocked in cases involving predicates such as 'happy' and 'bachelor', the alleged problem facing OQA_1 is resolved. For to say that 'happy'/'heureux', 'bachelor'/'unmmarried man', and the like are Pierre-style-scenario resistant is to say that the conceptual equivalence, or at least co-extensiveness, among the predicates in each pair is available upon reflection to any competent user of the pair. By analogy, Pierre-style scenarios are blocked in cases involving predicates in the two vocabularies at issue in the analyses of semantic naturalists. Although the purely descriptive predicate proposed on the right-hand side on any such analysis may, in fact, be a simple one such as 'happiness' or 'pleasure maximizing', the analysis could also feature a very complex predicate—perhaps of a disjunctive sort.[11] Either way, any correct claim about the content equivalence of

---

[11] A reductive naturalist of Jackson's persuasion may object to our casting of semantic analyses on the ground that they appear too simplistic. After all, they could feature on their right-hand side very complex disjunctions of purely descriptive terms. On this view, adequate naturalistic analyses

the terms featured in a naturalistic analysis ought to be available a priori to any rational thinker who is a competent user of those terms. Imagine Peter, a monolingual speaker of English who is both rational and a competent user of 'good' and 'pleasure-maximizing'. Peter is now considering a certain semantic naturalist claim to the effect that tokens of those terms instantiate the same semantic type. By analogy with the cases above ('happy'/'heureux', 'bachelor'/'unmarried man', etc.), we maintain that Peter ought to be able to settle this question just by thinking. If so, OQA_1 is in the clear, since predicates such as 'good' and 'pleasure-maximizing' are, after all, Pierre-style-scenario-resistant. *TMC*, the transparency thesis fueling that argument, remains unchallenged.

Yet it might still be thought that this line of reasoning is vulnerable to Frankena's (1939) objection against Moore's own argument: viz., that it begs the question against the reductionist program of semantic naturalists. But surely, just *who* is doing the question-begging is determined by where the burden of proof lies. Consider Peter again, who now is an avid fan of television's 'Jerry Springer Show', even though he does not really *like* the fact that he enjoys it. Although making fun of vulnerable people has considerable entertainment value, Peter thinks, it is achieved at a morally questionable price. Peter now sincerely asserts ' "The Jerry Springer Show" maximizes pleasure, but is not good.' Semantic naturalists willing to take Peter's tokens of 'good' and 'pleasure-maximizing' to be content equivalent would face a paradox. For they would be committed to denying at least one of the following: (1) that Peter is a competent speaker of English; (2) that he is sincere; or (3) that he is rational. Given that in common cases of this sort all three assumptions seem independently plausible, and that other equally common cases could be offered for equivalence claims involving different pairs of general terms in the two vocabularies of naturalistic analyses, there is room to argue that it is *the naturalist* who has the burden of proof. A mere rejection of the assumptions commonly made in light of such cases would simply beg the question. Furthermore, it counts against semantic reductive naturalism that, if this

---

are of the form, '*A* is right if and only if it has whatever [descriptive] property it is that plays the rightness role in mature folk morality'(1998, 151). This proposal is not, however, beyond dispute. For one thing, it attempts to ground the relevant analyses on *both* folk morality and meaning analysis. But there is room to ask, do such analyses depend on the a posteriori common-sense platitudes of a mature folk morality? Or are they rather a priori semantic equivalences between non-rigid descriptions? These seem to pull in opposite directions. Of course, the appeal to folk morality requires a complex analysans in order to preserve the view from the objection that the platitudes of common sense are often false. At the same time, since this theorist's analyses purport to capture *meaning equivalences* in the two relevant vocabularies, those analyses ought to square well with the intuitions of competent users of the terms/sentences involved. But currently, they don't. Maybe the theorist is right in claiming that there will be a convergence in a *mature* folk morality. Yet why should we accept this futuristic claim, given a plausible version of the open question argument? The burden of proof seems to be on the semantic naturalist.

thesis were correct, then Peter's assertion should be as paradoxical as those of Kripke's Pierre, since belief ascription in Peter's case would also be in tension with ascribing rationality to him. But belief ascription here seems tension-free: Peter simply believes that 'The Jerry Springer Show' maximizes pleasure but that it is not good.

In the absence of a convincing response by semantic naturalists, we may conclude that if tokens of 'good' and 'pleasure-maximizing' were content equivalent, then a competent thinker of both predicates who reflected long enough ought to be able to tell whether they are content equivalent—or, at least, coextensive. The Pierre-scenario objection to OQA_1 (our Moorean argument against the semantic theses of some reductive naturalists) is thus blocked.

VI

Although OQA_1 meets all conditions needed to defeat semantic theses of reductive naturalists—namely, being a non-question-begging argument that can transmit by entailment the apriority of premises to the conclusion that no such thesis is true—the argument falls short of refuting metaphysical theses of reductive naturalists.[12] Yet OQA_1 provides non-conclusive reasons for a view on the semantic properties of the relevant predicates that support OQA_2, our argument against metaphysical theses of reductive naturalists. OQA_2 starts out by maintaining that, given metaphysical reductive naturalism (MRN), some predicates in the two relevant vocabularies—say, 'good' and 'pleasure-maximizing'—must be coextensional. But the reasons brought about by our defense of OQA_1 suggest that such predicates qualify for being Pierre-style scenario resistant. This entails that any alleged co-extensiveness between them must be transparent to competent users that consider those predicates, which does not seem to be the case.

In order to defend the thesis that terms such as 'good' and 'pleasure-maximizing' are coextensive even when their coextensiveness fails to be transparent, the ethical naturalist holding MRN might argue that terms of these two sorts are similar in their semantic properties to pairs of coextensive natural-kind terms such as 'woodchuck' and 'groundhog', or 'water' and 'H_2O'. Such a claim would, however, commit that ethical naturalist to an implausible view of identity statements entailed by his attempted factual analyses—since, arguably, those statements should then have the same modal status as identifications in science involving natural-kind terms,

---

[12] The objection that the open question argument fails as a valid argument against metaphysical varieties of ethical naturalism was made independently by Harman (1977) and Putnam (1981). See Brink (1989, 2001) for a view on the a semantic properties of the relevant predicates that is vulnerable to the objections raised in this section.

in both their metaphysical and epistemic features. That is, if true, they should be necessarily so. At the same time, they should be epistemically contingent: i.e., knowable only *a posteriori*. But it is implausible that the identity statements of this ethical naturalist do have such a modal status. Here is the argument:

1 Given *MRN*, identity statements involving a value term and a purely descriptive term have the modal profile of theoretical identifications involving two natural-kind terms.

2 But such identity statements lack the modal profile of theoretical identifications involving two natural-kind terms.

Therefore,

3 *MRN* is false.

The theoretical identifications in science relevant to this argument are those containing two coextensional natural-kind terms. Whether or not terms of this sort turn out to be rigid designators is a controversial matter that falls beyond our concern here. For the purpose at hand, it suffices to note that they do seem *essentialist* in the sense that they appear to pick out structural properties of the substances and species falling within their extensions—often counted as hidden essences since they lie beyond the phenomenal qualities of those substances and species (Soames 2002). That a certain general term qualifies for being essentialist is shown by some well-known counterfactual scenarios such as Twin Earth cases. Given those cases, in any possible world where water exists, it is H_2O. Thus, the proposition expressed by instances of 'Water is H_2O' is not only true but necessarily so, in spite of any appearance of metaphysical contingency. Consistent with this intuition is the presumption that 'Water might not have been H_2O', 'Woodchucks might not have been groundhogs', and the like are self-contradictory. On the other hand, no such presumption arises when at least one of the general terms featured in the identity statement is not essentialist, as illustrated by 'Water might not have been the stuff flowing in our lakes and rivers'. Furthermore, the scenarios invoked to show the necessity of theoretical identifications in science also explain away any appearance of contingency by suggesting that it would stem from the epistemic possibility of conceiving structurally different substances and species which none the less have exactly the same phenomenal qualities.

Now compare 'Right is what maximizes pleasure', 'Good is what we desire to desire', or any other more complex identity statement of the sort that would have to be true if certain factual analyses of reductive naturalists were correct. None of these would seem to have the modal profile of the theoretical identifications just discussed—for, if they had it, then there would be compelling counter-factual scenarios supporting this. But such scenarios are not forthcoming. It is *not* clearly self-contradictory to say that an action is right even though it fails to maximize pleasure, or good even though it doesn't coincide with what we desire to desire. Plainly, such judgments are by no means incoherent—as can be seen, for example, from the unresolved conflicts in normative ethics between the fundamental moral intuitions of consequentialism, on the one hand, and of deontology on the other. But this strongly suggests that the predicates involved in those judgments are not of the essentialist sort needed to make the ethical naturalist's statements of identity relevantly analogous to theoretical identifications in science. If we are right, then there are good grounds to reject the reductive analyses of some metaphysical naturalists. The onus is now on them to show why we should accept a view that seems prima facie very implausible.

This objection generalizes, since at least in principle the same reasoning supporting that predicates such as 'good' and 'pleasure maximizing' are not coextensive could be offered for any other attempted analysis of value properties in terms of natural properties. It seems then that metaphysical reductive naturalism is faced with a *reductio* that runs as follows:

OQA_2

1 Given *MRN*, a certain value predicate such as 'good' and a descriptive predicate such as 'pleasure maximizing' are coextensive.

2 If 'good' and 'pleasure maximizing' are coextensive, then competent users of 'good' and 'pleasure maximizing' ought to be able to determine upon reflection that these predicates are coextensive, unless they are semantically analogous to natural-kind predicates.

3 But neither are competent users of 'good' and 'pleasure maximizing' able to determine upon reflection that those predicates are coextensive nor are such predicates semantically analogous to natural-kind predicates.

Therefore,

4 'Good' and 'pleasure maximizing' are not coextensive.

5 Steps (1) through (3) can be iterated for each attempted factual analysis of a value predicate into purely descriptive predicates.

Therefore,

6 *MRN* is false.

VII

In the end, it is tempting to speculate about what Moore himself would have thought of our casting the dispute in these terms and trying to offer a qualified defense of his argument by reconstructing it in these two different ways. Although he was optimistic in his early writings about the open question argument against naturalism, he later expressed disappointment. In 'Is Goodness a Quality', a 1932 paper read to the Aristotelian Society, he had this to say about his attempts to show the indefinability of 'good':

> In *Principia* I asserted and proposed to prove that 'good' (and I think I sometimes, though perhaps not always, was using this word to mean the same as 'worth having for its own sake') was indefinable. But all the supposed proofs were certainly fallacious; they entirely failed to prove that 'worth having for its own sake' is indefinable.   (Moore 1959, 98)

While it is true that his own *OQA* appears not to succeed as a proof of the indefinability of 'good', Moore was plainly up to more than that in the first chapter of *Principia*. Relevant to our concern here have been two other claims that Moore-inspired arguments have been shown to support: the rejection of reductive naturalism; and the defense of the autonomy of ethics. Despite Moore's own later judgment and those of many critics, we believe that properly construed open question arguments can succeed on these counts.

Works Cited

Baldwin, T., *G. E. Moore* (London: Routledge, 1990).

Ball, S. W., 'Reductionism in Ethics and Science: A Contemporary Look at G. E. Moore's Open Question Argument', *American Philosophical Quarterly*, 25 (1988), 198–201.

—— 'Linguistic Intuitions and Varieties of Naturalism', *Philosophy and Phenomenological Research*, 51/1 (March 1991), 1–38.

Bentham, J., *Introduction to the Principles of Morals and Legislation* [1789] (Buffalo, NY: Prometheus Books, 1988).

Boghossian, P., 'The Transparency of Mental Content', *Philosophical Perspectives*, 8 (1994), 33–50.

Brink, D. O., *Moral Realism and the Foundations of Ethics* (Cambridge: Cambridge University Press, 1989).

—— 'Realism, Naturalism, and Moral Semantics', *Social Philosophy and Policy*, 18 (2001), 154–76.

Burge, T., 'Our Entitlement to Self-Knowledge', *Proceedings of the Aristotelian Society*, 96 (1996), 91–116.

—— 'Reason and the First Person', C. Wright, B. C. Smith, and C. Macdonald (eds.), *Knowing Our Own Minds* (Oxford: Oxford University Press, 1998), 243–70.

Darwall, S, 'How Should Ethics Relate to (the Rest of) Philosophy? Moore's Legacy' in T. Horgan and M. Timmons (eds.), *Metaethics after Moore* (Oxford: Clarendon Press, 2006), 17–37.

Davidson, D., 'What is Present to the Mind?', *Philosophical Issues*, 1 (1991), (197–213).

Frankena, W. K., 'The Naturalistic Fallacy', *Mind*, 48 (1939), 464–77.

—— *Ethics* (Englewood Cliffs, NJ: Prentice-Hall, 1963).

Harman, G., *The Nature of Morality.* (New York: Oxford University Press, 1977).

Hutchinson, B., *G. E. Moore's Ethical Theory: Resistance and Reconciliation* (Cambridge: Cambridge University Press, 2001).

Jackson, F., *From Metaphysics to Ethics: A Defence of Conceptual Analysis* (Oxford: Clarendon Press, 1998).

_____ 'Cognitivism, A Priori Deduction, and Moore', *Ethics*, 113/3 (April 2003), 557–75.

Katz, J., *Sense, Reference, and Philosophy* (New York: Oxford University Press, 2004).

Kripke, S., 'A Puzzle about Belief', in A. Margalit (ed.), *Meaning and Use* (Dordrecht, The Netherlands: Reidel, 1979), 239–83.

Mackie, J. L., 'Possibilities of Analysis', in *Truth, Probability, and Paradox: Studies in Philosophical Logic* (Oxford: Clarendon Press, 1973), 1–16.

Moore, G. E., *Principia Ethica* [1903], rev. edn. (Cambridge: Cambridge University Press, 1993).

_____ 'The Conception of Intrinsic Value', in *Philosophical Studies* (London: Routledge & Kegan Paul, 1922), 253–75.

_____ 'A Reply to my Critics', in *The Philosophy of G. E. Moore,* ed. by P. A. Schilpp (Lasalle, Ill.: Open Court, 1942), 533–677.

_____ 'Is Goodness a Quality', in *Philosophical Papers* (London: George Allen & Unwin, 1959), 89–101.

_____ *Lectures on Philosophy*, ed. by C. Lewy (London: George Allen & Unwin, 1966).

Perry, R. B., *General Theory of Value* (Cambridge, Mass.: Harvard University Press, 1926).

Prior, A. N., *Logic and the Basis of Ethics* (Oxford: Clarendon Press, 1949).

Putnam, H., 'Is Semantics Possible?' [1970], in *Mind, Language And Reality: Philosophical Papers* 2 (Cambridge: Cambridge University Press, 1975), 139–52.

_____ 'Meaning and Reference', *Journal of Philosophy*, 70/79 (1973), 699–711.

_____ *Reason, Truth and History* (Cambridge: Cambridge University Press, 1981).

Scanlon, T. M., *What We Owe to Each Other* (Cambridge, Mass.: Harvard University Press, 1998).

Shafer-Landau, R., *Moral Realism: A Defence* (Oxford: Clarendon Press, 2003).

Snare, F., 'The Open Question as Linguistic Test', *Ratio*, 17 (1975), 123–9.

Soames, S., *Beyond Rigidity: The Unfinished Semantic Agenda of Naming and Necessity* (New York: Oxford University Press, 2002).

Strandberg, C., 'In Defence of the Open Question Argument', *The Journal of Ethics*, 8 (2004), 179–96.

Stratton-Lake, P. (ed.), *Ethical Intuitionism: Re-evaluations* (Oxford: Clarendon Press, 2002).

Sylvester, R., *The Moral Philosophy of G. E. Moore* (Philadelphia, Pa.: Temple University Press, 1990).

Vendler, Z., *Res Cogitans* (Ithaca, NY: Cornell University Press, 1972).

White, A., *G. E. Moore: A Critical Exposition* (Oxford: Basil Blackwell, 1958).

14

Non-naturalism

Robert Shaver

Non-naturalism has a musty reputation, redolent of Oxbridge dons delivering the opinions of the 'best and most enlightened of men' who perceive goodness just as mortals perceive yellowness (Ross 1939, 172; also Ross 1988, 41). In histories, it is noted chiefly as the theory so unacceptable that it inspired the non-cognitivists.

Traditionally, non-naturalism faces two sorts of objection.[1] The first is that non-naturalists picture 'a realm of moral qualities ... floating, as it were, quite free from anything else whatever' (Warnock 1967, 14).[2] A 'new world is revealed for our inspection ... mapped and described in elaborate detail ... [E]thics becomes the geography of a special world out of space and time' (Nowell-Smith 1954, 41). The non-naturalist claims to 'retur[n] like an explorer with tales from the kingdom of values' (Ayer 1954, 242). When Stevenson considers the objection to non-cognitivism that when we ask 'Is x good?' we ask for a 'unique sort of truth ... a truth which must be apprehended *a priori*', he replies by asking 'What is this truth to be *about*? For I recollect no Platonic Idea ... I find no indefinable property, nor do I know what to look for' (1937, 30). He aims to avoid 'multiplying entities beyond necessity' and the 'peculiar and occult subject matter' introduced by Moore (Stevenson 1944, 109, 108). Frankena sums up these worries: non-naturalists 'must believe in simple indefinable properties, properties that are of a peculiar non-natural or normative sort, a priori or nonempirical concepts, intuition, and self-evident or synthetic necessary propositions. All of these beliefs are hard to defend' (1973, 103). Call

---

[1] For a similar presentation of non-naturalism as subject to these two objections, see Philip Stratton-Lake's Introduction in P. Stratton-Lake (ed.), *Ethical Intuitionism* (Oxford: Clarendon, 2002), 1. I leave aside a third objection, that non-naturalism cannot properly explain moral motivation.

[2] For the definitive reply to this charge, see H. H. Cox, 'Warnock on Moore', *Mind*, 79 (1970), 265–7.

this the extravagance objection: non-naturalism has an extravagant ontology and epistemology.

The second objection is that 'the theory, appraised as a contribution to philosophy, seems deliberately, almost perversely, to answer no questions, to throw no light on any problem. One might almost say that the doctrine actually consists in a protracted denial that there is anything of the slightest importance to be said' (Warnock 1967, 12–13). Non-naturalism is 'unenlightening' since ' "X has the characteristic of obligatoriness" is just another way of saying "I ought to do X" ' (Nowell-Smith 1954, 43). '[A]ll intuitionist writers suffer from one difficulty: they are, on their own view, telling us only what we all know already' (MacIntyre 1966, 254).[3] Call this the cheapness objection: non-naturalism contributes nothing.

I shall spend most of the paper trying to rebut the extravagance objection. I close with thoughts on cheapness.

Three preliminaries:

First, following the (misleading) custom, I lump 'metaphysical' or supernatural analyses with 'naturalistic' ones.[4]

Second, I shall not consider how 'right' and 'good' are related or the question of exactly which moral concepts evade naturalistic analysis.

Third, I take Moore, Ross, Broad, and Ewing to be the core non-naturalists.[5]

I

Before considering the objections, I shall sketch two bits of non-naturalism: statements of the point of arguing for non-naturalism and some of the arguments themselves.

Moore writes that 'the main object of Ethics, as a systematic science, is to give correct *reasons* for thinking that this or that is good' (Moore 1903, 6). When he explains the importance of avoiding the naturalistic fallacy, he notes that those who make it give bad reasons for moral claims. '[I]f I am right, then nobody can foist upon us such an axiom as that "[p]leasure is the only good" or that "[t]he good is the desired" on the pretence that this is "the very meaning of the word" ' or by saying 'the very meaning of the word decides it' (Moore 1903, 7, 21). In *Ethics*, Moore writes that

---

[3] He adds '[t]hat they sometimes disagree about what it is that we all know already only makes them less boring at the cost of making them even less convincing.'

[4] For this usage, see C. D. Broad, *Five Types of Ethical Theory* (London: Routledge & Kegan Paul, 1930), 259.

[5] For Prichard, see n. 9. For difficulties in interpreting Broad, see Frankena's excellent 'Broad's Analysis of Ethical Terms', in P. A. Schilpp (ed.), *The Philosophy of C. D. Broad*, (New York: Tudor, 1959).

it is . . . very important that we should realize . . . that [subjectivist] views are false; because, if they were true, it would follow that we must take an entirely different view as to the whole nature of Ethics . . . from what has commonly been taken . . . [We] have assumed that the question whether an action *is* right cannot be completely settled by showing that any man or set of men have certain feelings or opinions about it   (1965, 54, 55, also 65, 96).

[T]he question [of naturalism] seems to me to be of great interest, because, if this is all, then it is evident that all the ideas with which Moral Philosophy is concerned are merely psychological ideas; and all moral rules, and statements as to what is intrinsically valuable, merely true or false psychological statements; so that the whole of Moral Philosophy and Ethics will be merely departments of Psychology   (Moore 1959b, 330).

Broad writes that

the importance of the question [of naturalism vs. non-naturalism] is this. If Non-naturalism is true, Ethics is an autonomous science with an irreducibly peculiar subject-matter . . . But, if Naturalism be true, Ethics is not an autonomous science; it is a department or an application of one or more of the natural or historical sciences   (1971c, 228).

Ewing writes that

[i]n order to establish ethical conclusions all that is needed will be to provide, in the case of theories which define ethical concepts in terms of the psychology of the speaker, a few introspections, and in the case of other naturalist theories a set of statistics about the actual feelings or desires of human beings, and these will *ipso facto* settle what is good or right beyond the possibility of contradiction. But this is not at all the method we follow in order to arrive at ethical conclusions   (1953, 90).

The main importance of [Moore's] contention [that goodness is a non-natural quality] lay in ruling out the views of all philosophers who . . . explained away the distinctive character of ethics and reduced it to a branch of some natural science, usually psychology, as you do if you analyse the fundamental concepts of ethics in terms of the concepts of that science. Like Kant, Moore insisted that ethics is autonomous, a branch of study with its own distinctive laws, not needed to apply for authority elsewhere . . . (Ewing 1966, 84).

Today, attention to arguments for non-naturalism is almost always confined to the open question argument.[6] But that is just one argument non-naturalists offer. All the non-naturalists stress that identifying moral concepts with naturalistic ones leads to problems—a loss of objectivity, or an inability to say things we think make

[6] For one example, see Michael Ridge, 'Moral Non-Naturalism', *The Stanford Encyclopedia of Philosophy* (Spring 2003), ed. Edward N. Zalta URL=<http//plato.stanford.edu/archives/Spr2003/entries/moral-non-naturalism/>

sense, or a moral epistemology we are convinced is wrong.[7] Broad writes, after stating various naturalistic analyses, that 'I do not know that there is any way of answering such contentions except by pointing out that they are not in accord with common sense and common usage and by asserting that the latter have a prima-facie claim to acceptance' (1952, 96). For example, 'x ought to be done' cannot be analysed as 'I like x' because different people uttering opposed ought-judgments can then both turn out to be right and because ought-claims could be confirmed (and only confirmed) by introspection (Moore 1965, 42, 46; 1959b, 333–6, 338; Ewing 1947, 5–10, 75; 1953, 84; Russell 1966, 20–1, 27; Ross 1988, 83, 95, 100; 1939, 23–4). 'x is good' cannot be analysed as 'x is approved of by the majority' because disputes over goodness could then be settled (and only settled) conclusively by doing a poll and because I sometimes judge that x is good while knowing that x is not approved of by the majority (Broad 1930, 114–15; Ewing 1947, 40–1, 59–62, 65, 67–8, 74; 1953, 83; 1966, 85; Moore 1966, 60; 1959b, 336; Ross 1988, 84; 1939, 25). 'x is wrong' cannot be analysed as 'God forbids x' because atheists can sensibly believe that some actions are wrong and because many believers think God forbids x because of x's wrongness (Moore 1966, 64–5; Ewing 1947, 106–9; 1953, 99–100). 'x is right' cannot be analysed as 'x best furthers human survival' or 'x is favoured by evolution' because many of our moral judgments are unconnected to conduciveness to survival and because, on some construals, it follows that whatever happens is right (Ewing 1947, 73; 1953, 88–9; 1942, 68–9; Carritt 1928, 33). Non-cognitivist analyses fail because moral disagreement is not merely disagreement in attitude; because asking for moral advice is not asking to be influenced or commanded; because moral claims keep their meaning even when, as in conditionals, the speaker is not expressing any attitude; because attributing truth values to moral claims seems necessary to our practice of judging some moral arguments to be valid or invalid; and because non-cognitivists cannot make room for moral judgments about the past or for weakness of will (Ewing 1947, 12–13; 1959, 10–19, 49; 1953, 106–8; 1973, 97, 103–4; Ross 1939, 33–4, 40–1; Moore 1968, 547).

Overall, non-naturalists have a certain conception of how moral inquiry proceeds (or, usually more clearly, how it does not proceed).[8] Their main goal is to protect the favoured procedures against changes that alternatives such as naturalism or non-cognitivism would bring.[9]

---

[7] By 'objectivity,' I mean, throughout, the view that apparently opposed moral judgments really are opposed, in the sense that both cannot be right.

[8] Ewing writes that 'it is often even more important to assert what something is not, that what it is, in order to eliminate mistakes' ('Recent Developments in British Ethical Thought', in C. A. Mace (ed.), *British Philosophy in the Mid-Century* (London: George Allen & Unwin, 1966), 83).

[9] Prichard is silent on the issues relevant to this paper. His focus is on threats from within moral theory (such as ideal utilitarianism) to what he takes to be the correct procedure, rather than on threats from metaethical positions such as naturalism or non-cognitivism.

II

I turn to ontological problems. I shall argue that (2.1) an extravagant ontology does not follow from the standard non-naturalist arguments; (2.2) it is unclear whether the non-naturalists had an extravagant ontology; and (2.3) an extravagant ontology is not required by the general non-naturalist project.

(2.1) It is often objected to non-naturalism that arguments to show that talk of goodness cannot be analyzed as talk of natural properties do not show that ascriptions of goodness commit us to adding non-natural properties to our ontology. There is Cornell: just as 'water' is not synonymous with 'H₂O' but water and H₂O are the same stuff, 'good' is not synonymous with some description of a natural property but goodness and some natural property are the same stuff.[10] Or there is Canberra: goodness is the natural property that fills the role specified by a priori truths that involve goodness and cannot, because these truths largely concern other normative concepts, be given a non-normative analysis.[11] If, however, non-naturalists have no wish to add non-natural properties to our ontology, this is not an objection, but rather a way of showing how non-naturalists can *avoid* ontological extravagance.

Indeed, it is hard to reconstruct an argument for an ontological view from the arguments the non-naturalists give. Of course, this in inconclusive—they might hold an ontological view without arguing for it, or falsely think arguments they give entail ontological conclusions. But these options are uncharitable, so it is worth showing the failure of the two careful attempts I know to give their arguments an ontological spin.

David Brink interprets non-naturalism as denying that moral properties are identical to, or constituted by, natural properties (1989, 160 n. 12, 162–4). Non-naturalists, he thinks, give (though did not 'clearly articulate') the following argument: there are no analytic connections between moral and natural properties; if moral properties were identical to, or constituted by, natural properties, this would entail a necessary connection between the moral and natural properties; all necessity is analytic; therefore moral properties are neither identical to, nor constituted by, natural properties (Brink 1989, 162–3, 165 n. 16).[12] He thinks that this reasoning

---

[10] See, e.g., Richard Boyd, 'How to be a Moral Realist,' in Geoffrey Sayre-McCord (ed.), *Essays on Moral Realism* (Ithaca: Cornell University Press, 1988); Peter Railton, 'Naturalism and Prescriptivity', *Social Philosophy and Policy*, 7 (1989), 151–74; David Brink, *Moral Realism and the Foundations of Ethics* (Cambridge: Cambridge University Press, 1989), 174–80.

[11] See esp. Frank Jackson and Philip Pettit, 'Moral Functionalism and Moral Motivation', *Philosophical Quarterly*, 45 (1995), 22–9.

[12] In a more recent paper, Brink continues to think that Moore wants an ontological conclusion, but thinks Moore might accept that moral properties are constituted by natural ones ('Realism, Naturalism, and Moral Semantics', *Social Philosophy and Policy* 18 (2001), 155–7, 161 n. 12). He again worries, however, that 'the intuitionist's reasons for accepting the semantic test of properties—that all necessity

is inconsistent with non-naturalist claims about supervenience (Brink 1989, 165 n. 16). But there is a different and fatal problem with ascribing this argument to the non-naturalists: they explicitly deny that all necessity is analytic. They think there are necessary, synthetic a priori truths. (Broad and Ewing both contribute to the general debate in epistemology over the synthetic a priori).[13] Indeed, this is one of the main tenets that divides them from their non-cognitivist opponents.[14] If non-naturalists did want ontological conclusions, they would need a different argument.

Philip Stratton-Lake suggests such an argument. He concedes that examples such as water and H$_2$O show that no ontological conclusion need follow from denying an analysis. But he argues that the concept of goodness differs from the concept of water in two ways. First, the concept of water is 'incomplete' in that it picks out surface features such as being clear and odourless, without saying anything about the nature of what explains these features. Second, the concept of water is a concept of a natural property. These two features of the concept of water make empirical investigation rather than a priori reflection suited for discovering its nature. This allows the possibility that, although a priori reflection does not show that water and H$_2$O are the same property, empirical investigation can show this. The concept of goodness is not incomplete: 'When we think of something as good, we do not think of it merely as ... picking out certain surface properties the property of goodness has, but think of it as having a distinctive characteristic' (Stratton-Lake 2002, 10).[15] Nor, given the open question argument, is the concept of goodness the concept of a natural

is analytic—may also undermine the claim that moral properties ... strongly supervene on, and are constituted by, natural properties' (161, n. 12). Like Brink, Russ Shafer-Landau thinks Moore moves from the open question argument to an ontological conclusion, but he does not give Brink's detailed reconstruction. Again like Brink, he notes that 'Moore did not explicitly defend this inference' (Russ Shafer-Landau, *Moral Realism* (Oxford: Clarendon, 2003), 57).

[13] See, e.g., A. C. Ewing, *The Fundamental Questions of Philosophy* (London: Routledge & Kegan Paul, 1951), 33–4; C. D. Broad, 'Are There Synthetic a Priori Truths?', *Proceedings of the Aristotelian Society*, Supp. 15 (1936).

[14] See, e.g., C. D. Broad, 'Is "Goodness" a Name of a Simple Non-Natural Quality?', 122–3, 'Some Reflections on Moral-Sense Theories in Ethics', 210–11, 'A Reply to My Critics', 306, 309–10, all in Broad, *Broad's Critical Essays in Moral Philosophy*, ed. David Cheney (London: George Allen & Unwin, 1971); W. D. Ross, *Foundations of Ethics* (Oxford: Clarendon, 1939), 35–8; or the reactions to Ewing by W. K. Frankena ('Ewing's Case Against Naturalistic Theories of Value', *Philosophical Review*, 59 (1948), 482); and Richard Robinson (Review of *The Definition of Good*, *Review of Metaphysics*, 1 (1948), 106–7, 112). Richard Brandt's criticisms of non-naturalism in *Ethical Theory* (Englewood Cliffs: Prentice-Hall, 1959) centre on finding examples of synthetic a priori claims in ethics (190, 197–201); J. D. Mabbott and H. J. McCloskey defend non-naturalism by defending the synthetic a priori (Mabbott, *An Introduction to Ethics* (London: Hutchinson, 1966), 92–5; McCloskey, *Meta-ethics and Normative Ethics* (The Hague: Martinus Nijhoff, 1969), 136–42).

[15] For a very similar argument, see Eric Gampel, 'A Defense of the Autonomy of Ethics: Why Value is Not Like Water', *Canadian Journal of Philosophy*, 26 (1996), 195–201.

property. As a result, there is no reason to think that empirical investigation is suited to discovering the nature of goodness, and so no reason to think that the property of goodness can be shown to be identical to some natural property.

I think this argument fails for two reasons. First, one can hold that the concept of goodness is incomplete. The 'surface features' it picks out are given by the a priori truths it enters into (as in the Canberra story). Broad even gives an account resembling this—the 'descriptive theory'—as 'the most satisfactory account of what I mean [by] "This is good."' The descriptive theory claims that 'x is good' means '[t]here is one and only one characteristic or set of characteristics whose presence in any object that I contemplate is necessary to make me contemplate it with approval, and x has that characteristic' (Broad 1985, 282, 283).[16] Here the concept of goodness is incomplete in that it points toward, but does not give, this characteristic.

Second, and more importantly, Stratton-Lake assumes that if there is no analysis of goodness in natural terms, and no empirical investigation, then there is no reason to think that, say, 'good' and 'maximizes happiness' refer to the same property. But there is a third alternative: a priori, but not analytic, investigation might show that 'good' and 'maximizes happiness' refer to the same property. Since non-naturalists welcome the synthetic a priori, this is a very live option for them.

I conclude that non-naturalists are not committed to an ontological view by the arguments they give.

(2.2) I think it is very unclear what ontological picture Moore, Ross, Broad, and Ewing have in mind. They spend almost all of their time saying what moral claims do not mean. If they intend an ontological picture, it is surprising that they offer so little. Moore's open question argument is often taken to be the non-naturalist argument for a special ontology.[17] But when Moore gives the argument, he writes of what is 'before our minds', 'two different notions', or our 'state of mind', without drawing any ontological conclusion (1903, 16–17).[18] Moore's conclusions 'amount to this:

---

[16] In effect, Broad relies on a single a priori truth—that I approve of things I take to be good—whereas Canberra relies on many a priori truths.

[17] See, e.g., Gilbert Harman, *The Nature of Morality* (New York: Oxford, 1977). 19; Hilary Putnam, *Reason, Truth and History* (Cambridge: Cambridge University Press, 1981), 206–7; Ridge, 'Non-Naturalism', 2, 6; Nicholas Sturgeon, 'Moore on Ethical Naturalism', *Ethics*, 113 (2003), 533, 'Ethical Intuitionism and Ethical Naturalism', in Stratton-Lake, *Intuitionism*, 196; Shafer-Landau, *Realism*, 57; Brink, 'Semantics', 155–6, *Realism*, 152, 162–3. Brink does think Moore might be content with moral properties constituted by natural ones ('Semantics', 157, 161).

[18] For an interpretation of Moore as drawing no ontological conclusions from his attacks on naturalism, see Stephen W. Ball's unjustly neglected 'Reductionism in Ethics and Science: A Contemporary Look at G. E. Moore's Open-Question Argument', *American Philosophical Quarterly*, 25 (1988), esp. 198, 200, 201–3, 206. Allan Gibbard thinks Moore's arguments secure only non-natural concepts, rather than non-natural properties, but he does not think this is the conclusion Moore intended ('Knowing What

That propositions about the good are all of them synthetic and never analytic' (1903, 7). When (often more cautiously) Ross, Broad, and Ewing give the open question argument, they, too, write of the 'notion in our minds', what is 'present to our minds', or what one has 'in mind', without drawing ontological conclusions (Ross 1988, 92–3; 1939, 13, 259; Broad 1971a, 113–14; Ewing 1947, 43). More generally, when Broad contrasts naturalism and non-naturalism, the distinction is in terms of analysis—it is whether 'ethical characteristics *can* be analysed without remainder into non-ethical ones' (Broad 1930, 257).[19]

The point that the ontology is very unclear can be made in another way. It is common, and I think correct, to note that in *Principia* Moore does not distinguish between concepts and properties.[20] For example, after giving arguments concerning our 'notions', 'ideas', 'meanings', 'objects of thought', and what we 'have in mind', Moore writes that 'I have said that "good" itself is not a natural property' (1903, 41). This is not presented as an inference from the arguments, but as a restatement of their conclusion. That Moore failed to distinguish concepts and properties is usually noted to explain how Moore could, wrongly, draw ontological conclusions from the open question argument. But if Moore did not draw the distinction, there is another, more charitable, possibility: he intends to speak of concepts throughout.[21] If Moore's talk of non-natural properties is read as talk of non-natural concepts, the open question argument does not fail in (one of) the ways in which it is taken to fail, and, as far as I can

to Do, Seeing What to Do', in Stratton-Lake, *Intuitionism*, 212, 216–17, 221; *Thinking How to Live* (Cambridge: Harvard University Press, 2003), ch. 2).

[19] For the same understanding, see Brandt's *Ethical Theory* chapter on non-naturalism.

[20] See, e.g., Putnam, *Reason*, 207. Part of the problem is that there is no easy way to signal talk of concepts (hence, recently, conventions such as using capital letters for concepts). Stratton-Lake thinks Moore and Ross did distinguish between concepts and properties, but his argument for this is not reassuring. He notes that they distinguish between 'an elucidation of the meaning of words and an account of the nature of the world with their distinction between proper verbal definitions and definitions of the sort they are interested in (i.e., metaphysical ones). A proper verbal definition of 'good' is simply an account of how most people use the word, whereas a metaphysical definition is one that tells us the nature of the thing of which the concept is a concept.' But Stratton-Lake admits that '[t]his is not quite the distinction between an analysis of a concept and an account of the nature of a corresponding property' ('Introduction', 9). And, indeed, it seems quite different: the intended distinction seems to be between a dictionary definition and what came to be called an 'analysis'. Thus, for example, in the pages Stratton-Lake refers to in Ross, Ross begins by writing that '[t]he purpose of this inquiry is to examine the nature, relations, and implications of three conceptions . . .' He continues by noting that 'general usage' is not decisive for his project 'where we are discussing the *meaning* of "right." ' That discussion is then pursued by arguing that ' "right" does not mean the same as "morally good"; and we can test this by trying to substitute one for the other' (W. D. Ross, *The Right and the Good* (Indianapolis: Hackett, 1988), 1–3).

[21] This is also suggested by Ball, 'Reductionism', 202 and (roughly) by Donald Regan, 'How to Be a Moorean', *Ethics*, 113 (2003), 652.

see, Moore loses nothing of worth to him. For example, he does not lose his arguments against naturalism, given that he construes naturalists as offering analyses.[22]

Here are three textual objections. The first can be met; the others are more problematic.

(a) In the unpublished preface to a revised edition of *Principia*, Moore says repeatedly that his point in *Principia* was that the predicate 'good' is not identical to any natural predicate or property.[23] *Principia*'s denial of an analysis is, he thinks, not so important. But the contrast Moore draws is not between ontology and analysis. The reasons for downplaying the denial of an analysis are that showing that 'good' cannot be analyzed (a) rules out a (possibly unobjectionable) analysis of 'good' in terms of other moral terms, (b) (objectionably) allows 'good' to be identical to an unanalyzable natural predicate or property, and (c) does not imply what Moore takes to be the most important thing to say, namely that goodness is a property 'which depends only on the intrinsic nature of states of things which possess it' (Moore 1993, 13–14, 6, 16). It remains important to claim that 'good' cannot be analysed '*in one particular way*,' namely, in terms of natural properties (Moore 1993, 14). And since the preface does not give an argument for thinking that 'good' is not identical to any natural predicates or properties, the most plausible reading is that Moore still relies on the arguments given before the preface, in *Ethics*, and around the time of the preface, in 'The Nature of Moral Philosophy', that aim to show that 'good' cannot be analyzed in terms of natural predicates or properties.[24] If he then inferred that 'good' is not identical to any natural property, he would be hasty. But if the denial of identity merely notes that the concepts are not identical, then it does follow from the arguments against an analysis in terms of natural properties.

(b) On my interpretation, Moore denies that goodness is a natural concept but not that goodness is a natural property. This requires a distinction between the natural and the non-natural. Moore makes various suggestions (always put in terms of properties). Sometimes, the suggestion raises no problem for my interpretation. For example, Moore suggests that a natural property is one 'with which it is the business of the natural sciences or of Psychology to deal' (1993, 13; also 1903, 40). To say that goodness is not dealt with by the natural sciences could be read as saying that the natural sciences

---

[22] See, e.g., G. E. Moore, *Principia Ethica* (Cambridge: Cambridge University Press, 1903), 37–8, 39–40, 41, 59.

[23] Later in the preface, Moore substitutes for this statement of his point a 'slightly different proposition' (G. E. Moore, 'Preface to the Second Edition', in Moore, *Principia Ethica*, revised edn., ed. Thomas Baldwin (Cambridge: Cambridge University Press, 1993), 21). His elaboration of this version of the point is incomplete in the preface and better developed in 'The Conception of Intrinsic Value' and in the Replies, so I leave it aside here.

[24] 'The Nature of Moral Philosophy' was written in 1921; Baldwin dates the preface as probably 1921 as well (Baldwin, 'Introduction' to his 1993 edition of *Principia*, x).

do not use the concept of goodness. It would not follow that goodness is a property over and above those properties dealt with by the natural sciences.[25] Unfortunately, Moore sometimes suggests different accounts of the natural/non-natural distinction. In *Principia*, his official account is that natural properties can exist in time by themselves, whereas non-natural properties cannot (Moore 1903, 41). Here, where the distinction is not between two ways of describing things, but rather between two different things, it seems that a non-natural concept must be a concept of a non-natural property, and being a non-natural property excludes being a natural property. Moore came to see that this account was 'utterly silly and preposterous', 'hopelessly confused' (1968, 582; 1993, 13)[26] But he did not recant it *because* it implied an ontological view, and that he gave it in the first place shows a willingness, if perhaps unreflective, to make ontological claims.

(c) In Ewing's *The Definition of Good*, as in Moore, Ross, and Broad, the issue is what we have 'in mind' or 'mean'. The issue is whether there is 'any concept different from those of the natural sciences'; 'I am committed to holding that there is at least one indefinable ethical term' (Ewing 1947, 42-5). Ewing wants 'only to exclude the possibility of reducing the central concepts of ethics to non-ethical terms'. 'All I am denying is that [naturalistic] statements could exhaust the meaning of the terms "good" or "ought"' (Ewing 1947, 48). In *Ethics*, he writes that '[i]n denying naturalism Moore . . . merely meant to point out the difference between good and the concepts belonging to psychology or to any other natural science' (Ewing 1953, 82). Most importantly, when Ewing considers objections to his view, they are always objections to indefinable or non-empirical concepts, rather than to any ontological picture (1953, 51–6). But (alas) sometimes he suggests ontology: the issue is whether there is 'a different property'; colours might be correlated with wave-lengths 'but this would not commit one to saying that the colour as seen was just the wave-length' (Ewing 1947, 42, 47). And sometimes he switches freely between 'concept' and 'property': 'a simple property or concept'; there is 'at least one indefinable concept of ethics. We are not dealing with a property that . . .'; it 'would not follow that "good" just *meant* "accompanied by this brain-modification" or that goodness *was identical with* the property of being accompanied by it' (Ewing 1947, 45, 48).[27]

Ewing is clearer in later work. The one detailed positive account of non-naturalism, given by Ewing in *Second Thoughts in Moral Philosophy*, is anxious to avoid a special

---

[25] For the same point, see Sturgeon, 'Moore', 552. Sturgeon gives a very useful account of Moore's suggestions for drawing the natural/non-natural distinction.

[26] For arguments against various proposals that invoke some intrinsic property of natural things, see Shafer-Landau, *Realism*, 58–9.

[27] A similar ambiguity afflicts Broad's use of 'characteristic'. For example, when Broad sums up his own view in *Five Types of Ethical Theory* (London: Routledge & Kegan Paul, 1930), 281, 'characteristic' seems best glossed in terms of concepts, but it is hard to read all of 'Is "Goodness"?' this way.

ontology. Ewing admits that once he, along with Moore and Ross, held that moral claims describe non-natural properties or relations (1959, 50; 1973, 101−2, 193−6).[28] But he argues that this is both mistaken and inessential to non-naturalism. The crucial non-naturalist claim is that concepts such as 'good' and 'right' cannot be replaced by purely empirical concepts (Ewing 1959, 50−5, 69, 76−7, 83, 96; 1973, 96, 101, 193−6). 'X is right' can be true, and not analyzable as (say) 'I like x', without there being an independent property of rightness. One might deny this on the ground that all true claims are made true on the model of 'x is round': it is made true by the roundness existing as a property of x. But not all true claims work this way. For example, some counter-factuals are true, but are not made true by separate counter-factual facts. They are made true by the actual world, but are not identical to claims about the actual world. The same, Ewing thinks, is plausible for 'right' (1959, 42−7, 53−5, 60, 63, 64, 100, 116, 118; 1973, 107, 194, 197).

This picture is not idiosyncratic to Ewing. He credits Raphael with the distinction between properties and concepts. Raphael writes that '[i]f it be true that ethical terms cannot be satisfactorily replaced by non-ethical to serve the purposes in fact served by ethical language, this does not necessarily imply that ethical terms stand for objects or characteristics that could not, in a different context, be correctly described by non-ethical terms' (Raphael 1955, 36; also 42−3).[29] The roots of the picture may lie in Moore. Ewing notes that both he and Moore claim that 'goodness is not part of the description of anything'. He adds that Moore 'probably . . . did not realize anything like the full implications of the admission' (Ewing 1959, 51 n.). Moore's claim has sometimes been cited as evidence of incipient non-cognitivism; expressing an attitude seems the obvious alternative to describing.[30] But Ewing's gloss on 'not a description' as 'not describing some further property' suggests another reading. An ascription of goodness might fail to be a description of the actual world without failing to take propositional form. This is indeed the view Moore, in his final statement on these issues, sees as the alternative to non-cognitivism. He supposes that, if one rejects non-cognitivism, one must explain the apparent difference in kind between goodness and (natural) properties such as roundness. His explanation is that '[p]roperties which

---

[28] One might take this to be definitive evidence that Ewing, at least, held a special ontology. But even in the earlier *The Definition of Good* (New York: Macmillan, 1947), he writes that '[t]here is obviously a sense in which one could give a complete description of something without saying whether it was good or bad, which fact shows goodness to be something different from an ordinary quality of the thing which is pronounced good . . . [F]ittingness is . . . not a part of [the thing's] factual nature' (200−1).

[29] Raphael does think, however, that non-naturalists have wrongly made this inference (D. D. Raphael, *Moral Judgment* (London: Allen & Unwin, 1955), 35, 43).

[30] For the charge of incipient non-cognitivism, see C. D. Broad, 'G. E. Moore's Latest Published Views on Ethics', in *Critical Essays*, 327−8; and Stephen Darwall, 'Internalism and Agency', *Philosophical Perspectives*, 6 (1992), 160−1.

are intrinsic properties, but *not* natural ones, are distinguished from natural intrinsic properties, by the fact that, in ascribing a property of the former kind to a thing, you are not describing it *at all*, whereas, in ascribing a property of the latter kind to a thing, you are always describing it *to some extent*' (Moore 1968, 591; also Moore 1959a, 274). Moore combines, then, the view that attributions of goodness are propositions and the view that ascribing goodness is not describing. Unfortunately, unlike Ewing, he does not flesh this out. He also seems willing to concede that his view that value is intrinsic commits him to what his opponents would describe as 'the erecting into a "metaphysical" entity of what is really susceptible of a simple naturalistic explanation' (Moore 1959a, 258). That is, again unlike Ewing, he does not take steps to avoid ontological commitments—though such steps seem necessary to explain how, absent non-cognitivism, an ascription of goodness can fail to be part of a description.

Overall, then, some non-naturalists sometimes say things that imply an ontological position, or confess that they once held such a position. But even in these earlier works, the position is idle, and, given the confusion between concepts and properties, perhaps unintended. As Ewing came to see, it is neither implied by arguments they give nor does its denial jeopardize their arguments against naturalism.

One result of my interpretation is that an alleged difference between Sidgwick and later non-naturalists is illusory.[31] Sidgwick is taken to be a rationalist: when I make a moral judgment, I am making a claim about what it is reasonable to do. Some think this makes him better off than later non-naturalists. Schneewind writes that Sidgwick lacks

a theory of the sort later put forward by Moore or Ross about the ontological status of what is known when we know that an act is right or good . . . [Sidgwick's] basic [normative] notion itself is not . . . a concept derived from perception of a unique non-natural property. It is the constraint imposed by reason, which in matters of theory is familiar enough through the laws of logic   (Schneewind 1977, 205, 222).[32]

But when one asks what point Sidgwick makes by analyzing moral claims in terms of reasons, the answer is that talk of 'reasons' marks just those features that later non-naturalists mark by talk of 'non-natural properties'. Sidgwick argues for rationalism by giving the arguments later non-naturalists give for non-natural properties: by

[31] For different arguments for the same conclusion, see Thomas Hurka, 'Moore in the Middle', *Ethics*, 113 (2003), 608–9.

[32] See also Roger Crisp, 'Sidgwick and the Boundaries of Intuitionism', in Stratton-Lake, *Intuitionism*, 59. For further criticism of the non-naturalists for adding properties rather than speaking of reasons, see Stephen E. Toulmin, *An Examination of the Place of Reason in Ethics* (Cambridge: Cambridge University Press, 1950), 23–8; Thomas Nagel, *The View from Nowhere* (New York: Oxford University Press, 1986), 144; T. M. Scanlon, *What We Owe to Each Other* (Cambridge: Belknap, 1998), 97; and Derek Parfit, 'Rationality and Reasons', in Dan Egonsson *et al.* (eds.), *Exploring Practical Philosophy: From Actions to Values*, (Aldershot: Ashgate, 2001), 19–20.

avoiding a naturalistic analysis, rationalism preserves objectivity, allows us to say things we want to say, and maintains a plausible moral epistemology (Sidgwick 1981, 26–32; 1889, 480–3; 1892, 89). If the later non-naturalists intend talk of 'non-natural properties' to secure these same goals, and do not add ontological claims, they do not differ from Sidgwick. (Not surprisingly, Broad and Ewing are friendly to rationalism.[33] No non-naturalist finds it a shortcoming of rationalism that it omits interposing a non-natural property between a thing's natural properties and the reasons these natural properties support. Ewing even offers this omission as an advantage of his view of 'good'.[34])

(2.3) I described the non-naturalists as arguing that identifying moral concepts with natural concepts leads to problems, particularly with objectivity and moral epistemology. This project is compatible with many ontological pictures. Provided the problems that come from identifying moral and natural concepts are avoided, the non-naturalist can admit that moral properties are realized by, or even identical to, natural properties.

A primary concern with avoiding these problems may also explain why Moore, Broad, and Ewing are tempted by, or sympathetic to, non-cognitivism (Moore 1968, 544, 546–7; Broad 1971a, 107–10; 1971b, 303–8; 1952, 100; Ewing 1959, 3, 33–7, 59; 1966, 95; 1973, 96, 102, 194). If making an ontological point really mattered to the non-naturalists, this would be bizarre. But if non-cognitivism could provide a credible account of objectivity—opposed moral claims really are opposed, though only in attitude—and of epistemology—say there are serious constraints on the justification of attitudes—the attraction makes sense.

One might object that an ontological difference between natural and moral properties is needed to explain why naturalistic analyses fail.[35] But since it is generally agreed that, say, 'water' cannot be analyzed as 'H_2O', there is no requirement that the explanation of a failure of analysis be ontological. And there are proposed explanations that bypass ontology. Brandt suggests that concepts taught by examples, without accompanying definitions, resist analysis (Brandt 1959, 159). Smith suggests that

---

[33] See A. C. Ewing, *Second Thoughts in Moral Philosophy* (New York: Macmillan, 1959), 17, 61, 63. Ewing thinks one needs a moral 'ought' in addition to the 'ought' of reasonableness, and it is this 'ought' that is used to define 'morally good'. But his argument turns on the ordinary prudential connotations of 'reasonable' and on the difference in force between 'reasonable' and 'obligatory', not on doubts about the tie between ought-judgments and reasons. See *Second*, 95–6, 111–14. For Broad, see Broad, 'Critical Notice of *An Examination of the Place of Reason in Ethics*', *Mind*, 61 (1952), 100–1.

[34] 'Certain characteristics are such that the fitting response to what possess them is a pro attitude, and that is all there is to it. We shall not be any better off if we interpolate an indefinable characteristic of goodness besides, for it is no easier to see that it follows directly from the nature of things that they are good than it is to see that it follows directly from their nature that they are fitting objects of a pro attitude' (Ewing, *Definition*, 172; also 157, 175, 201, *Second*, 52). See also Broad, 'Moral-Sense', 222.

[35] This is suggested in passing by Shafer-Landau (*Realism*, 66); and Sturgeon ('Intuitionism', 194).

naturalistic analyses fail because we learn one normative concept by learning, and seeing its connection to, many other normative concepts (Smith 1994, 55).[36]

I should add that one defender of non-naturalism, Russ Shafer-Landau, finds it important to defend the claim that moral properties are constituted by, and not identical to, natural properties. He takes the denial of identity to be definitive of non-naturalism. And constitution-but-not-identity does seem to be the view of many of the non-naturalists. Moore, for example, writes that 'if a thing is good ... then that it is so *follows* from the fact that it possesses certain natural intrinsic properties, which are such that from the fact that it is good it does *not follow* conversely that it has those properties' (Moore 1968, 588). Yet the constitution-but-not-identity view is separable from the project of avoiding the problems brought by a naturalistic analysis. It rests on substantive moral commitments shared by most, but not all, of the non-naturalists. Thus when Shafer-Landau argues for the constitution-but-not-identity view, he notes that a candidate natural property for rightness, such as maximizing happiness, (a) may not always be sufficient for rightness; (b) may not be the only way of making an action right; and (c) may be coextensive with rather than identical to rightness (Shafer-Landau 2003, 73–4). (c) is, of course, possible, but it is unclear why non-naturalists should care about distinguishing coextensiveness and identity when the issue is ontology rather than analysis. (a) and (b) follow from the ideal utilitarianism of Moore and Ewing or from Ross's theory of prima-facie duties, but not, say, from Sidgwick's utilitarianism. Moore concedes that, so far as his arguments against naturalism go, 'what we desire to desire' may be necessary and sufficient for goodness (1903, 16). Ross and Ewing allow that their attacks on analyzing 'right' or 'good' in terms of a single natural concept are separate from their (mainly anti-utilitarian) attacks on thinking there is a single necessary and sufficient condition for rightness or goodness (Ross 1939, 27–8, 57, 65; Ewing 1947, 47). This suggests that the constitution-but-not-identity view is best left optional.

III

I turn to epistemological problems concerning self-evidence and the synthetic a priori.

---

[36] Sturgeon's explanation of the autonomy of ethics might also be employed: moral claims cannot be inferred from (or analyzed by) non-moral ones, since any such inference relies on background moral assumptions—just as claims about unobservables cannot be inferred from claims about observables without reliance on background assumptions about unobservables. This explanation does not require an ontological difference between the two realms. (Sturgeon does argue that his explanation is unattractive if combined with a foundationalist epistemology, but I leave that aside here.) See Sturgeon, 'Intuitionism', 200–4.

Both non-naturalists and their critics often run together the thoughts that some moral claims are self-evident (knowable simply from understanding them) and that some are synthetic a priori. Rather than try to set out how these thoughts might be related, I shall (3.1) briefly consider why the non-naturalists held either view; (3.2) note that one epistemological criticism of non-naturalism turns on neither self-evidence nor the synthetic a priori, and that it fails; and (3.3) argue that non-naturalism is no worse off epistemically than naturalism. (There may, of course, be nothing wrong with self-evidence or the synthetic a priori. There has been excellent recent work by Robert Audi, Roger Crisp, Russ Shafer-Landau, and Philip Stratton-Lake defending self-evidence.[37])

(3.1) Broad argues that non-naturalists are committed to synthetic a priori knowledge.

Suppose that a person regards goodness as a non-natural characteristic, and admits that it is always dependent on the presence of certain natural characteristics that are good-making. Then, if he holds that the connection between a good-making characteristic and the goodness which it confers is *necessary*, he will be obliged to hold that there are *synthetically necessary* facts and that he knows some of them. He will therefore be obliged to admit that he can make *synthetically a priori* judgments   (Broad 1971a, 122−3; 1971d, 189).

Broad can be read in two ways. On the first, he concludes that the judgment is synthetic a priori because for a non-naturalist goodness is, as he has just argued, an 'a priori notion', in that it is 'not manifested in sensation or introspection' (Broad 1971a, 122). But elsewhere Broad notes that 'there can be empirical judgments which involve a priori concepts', such as 'friction *causes* heat' (Broad 1930, 266). So a second reading is more likely (and explains why Broad notes necessity): Broad assumes that necessary claims are known a priori.[38] But, if so, his argument for committing the non-naturalist to synthetic a priori claims fails, since we now think there can be a posteriori necessities.

There is, however, a better argument for non-naturalists to hold that moral knowledge is a priori. Non-naturalists try to protect what they take to be our ordinary practices of justifying moral claims. Where 'a priori' and 'a posteriori' mark the difference between performing thought experiments and systematizing common-sense morality, on the one hand, and taking polls, introspecting

---

[37] See Robert Audi, 'Intuitionism, Pluralism, and the Foundations of Ethics', in Walter Sinnott-Armstrong and Mark Timmons (eds.), *Moral Knowledge?* (New York: Oxford University Press, 1996); Crisp, 'Sidgwick'; Shafer-Landau, *Realism*, ch. 11; and Stratton-Lake, 'Introduction', 18−23. For a good earlier paper, see Caroline J. Simon, 'On Defending a Moral Synthetic *A Priori*', *Southern Journal of Philosophy*, 26 (1988), 217−33.

[38] For necessity as the explicit reason for attributing a priori connections to the non-naturalists, see Mabbott, *Introduction*, 92; or McCloskey, *Meta-ethics*, 96−7.

desires, and studying evolution, on the other, non-naturalists favour the a priori.[39]

Non-naturalists had two reasons for defending self-evidence. The first is that self-evident claims can block regress threats (Ewing 1947, 26; 1953, 120; 1959, 63–4). The second is that it simply seems true that some moral claims are self-evident. Broad, for example, suggests 'in any possible world painfulness would *pro tanto* make an experience bad' (1930, 282).[40] On the second suggestion, self-evidence is embraced, not because it is forced by other philosophical commitments, but rather again because, like a belief in objectivity, it is taken to be part of the ordinary moral practice non-naturalists try to protect. Whether either of these reasons is a good reason for embracing self-evidence depends on larger issues (such as the truth of foundationalism) that I leave aside here. Neither reason depends directly on denying a naturalistic analysis, so it is at least open for a non-naturalist, understood simply as one who denies such an analysis, to dispense with self-evidence.[41]

(3.2) One epistemological objection to non-naturalism does not target self-evidence or synthetic a priori claims. Consider some background. In defence of phenomenalism, Russell writes that '[v]erification consists always in the occurrence of an expected sense-datum . . . Now if an expected sense-datum constitutes a verification, what was asserted must have been about sense-data' (Russell 1926, 89). Ayer writes that 'we know that it must be possible to define material things in terms of sense-contents, because it is only by the occurrence of certain sense-contents that the existence of any material thing can ever be in the least degree verified' (Ayer 1952, 53). The epistemic principle is that claims put in one vocabulary can be evidence for claims in another vocabulary only if one vocabulary can be defined in terms of the other. This motivates not only phenomenalism, but similar analytic projects, such as replacing claims about the mental with claims about behaviour, or claims about unobservables with claims about observables.

In ethics, all sides agree that, if there can be evidence for a moral claim, this evidence consists in non-moral facts. No one thinks we have independent access to free-floating moral properties. Now say that claims put in one vocabulary can be evidence for claims in another vocabulary only if one vocabulary can be defined in terms of the other. It follows that either moral claims can be defined in non-moral terms or there

---

[39] Ewing does raise doubts about classifying moral judgments as synthetic a priori, but these doubts concern what 'synthetic a priori' suggests—'a priori' suggests that ethics is much like logic, and 'synthetic' suggests that ethical discoveries are 'discoveries of facts to be included in the description of the real'. Ewing agrees that moral judgments are neither analytic nor established merely by observation (*Second*, 70–1).

[40] See also, e.g., A. C. Ewing, *Ethics* (New York: Free Press, 1953), 121; Ross, *Right*, 29–30, *Foundations*, 320; McCloskey, *Meta-ethics*, 139–42.

[41] For an example of such a position, see Sturgeon, 'Intuitionism'.

cannot be evidence for moral claims. We must be naturalists or think, perhaps with the non-cognitivists, that there cannot be evidence for moral claims. This argument is used by Ayer and Strawson (to support non-cognitivism) (Ayer 1954, 236–7; Strawson 1949, 26–7).[42]

Before criticizing this argument, it is worth noting that it has a target. In *Principia*, Moore shockingly denies that there can be evidence for claims about what is intrinsically good. He thinks this follows from the indefinability of 'good' (Moore 1903, viii-ix, 77). This makes sense given acceptance of the epistemic principle: since claims about goodness cannot be replaced by claims in another vocabulary, nothing said in this other vocabulary can provide evidence.[43] (Moore's sympathy for the epistemic principle may also explain his attraction to phenomenalism.)

The problem with the argument is that the epistemic principle seems false. Ewing's example of counter-factuals again provides a good example: counter-factual claims cannot be translated into claims about the actual world, but claims about the actual world provide evidence for counter-factuals. Similarly, claims about behavior or observables count as evidence toward claims about mental states or unobservables, without the latter claims being translatable into the former. This objection to non-naturalism fails.

(3.3) It is hard to see how non-naturalism is epistemically disadvantaged. As Frankena argues, the naturalistic analysis that would remove subsequent epistemic difficulties is itself supported either by old-fashioned moral theorizing or by appeal to what we mean. In the former case, there is no epistemic advantage; naturalists are

---

[42] Ewing gives the analogy to phenomenalism and describes this as the 'chief motive' that leads people to naturalism (*Definition*, 54, also *Second*, 23–4). Unlike Moore, he is unsympathetic to phenomenalism (see, e.g., *Fundamental Questions*, ch. 4). He does not, however, attack the use of the epistemic principle in ethics, although his view of deductive inference as not always underwritten by meaning-connections between premises and conclusion would allow such an attack (*Fundamental Questions*, 30–3). (For Ewing's puzzling direct reply to the phenomenalism analogy, see *Definition*, 55.) In *Second Thoughts*, he argues that since a naturalist analysis fails to give a satisfactory account of what we mean, the naturalist neither shows that our claims are justified nor explains what makes her analysis correct (24–8).

[43] Sturgeon finds it puzzling how Moore moves from the simplicity of 'good' to the impossibility of evidence, and how Ayer moves from the failure of analysis of 'good' to unverifiability by inference ('Intuitionism', 189, 191, n. 19). The epistemic principle is one explanation. (For Moore, what does the work then is not simplicity, but the failure of analysis into natural claims.) Acceptance of the epistemic principle may also explain Russell's argument for non-cognitivism. 'The chief ground for adopting this view is the complete impossibility of finding any arguments to prove that this or that has intrinsic value . . . Since no way can even be imagined for deciding a difference as to values, the conclusion is forced upon us that the difference is one of tastes, not one as to objective truth . . . In a scientific question, evidence can be adduced on both sides . . . But in a question as to whether this or that is the ultimate Good, there is no evidence either way' (Bertrand Russell, *Religion and Science* (Oxford: Oxford University Press, 1961), 238, 229). Russell gives no argument for thinking there is no evidence, but acceptance of the epistemic principle, along with rejection of naturalism, would explain it.

employing just what non-naturalists are out to protect. Thus Perry—the paradigm naturalist—defends his definitions in terms of interests on the ground that they systematize common sense morality (1954, 133–6; 1950, 125–7).[44] Brandt defends his 'quasi-naturalist' definition in part by noting that it does not 'exclude, as necessarily irrelevant, any of the arguments actually used about particular ethical principles' (Brandt 1959, 266). Sharp defends his analysis of 'x is good' as 'x is desired upon reflection' by arguing that this reflects how we decide what is good (Sharp 1928, 409–11).[45] In the latter case, the naturalist must explain why we should continue to adhere to a moral principle just because it is 'enshrined in our moral discourse' and so again must engage in old-fashioned moral theorizing (Frankena 1973, 100–1).[46]

One might object that, even if naturalists and non-naturalists arrive at the same moral conclusions by the same moral theorizing, the naturalist still has an advantage. The naturalist offers his conclusion as an analysis, whereas the non-naturalist offers hers as synthetic a priori, and the latter category is suspect.[47] One reply is that, if the same arguments are given, whether the conclusions are classified as (unobvious) analyses or synthetic a priori truths may not matter. (The successful analysis is unlikely to look like 'to be a brother is to be a male sibling'.) And, even if it does, there seems more a difference than a straightforward advantage. For the naturalist must explain how the unobvious analysis is indeed an analysis. Where non-naturalists face the difficulty of defending the synthetic a priori, naturalists face the Paradox of Analysis.

One might also object that contemporary naturalists, such as Cornell, offer an alternative to old-fashioned moral theorizing. They sometimes suggest that identifications of moral and natural properties are to be made through a historical investigation of what natural properties causally regulate our use of moral terms. But

---

[44] Similarly, Sharp, who defines 'x is right' as 'x would be desired from an impersonal and benevolent point of view', defends his definition by arguing that it yields our moral judgments. See F. C. Sharp, *Ethics* (New York: The Century, 1928), chs. 6–8. Perry also argues by elimination, rejecting other definitions and the view that no definitions are to be had, and by noting that we think interests in, for example, cataracts, confer value on them (*General Theory of Value* (Cambridge: Harvard University Press, 1950), 124–5). Non-naturalists would not reject these epistemic strategies either.

[45] Similarly, Roderick Firth writes that 'we must try to determine the characteristics of an ideal observer by examining the procedures which we actually regard . . . as the rational ones for *deciding* ethical questions' ('Ethical Absolutism and the Ideal Observer', *Philosophy and Phenomenological Research*, 12 (1952), 332). David Lewis takes it as support for his analysis of 'x is good' as 'we desire to desire x' that (he claims) in practice we decide whether x is good by deciding whether we desire to desire it ('Dispositional Theories of Value', *Proceedings of the Aristotelian Society* sup. vol., 63 (1989), 131).

[46] Contrast Ridge: 'Since the naturalist holds that moral properties are either identical to or reducible to some subset of natural properties there need be no mystery about how we come to have some knowledge of those properties, even if there is some residual mystery as to how we discover that they are the moral ones' ('Non-naturalism', 7).

[47] I owe this objection to Russ Shafer-Landau.

this faces a popular objection similar to the non-naturalist objection to subjectivist analyses: if the use of the same moral term by different speakers is causally regulated by different natural properties, the speakers do not disagree with one another, even when it seems that they do.[48] In reply, some representatives of Cornell make alterations. Brink, for example, suggests two pictures. On one, the use of moral terms in question is not merely our actual use, but our use cleaned up in the usual coherentist way. We must first decide on the best moral principles and then see what natural properties causally regulate our use of the moral terms appearing in these principles. On the second picture, it is our intentions to refer, rather than causal regulation, that fix reference. He suggests that all speakers intend to adopt the moral point of view. Identifications of natural and moral properties then fall out of the correct conception and application of this point of view—a conception and application determined, again, in the usual coherentist way. On both pictures, as Brink stresses, old-fashioned moral theorizing is indispensable.[49]

It is also worth noting, contrary to the standard picture, that the non-naturalists (especially Ewing) are happy to give coherence considerations a role. 'The coherence test plays an essential part in confirming, amending, clarifying and extending what first presents itself as a more or less confused intuition' (Ewing 1947, 211, also 93; 1959, 72–3). 'We must not suppose that, because an intuition is not proved true by reasoning, therefore it cannot be supported by reasoning' (Ewing 1953, 117; also 116, 123). '[W]hen intuitive ethical views differ, use may be made of inference to support one or other of the clashing views, especially by showing that it fits well into a coherent ethical system' (Ewing 1947, 30). It is 'an argument against' a moral claim that it 'cannot be fitted into any systematic ethical theory' (Ewing 1947, 92). He argues at length that his prima-facie duties 'constitute a system' (Ewing 1947, 205, 203–11; 1959, 132–4, 143, 150; 1953, 117). More generally, 'the criterion of the truth of a theory of

---

[48] For one presentation of the objection, see Michael Smith, *The Moral Problem* (Oxford: Blackwell, 1994), 32–4.

[49] See esp. Brink, 'Semantics', 162, 168–9, 175. Some representatives of Cornell seem less conciliatory. Sturgeon, for example, thinks moral theorizing is no different from ordinary empirical theorizing. But the two grounds he offers would not bother non-naturalists. He notes that moral theorizing gives a role to empirical theses about, say, consequences or motivation, and that moral theorizing is empirical in the sense that it employs reflective equilibrium. Non-naturalists can accept both points while still opposing the sort of naturalistic position they oppose (and Sturgeon himself has no wish to defend that 'analytic' naturalism) ('Moore', 544–6). (There may be a substantive difference between Sturgeon and the non-naturalists, since Sturgeon seems to disapprove of thought experiments, at least when these are 'far-fetched and unrealistic' ('Moore', 545, n. 29). But his point seems to be that 'empirical evidence is needed to know whether a hypothetical example is realistic'. Even if one agrees that unrealistic thought experiments are bad, it does not follow that all the work has been done empirically, since the judgment made about a realistic thought experiment still seems to come 'just by thinking about it'.) For a worry about the suggestion that empirical status comes with use of reflective equilibrium, see Shafer-Landau, *Realism*, 60–1.

Ethics is its ability to make into a coherent system as much as possible of . . . common sense ethics' (Ewing 1953, 117; also 10−11).

IV

I close with two comments on the cheapness objection, that non-naturalism contributes nothing. First, the cheapness objection presupposes that there are problems which a naturalistic analysis is needed to solve. The model is Russell's theory of descriptions. Russell presents various puzzles. The solution to all of these puzzles is to substitute for the puzzling sentence a sentence with the same logical form but which avoids the puzzle. I have argued that leaving 'x is good' without a naturalistic analysis does not lead to special ontological or epistemological problems. If so, it may be true that non-naturalism is unhelpful, but this is not an objection, since a naturalistic analysis is no more helpful and it is not clear that any help is needed.[50]

Second, my understanding of non-naturalism makes it more popular but much less exciting. Most 'naturalists' today share the central non-naturalist opposition to any analysis in naturalistic terms. Non-naturalism is a distinct position, but the distinctness from most contemporary naturalism lies in accepting self-evidence and the synthetic a priori, not in views about analysis or ontology. The main non-epistemological division is between naturalists and non-naturalists, on the one hand, and non-cognitivists, on the other, though even here some non-naturalists were not so opposed to non-cognitivism, and recent non-cognitivists are eager to capture the objectivity and conditions on justification that non-naturalists defend.[51] But all this is not to give too much credit to non-naturalism. The 'analytic' naturalism which the non-naturalists target was never very lively—it takes some looking to find actual examples of analytic naturalism as opposed to the stock figure 'the naturalist'—and when it appears, off and on, in the person of Perry, Westermarck, or Waddington, and

---

[50] Stevenson claims that 'in order to answer the question "Is X good?" we must *substitute* for it a question which is free from ambiguity and confusion' (C. L. Stevenson, 'The Emotive Meaning of Ethical Terms', *Mind*, 46 (1937), 14). Stevenson does not explicitly state the ambiguities and confusions that call for substitution. The best candidate seems to be this. After stating his theory, he asks 'Does the omission of [emotive meanings] really lead people into errors? I think, indeed, that the errors resulting from such omissions are enormous' ('Emotive', 26). In the following section, intended to show the enormity of the errors, Stevenson argues that considering emotive meaning avoids the problems besetting 'traditional interest theories', which analyse 'x is good' as 'I like x' or 'we like x'. This, however, does not show that 'Is x good?' is ambiguous or confused. It shows only that one substitution for 'Is x good?' is poor, and that adding emotive meaning can improve it.

[51] Gibbard writes of his own view that the 'system that results mimics most closely the "non-naturalism" of G. E. Moore, Henry Sidgwick, A. C. Ewing, and others' (*Thinking*, xi).

gets crushed, this does not seem the titanic battle 'to stem the tide of subjectivism and naturalism' that Ewing views himself as waging (Ewing 1947, 212).[52] One gets the feeling that the non-naturalists exaggerated any hint of analytic naturalism because they took such delight in trotting out the arguments against it. Ross devotes twenty-four pages of his short *The Right and the Good* to Perry. In seventy-seven pages of Ewing's *The Definition of Good* criticizing subjectivism and naturalism, Perry is the only contemporary philosopher identified as either.[53] Sometimes the attempt to find an opponent is very forced: Moore reads Mill's claim of an evidential relation between being desirable and being desired as claiming that ' "good" means "desired" '; he ascribes to Kant the views that 'what [a free will] ought to do *means* nothing but its own law' and that ' "This ought to be" means "This is commanded" ' (1903, 66, 127, 128). In a sense, then, the cheapness objection is right—not because there are outstanding problems that a refusal to give an analysis looks away from, but because the main target of non-naturalism was largely a target of their own creation.[54]

References

Ayer, A. J., *Language, Truth and Logic* (New York: Dover, 1952).

———— 'On the Analysis of Moral Judgements', in Ayer, *Philosophical Essays* (London: Macmillan, 1954), 231–49.

[52] For Ewing on Waddington, see A. C. Ewing, 'The Relations between Science and Ethics', *Proceedings of the Aristotelian Society*, 42 (1942), 68–86. Once attacked, Waddington quickly renounced any definition of 'good' (Ewing, 'Relations', 68–9). The ideal observer theories offered by Field, Sharp, Firth, and Brandt would have been a more worthy target. (Broad himself defends such a theory in 'Moral-Sense', 206–22.) Ewing and (elsewhere) Broad very briefly raise the standard objection that the ideal observer gets characterized in normative terms (Ewing, *Definition*, 61, 67, *Second*, 20, *Value and Reality* (London: George Allen & Unwin, 1973), 101; Broad, *Five Types*, 262–3). Ewing also objects to Field's analysis of 'x is good' as 'x would be desired by everyone if they knew x's true nature' that there is no reason to think that everyone's desires would agree even given knowledge of x's true nature (*Ethics*, 87).

[53] Ewing does argue that the command theory of Stace and Kraft collapses into naturalism or subjectivism, but this is not what either seem to have intended (*Definition*, 16–18). Elsewhere, in passing, he adds Hume 'in some moods at least' ('Recent Developments', 85; also *Definition*, 41, *Ethics*, 92), following Broad (*Five Types*, 114–15). In *The Morality of Punishment* (London: Kegan Paul, Trench, Trubner & Co., 1929), (82) he mentions Leon Roth's *The Science of Morals* (London: Benn, 1928), but Roth's main point seems to be that ethics is a science in that it aims at system and in that experience is relevant (though he does seem to run together predictive and normative claims) (see Roth, *Science*, 57, 65, 74; 60, 82, 88; 63). The non-cognitivists inherited this tic: R. M. Hare is famous for attacking naturalism in *The Language of Morals*, but the closest he comes to naming a naturalist is the brief discussion of H. G. Bohnert's view that imperatives can be reduced to indicatives (*The Language of Morals* (Oxford: Oxford University Press, 1952), 7–8).

[54] Thanks to Ben Caplan, Roger Crisp, Danny Goldstick, Tom Hurka, Joyce Jenkins, and audiences at Manitoba and Toronto.

Audi, Robert, 'Intuitionism, Pluralism, and the Foundations of Ethics', in Walter Sinnott-Armstrong and Mark Timmons (eds.), *Moral Knowledge?* (New York: Oxford University Press, 1996), 101–36.

Baldwin, Thomas, 'Introduction' to Moore, *Principia Ethica*, revised edn., ed. by Thomas Baldwin (Cambridge: Cambridge University Press 1993), pp. ix–xxxvii.

Ball, Stephen W., 'Reductionism in Ethics and Science: A Contemporary Look at G. E. Moore's Open-Question Argument', *American Philosophical Quarterly*, 25 (1988), 197–213.

Boyd, Richard, 'How to be a Moral Realist', in Geoffrey Sayre-McCord (ed.), *Essays on Moral Realism*, (Ithaca: Cornell University Press, 1988), 181–228.

Brandt, Richard, *Ethical Theory* (Englewood Cliffs, NJ: Prentice-Hall, 1959).

Brink, David, *Moral Realism and the Foundations of Ethics* (Cambridge: Cambridge University Press, 1989).

——— 'Realism, Naturalism, and Moral Semantics', *Social Philosophy and Policy*, 18 (2001), 154–76.

Broad, C. D., *Five Types of Ethical Theory* (London: Routledge & Kegan Paul, 1930).

——— 'Are There Synthetic A Priori Truths?', *Proceedings of the Aristotelian Society*, supp. vol., 15 (1936), 102–17.

——— 'Critical Notice of *An Examination of the Place of Reason in Ethics*', *Mind*, 61 (1952), 93–101.

——— 'Is "Goodness" a Name of a Simple Non-Natural Quality?', in Broad, *Broad's Critical Essays in Moral Philosophy*, ed. by David Cheney (London: George Allen & Unwin, 1971a), 106–23.

——— 'A Reply to My Critics', in *Critical Essays* (1971b), 302–23.

——— 'Some of the Main Problems of Ethics', in *Critical Essays* (1971c), 223–46.

——— 'Some Reflections on Moral-Sense Theories in Ethics', in *Critical Essays* (1971d), 188–222.

——— 'G. E. Moore's Latest Published Views on Ethics', in *Critical Essays* (1971e), 324–50.

——— *Ethics*, ed. by C. Lewy (Dordrecht: M. Nijhoff, 1985).

Carritt, E. F., *The Theory of Morals* (London: Oxford University Press, 1928).

Cox, H. H., 'Warnock on Moore', *Mind*, 79 (1970), 265–9.

Crisp, Roger, 'Sidgwick and the Boundaries of Intuitionism', in Stratton-Lake, *Intuitionism* (2002), 56–75.

Darwall, Stephen, 'Internalism and Agency', *Philosophical Perspectives*, 6 (1992), 155–74.

Ewing, A. C., *The Morality of Punishment* (London: Kegan Paul, Trench, Trubner & Co., 1929).

——— 'The Relations between Science and Ethics', *Proceedings of the Aristotelian Society*, 42 (1942), 68–86.

——— *The Definition of Good* (New York: Macmillan, 1947).

——— *The Fundamental Questions of Philosophy* (London: Routledge & Kegan Paul, 1951).

——— *Ethics* (New York: Free Press, 1953).

——— *Second Thoughts in Moral Philosophy* (New York: Macmillan, 1959).

——— 'Recent Developments in British Ethical Thought', in C. A. Mace (ed.), *British Philosophy in the Mid-Century*, (London: George Allen & Unwin, 1966).

——— *Value and Reality* (London: George Allen & Unwin, 1973).

Firth, Roderick, 'Ethical Absolutism and the Ideal Observer', *Philosophy and Phenomenological Research*, 12 (1952), 317–45.

Frankena, William K., 'Ewing's Case Against Naturalistic Theories of Value', *Philosophical Review*, 59 (1948), 481–92.

_____ 'Broad's Analysis of Ethical Terms', in P. A. Schilpp (ed.), *The Philosophy of C. D. Broad*, (New York: Tudor, 1959), 537–61.

_____ *Ethics* (Englewood Cliffs, NJ: Prentice-Hall, 1973).

Gampel, Eric, 'A Defense of the Autonomy of Ethics: Why Value is Not Like Water', *Canadian Journal of Philosophy*, 26 (1996), 191–209.

Gibbard, Allan, 'Knowing What to Do, Seeing What to Do', in Stratton-Lake, *Intuitionism* (2002), 212–28.

_____ *Thinking How to Live* (Cambridge: Harvard University Press, 2003).

Hare, R. M., *The Language of Morals* (Oxford: Oxford University Press, 1952).

Harman, Gilbert, *The Nature of Morality* (New York: Oxford University Press, 1977).

Hurka, Thomas, 'Moore in the Middle', *Ethics*, 113 (2003), 599–628.

Jackson, Frank and Pettit, Philip, 'Moral Functionalism and Moral Motivation', *Philosophical Quarterly*, 45 (1995), 20–40.

Lewis, David, 'Dispositional Theories of Value', *Proceedings of the Aristotelian Society*, supp. vol., 63 (1989), 112–37.

Mabbott, J. D., *An Introduction to Ethics* (London: Hutchinson, 1966).

MacIntyre, Alasdair, *A Short History of Ethics* (New York: Macmillan, 1966).

McCloskey, H. J., *Meta-ethics and Normative Ethics* (The Hague: Martinus Nijhoff, 1969).

Moore, G. E., *Principia Ethica* (Cambridge: Cambridge University Press, 1903).

_____ *Ethics* (New York: Oxford University Press, 1965).

_____ 'The Conception of Intrinsic Value', in Moore, *Philosophical Studies* (Paterson: Littlefield, Adams & Co., 1959a), 253–75.

_____ 'The Nature of Moral Philosophy', in Moore, *Studies* (1959b), 310–39.

_____ 'Replies', in P. A. Schilpp (ed.), *The Philosophy of G. E. Moore* (La Salle, Ill: Open Court, 1968), 535–677.

_____ 'Preface to the Second Edition', in Moore, *Principia Ethica*, rev. edn., ed. by Thomas Baldwin (Cambridge: Cambridge University Press, 1993), 2–27.

Nagel, Thomas, *The View from Nowhere* (New York: Oxford University Press, 1986).

Nowell-Smith, P. H., *Ethics* (Harmondsworth: Penguin, 1954).

Parfit, Derek, 'Rationality and Reasons', in Dan Egonsson *et al.* (eds.), *Exploring Practical Philosophy: From Actions to Values* (Aldershot: Ashgate, 2001), 17–39.

Perry, R. B., *General Theory of Value* (Cambridge: Harvard University Press, 1950).

_____ *Realms of Value* (Cambridge: Harvard University Press, 1954).

Putnam, Hilary, *Reason, Truth and History* (Cambridge: Cambridge University Press, 1981).

Railton, Peter, 'Naturalism and Prescriptivity', *Social Philosophy and Policy*, 7 (1989), 151–74.

Regan, Donald, 'How to Be a Moorean', *Ethics*, 113 (2003), 651–77.

Raphael, D. D., *Moral Judgment* (London: Allen & Unwin, 1955).

Ridge, Michael, 'Moral Non-Naturalism', *The Stanford Encyclopedia of Philosophy*, ed. by Edward N. Zalta (Spring 2003 edn.), URL=<http//plato.stanford.edu/archives/Spr2003/entries/moral-non-naturalism/>

Robinson, Richard, 'Review of *The Definition of Good*', *Review of Metaphysics*, 1 (1948), 104–12.

Ross, W. D., *Foundations of Ethics* (Oxford: Clarendon, 1939).

_____ *The Right and the Good* (Indianapolis: Hackett, 1988).

Roth, Leon, *The Science of Morals* (London: Benn, 1928).

Russell, Bertrand, *Our Knowledge of the External World* (London: George Allen & Unwin, 1926).

―― *Religion and Science* (Oxford: Oxford University Press, 1961).

―― 'The Elements of Ethics', in Russell, *Philosophical Essays* (London: Allen & Unwin, 1966), 13–59.

Scanlon, T. M., *What We Owe to Each Other* (Cambridge: Belknap, 1998).

Schneewind, J. B., *Sidgwick's Ethics and Victorian Moral Philosophy* (Oxford: Clarendon, 1977).

Shafer-Landau, Russ, *Moral Realism* (Oxford: Clarendon, 2003).

Sharp, F. C., *Ethics* (New York: The Century, 1928).

Sidgwick, Henry, 'Some Fundamental Ethical Controversies,' *Mind*, 14 (1889), 473–87.

―― 'Is the Distinction Between "Is" and "Ought" Ultimate and Irreducible?', *Proceedings of the Aristotelian Society*, new ser., 1 (1892), 88–91.

―― *The Methods of Ethics* (Indianapolis: Hackett, 1981).

Simon, Caroline J., 'On Defending a Moral Synthetic A Priori', *Southern Journal of Philosophy*, 26 (1988), 217–33.

Smith, Michael, *The Moral Problem* (Oxford: Blackwell, 1994).

Stevenson, C. L., 'The Emotive Meaning of Ethical Terms', *Mind*, 46 (1937), 14–31.

―― *Ethics and Language* (New Haven: Yale University Press, 1944).

Stratton-Lake, Philip, 'Introduction', in Philip Stratton-Lake (ed.), *Ethical Intuitionism* (Oxford: Clarendon, 2002), 1–28.

Strawson, P. F., 'Ethical Intuitionism', *Philosophy*, 24 (1949), 23–33.

Sturgeon, Nicholas, 'Ethical Intuitionism and Ethical Naturalism', in Stratton-Lake, *Intuitionism* (2002), 194–211.

―― 'Moore on Ethical Naturalism', *Ethics*, 113 (2003), 528–56.

Toulmin, Stephen E., *An Examination of the Place of Reason in Ethics* (Cambridge: Cambridge University Press, 1950).

Warnock, G. J., *Contemporary Moral Philosophy* (London: Macmillan, 1967).

15

Beyond Moore's Utilitarianism*

Joshua Gert

Throughout his career, Moore is conspicuous as a self-critic. His rhetoric in the first edition of *Principia Ethica* against Bentham, Mill, Spencer, and others is often extremely harsh, but it is hardly less harsh when, a few years later, in the preface to the second edition, he assesses his own previous arguments. Even at the end of his career he is constantly accusing his former self of 'sheer mistakes' and of making claims that were 'certainly wrong' or 'utterly silly and preposterous'.[1] It therefore seems to me most in the spirit of Moore to carry on this form of criticism, and to assume that he is capable of making claims that are manifestly false. This is what I intend to do in what follows. For, like the latter Moore, I think the former Moore had many essential points essentially correct. Yet, like the latter Moore, I think the former Moore was confused in many ways, overlooked huge distinctions, and often offered us assumptions instead of arguments.

The primary purpose of this paper is not, however, historical. I want to defend a particular position—one that I have defended elsewhere in different ways.[2] But I do want to show how this position is related to a historically respectable position: Moore's. In particular, I want to show that the general perspective on ethics that Moore took, widened by certain philosophical innovations that have taken place since his last efforts, is quite consistent with a view that, at first glace, looks to be wildly at odds with anything Moore could possibly have come to endorse.[3]

---

* Thanks to Susana Nuccetelli and Gary Seay for comments on an earlier version of this chapter.

[1] 'Reply to My Critics', *The Library of Living Philosophers, Vol. IV: The Philosophy of G. E. Moore*, 3rd edn., ed. P.A. Schilpp (La Salle, Ill.: Open Court, 1968). For examples, see 548, 571, 581–2.

[2] In particular, see 'Problems for Moral Twin Earth Arguments', *Synthese* (forthcoming).

[3] That Moore almost came to endorse a Stevensonian emotivism should make it at least plausible that he could have been brought to endorse the view advocated below.

Here are come conspicuously Moorean ethical claims:

(1) 'Good' names a simple, unanalyzable, indefinable property.

(2) In this respect, 'good' is like 'yellow'.

(3) There is a diversity of things that are, in fact, good.

(4) Anything that is intrinsically good is always, and to the same degree, intrinsically good.

(5) Intrinsic goodness depends only on the intrinsic nature of that which possesses it.

(6) We cannot calculate the value of a whole simply by adding up the values of its parts.

(7) With regard to conduct, the right action is the one that will produce the most good.

Taken together, the four sections of this chapter will deal with each of the seven claims just listed, generally endorsing them in modified form. Section I explains how there might be a simple, unanalyzable normative property of the sort Moore envisioned, similar in certain respects to a secondary property like yellow. It also explains why we ought not be surprised if it should turn out to apply to a diversity of things. This then is a qualified defense of claims (1), (2), and (3). Section II defends a move from Moore's own isolation test for intrinsic value to a similar test that appeals to the notion of rationality instead of duty. Using this test, Section III defends claims (4), (5), and (6). Finally, Section IV diagnoses Moore's attraction to a maximizing utilitarian view, and rejects claim (7).

I The Simplicity of Goodness

One of the most celebrated of Moore's contentions is that good is simple and unanalyzable. This contention is also one with which Moore himself was very dissatisfied; and with reason.[4] But, despite his criticism, he does not abandon the general thesis that there is *some* unanalyzable property peculiar to ethics. The problem with such a view is that Moore provided us with no satisfying account of how we might have come to be acquainted with this property. To say, as he does, that we have 'direct apprehension' of goodness is no real solution, for we then need some account of how such direct apprehension is possible. And given the simplicity of the

---

[4] For expressions of this dissatisfaction, see the preface to the second edition of *Principia Ethica*, ed. Thomas Baldwin (Cambridge University Press, 1993 [1903]), 5–16.

property—whether it be goodness or something else—and the fact that it is not a natural property, he did not give us many prospects for such an account. Of course, Moore does offer us the analogy with yellow, and our direct apprehension of it. But this analogy has seemed flawed to many and, in any case, the simple assertion of an analogy is not very persuasive, given the obvious differences between color and value properties.[5]

What I would like to do in this section is offer Moore one account of how we might have some reason to trust our intuitions regarding the goodness of things, and also an account of the simple unanalyzability of goodness. I should emphasize that this is a preliminary account, cast in terms of goodness rather than some other normative notion, because it seems useful to proceed in steps. In offering this account, I will make use of Moore's own comparison of goodness with yellowness, but will try to justify reliance on that comparison, rather than simply taking it as given.

Suppose that yellowness is, as Moore held, a simple and unanalyzable property. How is it that we can come to know anything about it? One thing is clear: we do not come to know about it by being given a definition that contains an analysis. But nothing prevents us from making use of ostensive definitions: *that* is yellow. One problem with ostensive definitions, of course, is that they can be taken in many ways. Perhaps someone who receives such a definition will think that only the very specific shade of yellow that the ostended object has counts as yellow. Or, worse, perhaps he will think that 'yellow' is a name for the *shape* of the ostended object. These kinds of misinterpretations are corrected by further ostensions, and by correction when the language learner goes astray. The learner is *trained* in the use of the word, and *that* is how he comes to understand the word, and to be able to make justified claims about the yellowness of objects. Given the role that ostension plays in this story, it is important that the community of language speakers share a certain phenomenal response to the class of yellow things. But, despite the important role that uniformity of response plays, it is no part of the *meaning* of an ascription of yellowness to an object that the speaker, or people generally, have such a response to the object.[6] So 'yellow' is not subjective in the sense in which Moore understands that term.[7] This is an important result, since one point from which Moore never retreated was that goodness was not subjective in this sense.

If the story about how we come to learn the meaning of the word 'yellow' is reasonable, it may be possible to tell a similar story for the word 'good', at least for

---

[5] See, e.g., Simon Blackburn, *Essays in Quasi-Realism* (New York: Oxford University Press, 1993), 159—61.

[6] Moore himself is sensitive to the independence of origin and reference. He writes: 'the theory that moral judgments originated in feelings does not, in fact, lend any support at all to the theory that now, as developed, they can only be judgments *about* feelings' (*Ethics* (London: Oxford University Press, 1912, 74)).

[7] See 'The Conception of Intrinsic Value', *Philosophical Studies* (New York: Humanities Press, 1922), 253—75, at 254.

certain of its uses.[8] In the version of the story that involves goodness, we will have to assume that, just as in the case of yellowness, human beings have a common response to things that are good, or see them as saliently similar in a way that they need not be able to articulate. Of course, in both the case of color and the case of goodness, we cannot expect *everyone* to have the right sort of response or to see things as saliently similar when they are 'supposed to'. But as long as there is an overwhelming agreement among language users, these people can be identified, and their responses classified as defective. In the case of color, such people are called 'color blind'. And in the case of goodness, they are called 'crazy', or 'unreasonable', or 'irrational'.[9] What is the common response that plays the essential role here? Many would suggest that it is something like desire. My own view is that there are many goods to which many individuals, even if rational, might be indifferent: some people seek philosophical knowledge; others seek pleasure; and still others seek political power. All of these are rational pursuits, but it need not be irrational to refuse to take any pains at all to become philosophically illuminated, or to have political power. However, it does seem as though virtually everyone *understands why other people might make sacrifices to gain these things.* This *understanding* is a complex attitude, and may seem correspondingly implausible as a candidate for a basic response. In Section III I will suggest that this is because we ought not take 'good' as basic. But, for the moment, let these worries pass.

The above response-dependent, language-dependent, story allows us to understand why it is that people can reliably identify goodness where it exists. Moore, of course, has another story: the isolation test. This is a kind of recipe for thought experiments used to determine intrinsic value. Moore asks us to imagine a sort of god who has the ability to create a certain world, or no world at all. If it would be the duty of such a being to create the world—provided it did not think it wrong to do so—then that world is

---

[8] I have in mind the use according to which 'good' means roughly 'beneficial'. This helps to sidestep worries raised by Peter Geach, who rightly noted that what justifies the application of the word 'good' to something depends on what sort of thing it is. See Peter Geach, 'Good and Evil', *Analysis*, 17 (1956), 33–42. Later in the paper I will move from goodness to rationality. With this move it seems to me that Geach's worries simply disappear.

[9] Consistent with my own usage elsewhere, and with the usage of ethical theorists such as Stephen Darwall, Allan Gibbard, and Michael Smith, I use 'irrational' to pick out actions that, in a fundamental sense, one should never perform. They are actions that are not favored by sufficient reasons to justify performing them, given the reasons that disfavor them. There is no presumption that the agent herself *regards* the action as irrational, or invests the relevant reasons with their correct significance. Schizophrenic people, for example, often act irrationally in this sense, even if, relative to their distorted view of the world, their actions have a certain internal logic, and even if they (falsely) regard those actions as perfectly reasonable responses to the world. See Stephen Darwall, *Impartial Reason* (Ithaca: Cornell University Press, 1983) 215–16; Allan Gibbard *Wise Choices, Apt Feelings* (Cambridge: Harvard University Press, 1990), 49; Michael Smith, *The Moral Problem* (Cambridge: Blackwell, 1994), 150 ff. Moore himself uses 'rational' in this fundamental normative way, rather than to indicate anything about the agent's own normative assessment of her action. See his 'Reply to My Critics', 616.

intrinsically good, and so is the state of affairs that it manifests.[10] This procedure has struck many as ridiculous. Certainly it depends crucially on two extremely suspicious foundations: (1) that intuitions prompted by the odd proceeding of contemplating an extremely strange universe containing nothing but, say, a player-piano playing Beethoven, can give us a reliable indication of the value of the playing of a sonata; and (2) that value can be completely divorced from genuinely practical choice.

II Changing the Basic Normative Notion: From Goodness and Duty to Rationality

In fact, Moore's isolation test can be interpreted as a pump, not for intuitions about intrinsic goodness but for intuitions about the normative status of various choices. Even as early as the second edition of *Principia*, Moore was having doubts as to whether or not 'good' was the basic unanalyzable notion peculiar to ethics, suggesting that 'right' or 'duty' might have that honor.[11] However, once we see the basic normative predicate as one that applies not to states of affairs, but to actions, we need to recognize that there is more than one candidate for the most basic kind of normative assessment of action. Moore clearly thinks that the notions of moral rightness and wrongness are the most basic. But not only is the distinction between morality and rationality now widely accepted, so, too, is the idea that rationality rather than moral duty is the basic normative notion.[12] What this suggests is that the kind of intuitions we ought to be using in determining the values of various things are not intuitions regarding what a god would have a moral duty to choose, when such choices would have no effect on that god, but are intuitions about the choices that actual people could rationally make. For example, if it seems clear that it would be irrational to choose X over Y, regardless of any further consequences of the choice than the mere possession of X or Y by the agent, then we can say that Y has greater value than X.[13]

---

[10] 'Reply', 600.

[11] See *Principia Ethica: Revised Edition*, ed. by Thomas Baldwin, (Cambridge: Cambridge University Press, 1993), 5, 14. It may be worth noting that for Moore 'right', 'duty', 'what we ought to do', and 'obligatory' are virtually identical: when an act is the *only* right act available, it can be called our duty or obligation, and it can be said that we ought to do it.

[12] There is another current sense of 'rational', prominent in the work of Thomas Scanlon, according to which the rationality of an action is simply a formal matter of the action's being in line with the agent's own normative judgments, no matter how bizarre they might be. It should be obvious that, on this understanding, rationality is not the basic normative notion. We might easily try to persuade our friends to act irrationally in this sense, if we see that their normative judgments are confused. See Scanlon, *What We Owe to Each Other* (Cambridge: Harvard University Press, 1998), 25–7.

[13] I develop this idea in more detail in 'Value and Parity', *Ethics*, 114/3 (2004), 492–510.

The suggestion I am making, then, is that we keep the Moorean isolation test, but reconceive it in more human terms, and in terms of rationality. The advantages of such a procedure are many. The first has already been mentioned: there is an emerging consensus that rationality—in the objective sense that has to do with the reasons that favor and disfavor action, and not with the agent's possibly flawed assessment of these reasons—ought to be taken as a more basic normative notion than morality. If it is indeed *the* basic notion, as many now think, then we will, of course, not be able to rely on more basic normative notions in order to support our claims that certain choices are rational, and others irrational. So we will need something like the isolation test as our last court of appeal. Our thought experiments need only stipulate what the agent believes the choice to entail, and that the agent is reasonable in these descriptive beliefs. Since our actual judgments of the rationality of actual actions could often serve as instances of the reconceived isolation test, there is more reason to trust the intuitions that emerge from such thought experiments than there is to trust intuitions about the moral duties of an artificially limited god.

This last point might seem to show too much, at least if one claim of this chapter is that Moore had something right in the isolation test. For if our actual judgments of rationality are just as good as applications of the isolation test, why do we need an isolation test at all? There are two answers to this question. The first is that if we are concerned with the kind of practical rationality that is relevant to moral responsibility, free will, competence to give consent, and so on, then *often* such judgments will have no direct bearing on the relative values of the objects of those choices. For example, suppose someone saves the life of a stranger at great personal risk, but *merely* in order to appear on television. That may well be irrational: the result of a kind of obsession. But we shouldn't take that fact to show anything about the relative value of saving a stranger's life, and risking one's own life. When we evaluate actual actions, the etiology of those actions is relevant to our assessment of their rational status. But the isolation test allows us to ignore etiological peculiarities by asking 'Would it *ever* be rational to choose X over Y?' It allows us to consider *merely* the foreseeable consequences of the action. Would it ever be rational to choose to risk one's own life to save the life of a stranger? The answer seems to be 'yes', and this gives us information about the relative values of one's own life and a stranger's life: one's own life is not more important.

A second feature of an isolation test is that it avoids an obscuring factor present in many real-life choices: additional options. For example, when we use the isolation test and ask ourselves whether it would be rational to choose six months of extremely unpleasant chemotherapy in order to save one's own life, the answer clearly seems to be 'yes'. But in a real-life choice situation, it might well be irrational to choose the treatment. This would be the case if there were a third option that involved a less unpleasant but equally effective therapy. The general presence of a host of options in real-life choice situations can make one doubt that intrinsically good things have one of the features that Moore—I think correctly—attributes to them: invariant value. For if it can sometimes be rationally permissible to choose a certain medical treatment, and sometimes not, even when the treatment and the illness are precisely the same, then it might seem reasonable to conclude that the relative disvalues of the treatment and the illness change from context to context. But this conclusion seems mistaken to me, and it seemed so to Moore also.

The attraction of the rationality-based isolation test over Moore's duty-based version may explain the following uncharacteristically sensible claim of Moore's:

So long as I merely say that I use 'intrinsically good' to mean the same as 'worth having for its own sake', I think I am explaining fairly clearly how I use the term.[14]

This claim is quite natural and plausible, since here 'worth having' is naturally taken to mean 'worth an *agent's* having'.[15] Talk of what is worth having or getting, rather than of what one should produce, is best interpreted as what is *rational* to aim at having or getting, and this is what makes the above claim seem plausible. Interpreted in this way, goodness is to be understood as what it is rational to aim at getting for oneself. So we should replace Moore's isolation test with thought experiments in which we consider the rational status of various choices. Such a thought experiment does not require us to imagine that the person has the power to create universes, or that the person will not be affected by her choice. Indeed, because the rationality of a choice often depends very heavily on the effects of the choice on the *agent*, we should explicitly consider the effects on the agent.

If we are going to take our intuitions of rationality as epistemically reliable for the reasons suggested in Section I, we will need to understand either the notion of 'rational action' or the notion of 'irrational action' in a response-dependent way. My own view is that, since irrationality is far more salient than rationality, and is also the notion that has important practical consequences, it is irrationality that ought to be so understood. The relevant response, I have suggested elsewhere, is a kind of puzzlement—a mental red flag that goes up when we see other people acting in ways that we cannot unproblematically represent to ourselves in terms of the intentional pursuit of goals in light of the foreseeable consequences.[16] So let us take 'irrational' as our basic notion. 'Rational' will mean simply 'not irrational'.

---

[14] 'Is Goodness a Quality?', 95.

[15] Compare the following claim: 'We *can* consider with regard to any state of things whether it would be worth while that it should exist, even if there were absolutely nothing else in the Universe besides' (*Ethics*, 101). But what could it possibly mean for it to be *worth while* for something to exist? 'Worth *who's* while', one wants to ask Moore: 'the Universe's'?

[16] Joshua Gert, *Brute Rationalsity: Normativity and Human Action* (Cambridge University Press, 2004), ch. 7.

III Goodness and Badness

If we take irrationality as the basic normative notion, we can define the following derivative notions.

'Bad': Something is bad iff it would be irrational to choose to get it, if the alternative were getting nothing.

'Good': Something is good iff it would not be irrational to choose to get it, even if one had to get something bad as well, if the alternative were getting nothing.

The definition of 'good' here is a more precise version of the view that Moore hints at in the quotation given at the end of the previous section. For a good gloss on Moore's phrase 'worth having'—and one that makes sense of his appeal to the notion of worth—is 'worth some cost to have'.

The above definitions plausibly yield the following results. (1) Among other things, pain, disability, and death (understood as the end of conscious experience, and not a gateway to eternal bliss) are bad. (2) Among other things, pleasure, knowledge and abilities are good. It is important to note that these definitions are not symmetrical. Badness can, by itself, rationally compel a choice: a choice to get nothing. But goodness does not similarly compel. Goodness serves to mitigate the irrationality of a choice that would otherwise be irrational: it is what makes suffering a bad thing worth it. But mitigating the irrationality of a choice is not the same as rationally compelling that choice. Of course, this leaves it open that choosing nothing, rather than choosing some good thing, is irrational. But what is *definitional* of goodness is that good things are worth paying some price to get.

Why put things in this asymmetrical way? One reason is that it leaves it open that different rational agents might pursue different goods, all the while acknowledging that the things they are not pursuing *also* count as goods. A non-intellectual politician who is completely unmoved by the prospect of solving a certain philosophical problem, and who would not pay the smallest price to understand it, will typically not find it irrational if her philosopher friend forgoes a vacation in order to take advantage of an opportunity to talk to an expert in the field. Similarly, the philosopher might be totally indifferent to the prospect of political power, and yet might understand perfectly well why it is rational to spend a lot of one's own money and time in an effort to get elected. A plausible thing to say about these two cases is that the politician recognizes that abstract knowledge is a good, and the philosopher recognizes that power is a good. It will not do to try to homogenize the good here, and say that all that is really good is enjoyment, and that the philosopher enjoys solving intellectual problems while the politician enjoys solving (or creating) practical ones.

Both philosopher and politician can convincingly deny that enjoyment has much to do with their activities. With regard to badness, however, this sort of latitude doesn't seem as compelling. That is, while the philosopher can regard political power as a good, and yet refrain from regarding those who ignore it as irrational, if we regard something as *bad*, then we do not seem to have this latitude. Failure to choose an acknowledged good simply does not seem irrational in the same way that choosing an acknowledged evil does.

Even though these definitions of good and bad require us to imagine an agent acting in such a way as to get these things for *herself*, nothing in the definitions implies that, 'from my point of view' your pain is not bad. Indeed, the opposite is true. According to the account, it is pain that is bad—not just my pain for me and your pain for you. For it is the prospect of getting pain—not *my* pain, but pain—that makes it irrational for you, or me, to refuse to take a certain medical treatment. Compare: something is monetarily valuable if having it can make someone rich. Gold fits this definition: not my gold or your gold, but gold by itself, even though it is only particular people who can be made rich by possession of particular samples of it. Similarly, a substance is carcinogenic if it can cause someone to have cancer, an object is too hot to touch if it can burn someone, and so on. This point is obscured in the case of 'good' by the fact that something can indeed be good 'for you' but not good 'for me'. But this need only mean that, because of the peculiarities of my constitution or situation, my possession of something that is not itself intrinsically good would cause me to have something that is intrinsically good, while it would not do so for you. For example, if you like spicy food and I do not, then a certain meal might be good for you, but not for me. But it is not spicy food that is intrinsically good here. Rather, it is the pleasure you get in eating it. If I could get that pleasure, it would be 'good for me' too. Perhaps the point is even clearer in the case of bad things: if I am allergic to nuts, and you are not, then nuts are bad for me, but not for you. But this says nothing about the intrinsic value of nuts. Rather, it is a result of the intrinsic badness of discomfort and death, and of my particular constitution.

Suppose that we accept the preceding account of goodness and badness in terms of the rationality of action. It might seem that, using this definition, we could discover what things were, in fact, good and bad—make a catalogue, as it were—and then, for convenience, appeal to this catalogue in order to calculate the rational status of actions. And it might seem that such a calculation would amount to a mere summing of the values of the good things, and subtracting of the values of the bad things. What this suggestion ignores, however, is the relevance of the way in which the goods and evils are related to the action. That is, an action may be productive of a certain amount of pain, and a certain amount of pleasure. Assuming, plausibly, that pain is bad and pleasure good, we still may not know the rational status of the action until we know *who* will suffer the pain, and *who* will enjoy the pleasure. For it may make a great deal of difference whether it is the agent herself who will experience one or the other, or neither or both, of these important consequences. Suffering a great deal of pain for a small pleasure seems irrational, but it does not seem irrational—only immoral in the extreme—to cause a great deal of pain to someone else, in order to experience a small pleasure oneself. Our moral intuitions, together with a confusion of morality and rationality, may obscure this. But it ought to be very clear that while it would typically be irrational to break both of one's own legs to earn enough money for a very pleasant two-week vacation, Mafia hit-men are not acting irrationally in breaking *other people's* legs for the same compensation.

The example of the Mafiosi, chosen to provide a dramatic illustration of the importance of knowing *who* will suffer the harms an action causes, may suggest that the pains of other people are completely irrelevant to the rational status of one's own action. But that is not true. For if it would be rational to suffer certain pains to prevent a risk of death to oneself, so, too, would it be rational to suffer those pains to prevent a similar risk of death to someone else: even a stranger. No one regards altruistic action, within very broad limits, as irrational. But neither do people regard the mercenary actions of Mafiosi as irrational, at least when those Mafiosi are careful. What precisely is the relation, then, between rational status, good and bad consequences, and the self/other distinction? Elsewhere I have argued for a principle of practical rationality very similar to the following.[17]

> P: An action is irrational iff
>> (a) it will cause *the agent* to suffer something bad, and
>> (b) it will not bring any compensating good, or prevent anything at least as bad, for *anyone*.[18]

Clause (b) here specifies the kinds of considerations that can rationally *justify* an agent in suffering some bad thing. But such considerations do not rationally *require* an agent to do so: they function much like considerations of self-defense in the moral domain. Thus, if an action will not cause the agent to suffer something bad, it cannot count as irrational. But even if it *will* cause the agent to suffer something bad, it need not be irrational: for someone may receive a compensating benefit. This is how principle P accommodates both our intuitions about the Mafiosi, and about altruistic people. Admittedly, principle P goes against popular maximizing conceptions of rationality.

---

[17] *Brute Rationality.* For purposes of clarity I here omit a number of necessary qualifications. This characterization of practical rationality has its roots in the work of Bernard Gert. See, e.g., Bernard Gert, 'Rationality, Human Nature, and Lists', *Ethics*, 100 (1990), 279–300.

[18] One might wonder whether this account could capture the rationality of making small sacrifices to honor a dead parent's wishes, or to keep a death-bed promise. A brief answer is that judgments of rational status are basic to the view on offer here. Should these small sacrifices count as rational, it will then turn out that we should classify being able to honor a parent, or keep a promise, as goods.

But by itself that is not really an objection to it. Principle *P* seems much better than maximizing views with regard to capturing the kinds of actions normal people would call 'stupid', 'crazy', 'irrational', 'silly', 'wrongheaded', and so on. It also does a better job of capturing the kinds of actions we take to be relevant to questions of moral responsibility, free will, and so on: paradigm instances of irrational action, according to P, will include actions that result from compulsions and phobias. It allows that it is rational to make altruistic sacrifices, but also that it is rational to be quite selfish. The asymmetry at the heart of principle *P* will certainly offend a certain sort of philosophical sensibility. But I strongly believe that such a sensibility deserves to be offended. And, in any case, Moore himself was sensitive to the asymmetries of a similar sort in the moral domain. He claimed, for example, that 'pity for the undeserved suffering of others' and 'endurance of pain to ourselves . . . seem to be undoubtedly admirable in themselves'.[19] But I doubt that he would count self-pity as admirable, or, for that matter, contempt for the pain of others. The asymmetry here would not trouble him in itself, as long as it seemed well supported by intuition.[20] And, indeed, it does so seem. Once one admits this, as Moore has done, it seems very hard to defend the idea that such asymmetries do not matter in the case of judgments of rationality.

But if it matters to the rationality of an agent's action whether the pain that it will produce will be suffered by the agent, or by someone else, then don't we need to give up Moore's *invariance thesis*: that anything that is intrinsically good (or bad) is always, and to the same degree, intrinsically good (or bad)? And since any application of principle *P* to a particular action will require us to know *who* will be getting the various harms and benefits, don't we need to give up Moore's *narrow dependence thesis*: that intrinsic goodness (or badness) depends only on the intrinsic nature of that which possesses it? The answer is that we need give up neither of these theses. The asymmetry in principle *P* is as far from implying the variability or context-dependence of goodness or badness as was the fact that goodness and badness were defined by reference to what the *agent* would suffer or enjoy as the result of her action. Calculations of rational status, according to P, depend on two things: the magnitude of the various goods and evils that the action will produce; *and* the question of who will suffer or enjoy those goods and evils. Such a calculation presupposes, rather than undermines, the idea that the goodness of a good consequence, or the badness of a bad one, are independent of the question of who will suffer or enjoy them. What is not independent of such a question is only the *rational status* of the action.

Still, the fact that the badness of a bad consequence is independent of the question of who will suffer it only *clears the way* for the truth of Moore's invariance thesis. So we can still wonder whether we have any positive reason to believe the thesis is actually true. First, we should admit that our definition of 'bad', though it automatically yields

---

[19] *Principia Ethica*, 217. [20] See, e.g., *Principia Ethica*, 222.

the result that anything bad is always and everywhere bad, only does this for the trivial reason that our test for badness abstracts from context completely. That is, it only asks us to consider whether it would be irrational to choose the bad thing over nothing at all. If the answer to this question is 'yes' for some particular thing, it will always be 'yes', because the context in which we ask the question plays no role. This way of meeting the first part of the invariance thesis is not very satisfying. What we need is a conception of what it is for something to *manifest a degree of badness in a context*. Only with such a conception can we ask the essential question: whether something that manifests badness in one context must manifest it to the same degree in all others. As a first step towards such a conception we need an account of a bad thing's *degree* of badness.

Here is my suggestion. To assign degrees of goodness and badness to the consequences of a particular action is to commit oneself to various counter-factuals regarding the status of that action, were those consequences eliminated, augmented, or diminished in various ways. An analogy with weight will make things clearer. If we are given an unmarked balance and a large collection of variously sized pieces of different metals, we can, with a little ingenuity, work out rough assignments of weight—taking some particular piece as a standard unit. How do we do this? We weigh different collections of pieces against each other, and see which collections are heavier than others. Then we remove weights and see what difference that makes. All of these operations make one crucial presupposition: that any given piece of metal always makes the same contribution. If we make the contrary assumption—that a given bit of metal might be heavier in one context than in another—then there is no hope at all of justifying our assignments of weight even in particular cases, except to say that this *single* piece is (here) heavier than that *single* piece. In cases in which one side of the balance has more than one piece of metal on it, we would be unable to talk (sensibly) about the weight of each piece. For there would be nothing to justify an assignment of $(1, 4)$ to a pair of pieces of metal on one side of the balance, as opposed to $(2, 3)$ or $(3, 2)$. What justifies an assignment of $(1, 4)$ to two pieces is the fact that if we continue to assign these two values in *other* contexts, our predictions are borne out.[21]

In light of the above claims about weight, my conclusion is that anyone who is willing to concede that rational status is a function of the degrees of goodness and badness of its consequences is similarly committed to the idea that those consequences keep their degrees of goodness or badness from context to context.

---

[21] In fact, this explanation simplifies the physical phenomena a bit. The weight of an object does vary from context, since it is a function of mass and the strength of the local gravitational field. But this concession does nothing to undermine the force of the current argument. For even if weight does change from context to context, it changes as a function of a stable mass value and a gravitational field that is stably calculable as a function of other masses. Without the assumption that mass remains stable, and the assumption that the law of gravity is also constant, it would make no sense to assign particular masses or gravitational forces in particular cases.

Otherwise assignments of particular degrees of goodness and badness even in particular contexts lack justification. Indeed, without this assumption of stability, assignments of particular degrees of goodness or badness in particular cases lack not only justification but sense. One crucial assumption here, of course, is that it makes sense to talk about degrees of goodness and badness at all, even in particular cases. But I am content to address my argument only to those who share this assumption. Given that even the arch-particularist Jonathan Dancy can be counted as a member this group, I am confident that the argument has wide scope.[22]

Now to the narrow dependence thesis. It is not entirely clear what the narrow dependence thesis amounts to for Moore. In his own terms, it can be expressed as the thesis that value is an intrinsic property.[23] And a property is intrinsic if 'the question whether a thing possesses it, and in what degree it possesses it, depends solely on the intrinsic nature of the thing in question'.[24] This is not very helpful unless we have a prior grasp on intrinsic nature. I propose to sidestep this complication by discussing the most obvious way in which the value of something might clearly *not* be intrinsic: it might depend on the degree to which the agent desires it. If my argument against this possibility is convincing, it should provide a template for arguing against all of the most tempting variations on this theme. The temptation to think that value depends on the desire of the agent stems from cases of the following sort. Suppose that two separate agents are acting in a way that will cause each of them to suffer the same bad consequence. This implies that, without the prospect of bringing someone a compensating good, or of helping someone avoid something at least as bad, each of these agents will be acting irrationally. But suppose that each agent's action will, indeed, bring a stranger something that we consider a compensating good. Now we can introduce the element that suggests a relativity of goodness to the desires of the agent: the first agent, Polly, chooses to suffer the bad thing *because* of the good her action will produce; while the second agent, Carl, chooses to suffer the bad thing *despite the fact* that his action will produce some good for the third person (perhaps Carl hates this person). Because Polly's action seems rational, and Carl's irrational, it seems that we should conclude that the 'good' that the third person will receive is only really good in Polly's case, and not in Carl's. This, if true, would undermine the narrow dependence thesis. Happily, it is not true. Carl is indeed acting irrationally, but the action he is performing is not irrational in the relevant sense. When we engage in our thought experiments in order to determine whether something is bad or good, we do not ask ourselves if it would be irrational for any particular person to choose the candidate

---

[22] See Jonathan Dancy, *Ethics Without Principles* (Oxford: Oxford University Press, 2004). At least Dancy holds that reasons have strength values in particular contexts, and that reasons and value are very intimately related.

[23] At least as Moore later used the terms 'intrinsic' and 'property'. See his 'Reply', 585.

[24] 'The conception of intrinsic value', 260.

bad thing over nothing, or to choose the package of an acknowledged bad thing and a candidate good thing. Rather, we ask ourselves whether *anyone could* make such a choice rationally. A broken arm counts as a bad thing because *no one could* rationally choose it, rather than choosing nothing, if the choice were only between these two options.[25] And certain bits of abstract knowledge count as good things because *someone could* choose to suffer sleepless nights and a certain amount of frustration, and so on, in order to get them. That Carl is not motivated by the prospect of producing something good does nothing to undermine the claim that it is, nevertheless, good, and that its goodness is part of what makes Polly's action rational.

IV Rejecting Utilitarianism

So far I have been defending a view that could, with some plausibility, be called Moorean. At least many of my conclusions are very similar to a number of Moore's distinctive claims, whether or not Moore himself would have appreciated my attempts to argue for them on his behalf. In this final section, however, I want to pattern myself after Moore in a different way: as a harsh critic of Moore. In particular, I want to argue that (a) Moore gives us no reason at all in support of the utilitarian view he favors; that (b) his own adherence to it may have been the result of the intersection of a number of confusions; and that (c) in some cases even Moore cannot adhere strictly to his own stated views. What are those views? Here are two clear expressions:

'[D]uty', therefore, can only be defined as that action, which will cause more good to exist in the Universe than any possible alternative.

[T]he term duty is certainly so used that, if we are subsequently persuaded that any possible action would have produced more good than the one we adopted, we admit that we failed to do our duty.[26]

Why is Moore so certain that it is, in fact, our duty to produce as much intrinsic good as possible? Nowhere does he offer any argument for this claim. All he does is repeat, with varying degrees of vehemence, that he finds it self-evident.[27] And, at least if he did not change his mind from the time at which he wrote *Principia*, this means that he thinks that there *are* no reasons for it.[28] In any case, and whatever the link

---

[25] Of course, it can be rational to choose a broken arm in order to get other things, such as exemption from a dangerous military assignment. But then the choice is simply a different one than the simple choice of the thought experiment.

[26] *Principia Ethica*, 148, 150. See also 'Reply', 575, *Ethics*, 97, 119–21, 143.

[27] *Ethics*, 97, 112, 143; *Principia*, 24–5, 42.   [28] *Principia*, 144.

between self-evidence and the existence of reasons might be, one thing seems clear: the fact that Moore finds his definition of duty self-evident is no reason to suppose that it is true, especially given the existence of many other philosophers for whom its denial is either equally self-evident, or actually supported by positive argument. Why was Moore so firmly persuaded of this doctrine, given that he never offered any reason in its favor? Of course, any answer to this question must be highly speculative, but I would like to suggest that it was partly the result of a failure to pay sufficient attention to the notion of *practical rationality*, as distinct from the notion of *morality*. If rationality is distinct from (though, of course, related in important ways to) morality, then it is likely that goodness and badness will be related to rationality in ways that are different from the ways in which they are related to morality. And if they are most directly related to rationality—as has been suggested above—then maximizing views of morality will be easier to avoid.

One of the most obvious reasons for supposing that rationality and morality are distinct is that it is plausible to suppose that many instances of immoral action are not irrational. Indeed, to the extent that we want to hold those who commit very immoral actions fully responsible, we ought not regard them as having acted very irrationally.[29] Moore may have missed this point because of his purely formal account of free will, according to which we act freely when we would have acted differently *if* we had chosen to act differently, quite independently of whether or not we *could* have so chosen.[30] On this view, the gambling addict is acting freely as he gambles away his last dollar; as is the agoraphobe, even though he finds it impossible to cross the threshold of his doorway. For both the addict and the phobic would have acted differently *if* they had chosen to. This is not the place to argue for an alternative account of free will and moral responsibility. However, it is the place to suggest that the notion of rationality will have some place in such an account. For example, one kind of unfree act might be an act that is the result of an irresistible desire, where 'irresistible' here should be taken to mean 'sufficiently strong that one's awareness of reasons that would make it irrational to act on the desire would be psychologically incapable of dissuading one from acting'.[31]

If one does not separate rationality from morality, and one asks oneself the question 'Faced with two options, one of which will produce more good than the other, which should I pick?', it may seem that the only possible answer must be 'The one that will

---

[29] Of course, we can hold people morally responsible even if they are acting irrationally. But some forms of irrationality do mitigate blame, and an identification of morality and rationality will make this hard to understand.

[30] *Ethics*, ch. VI.

[31] For an account of disabilities of the will in these terms, see Timothy Duggan and Bernard Gert, 'Voluntary Abilities', *American Philosophical Quarterly*, 4 (1967), 127–35; and 'Free Will as the Ability to Will', *Noûs*, 13 (1979), 197–217.

produce the most good'. One reason for this is that morality very plausibly requires a certain sort of impartiality, and one obvious interpretation of impartiality involves the idea of giving each person the same *weight*. Conceived in this way, it seems that the calculations relevant to morality will be weighted sums of the goods had by all relevant people, and that the weights should be the same for all human beings. It is true that this presupposes that the only good things will be things that can be 'had' by individual people (so that, for example, fair distributions will not count as basic goods). But Moore explicitly endorses this assumption, writing that 'nothing but an experience *can* be "intrinsically good", since nothing but an experience can be "had" in the sense in which an experience is "had" '.[32]

But if rationality and morality are clearly distinguished, it is possible to ask which of two options one should *rationally* choose. And even if one of the options will produce the most good, it does not seem in any way obvious that one is rationally required to choose it, particularly if the bulk of that good will be enjoyed by other people, and will come at one's own significant expense. Sidgwick, from whom Moore took many of his ideas, was clear about this: that, rationally, there is no way to adjudicate between the egoistic and the utilitarian 'methods of ethics'. Both Sidgwick and Moore saw the conflict of these two views as somehow problematic, but, in fact, one relatively easy way of defusing it is simply to admit that there is no rational *conflict* here at all: that while *morality* might sometimes prohibit acting in a completely self-interested way, *rationality* explicitly allows both selfish and selfless behavior. This latter claim is hardly controversial, it seems to me, among normal people.

Moore does, indeed, seem to have thought that morality and rationality amounted to essentially the same thing, which would have prevented him from seeing this solution to the dilemma. For example, he holds the following claims not merely to be logically equivalent, but to be identical.

It would have been the duty of this agent . . . to make this choice.
This agent, if he had a rational will, would have made this choice.[33]

Nor is Moore's use of 'rational will' here meant to indicate any special technical notion, or to name any contentious mental faculty. Rather, according to Moore 'to say that so and so has a rational will just *means* that he makes the choices which he ought to make, or (in other words) which it is *rational* to make'.[34] Here is one place where it does not seem unfair to charge Moore with a 'sheer mistake'. If Moore were right, then according to his own tests for identity of meaning, it would be impossible to ask whether or not it might sometimes be rationally permissible to act in contrary to one's moral duty. Of course, many philosophers—Kantians in particular—have argued,

---

[32] 'Is Goodness a Quality?', *Philosophical Papers* (London: George Allen & Unwin 1959), 89–101, at 95.
[33] 'Reply to My Critics', 616.   [34] Ibid.

heroically, that the answer to this question is 'No'. But many others have argued for the more common-sensical affirmative answer. Michael Smith, for example, goes so far as to claim that 'a theory of rational action that suggested otherwise would be flawed in a quite decisive way'.[35]

If we agree with Michael Smith here, and distinguish sharply between morality and rationality, then we can keep much of Moore's general view, including a version of the isolation test, and yet hold that the notions of good and bad are most directly related not to morality but to rationality. This move allows us much more theoretical space in which to develop a moral theory. What kind of theory should we favor? To close this chapter, I would like to point out that Moore himself sometimes departs from his own hard-line act utilitarianism. Taken together with some of the earlier modifications to Moore's view, we can take our cue from his 'lapses' to suggest a more plausible moral theory. Moore's lapses have to do with the relevance of rules. He admits that many of the kinds of actions that only *generally* produce the best consequences are still such that an agent *ought always* to perform them. As he puts it:

[T]hough we may be sure that there are cases where the rule should be broken, we can never know which those cases are, and ought, therefore, never to break it.
With regard to actions of which the *general* utility is thus proved, the individual should *always* perform them.[36]

It is clear from these two claims that Moore is making no distinction between 'should' and 'ought', and it is therefore equally clear that he is claiming that, with regard to conduct, it is sometimes true that we ought to act in ways that, as a matter of fact, will not produce the best consequences. Indeed, even when we ourselves think that the action will not produce the best consequences, Moore still counsels us to adhere to the rule.

Moore, then, can at least on some occasions be read as a kind of rule-utilitarian. Such a reading, even taken alone, is likely to bring his views more into line with the first-order moral judgments of normal people. But we can do more than this. Recall that by taking judgments of rationality as basic, we were able to define 'good' and 'bad' in a slightly asymmetric way. In particular, bad things were rationally compelling in a way that good things were not: bad things are irrational to choose without some justification; and good things provide that justification. Now, one feature of morality that has typically been difficult for utilitarians to capture has been the distinction between the morally permissible and the morally supererogatory. Another feature, which utilitarians are more likely to mention, is impartiality.[37] If we take the notion of

---

[35] Michael Smith, 'Bernard Gert's Complex Hybrid Conception of Rationality', in R. Audi and W, Sinnott-Armstrong (eds.), *Rationality, Rules, and Ideals: Critical Essays on Bernard Gert's Moral Theory* (Lanham, Md., Rowman and Littlefield, 2002), 121.

[36] *Principia Ethica*, 162–3, 182.   [37] See Mill, *Utilitarianism*, ch. 5.

rationality as basic, and incorporate the notions of rules and impartiality, we can offer the following rough skeleton of a moral theory: it is the system of rules that would be favored by impartial rational people.[38] Given our assumption that good things can justify without compelling, these rules will primarily serve to prohibit the harming of other people. This essentially prohibitive orientation of moral rules will give moral agents a lot of latitude. For even impartial rational people will be able to differ in the degree to which they are motivated to promote the good of others. Supererogatory action then might be that class of action that reflects a greater degree of such concern.

[38] This is the one-sentence version of Bernard Gert's moral theory. For the full view, see his *Morality: Its Nature and Justification* (Oxford: Oxford University Press, 2005). For the pocket-sized version, see his *Common Morality* (Oxford: Oxford University press, 2004).

16

Moore's Account of Vindictive Punishment: A Test Case for Theories of Organic Unities

Jonathan Dancy

I

The final chapter of G. E. Moore's *Principia Ethica* contains a fascinating discussion of what Moore calls 'vindictive punishment'.[1] Moore's views are worth extended treatment in their own right. But theorists of punishment have not given them the attention they deserve, and I can hardly claim that I will be doing so in this paper. My purpose is rather to treat punishment as a sort of test case in a debate about the right way to understand organic unities. An organic unity is a whole, or complex, whose value is not, or at least need not be, identical to the sum of the values brought to it by its parts. An obvious example is that of a recipe which seems to be much improved by the addition of a little salt, supposing the value of the pinch of salt to be far less than the value that it adds or brings to the recipe. The idea of the value brought to the whole by a part is important, because it seems possible for a part to have value which it does not contribute to the whole—which it hugs to itself, as it were. An example here might be a charming brooch which clashes with the blouse to which it

---

[1] The two extant editions of this work, the original edition (Cambridge: Cambridge University Press, 1903), and the Revised Edition (ed. T. Baldwin, 1993), have different pagination, which is inconvenient; so in references I will always give the relevant section number, followed by page references to both editions, thus: *PE* §1, 1/53.

is attached, so to that the value of the whole outfit is less than the value of either blouse or brooch. If this is the right way to describe the situation, it is easy for a whole to have less value than the sum of the values of its parts, because some of the latter value may be withheld, and not passed upwards. But this possibility is not what the friends of the organic were primarily thinking of. What most impressed them was the idea that even if one only considers the value that the parts bring to the whole, or pass upwards, the whole may have more value than comes to it from its parts—or less.

There is a debate about the right way to understand organic unities. There are two views, which have come to be called 'intrinsicalism' and 'variabilism'. Moore is an intrinsicalist; I am a variabilist. Now it would be nice to begin my discussion of the debate between these two positions with an example of each, to fix ideas. But since each position denies the coherence of the other, this cannot be done without begging central questions. So I will have to proceed with a rather abstract account of the two views.

Intrinsicalists suppose that parts retain their intrinsic value as they move from whole to whole; this is not terribly contentious—many would say as much. But they also suppose that even if the parts do not acquire any new value as they enter a new whole, still the value of the whole can be increased by their presence *more* than can be explained by simple appeal to the value that the parts have there. In this sense, parts can contribute value that they have not got. In fact, a whole can be the better for the presence of a part even if the part itself has no value at all, either there or anywhere else. The salt adds more value to the recipe than it itself has *in that context*.

Now, in fact, Moore held that there are only two sorts of value: intrinsic value and instrumental value. Thinking this, and thinking that intrinsic value cannot be affected by changes in context, and thinking that the relation between part and whole is not instrumental, Moore concluded, very reasonably, that parts cannot change in value as they move from whole to whole, because that sort of change could change neither instrumental nor intrinsic value. So when we are trying to understand the part–whole relationship and organic unities, everything has to be done in terms of intrinsic value. I say that this was reasonable; but, in fact, Moore went a bit further, for he held that intrinsic value is essential value. He writes elsewhere:

it is impossible for what is strictly one and the same thing to possess that kind of value at one time, or in one set of circumstances, and not to possess it at another; and equally impossible for it to possess it in one degree at one time, or in one set of circumstances, and to possess it in a different degree at another, or in a different set.   (1922, 260−1)

This is not quite so reasonable. The most natural way of understanding intrinsic value is as that part of the value of an object which is grounded in intrinsic properties of that object—in what Moore calls the object's 'intrinsic nature' (see, for example, Moore 1922, 274). But intrinsic properties include the object's particular size and shape, it would seem, and these are surely capable of change. If so, there is no reason to deny that an object's intrinsic value can change; what it can't do, we might say (though I won't, in fact, say this), is change when the intrinsic properties that are its ground remain constant. But Moore, as the quotation above shows, seems to go further than that and, in going further, he goes too far.

Variabilists take the view that parts can change in value as they move from whole to whole. Most variabilists hold this view because they suppose that there are more sorts of value than the two that Moore was willing to allow. They think that, in addition to the intrinsic and the instrumental, there are other sorts of value, which can be called 'extrinsic'. It is best, I think, to classify the instrumental as one sort of extrinsic value.[2] But there are other sorts. The most obvious are symbolic and sentimental value, which, as far as I can see, are neither instrumental nor intrinsic. The question, then, is whether, in addition to extrinsic symbolic and sentimental value, there is another sort of extrinsic value, 'value-as-a-part'. If there is, I can see no reason why such value should not change as the bearer moves from whole to whole. This gives us constant intrinsic value, supposedly, and variable extrinsic value. With this weaponry, we are less likely to say that parts can contribute value that they have not got; for we now have the option of supposing that *all* the value that a part contributes is value that it itself has in that whole, even though it won't necessarily have that same value elsewhere. Any difference between the value contributed to one whole and to another will be explained by appeal to differences in the extrinsic values enjoyed by that part in those two wholes; that is, by appeal to the differences between its value as a part of one whole and its value as a part of the other.

Before entering into the substantial debate between intrinsicalism and variabilism, I want to make a couple of comments. The first is that all this talk of parts and wholes, and of a part contributing value to a whole, is pretty peculiar. But does its peculiarity vitiate the debate? I don't think so. However we express the matter, we think that the value of an object is to be explained by appeal to 'features' of that object, or of the situation in which it stands. These 'features' are the characteristics which make it good, and this 'making-good' is something that each of several features can do at the same time. By this, we don't mean that each severally succeeds in making the object good overall. We mean, rather, that each contributes to the value of the object, or, as we might say, raises the object's value. This talk of contribution can be understood less metaphorically in terms of explanation, but there are two ways of doing that. As the intrinsicalist sees things, if the value of the object could be explained entirely in

---

[2] This suggestion would be disputed by those who hold, with Ross and Prichard, that instrumental value is no sort of value at all: it is possible to think that to be instrumentally valuable is just to be a means to something that is of value, without allowing that to be such a means is a way of being valuable. See W. D. Ross, *The Right and the Good* (Oxford: Clarendon Press, 1930), 133.

terms of the values of the various features, there would be no organicity. But there is organicity, because there are cases where the value of the object is to some extent explained in terms of the presence of the various features but not in terms of their value, either because they have no value here (or not enough) or because we do not appeal to their value in our explanation of the value of the object. What is more, there are no cases where the value of a part changes as it moves from one whole to another. As variabilists see things, by contrast, there are no organic wholes of the intrinsicalist's sort at all. The only possibility is that, though the explanation of the value of the whole is run entirely in terms of the values of the parts, those parts need not have the same value here as they have elsewhere.

My second comment is that, though the debate about organicity has always been conducted within the theory of value, so far as I know, it is, in fact, of wider significance. It is a debate about the possibility of certain structures and, as such, it has repercussions elsewhere in philosophy. To take the most glaring instance: there is strong similarity between the present debate, which in the most general terms can be thought of as a debate about practical purport, and a familiar debate in the theory of meaning about semantic purport. Must the meaning of the whole be entirely explained in terms of the semantic contributions of the contributing parts? Can such parts 'change' their meaning as they move from context to context? Can they contribute meaning that they have not got? Do we need a distinction between variant (extrinsic) and invariant (intrinsic) meaning, and must we suppose that in the absence of invariant meaning, there is no meaning at all? These questions in the theory of meaning may seem peculiar, but I take them to be strongly analogous to the questions we shall be discussing in the theory of value.

II

So far I have suggested that there are two approaches to organic unities: the intrinsicalist; and the variabilist. But this does not by itself lead to any substantial debate. If the question is whether we should understand the relevant phenomena in terms of changes in the values of parts as they move from whole to whole, or in terms of a difference between the sum of the values of the parts *in the whole* and the overall value of the whole, the answer might be that we need both conceptions. Some wholes are to be understood in one way, and others in the other. But the fact is that neither side in the debate is willing to be so conciliatory. Each side comes with an argument, and the two arguments are designed to show not just that there are no instances of the opposing conception, because that conception is incoherent. In this section I consider the arguments on either side.

Moore's argument is as follows:

> Thus we may easily come to say that, *as* a part of the body [the arm] has great value, whereas *by itself* it would have none . . . But in fact the value in question obviously does not belong to *it* at all. To have value merely as a part is equivalent to having no value at all, but merely being a part of that which has it. Owing, however, to neglect of this distinction, the assertion that a part has value, *as a part*, which it would otherwise not have, easily leads to the assumption that it is also different, as a part, from what it would otherwise be; for it is, in fact, true that two things which have a different value must also differ in other respects. Hence the assumption that one and the same thing, because it is a part of a more valuable whole at one time than at another, therefore has more intrinsic value at one time than at another, has encouraged the self-contradictory belief that one and the same thing may be two different things, and that only in one of its forms is it truly what it is. (*Principia Ethica*, §22, 35/86–7)

This is a *most* peculiar argument. The crucial claim is that there is no such thing as value-as-a-part, in the third sentence. (This claim is structurally identical to the Prichard/Ross claim that there is no such thing as instrumental value.) It may be that this claim is not supposed to be supported by the rest of the quotation.[3] But if one is tempted to suppose that there is such a thing as extrinsic value, and that value-as-a-part is of that sort, what is said here to persuade one otherwise? The last sentence says that a contradiction follows from supposing that one and the same thing can have different intrinsic value in different situations. But that is irrelevant. To make it relevant, I suggest that we remove the word 'intrinsic' from the last sentence, and replace it by 'non-instrumental'. (It is obviously coherent to suggest that something can vary in instrumental value from context to context.) This should not damage Moore's argument, because he thought that all value was either intrinsic or instrumental. The question is whether this passage provides independent support for that view. I take it that, to the extent that there is any such support, it comes from the claim about supervenience. If you suppose that something which is a (contributory) part of a valuable whole therefore has something worth calling 'value-as-a-part', you end up with a contradiction, because two things that have different value must differ in other respects. But the whole idea was that the part does not change in any way as it moves from whole to whole; and, if not, it cannot change in value either. If it changes in value, it necessarily ceases to be what it was.

But is it true that two things that have different non-instrumental value must differ in other respects? No. For all we have yet been told, it is possible for changes elsewhere

---

[3] The next sentence is a bit ambiguous in tone, because the phrase 'easily leads' might be supposed to imply that the relevant inference is unsound. On that reading, Moore would be rehearsing an objection which he himself does not accept. But Moore's general practice in *PE* tells against this reading. He *always* speaks of the whole being better for the presence of the part, and never suggests that the part might be more valuable here than it is elsewhere. See §§18, 55, 57, 117, 119, 121, 122, at pp. 29/80, 92/144, 194/243, 197/245–6, 202/250–1, 203/252.

to affect something's value without altering that thing in any other way. I have argued elsewhere that Moore has adopted too limited a conception of supervenience. He assumes that an object's value must supervene on the other properties *of that object*; but there is a wider conception of supervenience under which an object's value supervenes simply on other properties, which may or may not be properties of that object. If this wider conception is defensible, as I suppose, it is not true that 'two things which have a different value must also differ in other respects'. And with that, Moore's argument collapses. This leaves us with the three or four potential sorts of extrinsic value that I mooted in the previous section: value-as-a-part, symbolic and sentimental value, and instrumental value.

So Moore's attempt to destabilize the opposition fails. But what about the argument in the other direction, the variabilist's attempt to show that the intrinsicalist picture of the organic is incoherent? This argument focuses on the idea that a part can contribute value that it has not got. (It allows that a part can fail to contribute value that it has got.) Moore's view is that the presence of the part can be important for the value of the whole, vital even though the part itself remains totally valueless. But this seems to fly in the face of what one might call the essential link between values and reasons. It does not matter for the point exactly how one expresses, or tries to capture, that link. In rough terms, the idea is that where there is value there are reasons of certain sorts, and vice versa. If something is of value, one will have reasons to preserve, promote, admire, approve, respect, or honour it; and if one has such reasons, it must be that the relevant object has some value, or is valuable in some respect. I have expressed this rather vaguely, intentionally. There are all sorts of different views about the nature and the tightness of the link between values and reasons, right up to the 'buck-passing' view which understands an object's being valuable just as its having features that give us reasons to protect, promote . . . it. We should also bear in mind various possible exceptions to the rule that values and reasons are essentially connected. But none of these niggles does anything to undermine the existence of a *general* tie between values and reasons; or, if they do, they do not address the case we are here considering, namely the intrinsicalist suggestion that we might have considerable reason to protect *here* a feature which itself has no value at all here, because of the value which its presence generates in the whole of which it is a part. Whether we say, with the buck-passers, that for us to have those reasons is just what it is for the feature to be of value, or hold the weaker view that it is incoherent to deny all value to something which is, in the context, so important, we get the same result. Something which it is important to protect in a certain context must be of value in that context. And this rules out the possibility that a part can contribute value which it has not got.

III

In all this I have been allowing something that I now wish to dispute. This is the idea, common to intrinsicalists and variabilists, for all I have said so far, that the intrinsic value of an object must remain unchanged so long as the intrinsic qualities that are its ground do not change. Intrinsic value, we have been supposing, is to this extent persistent. So to find such value we have to find something whose value is completely insensitive to changes in other things, unless those changes lead to changes in the object's own intrinsic nature. In this section I want to suggest that this picture is, at best, optional. There is a conception of intrinsic value which allows such value to vary even when its intrinsic ground remains invariant.

This may come as something of a surprise, but actually I think it should not. The picture that I am disputing results from unwarily supposing that the only thing relevant to the generation of value, as one might put it, is the ground for that value. But it might be that though we hold that ground unchanged, changes elsewhere will suffice to undermine the ability of the ground to generate the relevant value, so that the ground will remain but the value vanish. If so, we will get something worth calling intrinsic value, because its ground consists entirely in intrinsic features of the object, but which may vary independently of those features. (Only in the sense that we can retain those features but lose the value, of course.) There will be variable intrinsic value.

How is this possible? As I see it, the grounding relation itself is one that is sensitive to potential changes in the surroundings. There can be conditions necessary for the grounds to do their grounding work, which are not themselves among the grounds. These features, which I call enabling conditions, are conditions in the absence of which the grounding features still remain, but whose presence is required for the grounding, that is, for the generation of the value, to occur. Take the enabling conditions away and the value vanishes, even though the enablers themselves are not part of the ground; they are doing another job. The matter is a bit like (but not entirely like, because of the difference between causal and non-causal relations) the relation between the actors on the stage and the lighting engineers and the other support staff in a theatre. The activities of the support staff are required for the actors to play *their* role; but this does nothing to turn the support staff into members of the cast. The same structure is to be found in the theory of value (and, I would say, everywhere where there is normativity). There are two roles: the grounding role; and the enabling role. It is one thing to play a certain role, and another to enable something else to play that role. But, given this distinction, we immediately derive a variabilist conception of intrinsic value. To guarantee the persistence of a value, we need not only the persistence of the ground but also that of the relevant enablers. But the enablers themselves may be features of other objects. If so, an object that is intrinsically valuable may lose all value as a result of changes in other objects, even though its own intrinsic properties remain unchanged.

My description of this possibility has so far been entirely abstract. The best example I know, which I owe largely to Frances Kamm, is that of a joke about someone, where the value of the joke (its humour) vanishes if the joke is told behind that person's back. That the butt of the joke is present is required for the joke to have the value it does, but it does not itself contribute to the humorousness; it is not among the funny things.

This gives us a conception of intrinsic but variant value. I am mentioning it here only for the sake of completeness. At most we should say of it what Ross says of the doctrine of organic unities itself: 'The importance of the doctrine so far as its application goes is somewhat doubtful. But its truth in the abstract seems unquestionable' (1930, 72).

Of course, there may remain some objects which have a very special sort of intrinsic value that is genuinely invariant, so long as their intrinsic properties remain unchanged. These will be ones such that the enabling conditions for the relevant value, if any, consist in *further* intrinsic properties of the value-bearer concerned. Perhaps there are, indeed, such specially valuable objects. My point is only that there is no need, so far as the structure of value goes, for any such things. It might be that there are plenty of things of value, even of intrinsic value, while this transcendental category remains entirely empty.

One interesting aspect of the distinction between enablers and value enabled is that the enablers themselves will have value, because of the link between values and reasons. There is reason to protect something whose presence is required for the existence of a value. So an enabler for a value will itself be of value. This doesn't seem to me to introduce any theoretical problems. It is not as if something in the theory of organicity is thereby destabilized, for the value of any enabler will not itself be contributed to the value of the whole. It is of value in the circumstances, but it does not pass its value upwards to the whole, part of whose value it is enabling. My present point is only that what one might call 'value as an enabler' is another form of non-intrinsic value, to be put beside the instrumental, the symbolic, and the rest.

IV

After that methodological digression, I return to the main theme. We had two conceptions of organicity, and two arguments. I purported to dispose of one of those arguments, leaving the other one master of the field, and with it the variabilist conception of organic unities. But there is an alternative view, promoted by Thomas

Hurka, among others, which holds that we need both conceptions.[4] On this view, both of the arguments must be flawed, but this does nothing to destabilize the conceptions those arguments were designed to promote. All it means is that the other conception, the one attacked, remains unimpugned. If that were so, there would be two possibilities, not just one. And Hurka claims that this is just as well, because some actual organic unities need to be understood in one way, and others in the other. Why insist that only one way is possible? There is no reason, once the two arguments have been seen off.

As an example that fits variabilism, I would offer a mosaic. A mosaic consists of lots of little stones which were, before the prospect of the mosaic came along, utterly worthless (let us say). However, once placed in the mosaic each one (like the pieces of a jigsaw puzzle) acquires a new importance. It is difficult to get this part of the story quite right, because we don't want to award to each part more than its share in the value of the whole; but I assume that there is some way of sorting this out. Anyway, Hurka would have no trouble with any of this and, indeed, he offers a clutch of further examples to the same end. His point, however, is that there are some cases which cannot be handled in the variabilist way. The rest of the present paper is devoted to considering his main example, which is that of vindictive punishment. The interest of this example, in the present context, is that Moore offers in chapter 6 of *Principia Ethica* an extended intrinsicalist treatment of punishment as a good which consists entirely of bad parts. The idea is that variabilists, if they want to turn the same trick, will have to say that if the whole is good the parts must be good, and that this is so counter-intuitive as to be impossible.

Suppose, for a moment, that we try to understand punishment in a standard consequentialist manner but without appeal to organic unities. The crime itself is bad, we may admit; and the punishment is also bad, since it amounts to an increase of nastiness in the world. If we are to justify making things worse by adding one bad thing to another, we will have to find some other respect in which, by making them worse in this way, we are also making them better; and whatever increase in value we find must be greater than the decrease involved in the punishment itself. This is very much the picture we find in Bentham, for instance; Bentham is clear that punishment is itself mischief, as he puts it. It is only worth inflicting if by doing so we secure a greater good than the punishment is a harm.

Now this is not the only way in which a consequentialist might be thinking about punishment. It is possible to think of the act of punishment as having intrinsic value as well as instrumental value. So instead of saying that we will have to find some way in which, in addition to making things worse, we also make them better, we might look for some other feature of the act of punishing that makes that act intrinsically, not

---

[4] T. Hurka, 'Moore in the Middle', *Ethics*, 113 (2003), 599–628.

instrumentally, valuable. Consequentialists are, after all, allowed to ascribe intrinsic value to actions as well as to consequences of those actions; and they might seek to take advantage of that freedom in this case. The problem, however, is to see what feature of the action might be capable of being good enough to do the trick.

If we look at the matter in terms of organic unities, it all looks different. Moore approaches it with a distinction between what is valuable or good on the whole and what is valuable or good as a whole. For something to be valuable on the whole is for the world to be better for its existence, all things considered. '... the value which a thing possesses *on the whole* may be said to be equivalent to the sum of the value which it possesses *as a whole, together with* the intrinsic values which may belong to any of its parts (214/263). But a combination that is bad on the whole may yet be valuable as a whole, and would be if 'there arises from the combination a positive good which is greater than the *difference* between the sum of the two evils and the demerit of either singly' (215/263). So a combination of two evils is good as a whole if the gain from putting the two parts together is greater than the loss incurred by the addition of the second evil. But a combination of two evils might still be such that the two parts are together worse than the combination is better, so that the world is overall still the worse for the combination, and that would mean that despite being good as a whole it remains bad on the whole, not good.

A numerical, and therefore necessarily artificial, example might help. Suppose we are dealing with units of goodness. The crime scores -5, and the punishment scores -2; but the combination of crime and punishment together has an independent score of $+3$ (this is its value as a whole). This means that when we punish the crime we turn an overall score of -5 to one of -4. The situation is still bad on the whole, because our overall score is a minus one, but it is less bad than it would have been if we had left the crime unpunished. So we were right to punish, and would have been wrong not to, even though in punishment we add evil to evil.

So in punishment one evil is added to another in such a way, we hope, that the combination is good as a whole; it would be good on the whole if the combination were more valuable than the disvalue of the punishment. This being so, by adding the punishment to the crime we would leave things better than they would have been—though not better than if the crime had not been committed. Moore concludes: 'If pain be added to an evil state of either of our first two classes, the whole thus formed is *always* better, *as a whole*, than if no pain had been there; though here, if the pain be too intense, since that is a great evil, the state may not be better *on the whole*. It is in this way that the theory of vindictive punishment may be vindicated' (PE, 214).

The idea, then, is that we can make things better by adding one evil to another. Of course, in making them better all we are normally doing is making them less bad. Crime punished is better than crime unpunished. But this does not normally mean that a punished crime is overall a good, good on the whole; it is merely less bad than an unpunished one. And if the punishment is excessive, even this would not be true; the addition of excessive punishment will generate a combination that is not even good as a whole, since the disvalue added by the punishment will exceed the value added by the combination in the light of the appropriateness of punishment to crime. In our numerical example above, if the punishment comes in at -4, but the combination of crime and punishment remains at $+3$, the punishment just makes things worse, since it turns an overall -5 into -6. This is genuine mischief.

So what Moore ends up saying is that, though punishment is an intrinsic evil, a combination of crime and punishment may be intrinsically good as a whole. It won't be good on the whole (even if it is better on the whole than the unpunished crime), since we would be right to prefer a world with neither crime nor punishment to one with crime and punishment. So our ranking is: best, neither crime nor punishment; second best, both crime and punishment; worst, crime alone. This is a justification of vindictive punishment that is not run extrinsically, in terms of causal relations to intrinsically valuable consequences. That is, it is a justification of punishment that is based on the appropriateness of punishment to crime, not in terms of the hoped-for social or other consequences of inflicting the punishment.

This is all rather clever. To see how clever, we should return to the difference between Moore and the advanced consequentialist who wants to appeal to the fact that actions can be among the intrinsic goods in order to avoid a merely instrumental justification of vindictive punishment. This consequentialist has to find some feature of the punishing (rather than of the consequences of the punishing) that makes it good, and good enough to counteract the badness of the pain inflicted. Moore, by contrast, looks at the relation between punishment and crime, and thereby succeeds in showing that a consequentialist can adopt a conception of punishment which strongly resembles that of the retributivist. For even if we do not allow an independent intrinsic value to the relation of fittingness or appropriateness which obtains between punishment and crime, as the retributivist may seek to do, we are at least awarding value to a *combination* whose parts fit each other in an appropriate way.

Having distinguished Moore's views from those of a standard consequentialist, we might find it worth while to contrast them also with those of Ross,[5] because there is a sense in which Moore sits in between standard consequentialism, on the one hand, and intuitionism, on the other, at least with respect to punishment. Ross considers, but rejects, a possible intuitionist understanding of the duty of punishment as an instance of the more general duty of producing as much good as we can. The good in

---

[5] Ross's views are given in the 2nd appendix to ch. 2 of *The Right and the Good*.

question would be 'a certain relative arrangement of virtue, vice, pleasure and pain'. But Ross objects that, first, the right arrangement for a particular person would be not what is right in the limited context of that person's having committed a crime but what is right considering the balance of their life as a whole, which it is quite beyond our ability and that of the courts to determine. And he adds to this the thought that it is not the business of the state to attempt to create such a balance in the lives of individual trangressors. States should limit themselves to protecting the most important rights of individuals transgressed against. They cannot, therefore, be held to have a general prima-facie duty to punish the guilty, if that is supposed to be an instance of the more general prima-facie duty to do as much good as they can. For states do not have this latter duty; their duty is only to 'consult the general interest' when they look for ways of protecting the rights of the individual. We need a different account, therefore, and it must be one consistent with Ross's overall theory of prima-facie duties.

Ross's own answer is that the state's duty to punish is an instance of the duty to keep one's promises. The state, he claims, makes promises to the injured person and his friends, and to society at large. To the injured person is promised compensation and the satisfaction of knowing that the offender has not gone scot-free. To society is promised both this satisfaction and a degree of protection against further offences. This accounts for the prima-facie *duty* to punish, and it does so in a way that consequentialists supposedly cannot borrow, for they necessarily distort the prima-facie duty to keep one's promises. The *right* to punish is established by the claim that those who infringe the prima-facie rights of others to life, liberty, or property thereby lose their own prima-facie rights to these things, and the state has no such prima-facie duty to spare them as it does to spare the innocent.

Ross claims that:

There is thus a distinction in kind which we all in fact recognize, but which utilitarianism cannot admit, between the punishment of a person who has invaded the rights of others and the infliction of pain or restraint on one who has not.   (1930, 60)

This does not mean that the state may never inflict pain or restraint on those who have not invaded the rights of others. 'The interests of society may sometimes be so deeply involved as to make it right to punish an innocent man "that the whole nation perish not"' (1930, 61). In this Ross agrees with the consequentialists, including Moore. It is in the explanation of it that he differs. All agree that there is something very bad about punishing the innocent. But when we ask why, the standard consequentialist has to scrape the barrel; Moore talks about an absence of a certain organic unity, a certain failure of value; and Ross talks about the infringement of a prima-facie right. That prima-facie right is a form of protection of the individual that is absent from Moore's account.

V

For present purposes, however, the question is to what extent Moore's success tells in favour of his account of organic unities. Is it that no such account is available to the variabilist? If so, we have here a significant strike against variabilism's claims to be *the* correct way of understanding the organic. And that is how Hurka sees things. He writes:

A pure variability view must say that in this case the pain is 'transvalued' from bad to simply good, which implies that our emotional response to it should be simple pleasure. But this is not right: the morally best response to deserved suffering is somber, mixing satisfaction that justice is done with regret at the infliction of pain. By making deserved pain still bad as pain, the [intrinsicalist] view captures this important [truth].   (2003, 606–7)

Hurka has two points here, I think. Suppose that we want to say that the pain cannot contribute a value it has not got, and that all value belonging to the whole must somehow be distributed among the contributing parts. It looks as if, with the purpose of emerging with the result that the complex [crime + punishment] is better than the crime alone, we will have to say that the pain inflicted is good—when it plainly is not good. Indeed, its not being good is the whole point. We want to inflict something bad on our punishee; if our analysis turns the pain from bad to good, inflicting that pain would hardly be punishment, but rather the donation of an unmerited good. No, Moore was right: we need to find a way of having it that the addition of something bad can make things better, without this having the result that the bad thing we have added is somehow turned good in the process.

The second point concerns the appropriate moral attitude to the punishment of crime, where that involves inflicting pain. Ordinarily we would suppose that a mixed reaction is called for, involving, as Hurka says, satisfaction that justice is done (which is a good) with regret at the pain inflicted. But we can only keep this mixed attitude going if the pain inflicted is bad, not good.

How can the variabilist reply? Taking the second point first, we should distinguish between the painfulness of the pain, and the goodness or badness of inflicting that pain. A mixed attitude to punishment is certainly called for; unalloyed pleasure seems certainly to be out of place. But I suggest that the mixed attitude can be cast rather differently from the way that Hurka imagines. What we want is regret at the whole situation, but satisfaction that proper penalty is exacted. The painfulness of the punishment is not itself to be regretted, since it is exactly what is called for in the situation. It is good (or at least makes things less bad) that the punishee should suffer in this way, given his crime. And all that this shows is that suffering is not always something to be regretted. Nobody is suggesting that the pain itself is not nasty, of course; there is no suggestion that the person receiving it should somehow welcome it. The suggestion is rather that we should not be thinking of the pain as a necessary evil, but rather as something appropriate to the situation, and without which things would be worse rather than better.

What, then, for the more structural point, that we are in danger of turning the pain inflicted into an unmerited good? Here I want to introduce a rather different distinction. One thing lurking in the back of this debate is the idea that pain is an intrinsic or essential evil, and that we should reject any theory that converts it into something which is, on occasions, to be welcomed. The idea should remind us of recent discussions of the prosperity of the wicked.[6] Suppose we say that their prospering is not a good at all, but an evil. In doing that, we destroy the very thing we were trying to understand. We started out thinking that prosperity is something the wicked do not deserve. But we lose that thought if we announce that prosperity for them is not the good it would be for others. It can only be something they do not deserve if it is still a good when they get it.

I suggest that we assess this argument by recasting its talk of good and bad in terms of reasons. There are various theses which I would wish to preserve in any eventual analysis. First, we have sufficient reason to prevent the wicked from prospering and no reason to promote their prosperity, and so the prosperity of the wicked is not a good (because of the link between reasons and values). Second, prosperity is 'unfitting' to the wicked, which is to say that it is wrong, or bad, that they should prosper (by definition of what it is for something to be in this sense unfitting). Third, that it is not good that the wicked should prosper does not show that their prosperity is not a good *for them*. So, fourth, it is possible that though their prosperity is a good for them, it is not good that they should prosper. This conclusion fits the pattern of the reasons. For they may have sufficient reason to preserve their prosperity, though we have no reason to do so, having indeed sufficient reason to prevent them from prospering—which is where we started.

We cannot hope to argue here that prosperity is not a good for the wicked. For we can define what is to count as prospering for the purposes of the argument simply in terms of something that is *allowed* as a good for the wicked. There must be some such thing, for example, health or comfort. Health is a more tricky one, because it is not clear that we have reason to prevent the health of the wicked. Let us allow, then, that comfort is a good for the wicked, so that they prosper to the extent that they are comfortable. We are saying that their comfort is something which *they* may have sufficient reason to preserve, though *we* have no reason to do so; indeed, we have sufficient reason to prevent it where we can. In terms of value, I conclude that the prosperity of the wicked is a good for them, but not good. It is not good that they should have this thing that is a good for them.

---

[6] See, e.g., N. Lemos, *Intrinsic Value: Concept and Warrant* (Cambridge: Cambridge University Press, 1994).

Mutatis mutandis, I would say that the pain of the punishee is a good, something we have reason to welcome, inflict, or insist on, even though (and indeed because) it is not a good for him, and he has reasons to get out of it if he can.

Returning now to the question of the appropriate attitude: having announced that we should not regret the pain inflicted, despite its being bad for him, I do not need to think that the proper attitude to the inflicting of that pain is unmixed pleasure. The sort of sombre response that Hurka wants to keep in place is still available, since we must recognize that what we are doing, though good, is not good for the punishee. One can retain some sense of identification with the recipient and the pain that is being imposed on him (ouch!), even though one thinks that the imposition of that pain is all for the good. And this is another source of sombreness, in addition to regret that the situation has arisen in the first place.

VI

Even if this variabilist response is thought acceptable, there remain two subsequent difficulties to be dealt with, or rather one difficulty which comes in two stages. We have decided that the punishment is good since it is to be welcomed, in the context of the crime, and that the combination of crime and punishment is better than the crime alone, i.e., than the crime unpunished. But we are in danger of having manœuvred ourselves into a position in which we find ourselves saying that the crime also is good. There is a symmetry here: just as crime without punishment is worse than crime with punishment, so punishment without crime is worse than punishment with crime. Such structures persuaded us that the punishment, when put together with the crime, makes things better, and therefore itself acquires positive value; and we should surely say the same of the crime. After all, our earlier ranking order was incomplete: the crime alone is worse than the crime + punishment, which is itself worse than what is best, namely having neither crime nor punishment. But the punishment alone is surely a lot worse than the crime alone, and so comes at the very bottom of the scale; most of us would prefer to leave some crimes unpunished if this is the only way to ensure that nobody is punished for a crime they did not commit. On this basis, adding the crime to the punishment improves the situation, or at least reduces its disvalue, more than does adding the punishment to the crime. All the more reason, then, to think that if the punishment is good in the context of the crime, the crime is good in the context of the punishment. But then (and this is the second stage), if each is for the better in the context of the other, won't the combination have to be positively good, since it consists of good elements in an appropriate relation? And wouldn't it be rational (or even morally required) for someone, knowing that he will end up punished for a crime that he has not committed, to go out and commit it so as to reduce the number of unpunished crimes, or at least makes things less bad than they would otherwise be? And would it not also be rational (and morally required, again) for us to go about encouraging crimes whose authors we know are going to be detected and convicted, in order to increase the sum total of value? These questions are a sure sign that something has gone wrong somewhere.

Moore's intrinsicalist position is in good shape on both these points. For him, the pain inflicted is bad, and so is the crime, though the combination of the two is good as a whole and less bad on the whole than either separately. But is the variabilist in trouble here?

The obvious way of proceeding is to attack the first stage of the difficulty. Part of the pressure derives from the fact that it is hard to think that the crime is genuinely bad when the world is the better for its presence. But, in fact, it is possible for an evil to be such that the world is better for its presence, if the world would have been even better for its absence. It might look as if this is not our case, for we are imagining starting from the combination of crime and punishment and subtracting the crime—which makes things worse than they were before. On this picture, things are not better for the absence of the crime. But that is a distorted perspective. What we should be saying is that though things are the better for the presence of the crime, they would have been even better for its absence. How could this be? The answer is that this could occur even if something that with the crime was good would have been bad without it—so long as without the crime that further thing would not have occurred at all. And that is, of course, the normal case; without the crime, there would have been no punishment.

The other thing to bear in mind here is that, on the variabilist picture, by inflicting the punishment we may perhaps diminish the disvalue of the crime, but we don't render it positively good. The combination of crime + punishment is not a good of any sort; it is merely less bad than either part alone. It would have been far better to have had neither than both. There is no danger that we ought to go about maximizing the number of punished crimes, by encouraging crimes whose authors we know are going to be detected and convicted, in order to increase the sum total of value.

Perhaps the crucial mistake, though, was to think that because the punishment, when put together with the crime, makes things better, it therefore itself acquires positive value, since its presence is to be welcomed rather than regretted; and that we should surely say the same of the crime. The reply to this should be that a feature which makes things less bad need not itself be positively good, if that means that we should seek to have more such things. We should distinguish between a good feature and a mitigating feature. Add the punishment to the crime and each becomes less bad than it would otherwise be—in the case of the punishment, it becomes a lot less bad because punishing the innocent is so dreadful; in this way it becomes possible that their combination is less bad than either would be alone.

Variabilists are only condemned to holding the punishment positively good if they take the crime to remain as bad as before, whether punished or not. For if they took that line, they would have to find a positive good to set against a persistent positive evil. But that is not a picture that should recommend itself to them. What they should say, of course, is that in the context of the crime, the punishment is much less bad than it would otherwise be—and the same is true in reverse of the crime, even if not to the same degree. It is quite possible that the disvalue of the crime is reduced by the addition of something which is still a disvalue, in a way that leaves the combination still bad, but less bad than the crime would have been alone. This is the true variabilist picture of vindictive punishment.

Still, isn't it the case that if I know that I am going to be punished anyway, I have good reason (of a certain sort—a reason of justice) to commit the crime, since the complex [crime + punishment] is more just than the punishment alone? First, this scenario can occur even for Moore, if the figures come out right—as they can do. Second, this question is asked from a peculiarly objective standpoint, one encouraged by consequentialist talk of how well the world is going. Deontologists would not find very attractive the idea that I should help the world get along better by committing a crime. So this 'consequence' of organicity is actually a consequence only of an organic consequentialism, not of organicity as such. What is more, on any theory we might face the problem whether, if I know that I will be punished anyway, and that the injustice of this undeserved punishment is greater than would have been the injustice of the crime, I should commit the crime in order to reduce the injustice in the world. *This* question does not even need any sort of appeal to organicity to get going.[7]

References

Dancy, J. *Ethics Without Principles* (Oxford: Clarendon Press, 2004).

Hurka, T., 'Moore in the Middle', *Ethics*, 113 (2003), 599–628.

Lemos, N., *Intrinsic Value: Concept and Warrant* (Cambridge: Cambridge University Press, 1994).

[7] I am very grateful to many friends and colleagues who have tried to help me with this paper, which is my final effort on a topic with which I have been struggling for quite a while. Philip Stratton-Lake deserves a special mention.

Moore, G. E., 'The Conception of Intrinsic Value', in his *Philosophical Studies* (London: Routledge & Kegan Paul, 1922), 253–75.

——— *Principia Ethica* (Cambridge: Cambridge University Press, 1903); rev. edn., ed. by T. Baldwin (Cambridge: Cambridge University Press, 1993).

Ross, W. D., *The Right and the Good* (Oxford: Clarendon Press, 1930).

INDEX